P.

FUNDAMENTALS OF COMPUTERS

THIRD EDITION

V. RAJARAMAN
IBM Professor of Information Technology,
Jawaharlal Nehru Centre for Advanced
Scientific Research, Bangalore
and
Honorary Professor, Indian Institute of Science,
Bangalore

Prentice-Hall of India Private Limited
New Delhi - 110 001
2000

Rs. 125.00

FUNDAMENTALS OF COMPUTERS, 3rd Ed.
by V. Rajaraman

ISBN-81-203-1531-6

The export rights of this book are vested solely with the publisher.

Twenty-fourth Printing (Third Edition)   ...   ...   **November, 2000**

Published by Asoke K. Ghosh, Prentice-Hall of India Private Limited, M-97, Connaught Circus, New Delhi-110001 and Printed by Mohan Makhijani at Rekha Printers Private Limited, New Delhi-110020.

*In memory of
my uncle
Dr. P.S. Viswanathan*

Contents

Preface

A student must understand how a computer functions in addition to knowing how to program it. The main objective of this book is to explain to a beginner how a computer works. Computer salesmen and advertisers have the tendency of using numerous obscure technical terms to describe computers. Very often such jargon overwhelms many managers and computer users because they do not understand it; thus another objective of this book is to explain in a simple language what many of these terms really mean. Hardware and software components of a computer are both important for its functioning and thus both these aspects are explained in this book.

This book is intended as a text for a course on 'Fundamentals of Computers' to be taught concurrently with courses on programming. It would thus be useful for the first course in computers taught in bachelors and master's courses in computer applications (BCA and MCA). Rapid advances in computer technology have made it imperative for all engineers to understand the hardware features of computers besides knowing how to program them in a high level language. A core course is being introduced in undergraduate engineering curricula on fundamentals of computers, and this book would be appropriate for this course. In view of the extensive use of computers in business and industry, students in schools of management require a course on computers, and this book would be appropriate for such a course. There is a trend to introduce computer science as a subsidiary subject in B.Sc. courses and this book can also be used as a text in this course.

Besides its use as a text, this book would also provide managers, engineers and scientists a basic introduction to the hardware and software of computers. This knowledge is essential to appreciate the power and weaknesses of computers and to select appropriate applications and hardware.

This book was evolved from a set of notes used by the author in various courses, and they are thoroughly class-tested. These notes have been used for concurrent reading in short intensive programming courses, in computer appreciation courses for managers and engineers, and in undergraduate programmes for engineers.

The first two editions of this book received excellent support from the readers and was highly acclaimed. A number of suggestions were also received from the readers. This third edition has been written by extensively revising the second edition. The basic structure of the book has been retained. All chapters were thoroughly reviewed and a number of chapters were rewritten to conform to the changes that have taken place in computer technology.

The book begins with a chapter that explains the concept of computer algorithms, computer structure and programming languages. It is followed by a chapter discussing how various types of data are represented and stored in a computer. The next chapter describes various devices used to input data and programs to computers and the devices used to write the results of computation. Chapter 4 discusses the properties of storage devices used to fabricate computer memories. It also describes the structure of different types of memories. In Chapter 5, the logical structure of a processor (also known as the *Central Processing Unit*) of a computer is presented. A small hypothetical computer is used to explain the basic ideas in the design of processors. The next chapter discusses how binary arithmetic operations are carried out by a computer. Chapter 7 introduces boolean algebra to describe how logical operations are carried out. Concepts of boolean algebra are used to illustrate the design of arithmetic and logic circuits. The next chapter describes how I-O units, the memory and the processor are interconnected and the methods used to alleviate the speed mismatch between these units.

Chapters 9 and 10 are mainly concerned with the software of computers. Chapter 9 introduces the need for high level languages for computers and briefly describes a number of popular languages. Chapter 10 presents the important concept of operating systems. It explains how various units are co-ordinated and their functioning overlapped using software aids.

Chapter 11 is concerned with microcomputers. In view of the rapid growth of microcomputer applications we have devoted a full chapter to this topic and explained the logical structure of microprocessors, the architecture of microcomputers and their applications. Chapter 12 explains how computers are classified as Laptop (or notebook) computers, PCs, Workstations, Mainframes, Distributed and Parallel Computers, and as first, second, third, and fourth generation machines.

The last two chapters are recent topics not usually found in most 'first books' on computers. Chapter 13 deals with communications and computers. We discuss basic concepts of communication technology and how computers are connected together as a network using communication media. New material on the Internet, Local Area Networks, Fibre Optic Networks, Wireless Networks and ATM Networks has been added to this chapter. Chapter 14 introduces the important area of interactive computer graphics. Various input and output devices to accept and display pictures are described. An overview of applications of graphics and software for graphics is presented. The book concludes with a glossary of technical terms. The presentation in this book is aimed at self-study. Each chapter ends with an extended summary and a large number of review questions.

The author would like to thank Prof. C.N.R. Rao, President, Jawaharlal Nehru Centre for Advanced Scientific Research, Bangalore, for providing the support which made this writing feasible. Sincere thanks are extended to Dr. T. Viswanathan for reading the first edition of the manuscript and for a number of valuable suggestions. Thanks are due to Dr. Thomas Chacko for many suggestions which enabled the author to improve the style of presentation.

The author would like to thank all the staff members of the Supercomputer Education and Research Centre, Indian Institute of Science, Bangalore, for their cooperation. Special thanks are due to Ms. T. Mallika, for an excellent job of typing the revisions of the second edition of the manuscript.

Lastly the author would like to express his affectionate appreciation to his wife Dharma for critical reading of the book and her dedicated support in writing this book.

Bangalore   **V. RAJARAMAN**
January, 1999

1

Computer Basics

Computers are now affecting every sphere of human activity and bringing about many changes in industry, government, education, medicine, scientific research, law, social sciences and even in arts like music and painting. They are presently used, among other applications, to

- Design buildings, bridges and machines
- Control space vehicles
- Assist in Railway reservation
- Control inventories to minimize material cost
- Grade examinations and process results
- Aid in teaching
- Systematically store and quickly retrieve data on crimes and criminals
- Play games like chess and video games

The areas of applications of computers are confined only by limitations on human creativity and imagination. In fact any task that can be carried out systematically, using a precise step-by-step method, can be performed by a computer. Therefore it is essential for every educated person today to know about a computer, its strengths, its weaknesses and its internal structure. The main objective of this book is to explain these in a simple language.

1.1 ALGORITHMS

In order to solve a problem using a computer it is necessary to evolve a detailed and precise step-by-step method of solution. Step-by-step methods for solving problems are not new or peculiar to computers. They have been in use for a very long time, and in almost all walks of life. One such method, taken from a popular magazine, is given as Example 1.1.

Example 1.1   Recipe for potato bondas

Ingredients

Potatoes 250 gms., Chopped onions 3 (small), Finely chopped chillies 5, Gram flour 100 gms., Oil for Frying, Water for batter, Salt 2 teaspoons.

1

Method

Step 1:   Boil potatoes till cooked, peel and mash them until they are soft.

Step 2:   Mix onions, green chillies and salt with the mashed potatoes.

Step 3:   Take little portions of the mixture and make small balls.

Step 4:   Mix gram flour, water and a little salt and beat well till a smooth and creamy batter is obtained.

Step 5:   Dip the potato balls in the batter. Take out and deep fry in oil on a low fire.

Step 6:   Take out when the balls are fried to a golden brown colour.

Result

A dozen potato bondas ready to be served hot with tomato sauce.

The recipe given above has the following properties:

1. It begins with a list of ingredients which we may call the *inputs*.

2. A sequence of instructions is given to process the inputs.

3. As a result of carrying out the instructions, some *outputs* (namely Potato bondas) are obtained.

The instructions given to process the inputs are, however, not precise. They are ambiguous. For example, in Step 4, we are instructed to "beat well till a smooth and creamy batter is obtained". The interpretation of "smooth and creamy" can vary from person to person. Due to such imprecise instructions, different persons following the same recipe with the same inputs can produce potato bondas which differ in size, shape and taste!

We will now examine another step-by-step procedure (again taken from a popular magazine).

Example 1.2   *A procedure to knit a sweater*

Materials required

Needles No. 12—2, Wool 4 ply — 9 balls.

Method

Step 1:   Cast on 133 stitches.

Step 2:   Repeat Steps 3 and 4, 11 times.

Step 3:   Knit 2, * Purl 1, Knit 1, Repeat from * to last stitch, Knit 1.

Step 4:   Knit 1, * Purl 1, Knit 1, Repeat from * to End.

. . . .

. . . .

(Similar Steps)

Result

A sweater.

The above example illustrates the following points:

1. This procedure has inputs, a set of steps to process the inputs to produce an output.

2. The procedure is more precise and unambiguous than the recipe for potato bondas. There is very little chance for misinterpretation.

3. The number of different types of instructions used in the procedure is very few. If one knows how to knit, how to purl, cast stitches on or off needles, and count, then any sweater can be knit.

4. By a proper permutation and combination of this elementary set of instructions a virtually infinite number of patterns for sweaters may be created. For example if Step 3 is made "Knit 1, * Knit 1, Purl 2, Repeat from * to last stitch" the pattern of the sweater will be entirely different.

The preciseness of the instructions combined with their small variety makes it possible to design a machine which can knit automatically. In fact, a forerunner of the modern computer was a loom designed by a French engineer, called Jacquard, in 1801, which could be 'programmed' to create a large number of patterns. The program consisted of cards with specific patterns of holes in them which would control the loom.

We have illustrated two simple step-by-step methods of solving problems. We will now explain when a step-by-step method can be called an *algorithm*.

The origin of the word algorithm has been hotly debated. It is, however, generally accepted among mathematicians that it comes from the name of a famous Arab mathematician Abu Jafar Mohammed ibn Musa al-Khowarizmi (*circa* 825) (literally meaning father of Jafar Mohammed, son of Moses, native of al-Khowarizm) who wrote the celebrated book *"Kitab al jabr Walmuqabla" (Rules of Restoration and Reduction)*. The last part of his name al-Khowarizmi was corrupted to *algorithm*. An algorithm may be defined as a finite sequence of instructions (to solve a problem) which has the following five basic characteristics:

1. An algorithm begins with instruction(s) to accept *inputs*. These *inputs* are processed by the subsequent instructions in the algorithm.

2. The *processing rules* specified in the algorithm must be precise and unambiguous. In other words, the instructions must not be vague. It must also be possible to carry them out. For example the instruction "Go to hell" is precise, but cannot be carried out.

3. Each *instruction* must be sufficiently *basic* such that it can, in principle, be carried out in finite time by a person with paper and pencil.

4. The total *time* to carry out all the steps in the algorithm must be *finite*. As algorithms may contain instructions to repetitively carry out a group of instructions, this requirement implies that the number of repetitions must be *finite*.

5. An algorithm must produce one or more *outputs* (namely the result of processing the inputs).

Based on the above definition we see that the recipe of Example 1.1 does not qualify as an algorithm as it is not precise. The knitting pattern, on the other hand, does qualify.

We will now evolve a step-by-step procedure to solve an information processing job. The problem is to find the average number of vowels occurring in a short passage.

Example 1.3 *Procedure to find the average number of vowels in a passage*

Step 1:   Let Number of characters = 0

Step 2:   Let Number of vowels = 0

Step 3:   Repeat Steps 4, 5, 6 and 7 until end of passage is reached.

Step 4:   Read one character from the passage.

Step 5:   Add 1 to Number of characters.

Step 6:   If the character is any one of the letters A, E, I, O, U, a, e, i, o, u, add 1 to Number of vowels.

Step 7:   Move to next character.

Remark: Step 8 is reached when no more characters are left in the passage. Otherwise we go back to Step 4.

Step 8:   Average Number of Vowels = $\dfrac{\text{Number of vowels}}{\text{Number of characters}}$

Step 9:   Write Average Number of vowels, Number of characters.

Step 10: Stop.

This step-by-step procedure qualifies as an algorithm as:

(i) It has an input, namely, the passage to be examined.

(ii) The processing steps are precisely specified.

(iii) Each instruction is basic and can be carried out by a person with paper and pencil.

(iv) The procedure terminates when the end of passage is reached. The total number of steps carried out is finite.

1.2 A SIMPLE MODEL OF A COMPUTER

If a machine is to be built to carry out the algorithm of Example 1.3, it should have the following features:

(i) It should be able to interpret each of the instructions in the algorithm and carry it out.

(ii) It should be able to read a text consisting of a set of characters.

(iii) It should be able to add and divide.

(iv) It should be able to compare a character read from the passage with the letters A, E, I, O, U, a, e, i, o, u and if it matches, to add 1 to the number of vowels.

(v) It should be able to store (or remember) computed values.

(vi) It should be able to write (or output) the answers obtained.

(vii) If the steps in the algorithm are to be carried out *automatically* without human intervention the entire algorithm must be *stored* for reference. As the algorithm is also repetitive, that is, a set of steps are carried out again and again until a condition is satisfied, it is necessary to have all the steps in the algorithm stored in a storage unit.

A computing machine designed to carry out algorithms for information processing thus has the configuration of Fig. 1.1. Referring to Fig. 1.1 it is seen that an *input unit* is provided to read the algorithm and the data to be processed by the algorithm. The *memory unit* stores the algorithm and computed values. The *processing unit* interprets the instructions and carries them out. It has the capability to perform arithmetic operations, character manipulation operations, and logical operations. The *output unit* prints or displays computed results.

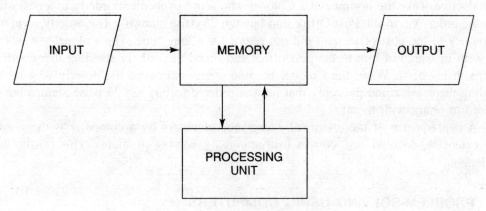

Fig. 1.1   Organization of a computer.

In Example 1.2, it was seen that it is possible to develop an enormous number of different interesting patterns by permuting and combining a few basic types of instructions. The same principle is used in building computers. Thus by using a computer's processing unit which can interpret and execute as few as ten different operations, it is possible to perform a large variety of information processing tasks.

1.3   CHARACTERISTICS OF COMPUTERS

The interesting features of a computer are:

1. Computers are built to carry out a small variety of instructions. It is not necessary to have more than about 100 distinct instructions even for a very powerful machine.

2. Instructions are extremely simple; e.g., add, subtract, read a character, write a character, compare numbers, characters, etc.

3. Most instructions are carried out in less than a millionth of a second.

4. Instructions are carried out obediently with no questions asked.

5. Instructions are carried out without any mistakes.

A computer may thus be thought of as a servant who would carry out instructions obediently, uncritically, at a very high speed, and without exhibiting any emotions. As human beings, we use judgement based on experience, often on subjective and emotional considerations. Such value judgements often depend on what is called sound "commonsense". As opposed to this, a computer exhibits no emotions and has no commonsense. An algorithm may be written for a computer to compose music based on rules of composition, but the computer cannot judge the quality of the resultant music. It must be clearly understood that computers are machines which can be programmed to follow instructions; they don't have their own priorities and judgements. Computers are machines which can help mankind in many ways; but they do not threaten us.

Being obedient without exercising 'commonsense' can be very annoying and unproductive. Take the instance of a Colonel who sent his obedient orderly to a post office with the order "Go to the Post Office and buy ten 25 paise stamps". The orderly went with the money to the post office and did not return for a long time. The Colonel got worried and went in search of him to the post office and found the orderly standing there with the stamps in his hand. When the Colonel became angry and asked the orderly why he was standing there, pat came the reply that he was ordered to buy ten 25 paise stamps but not ordered to return with them!

A consequence of the uncritical acceptance of orders by a computer is the need to give extensive, detailed, and correct instructions for solving problems. This can be quite challenging.

1.4   PROBLEM-SOLVING USING COMPUTERS

In order to solve a problem using a computer the following steps are followed:

1. The given problem is analyzed.

2. The solution method is broken down into a sequence of elementary tasks.

3. Based on this analysis an algorithm to solve the problem is formulated. The algorithm should be precise, concise and unambiguous. Based on our discussions we realize that algorithm formulation is difficult and time-consuming.

4. The algorithm is expressed in a precise notation. An algorithm expressed using a precise notation is called a *computer program*. The precise notation is called a *computer programming language*.

5. The computer program is fed to the computer.

6. The computer's processing unit interprets the instructions in the program, executes them and sends the results to the output unit.

We will now consider an example of formulating a computer algorithm and write a computer program corresponding to the algorithm.

Example 1.4   The task

Find out the highest marks obtained in an examination and the roll number of the student obtaining the highest marks. For simplicity it is assumed that only one student obtains the highest marks.

Input

We first decide the format in which the marks would be presented. We assume that each student's paper will have a roll number and total marks obtained.

Method

Having decided the data format, we formulate the steps needed in a procedure to pick the highest marks.

Step 1:   Read the first student's paper and note down the roll number and the marks. This is the highest marks found so far.

Step 2:   Repeat Steps 3 and 4 until no more papers are left.

Step 3:   Read the next student's paper. Compare the marks in this paper with the highest marks found so far.

Step 4:   If the marks read in Step 3 is greater than the highest marks noted, then erase that and replace it by the marks read in Step 3 and replace the roll number noted down earlier by this new roll number. Else do not do anything.

Remarks: As soon as all papers have been examined we go to Step 5. Until then Steps 3 and 4 are repeated.

Step 5:   Print the roll number and the maximum marks noted.

1.4.1   Flowchart

Having obtained an algorithm for solving the problem, we express the algorithm in a pictorial form called a *flowchart*. The flowchart is primarily used as an aid in formulating and understanding algorithms. The sequencing of instructions and repetition of groups of instructions may be quickly seen by inspecting a flowchart. The flowchart for the algorithm of Example 1.4 is given as Fig. 1.2 (page 8).

For easy visual recognition, a standard convention is used in drawing flowcharts. In this standard convention the following shapes are used for various blocks in a flowchart.

(i) Rectangles with rounded ends are used to indicate START and STOP.

(ii) Parallelograms are used to represent input and output operations.

(iii) Diamond shaped boxes are used to indicate questions asked or conditions tested based on whose answers appropriate exits are taken by a procedure. The exits from the diamond shaped box are labelled with the answers to the questions.

(iv) Rectangles are used to indicate any processing operation such as storage and arithmetic.

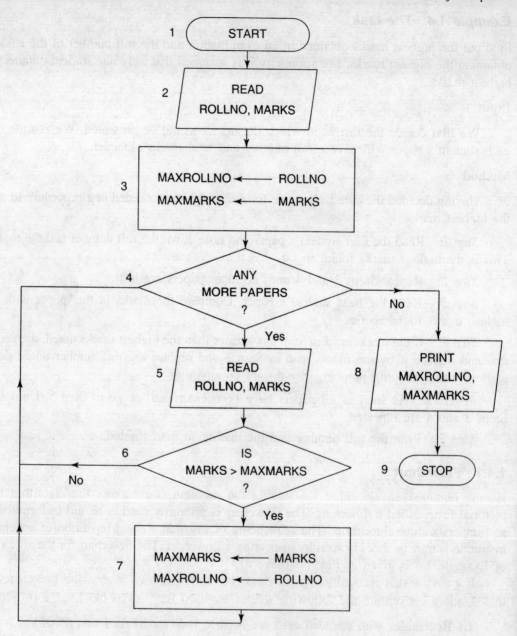

Fig. 1.2 A flowchart giving the method for picking the highest marks.

1.4.2 A Program

The next step is to express the flowchart in a more precise and concise notation called a *programming language*. A computer program corresponding to the flowchart of Fig. 1.2 written in a programming language called *Pascal* is given below:

A reader need not worry if he or she does not understand the notation used to express the algorithm. It has been given only to let the reader appreciate what a program looks like.

```
PROGRAM HIGHMARKS (INPUT, OUTPUT);
Var MAXROLLNO, MAXMARKS, ROLLNO, MARKS : integer;
begin
     READLN (ROLLNO, MARKS);
     MAXMARKS  := MARKS;
     MAXROLLNO := ROLLNO;
     While not EOF (INPUT) do
     begin
     READLN (ROLLNO, MARKS);
     if  MARKS > MAXMARKS then
        begin
        MAXMARKS  := MARKS;
        MAXROLLNO := ROLLNO
        end;
     end;
     WRITE (MAXROLLNO, MAXMARKS)
end.
```

The above program is a straightforward translation of the flowchart. It uses a precise notation which should be learnt by a programmer.

1.4.3 The Working of a Computer

Having shown how to obtain an algorithm and a program to solve the given problem (Example 1.4), we will now illustrate how the algorithm is executed by a computer. The model of the computer shown in Fig. 1.1 will be used for illustration.

We will assume that the flowchart of Fig. 1.2, is first read by the input unit and stored in the computer's memory. (Strictly speaking, a program, and *not* a flowchart is read and stored in a computer's memory. We use the flowchart, instead of the program, only because the reader may not know a programming language.) The data to be processed, namely a set of papers, each with a roll number and marks, are queued up at the input unit in the order in which they would be used by the flowchart (see Fig. 1.3).

The processing unit of the computer reads from the memory the first block in the flowchart, which says 'START'. This instruction gets all the units in the computer ready. After this, the processing unit retrieves from the memory the next instruction given in the flowchart (block 2 Fig. 1.2) which states:

READ ROLLNO, MARKS

This command is interpreted as "Read the first number from the data record waiting at the top of the queue at the input unit. Label a box in memory as ROLLNO. Clear it and store in it the number read. Similarly store the second number from the data record in a memory box labelled MARKS. Figure 1.3(b) illustrates this.

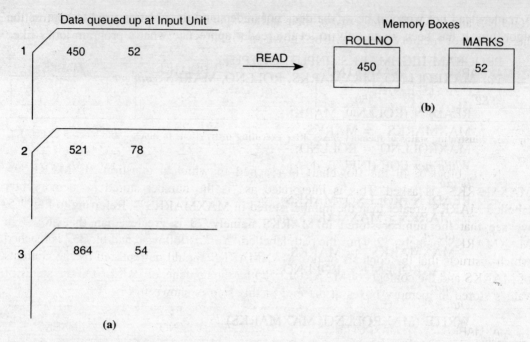

Fig. 1.3   Illustrating data queued up in an input unit and the result of executing READ instruction.

The next block (block 3 Fig. 1.2) is now taken up for execution. It is interpreted as: "clear a memory box and label it MAXROLLNO. Copy into it the contents of memory box ROLLNO. Clear another memory box and label it MAXMARKS. Copy into it the contents of box MARKS". Figure 1.4 illustrates this.

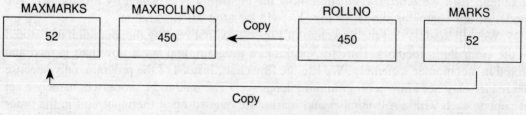

Fig. 1.4   Illustrating status of memory boxes after executing instructions in block 3 of flowchart of Fig. 1.2.

Following the flowchart, the next block (block 4) asks the question: "Any more papers?" This is interpreted by the processing unit and it checks if there are any more papers queued up at the input unit. Papers 2 and 3 (Fig. 1.3a) would still be there and the answer to the question is "Yes". The path labelled "Yes" is thus followed and block 5 in the flowchart is taken up for execution. It states:

READ ROLLNO, MARKS

It is interpreted as before and the numbers in the paper waiting at the top of the queue in the input unit, namely paper 2 (Fig. 1.3), are read and the values in it are stored in boxes

ROLLNO and MARKS *after erasing* their earlier contents. After executing this instruction the contents of memory boxes will be shown in Fig. 1.5.

Fig. 1.5 Illustrating status of memory boxes after executing instructions in block 4 and block 5 of Fig. 1.2.

Next, block 6 in the flowchart is reached in which a question "Is MARKS > MAXMARKS" is asked. This is interpreted as "Is the number stored in memory box labelled MARKS greater than the number stored in MAXMARKS?". Referring to Fig. 1.5, we see that the number stored in MARKS namely 78 is greater than that stored in MAXMARKS, namely, 52. Thus the path labelled "Yes" is followed and block 7 is reached which instructs that the contents of box MAXMARKS should be replaced by the contents of MARKS and the contents of MAXROLLNO by the contents of ROLLNO. The status of values stored in memory boxes at the end of this step is shown in Fig. 1.6.

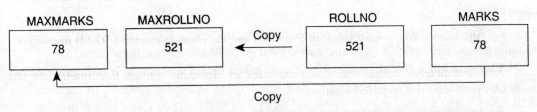

Fig. 1.6 Status of memory boxes after executing instructions in blocks 6 and 7 of Fig. 1.2.

The path leading out of block 7 in the flowchart leads back to block 4 of the chart. Executing block 4 we see that a paper is still left. Executing block 5, the numbers 864 and 54 are read into ROLLNO and MARKS respectively (Fig. 1.7). Executing block 6 we see that 54 stored in MARKS is less than 78 stored in MAXMARKS. Thus the "No" path is taken out of block 6 and we reach block 4.

Fig. 1.7 Status of memory boxes after the last record in the input is read.

When block 4 is executed we see that no more papers are left in the input queue. Thus execution of block 4 gives an answer "No" and we reach block 8 of the flowchart. The instruction in block 8 commands that the contents of boxes MAXROLLNO and MAXMARKS are to be printed by the output unit. Thus the numbers 521 and 78 are printed. After doing this, the instruction in block 9 is reached which stops computation.

1.4.4 Stored Program Concept

The model of computer used in this section was first proposed by John Von Neumann, a chemical engineer turned computer scientist, in 1945. The major contribution of Von Neumann is the idea of storing the program and the data in the same memory. Storing of programs in memory is essential if a series of instructions is to be repetitively carried out. For instance, in Example 1.4, after Steps 3 and 4 are carried out the algorithm returns to the previous Step 3 if more papers are left in the input. The previous step cannot be carried out unless it is "stored" and is available for reference in the memory.

Storing a program in memory also makes the operation of computers *automatic*. Unlike a calculator where one has to press buttons after each operation is carried out the instructions stored in the memory of a computer are taken one-by-one automatically to the processing unit, interpreted and executed without human intervention.

SUMMARY

We summarize now the main concepts presented in this chapter:

1. In order to solve a problem using a computer it is necessary to evolve an algorithm.

2. An algorithm is a finite sequence of instructions. Each instruction is precise, unambiguous, and capable of being carried out by a machine in a finite time.

3. A computer is a machine which executes an algorithm written to process data fed to it and produces the required results.

4. An algorithm is expressed in a graphical form known as a flowchart. A flowchart is mainly used to aid understanding of algorithms.

5. A programming language is a precise notation used to express algorithms. An algorithm expressed in a programming language is called a computer program.

6. A computer is designed using four basic units to enable it to process data. It has an *input unit* which accepts the data and the program to process the data. It stores these in a *memory unit*. The program retrieved from the memory unit is interpreted and executed by a *processing unit*. The results of computation are stored in memory and printed using an *output unit*.

7. Storing a program in memory is essential to formulate concise, repetitive, algorithms and for automatic program execution.

8. The main characteristics of a computer are its speed, accuracy, versatility to perform a variety of tasks, automatic program execution without human intervention and its capacity to carry out repetitive jobs routinely any number of times.

REVIEW QUESTIONS

1.1 Pick out a recipe from a popular magazine and express it as a step-by-step procedure.

1.2   Explain why a procedure given for a recipe in a cook book may not be termed an algorithm.

1.3   What is the basic difference between a procedure given for knitting a sweater and a recipe?

1.4   Explain the term algorithm.

1.5   What is a programming language?

1.6   What is a computer program?

1.7   Draw a block diagram of a computer. Explain the function of each of the blocks.

1.8   Example 1.4 is a procedure to find the highest marks obtained in a class. Modify it to find the lowest marks obtained.

1.9   Modify the procedure of Example 1.4 to find the average marks of a class.

1.10 Obtain a flowchart corresponding to the algorithm of Exercise 1.9. Using the model of a computer presented in this chapter, explain how a computer will find the average marks.

1.11 In obtaining the algorithm for Example 1.4 it has been assumed that the maximum marks is obtained by only one student. How would you modify the algorithm to find out the roll number of all the students who obtain the maximum marks?
Hint: Assume that we can re-read the data records.

1.12 Devise a flowchart corresponding to the algorithm of Example 1.3 given in the text.

1.13 Using the model of a computer explain how this flowchart will be executed by a computer.

1.14 Formulate an algorithm to find the average number of occurrences of each of the letters Q, X, Y, Z in an English passage.

1.15 Obtain an algorithm to find the average number of letters in each sentence in an English passage.

2

Data Representation

In order to discuss how data is processed by a computer, we should first understand the form in which data is stored in its memory. In this chapter we shall see how data is transformed or coded to facilitate its storage and processing.

There are two basic types of data which are stored and processed by computers; namely *characters* and *numbers*. Characters include letters and special symbols. For example, computers may be programmed to read a list of names, sort them in alphabetical order and print the sorted list. A list of names, such as SIVA, RAMA, KRISHNA read by an input unit would be stored in memory, sorted by the program in alphabetical order and printed as the list KRISHNA, RAMA, SIVA. The data processed in this case are *strings of characters,* the strings being SIVA, RAMA and KRISHNA.

The other type of data are decimal numbers such as 1234, 485 etc. Numbers are processed using arithmetic operations such as add, subtract, multiply and divide. In this case we assign *values* to numbers and the processing results in new values.

The characters and numbers fed to a computer, and the output from the computer, must be in a form which is usable by people. For this purpose natural language symbols and decimal digits are appropriate. These constitute the *external data representation.* On the other hand, the representation of data inside a computer must match the technology used by the computer to store and process data. Thus we should first determine the most appropriate *internal representation of data* and then specify unique transformation rules to convert external representation to internal representation and vice versa.

2.1 REPRESENTATION OF CHARACTERS IN COMPUTERS

Physical devices used to store and process data in computers are *two-state* devices. A switch, for example, is a two-state device; it can be either ON or OFF. Very reliable recording and reading on a magnetic surface is achieved when the surface is magnetized in either one of two opposite directions. The two states in this case are magnetic poles aligned left to right (S→N) and right to left (N←S). Electronic devices such as transistors used in computers function most reliably when operated as switches, that is either in a conducting mode or in a non-conducting mode. Thus all data to be stored and processed in computers are transformed or coded as strings of two symbols, one symbol to represent each state. The two symbols normally used are 0 and 1. These are known as *bits,* an abbreviation for *bi*nary dig*its*.

There are 4 unique combinations of two bits, namely:

00   01   10   11

There are $2 \times 2 \times 2 = 8$ unique combinations or strings of 3 bits each and they are:

000   001   010   011   100   101   110   111

Each unique string of bits may be used to represent or code a symbol. In order to code the 26 capital letters of English at least 26 unique strings of bits are needed. With 4 bits there are only 16 ($2 \times 2 \times 2 \times 2 = 16$) unique strings of 4 bits and thus 4 bits are not sufficient. Five bits, however, are sufficient as 32 ($2 \times 2 \times 2 \times 2 \times 2 = 32$) strings of 5 bits each can be formed. Twentysix out of these 32 strings of 5 bits may be picked to code the 26 letters as illustrated in Table 2.1.

Table 2.1   Illustrating the coding of English letters

Bit string	Letter	Bit string	Letter
0 0 0 0 0	A	1 0 0 0 0	Q
0 0 0 0 1	B	1 0 0 0 1	R
0 0 0 1 0	C	1 0 0 1 0	S
0 0 0 1 1	D	1 0 0 1 1	T
0 0 1 0 0	E	1 0 1 0 0	U
0 0 1 0 1	F	1 0 1 0 1	V
0 0 1 1 0	G	1 0 1 1 0	W
0 0 1 1 1	H	1 0 1 1 1	X
0 1 0 0 0	I	1 1 0 0 0	Y
0 1 0 0 1	J	1 1 0 0 1	Z
0 1 0 1 0	K	1 1 0 1 0	
0 1 0 1 1	L	1 1 0 1 1	
0 1 1 0 0	M	1 1 1 0 0	Not
0 1 1 0 1	N	1 1 1 0 1	used
0 1 1 1 0	O	1 1 1 1 0	
0 1 1 1 1	P	1 1 1 1 1	

Information processing using computers requires processing of not only the 26 capital English letters but also the 26 small English letters, 10 digits and around 32 other characters, such as punctuation marks, arithmetic operator symbols, parentheses etc. Total number of characters to be coded is thus: $26 + 26 + 10 + 32 = 94$. With strings of 6 bits each it is possible to code only $2^6 = (64)$ characters. Thus 6 bits are insufficient for coding. If we use strings of 7 bits each we will have $2^7 = (128)$ unique strings and can thus code up to 128 characters. Strings of 7 bits each are thus quite sufficient to code 94 characters.

Coding of characters has been standardized to facilitate exchange of recorded data between computers. The most popular standard is known as ASCII (*American Standard Code for Information Interchange*). This uses 7 bits to code each character. Besides codes for characters, in this standard, codes are defined to convey information such as end of line, end of page, etc., to the computer. These codes are said to be for non-printable control characters. Table 2.2 gives the ASCII code for both printable and non-printable control characters. Columns 1 and 2 are non-printable codes. The entry CR, for example, indicates carriage return (or end of line) control character. The most significant bits of the code are given in Table 2.2 as column headings and the least significant bits of the code are row headings. Thus the code for A, for example, is identified from the table by finding the column and row bits. The column gives bits 100 as bits b_6 b_5 b_4 and the row gives bits 0001 for b_3 b_2 b_1 b_0.

Table 2.2 ASCII code for characters

Least significant bits of code $b_3 b_2 b_1 b_0$	Most significant bits b_6 b_5 b_4							
	000	001	010	011	100	101	110	111
0 0 0 0	NUL	DLE	SPACE	0	@	P		p
0 0 0 1	SOH	DC1	!	1	A	Q	a	q
0 0 1 0	STX	DC2	"	2	B	R	b	r
0 0 1 1	ETX	DC3	#	3	C	S	c	s
0 1 0 0	EOT	DC4	$	4	D	T	d	t
0 1 0 1	ENQ	NAK	%	5	E	U	e	u
0 1 1 0	ACK	SYN	&	6	F	V	f	v
0 1 1 1	BEL	ETB	'	7	G	W	g	w
1 0 0 0	BS	CAN	(	8	H	X	h	x
1 0 0 1	HT	EM	)	9	I	Y	i	y
1 0 1 0	LF	SUB	*	:	J	Z	j	z
1 0 1 1	VT	ESC	+	;	K	[	k	{
1 1 0 0	FF	FS	'	<	L	\	l		
1 1 0 1	CR	GS	–	=	M	]	m	}
1 1 1 0	SO	RS	.	>	N	∧	n	~
1 1 1 1	SI	US	/	?	O	—	o	DEL

Thus the code for A is:

$$b_6 \; b_5 \; b_4 \; b_3 \; b_2 \; b_1 \; b_0$$
$$1 \; 0 \; 0 \; 0 \; 0 \; 0 \; 1$$

The internal coded representation of the string RAMA J is:

1010010	1000001	1001101	1000001	0100000	1001010
R	A	M	A	SPACE	J

Observe that the blank between RAMA and J also needs a code. This code is essential to leave a blank between RAMA and J when the string is printed.

In addition to ASCII, another code known as ISCII (Indian Standard Code for Information Interchange) has been standardized by the Indian Standards Organization. The full description of this code is available in the document IS:13194-91 published by the Indian Standards Organization. It is an 8 bit code which allows English and Indian script alphabets to be used simultaneously. It retains the standard ASCII code for English. It extends Table 2.2 by adding columns 1010, 1011 upto 1111 (Observe that Table 2.2 as shown has columns 0000 to 0111 only). With this addition it is possible to define 96 more characters.

A common code for all Indian languages is feasible as all Indian scripts have a common origin from the Brahmi script. The phonetic nature of Indian languages is used to design the keyboard. All consonants have an implicit vowel. For example क = क् + अ. Thus a consonant such as कि is split into क् + इ. Using this idea the consonants and vowels are separated. Two character codes are therefore needed for a consonant.

A string of bits used to represent a character is known as a *byte*. Characters coded in ISCII need 8 bits for each character. Thus a byte, in this case, is a string of 8 bits. A character coded in ASCII will need only 7 bits. The need to accommodate characters of languages other than English was foreseen while designing ASCII and thus 8 bits were specified to represent characters. Thus a byte is commonly understood as a string of 8 bits.

2.2　REPRESENTATION OF INTEGERS

In the last section we saw how characters and strings of characters are represented internally in a computer. Decimal digits are also considered as characters and codes are assigned to them. These codes for digits are primarily used when digits are used merely as symbols with no "value" assigned to them. For example, the string, MYX4885 is the registration number of a car, which has both letters and digits. In this string the digits have no 'value' in a conventional sense. If we want to store decimal numbers in a computer and perform arithmetic operations on them, the representation must have a value assigned to the numbers. In order to do this, we *convert* a decimal number to another number which uses only the symbols "0" and "1" and has a value which is equal to that of the given decimal number.

Consider, for example, the decimal number 4903. The value of each digit in this number is determined by:

(i) The *digit* itself

(ii) The *position* of the digit in the number

(iii) The *base* or *radix* of the number system.

The base of a number system is defined as the number of distinct symbols used to represent numbers in the system. The decimal system uses the ten symbols 0, 1, 2, 3, 4, 5, 6, 7, 8, and 9 and its base is thus ten.

Given a decimal integer, we assign it a value by first assigning weights to each digit position. The weights are unity for the right most digit, ten, hundred, thousand, and so on for successive digits to its left.

We multiply each digit by its weight and add all products to obtain the value of the number. The value of the decimal number 4903 is calculated as:

$$
\begin{array}{ccccccccl}
4 \times 1000 & + & 9 \times 100 & + & 0 \times 10 & + & 3 \times 1 & \\
4000 & + & 900 & + & 0 & + & 3 & = 4903 \\
\text{Thousands} & & \text{Hundreds} & & \text{Tens} & & \text{Units} & \\
\text{position} & & \text{position} & & \text{position} & & \text{position} &
\end{array}
$$

The notation used to express numbers described above is known as the *positional system*.

If a number system has only two symbols, then its *base* is 2. Such a system is known as a *binary* system. The two symbols used in the system, namely, 0 and 1 are binary digits or *bits*. Numbers in this system are strings of bits. For example, a binary number is shown below:

$$1 \ 0 \ 1 \ 0 \ 1$$

$$\downarrow \qquad\qquad\qquad\qquad \downarrow$$

Most significant   Least significant

bit   bit

The right most bit is called the *least significant bit* and the left most bit the *most significant bit*. The weights assigned to bits in this system are powers of 2, namely $2^0 = 1$, $2^1 = 2$, $2^2 = 4$ etc. In order to find the decimal value of a binary number, we multiply its least significant bit by the weight 1, the next bit to its left by 2 and so on. Thus the decimal value of the binary number 10101 is calculated as shown below:

1		0		1		0		1
1×2^4	+	0×2^3	+	1×2^2	+	0×2^1	+	1×2^0
16	+	0	+	4	+	0	+	1 = 21

As another example, the binary number 10010101 is converted to its decimal equivalent as shown below:

$$(1 \times 128) + (0 \times 64) + (0 \times 32) + (1 \times 16) + (0 \times 8) + (1 \times 4) + (0 \times 2) + (1 \times 1) = 149$$

Counting in the binary system is similar to that in decimal. In decimal we start from 0, add a 1, obtain 1 and continue adding 1 successively till we reach 9. As the base of the system is ten, there are no further symbols. Thus when we add 1 to 9 we count 10. The 1 becomes the *carry* to the tens position in the decimal system. Similarly we count 100 after reaching 99. Counting in binary system is similar and proceeds as follows:

$$0, 1, 10, 11, 100, 101, 110, 111, 1000, 1001. \ . \ . \ . \ .$$

Table 2.3 shows the binary counting sequence. Observe that we require 3 bits to represent decimal numbers 0 to 7 and 4 bits to represent 8 and 9. Thus, on the average

Table 2.3   Binary counting sequence

Binary number	Decimal equivalent	Binary number	Decimal equivalent
0	0	1001	9
1	1	1010	10
10	2	1011	11
11	3	1100	12
100	4	1101	13
101	5	1110	14
110	6	1111	15
111	7	10000	16
1000	8	10001	17

$\dfrac{8 \times 3 + 2 \times 4}{10} = 3.2$ binary digits are required to represent a decimal digit. This is somewhat similar to the statement: "The average number of children in a family is 2.5". What we mean by the statement: "a decimal digit is represented on the average by 3.2 bits" is that, if we convert a large number of decimal numbers and obtain their binary equivalents, the number of bits in each binary equivalent would be approximately 3.2 times the number of digits in the corresponding decimal number.

Just as powers of 10 are important in the decimal system of enumeration powers of 2 are important in binary system. We thus give in Table 2.4 powers of 2 and their decimal equivalents. The abbreviation K in Table 2.4 stands for 1024 which is approximately

Table 2.4 Powers of 2

Power of 2	Decimal equivalent	Abbreviation	Power of 2	Decimal equivalent	Abbreviation
2^0	1		2^{11}	2048	2K
2^1	2		2^{12}	4096	4K
2^2	4		2^{13}	8192	8K
2^3	8		2^{14}	16384	16K
2^4	16		2^{15}	32768	32K
2^5	32		2^{16}	65536	64K
2^6	64		2^{17}	131072	128K
2^7	128		2^{18}	262144	256K
2^8	256		2^{19}	524288	512K
2^9	512		2^{20}	1048576	1M
2^{10}	1024	1K	2^{21}	2097152	2M

1000, a *Kilo*. Thus the notation 16K means $16 \times 1024 = 16384$. The abbreviation M (Mega) stands for $1024 \times 1024 = 1048576$. The abbreviation G (Giga) is used to represent $1024 \times 1024 \times 1024$ which is nearly a billion.

2.3 REPRESENTATION OF FRACTIONS

So far we have considered decimal and binary integers. Decimal fractions are interpreted as follows:

$$0.235 \quad = \quad 2 \times 10^{-1} \quad + \quad 3 \times 10^{-2} \quad + \quad 5 \times 10^{-3}$$

Decimal point   One-tenth position   One-hundredth position   One-thousandth position

Observe that negative powers of 10 are used as weights to multiply the digits in the fractional part of the number.

A binary fraction is represented by a string of 1s and 0s on the right of a binary point. The bits are multiplied by negative powers of 2 to obtain the decimal value of the binary fraction as shown below:

$$0.1011 \quad = 1 \times 2^{-1} \quad + \quad 0 \times 2^{-2} \quad + \quad 1 \times 2^{-3} \quad + \quad 1 \times 2^{-4}$$

$$\text{Binary point} \; = \quad {}^{1}\!/_{2} \quad + \quad 0 \quad + \quad {}^{1}\!/_{8} \quad + \quad {}^{1}\!/_{16}$$

$$= \; {}^{11}\!/_{16} \quad = 0.6875 \text{ (in decimal)}$$

We give below some more examples of binary numbers and their decimal equivalents:

(i) $(111011.101)_2 = 1 \times 2^5 + 1 \times 2^4 + 1 \times 2^3 + 0 \times 2^2 + 1 \times 2^1 + 1 \times 2^0$
$$+ \; 1 \times 2^{-1} + 0 \times 2^{-2} + 1 \times 2^{-3}$$
$$= 32 + 16 + 8 + 2 + 1 + {}^{1}\!/_{2} + {}^{1}\!/_{8}$$
$$= (59.625)_{10}$$

(ii) $(11000.0011)_2 = 1 \times 2^4 + 1 \times 2^3 + 0 \times 2^2 + 0 \times 2^1 + 0 \times 2^0$
$$+ \; 0 \times 2^{-1} + 0 \times 2^{-2} + 1 \times 2^{-3} + 1 \times 2^{-4}$$
$$= 16 + 8 + {}^{1}\!/_{8} + {}^{1}\!/_{16}$$
$$= (24.1875)_{10}$$

Note that we have used the subscript 2 to indicate that the number is binary, and the subscript 10 to indicate that the number is decimal. This notation to represent the base of a number is useful to prevent misinterpretation of numbers.

2.4   HEXADECIMAL REPRESENTATION OF NUMBERS

The average number of bits needed to represent a decimal digit is 3.2, as pointed out in Section 2.2. Thus the binary equivalent of a 10-digit number will be approximately 32 bits long. It is difficult to write such long strings of 1s and 0s and convert them to equivalent decimal numbers without making mistakes. The *hexadecimal* system, which uses 16 as base, is a convenient notation to express binary numbers. This system, by definition, uses sixteen symbols, viz., 0, 1, 2, 3, 4, 5, 6, 7, 8, 9, A, B, C, D, E, F. Note that the symbols A, B etc. now represent numbers. As 16 is a power of 2, namely 2^4, there is a one-to-one correspondence between a hexadecimal digit and its binary equivalent. We need only 4 bits to represent a hexadecimal digit. Table 2.5 gives a table of hexadecimal digits and their binary and decimal equivalents.

Table 2.5   Binary hexadecimal and decimal equivalents

Binary number	Hexadecimal equivalent	Decimal equivalent	Binary number	Hexadecimal equivalent	Decimal equivalent
0000	0	0	1000	8	8
0001	1	1	1001	9	9
0010	2	2	1010	A	10
0011	3	3	1011	B	11
0100	4	4	1100	C	12
0101	5	5	1101	D	13
0110	6	6	1110	E	14
0111	7	7	1111	F	15

A binary number can be quickly converted to its hexadecimal equivalent by grouping together successively 4 bits of the binary number starting with the least significant bit and replacing each 4 bit group with its hexadecimal equivalent given in Table 2.5. The examples below illustrate this.

Examples

(i) Binary number   0111   1100   1101   1110   0011

    Hexadecimal equivalent: 7   C   D   E   3

(ii) Binary number   001   0001   1111   0000 · 0010   1100

    Hexadecimal equivalent: 1   1   F   0 · 2   C

Observe that in Example (ii) above, groups are formed from left to right for the fractional part of the number and from right to left for the integer part. If the number of bits in the integer part is not a multiple of 4, we insert *leading 0s,* as leading 0s have no significance for the integer part. If the number of bits in the fractional part is not a multiple of 4, then we introduce *trailing 0s,* as trailing 0s have no significance in the fractional part.

Conversion from hexadecimal to decimal system is simple. It uses the fact that the base of the hexadecimal system is 16. We give below two examples of hexadecimal to decimal conversion.

Examples

(i) $(D6C1)_{16}$
$$= D \times 16^3 + 6 \times 16^2 + C \times 16^1 + 1 \times 16^0$$
$$= 13 \times 16^3 + 6 \times 16^2 + 12 \times 16 + 1 \times 16^0$$
$$= 53248 + 1536 + 192 + 1$$
$$= (54977)_{10}$$

(ii) $(F9A \cdot BC3)_{16}$
$= F \times 16^2 + 9 \times 16^1 + A \times 16^0 + B \times 16^{-1} + C \times 16^{-2} + 3 \times 16^{-3}$
$= (15 \times 256) + (9 \times 16) + (10 \times 1) + 11/16 + 12/256 + 3/4096$
$= 3840 + 144 + 10 + 11/16 + 12/256 + 3/4096$
$= (3994.7351074)_{10}$

2.5 DECIMAL TO BINARY CONVERSION

As mentioned at the beginning of this chapter, external to the computer we use decimal numbers whereas internally we use binary representation. We thus have to convert decimal to binary. The method of converting a decimal integer to its binary equivalent is based on the fact that any decimal integer may be expressed as a sum of powers of 2 as shown below:

$$d = (23)_{10} = (1 \times 2^4) + (0 \times 2^3) + (1 \times 2^2) + (1 \times 2^1) + (1 \times 2^0)$$

$$= (10111)_2$$

The easiest way to find the coefficients of the powers of 2 is to divide the given number by 2 and the successive quotients by 2. Division is terminated when a quotient becomes zero. The binary equivalent of the decimal number is given by the sequence of remainders obtained during division. The least significant bit of the binary number is the first remainder obtained and its most significant bit is the last remainder. The procedure is illustrated below:

Example

    (i) Find the binary equivalent of $(23)_{10}$

2	23	*Remainder*	
2	11	1	⟶ Least significant bit
2	5	1	
2	2	1	
2	1	0	
	0	1	⟶ Most significant bit

The binary equivalent is thus: $(10111)_2$

    (ii) Find the binary equivalent of 36

2	36	*Remainder*	
2	18	0	⟶ Least significant bit
2	9	0	
2	4	1	
2	2	0	
2	1	0	
	0	1	⟶ Most significant bit

$(36)_{10} = (100100)_2$

Decimal to hexadecimal conversion is similar. In this case 16 is used as the divisor instead of 2. The following examples illustrate decimal to hexadecimal conversion.

Example

    (i) Find the hexadecimal equivalent of $(23)_{10}$

16	23		
16	1	7	⟶ Least significant hex-digit
	0	1	⟶ Most significant hex-digit

$(23)_{10} = (17)_{16} = 1 \times 16 + 7 \times 16^0 = (23)_{10}$

(ii) Find the hexadecimal equivalent of $(41819)_{10}$

		Decimal remainders	Hexadecimal equivalent	
16	41819			
16	2613	11	B	⟶ Least significant hex-digit
16	163	5	5	
16	10	3	3	
	0	10	A	⟶ Most significant hex-digit

$(41819)_{10} = (A35B)_{16}$

Decimal fractions may also be converted to binary. The method is based on observing that a decimal fraction is expressed as a sum of negative powers of 2. Successive multiplication of the fraction by 2 would give the coefficients of the negative powers of 2.

Example

$$(0.8125)_{10} \quad = 0.5 + 0.25 + 0.0625$$
$$= 1 \times 2^{-1} + 1 \times 2^{-2} + 0 \times 2^{-3} + 1 \times 2^{-4}$$

$$2 \times 0.8125 \quad = 1 + (1 \times 2^{-1} + 0 \times 2^{-2} + 1 \times 2^{-3})$$
$$= 1 + 0.625$$

$$2 \times 0.625 \quad = 2\,(1 \times 2^{-1} + 0 \times 2^{-2} + 1 \times 2^{-3})$$
$$= 1 + (0 \times 2^{-1} + 1 \times 2^{-2})$$
$$= 1 + 0.25$$

$$2 \times 0.25 \quad = 2\,(0 \times 2^{-1} + 1 \times 2^{-2})$$
$$= 0 + 0.5$$

$$2 \times 0.5 \quad = 2 \times 2^{-1}$$
$$= 1$$

Thus $(0.8125)_{10} = (0.1101)_2$

It is clear from the above example that if we multiply a decimal fraction by 2, the integer part of the answer will be the most significant bit of the binary fraction. The fractional part of the answer is multiplied by 2 to obtain the next significant bit of the binary fraction. The procedure is continued till the fractional part of the product is 0. The method is illustrated below with examples:

Example

(i) Find the binary equivalent of $(0.5625)_{10}$

	Product	Integer part of product

$$0.5625 \times 2 = 1.125 \qquad 1 \longrightarrow \text{Most significant bit}$$
$$0.1250 \times 2 = 0.25 \qquad 0$$
$$0.2500 \times 2 = 0.5 \qquad 0$$
$$0.5 \quad\ \times 2 = 1.0 \qquad 1 \longrightarrow \text{Least significant bit}$$
$$(0.5625)_{10} \ = (0.1001)_2$$

(ii) Find the binary equivalent of 0.3

	Product	Integer part of product

$$0.3 \times 2 \quad 0.6 \qquad 0 \longrightarrow \text{Most significant bit}$$
$$0.6 \times 2 \quad 1.2 \qquad 1$$
$$0.2 \times 2 \quad 0.4 \qquad 0$$
$$0.4 \times 2 \quad 0.8 \qquad 0$$
$$0.8 \times 2 \quad 1.6 \qquad 1$$

- -

$$0.6 \times 2 \quad 1.2 \qquad 1 \qquad\qquad \text{Recurs beyond this point}$$

Thus $(0.3)_{10} = (0.01001(1001))_2$

This example shows that the binary fraction equivalent of a terminating decimal fraction may not terminate.

Converting decimal fractions to hexadecimal fractions is similar. In this case we multiply the decimal fraction by 16.

Example

(i) Find the hexadecimal equivalent of $(0.5625)_{10}$

	Product	Integer part

$$0.5625 \times 16 = 9.0000 \qquad 9$$

Thus $(0.5625)_{10} = (9)_{16}$

(ii) Find the hexadecimal equivalent of $(0.3)_{10}$

	Product	Integer part of product	Hex-digit

$$0.3 \times 16 \qquad\quad 4.8 \qquad\qquad 4 \qquad\qquad 4$$
$$0.8 \times 16 \qquad\quad 12.8 \qquad\qquad 12 \qquad\qquad C$$

- -

$$0.8 \times 16 \qquad\quad 12.8 \qquad\qquad 12 \qquad\qquad C \qquad \text{Recurs beyond this point}$$

Thus $(0.3)_{10} \quad = (0.4CCC. \ . \ . \ .)_{16}$

2.6 ERROR-DETECTING CODES

Errors may occur in recording data on magnetic surfaces due to bad spots on the surface. Errors may also be caused by electrical disturbances during data transmissions between units. It is thus necessary to device methods to guard against such errors. The main principle used for this purpose in coded data is the introduction of extra bits in the code to aid error-detection. A common method is the use of a *parity check bit* along with each character code. A parity check bit is appended to the 7 bits of the code of each character in such a way that the total number of 1s in each character code is *even*. For instance, the ASCII code of the letter E is 1000101. The number of 1s in this string is odd. A parity check bit 1 is appended to this string to obtain a code which is now 8 bits long and has an even number of 1s in it. If the ASCII code of a character has already an even number of 1s in it, then the parity check bit appended is 0. For example, the ASCII code of A is 1000001 and its code with an appended parity check bit is 10000010. All characters now have 8 bit codes including the parity check bit. Whenever a character is read from storage or received from a remote location, the number of 1s in its code is counted. It has to be even. If it is odd, then at least one bit is wrong. A *single* error in any of the eight bits of the code will definitely be detected. Two errors cannot be detected by this scheme as the total number of 1s in the code will remain even after two bits change. As the probability of more than one error occurring is in practice very small this scheme is commonly accepted as adequate.

Instead of appending a parity check bit which makes the total number of 1s in the code even, one may choose to append a parity check bit which makes the total number of 1s in the code odd. Such a parity check bit is known as an *odd parity check* bit. This scheme also facilitates detection of a single error in a code.

Codes have also been deviced which use more than one check bit to not only detect but also correct errors. These are called *error-correcting codes*. We will not discuss these codes in this book. Interested readers may refer to [2] given among references.

SUMMARY

1. As the physical devices used for storage and processing of data in computers are two-state devices, it is necessary to transform or code all data using only two symbols.

2. The two symbols used are, by convention, the digits 0 and 1. These are called "binary digits" or "bits" for short.

3. The number of unique strings possible in a code with 2 bits in each string is 4. These strings are 00, 01, 10 and 11. In general the number of unique strings with n bits in each string is 2^n. Each string in this set of strings may be used to code or represent one character. There are 128 unique strings with 7 bits each.

4. The American Standards Institution has evolved a standard code to represent characters to be stored and processed by computers. This code, called ASCII, uses 7 bits to represent each character. The ASCII code defines codes for English letters (capital and

small), decimal digits, 32 special characters and codes for a number of symbols used to control the operation of a computer. The symbols used for control are non-printable.

5. Decimal numbers are coded depending on the manner in which they are to be processed by the computer. If they are used merely as symbols without any attached values, such numbers (e.g., motor car registration numbers, post codes, telephone numbers etc.) are *coded* using the ASCII code. If values are to be assigned to decimal numbers and if they are used as operands in arithmetic operations, then they are *converted* to equivalent binary numbers.

6. Binary numbers are formed using the positional notation. Powers of 2 are used as weights in the binary number system. A binary number 10111, for example, has a decimal $value = 1 \times 2^4 + 0 \times 2^3 + 1 \times 2^2 + 1 \times 2^1 + 1 \times 2^0 = 23$.

7. A decimal number is converted into an equivalent binary number by dividing the number by 2 and storing the remainder as the least significant bit of the binary number. The quotient is divided by 2 and the remainder becomes the next bit of the binary number. This procedure is continued till the quotient becomes 0. The binary equivalent of 9, for example, is 1001.

8. High-valued binary numbers will be represented by a long sequence of 0s and 1s. A more concise representation is obtained using the hexadecimal notation. The base of the hexadecimal system is 16 and the symbols used in this system are: 0, 1, 2, 3, 4, 5, 6, 7, 8, 9, A, B, C, D, E, F. Strings of 4 bits have an exact equivalent hexadecimal value. This facilitates conversion of binary numbers to hexadecimal numbers. For example, the binary number 101 1101 1011 1110 0011 0100 is equal to the hexadecimal number 5DBE34.

9. Decimal fractions may be converted to binary fractions.

10. Errors may occur while recording and reading data and when data is transmitted from one unit to another unit in a computer. Detection of a single error in the code for a character is possible by introducing an extra bit in its code. This bit, known as the parity check bit, is appended to the code. This bit is chosen so that the total number of 1s in the new code is even. If a single bit is incorrectly read, written or transmitted, then the total number of 1s in the corrupted code would become odd thereby indicating an error.

REVIEW QUESTIONS

2.1 What is the meaning of the term "external representation" of data?

2.2 What are the considerations that govern the selection of a representation for storing and processing data in a computer?

2.3 Why are binary digits used to code data to be stored in a computer?

2.4 How many unique strings are there with 6 bits in each string?

2.5 If the capital English letters, digits and 16 special characters are to be coded as strings of bits, how many bits will be required for each string?

2.6 What is ASCII code?

2.7 How many bits per character does ASCII code use?

2.8 Why are not-printable characters assigned code in ASCII?

2.9 Define a byte.

2.10 What is ISCII?

2.11 Under what circumstances are decimal digits coded using ASCII?

2.12 Under what circumstances are decimal numbers converted into binary numbers?

2.13 What is the difference between the bits used in a code such as ASCII and the bits used in binary numbers?

2.14 Find the decimal values of the following binary numbers:
1011010, 0101111, 111111 and 100001.

2.15 What are the binary equivalents of the decimal numbers 7, 20, 31, 64?

2.16 In octal number system, the symbols used are 0, 1, 2, 3, 4, 5, 6, 7. What is the base of the system?

2.17 What is the binary equivalent of the octal number 723?

2.18 What is the octal equivalent of the binary number 10001010101?

2.19 What are the decimal equivalents of the following binary fractions:
0.01101, 0.11010, 0.00011?

2.20 What are the binary equivalents of the following decimal fractions:
0.7625, 0.8, 0.245?

2.21 What is the decimal equivalent of the octal fraction 0.647?

2.22 What is the octal equivalent of the decimal fraction 0.789?

2.23 What is the advantage of using hexadecimal numbers?

2.24 Convert the following binary numbers to hexadecimal:
100101010101, 0101110111101, 1011000001.

2.25 What are the decimal values of the hexadecimal numbers found in the previous question?

2.26 Convert the following binary numbers to hexadecimal and then to decimal:
1000100101.1101011, 101001011111.0010001

2.27 Convert the following decimal numbers to hexadecimal:
285.48, 3452.645, 678920.45

2.28 What is the purpose of using a parity check bit?

2.29 Write down the ASCII codes for H, T and 7. Add even parity check bit to each code. Explain how a single error will be detected in each code.

3

Input/Output Units

In the previous chapter we discussed methods used to store data in a computer. Data to be processed by a computer usually originate as written documents. For example, if the average marks obtained by a student in an examination is to be computed, the data will originate as a document which will contain the roll number of the student, his name, and the marks obtained by the student in each subject. The data has to be first converted to a form which can be read by an input unit of the computer. This form is known as *machine readable form.* The data in machine readable form is read by an input unit, transformed to appropriate internal code and stored in the computer's memory.

The processed data stored in the memory is sent to an output unit when commanded by a program. The output unit transforms the internal representation of data into a form which can be read by people. For example, after processing the marks of a student, the output would be the roll number of the student, name, marks in each subject, average marks and passing division. This result would be printed in a nice format by the output unit. Figure 3.1 illustrates the various states in data transformation.

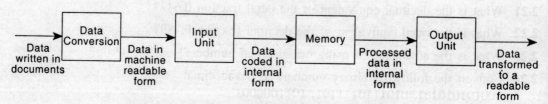

Fig. 3.1 Illustrating steps in data input and output.

In this chapter we will examine the functioning of a variety of input and output units used by computers.

3.1 DESCRIPTION OF COMPUTER INPUT UNITS

The input and output units of a computer are normally abbreviated as I/O units. There are a variety of input units which are used by computers. Some of them are general purpose, that is, they may be used by any computer. The most commonly used units of this type are magnetic floppy disc readers and keyboard of video terminals. Special purpose units are magnetic ink character readers, optical mark readers, optical character readers and bar code readers. We will briefly describe these methods used to input information to computers.

3.1.1 Key to Floppy Data Entry System

In this system, data from documents is recorded on a magnetic medium called a *floppy disk*. A floppy disk is made of a flexible circular disk of plastic (diameter 3.5 inches) coated with a magnetic material. The disk is enclosed in a square hard plastic cover and weighs about 20 grams. Each floppy disk can store approximately one million characters. An average page of a book has about 2500 characters. Thus one can store the contents of a 400 page book in one floppy disk.

Data is recorded on a floppy disk using a *personal computer* abbreviated as PC. A PC has a keyboard similar to a standard typewriter keyboard with additional control keys. It also has a display which displays each character keyed in. A floppy disk is inserted in a slot on the machine. A clicking sound indicates that the floppy disk is firmly held by a spindle. When a switch is turned ON, the disk is rotated at a constant speed of about 360 revolutions per minute by a motor. A magnetic head is positioned touching the disk. This head magnetizes the surface of the disk below the head. When a binary 1 is to be stored, the information is sent to the head, and it magnetizes a spot below with left to right pole alignment (S→N). Similarly the binary 0 is stored with right to left pole alignment (N←S). Information is thus stored along a circular track as a series of magnetized spots (see Fig. 3.2).

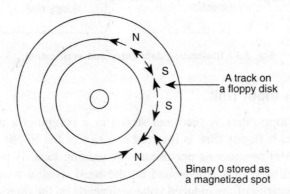

Fig. 3.2 Information stored on a floppy disk along a set of concentric tracks.

A data entry operator records data from the source document on the floppy disk by depressing appropriate keys on the keyboard. To facilitate data entry a blank form with appropriate number of columns and headings is displayed on the screen. The keyed data are held in temporary storage in a coded form till all 80 characters are entered. If an error is made in entering a data item, the operator can back-space and re-enter it. The operator gives a command to save when the data is ready to be entered on the floppy disk. The coded characters are sent to the recording head of the floppy disk and they are recorded along a circular track. When a track is full, the head moves to the next concentric track.

Data entered on a floppy disk should be verified to detect and correct any errors made by the data entry operator. This is done by giving the source document to another data entry operator and asking him to enter it on another floppy disk. The two floppy disks are then inserted in a personal computer and a program reads corresponding records from the two disks and compares them. If they do not match the record which does not match is displayed on the screen. It is then corrected by the operator by referring to the source document. Thus the final data entered is correct. Figure 3.3 illustrates data entry and verification when floppy disks are used to store data.

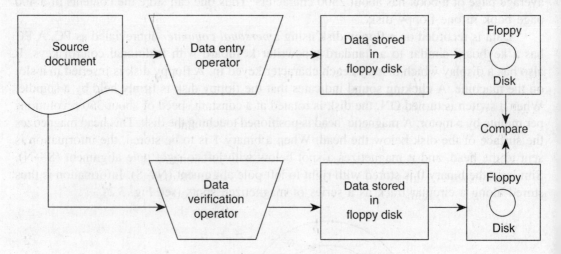

Fig. 3.3   Illustrating data entry and verification.

3.1.2   Floppy Disk Input Unit

Data recorded on a floppy disk is read and stored in a computer's memory by a device called a floppy reader. A floppy disk is inserted in a slot of the floppy input unit. The disk is rotated at around 360 revolutions per minute. A reading head is positioned touching a track. A voltage is induced in a coil wound on the head when a magnetized spot moves below the head. The polarity of the induced voltage depends on the direction of magnetization of the spot under the head. The polarity of voltage when a 1 is read is opposite to the voltage when a 0 is read. The voltage sensed by the head coil is amplified, converted to an appropriate signal and stored in the computer's memory.

3.1.3   Video Terminals (VDU)

A video terminal or a video display unit consists of a television screen and a keyboard similar to a typewriter keyboard with additional control keys. When a key is pressed, the corresponding character is displayed on the screen. Simultaneously a cursor moves to the position where the next character will be displayed. A cursor is a small arrow, underline or a small square which can be moved horizontally or vertically to indicate the position of a character.

The cathode ray television tube is scanned by an electron beam to create a raster of horizontal lines. The intensity of the electron beam is increased at certain moments creating bright spots on the face of the tube. Each character is displayed by a matrix of 5 horizontal and 7 vertical dots. Figure 3.4 illustrates one such character.

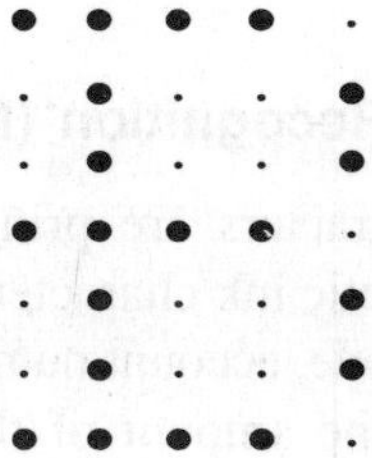

Fig. 3.4   A 7 × 5 dot matrix to display characters (the letter B is displayed here).

A display normally has 80 characters per horizontal line and 24 such lines on the screen.

When a key on the keyboard is pressed, the corresponding character is displayed on the screen and simultaneously an appropriately coded series of electrical pulses are sent to the computer's memory. If a wrong key is pressed, the operator can back-space and re-type the correct character. Some terminals have built into them some computing power and extra storage, allowing sophisticated editing of information before it is sent to the computer.

Video terminals used for bulk data entry often display a blank form type outline with column headings to facilitate data entry.

Figure 3.5 illustrates a typical video display unit used with computers.

Fig. 3.5   ELT 320 video display terminal.   (*Courtesy*: Digital Equipment Corporation)

3.2 OTHER INPUT METHODS

There are some more specialized input methods which are occasionally used. These are briefly described in the following part:

3.2.1 Magnetic Ink Character Recognition (MICR)

In this method, human readable characters are printed on documents (such as cheques) using a special magnetic ink. A magnetic ink character reader can recognize such characters. In a cheque, for instance, the branch code, account number, and cheque number are preprinted at the bottom using magnetic ink. The amount of the cheque is later entered by a clerk using a machine which prints the amount with magnetic ink. The cheque itself can now be read using a special input unit which can recognize magnetic ink characters. This method eliminates the need to manually enter data from cheques into a floppy. Besides saving time, this method ensures accuracy of data entry. Figure 3.6 illustrates magnetic ink character fonts.

3.2.2 Optical Mark Reading and Recognition (OMR)

In this method special preprinted forms are designed with boxes which can be marked with a dark pencil or ink. Each box is annotated distinctly so that the user clearly understands

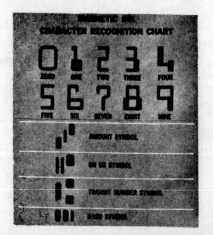

Fig. 3.6 Photograph of magnetic ink characters.

what response he is marking. Such a document is read by a document reader which transcribes the marks into electrical pulses which are transmitted to the computer.

These documents are applicable in areas where responses are one out of a small number of alternatives and the volume of data to be processed is large. Thus they are used for

(i) Objective type answer papers in examinations in which large number of candidates appear.

(ii) Market surveys, population surveys etc., where responses can be restricted to one or more out of a few possibilities.

(iii) Order forms containing a small choice of items.

(iv) Time sheets of factory employees in which start and stop times may be marked.

The advantage of this method is that information is entered at its source and no further transcription is required. This minimizes unreliability of data. The main disadvantage is the need for accurate alignment of printing on forms and the need for good quality expensive paper. The form cannot be redesigned frequently because any change will require reprinting of the form, which is expensive.

3.2.3 Optical Character Recognition (OCR)

An optical scanner is a device used to read an image, convert it into a set of 0s and 1s and store this in computer's memory. The image may be a handwritten document, a typed or a printed document or a picture. We will now explain how this conversion is done. Assume that the image is drawn on a graph sheet. If there is a dark spot at an intersection of a horizontal and a vertical line of the graph (called a grid point) the image is represented by a 1. If there is no dark spot at a grid point it is represented by a 0. The representation of the drawing of Fig. 3.7 as 0s and 1s is shown in Fig. 3.8. This representation is called the *bit map* of the image. Each bit in the representation of the image is called a pixel (a picture element).

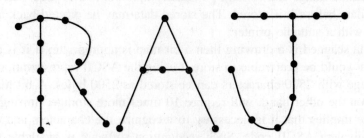

Fig. 3.7   A figure scanned.

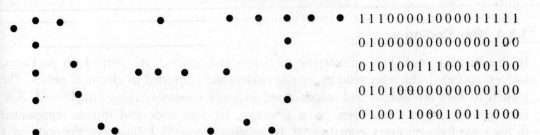

1110000100001111

0100000000000100

0101001110010010 0

0101000000000100

0100110001001 1000

Fig. 3.8   Bit map representation of Fig. 3.7.

An optical scanner converts an image to an equivalent bitmap representation. There are two types of scanners. One is a hand held scanner and the other a flat bed scanner. A hand held scanner is around 13 cm long and 15 cm wide with a handle to enable it to be held conveniently in hand. A set of light emitting diodes is enclosed in it. It is placed over the material to be scanned and slowly dragged from the top to the bottom. The light emitted by the diodes are not reflected by black lines and are reflected by white areas. The material is converted and stored as a bit map. If the scanner is moved slowly (2.2 cm/second) the image is converted into 400 bits per inch (160 bits per cm) and stored. The hand held scanner is an inexpensive device costing around Rs. 3000/-. The scanner has to be dragged very steadily and carefully over the material. If it is not dragged carefully the conversion of the material into a bit map will not be correct. It is thus used only in cases where high accuracy is not needed. Typical applications are to store images and reproduce them in publications.

A flat bed scanner consists of a box with a glass plate on top and a cover which covers the glass plate. The document to be scanned is placed above the glass plate. The light beam is situated below the glass plate and is moved from left to right horizontally. After scanning one line the beam moves up a little and scans the next line. It takes about 20 second to scan an entire page of size 21 cm × 28 cm. The contents of the page is stored as a bit map of 400 dots per inch. Each dot may be encoded as just 1 bit. If different shades from black to grey to white are to be encoded then 4 bits are used to represent each dot. The scanner can also store colour images. A 24 bit representation for each dot is used to represent a maximum of 256 colours. The scanner can be connected to a computer and the bits may be stored in it. As each scanned image can contain potentially upto 300K bits/page, software is used to compress the data before it is stored. The stored data may be printed back as an image by the computer with a suitable printer.

If the data scanned is a drawing then a bit map is appropriate. If it is a printed page, for example, it would be preferable to store it using the ASCII representation of characters, as a typical page with 2500 characters can be stored as 2500 bytes. A bit map of the same printed page, on the other hand, will require 10 times more storage. Storing the text using an ASCII code implies that it is necessary to recognize the characters and convert the bit map to an equivalent ASCII code. Such recognition software is available for texts using standard type fonts. If the printed matter contains italics, bold face letters and other special fonts then the recognition software does not work effectively. There is yet no fully automated recognition software to convert hand written text to ASCII.

3.2.4 Bar Coding

In this method small bars of varying thickness and spacing are printed on packages, badges, tags etc., which are read by optical readers and converted to electrical pulses. The pattern of bars are unique and standardized in some countries. For example in U.S.A. each grocery product has been given a unique 10 digit code and this is represented in bar code form on every container of the product. Figure 3.9 illustrates bar code on a product.

Fig. 3.9 Photograph of bar coding for products.

3.2.5 Speech Input Unit

A unit which takes as its input spoken words, and converts them to a form which can be "understood" by a computer is called a speech input unit. By understanding we mean that the unit can uniquely code (as a sequence of bits) each spoken word and can interpret and initiate action based on the word. Giving a spoken command is much quicker than typing out such a command. Speech input unit is particularly useful in situations where commands are to be given to a remote computer using a telephone or when one's hands are not free.

Speech input units may be classified as:

(a) Single word recognition unit, and

(b) Continuous speech recognition unit.

By a single word recognition we mean recognizing single word commands such as STOP, START, ONE, YES, NO etc. By continuous speech we mean a sentence spoken continuously such as WHAT TIME DOES SHATAPDI EXPRESS ARRIVE? Recognizing single words is easier than recognizing spoken sentences. Speech input unit may be further classified as

(i) Speaker dependent, and

(ii) Speaker independent.

A speaker dependent unit is designed to recognize the speech of a particular person, whereas a speaker independent unit recognizes the spoken input of any person. Speaker dependent units are easier to design and have been designed to recognize both single word and continuous speech using a limited vocabulary. In this case the unit is "trained" by the specified user to recognize his/her speech. Speaker independent units are much more difficult to build. Speaker independent units have been designed for recognizing single words. Speaker independent continuous speech units for limited purposes such as simple enquiry are being designed but are not widely available as commercial products.

3.3 COMPUTER OUTPUT UNITS

There are three principal devices to output information from a computer. These are: a printer, a video terminal and a computer output microfilm. Of these three, printing is the most common method. Microfilming is expensive and used only in special cases.

3.3.1 Printers

Computer printers fall into two main categories, namely, line printers and serial character printers. A line printer prints a complete line at a time. Printing speeds vary from 150 lines to 2500 lines per minute with 96 to 160 characters on a 15 inch line. Six to eight lines per vertical inch are printed. One may buy printers with a variety of character sets. Usually 64 and 96 character sets are used with English letters. Printers are available in almost all scripts, e.g., Japanese, Arabic, Cyrillic (Russian) etc.

There are two types of line printers. These are the *drum printers* and the *chain printers*. A drum printer consists of a cylindrical drum. The characters to be printed are embossed on its surface. One complete set of characters is embossed for each and every print position on a line. Thus a printer with 132 characters per line and a 96 character set will have on its surface $132 \times 96 = 12672$ characters embossed (see Fig. 3.10).

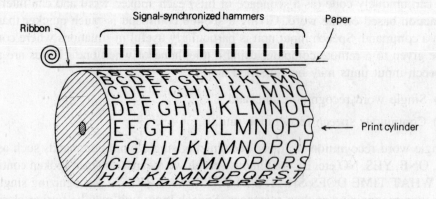

Fig. 3.10 Printing cylinder of a drum printer.

The codes of all characters to be printed on one line are transmitted from the memory of the computer to a storage unit in the printer. The storage unit called a *printer buffer register* can normally store 132 character codes. The printer drum is rotated at a high speed. A set of print hammers, one for each character in a line, are mounted in front of the drum. The position of each character on a band of the drum surface is coded using its angular displacement from the origin. A character is printed by striking a hammer against the embossed character on the surface. A carbon ribbon and paper are interposed between the hammer and the drum. As the drum rotates, the hammer waits, and is activated when the character to be printed at that position (as given in the print buffer register) appears in front of the hammer. Thus the drum would have to complete one full revolution for a line to be printed. This is called "on the fly" printing as the drum continues to rotate at a high speed when the hammer strikes it. Thus the hammer must strike very quickly and must be accurately synchronized with drum movement. If the hammer striking is mistimed, then the printed line looks wavy and slightly blurred. Printer drums are expensive and cannot be changed often. Thus drum printers have a fixed font.

3.3.2 Chain Printers

A chain printer has a steel band on which the character sets are embossed. For a 64 character set printer, 4 sets of 64 characters each would be embossed on the band. For printing a line, all the characters in the line are sent from the memory to the printer buffer register. The band is rotated at a high speed. As the band rotates, a hammer is activated when the desired character as specified in the buffer register comes in front of it. For a printer with 132 characters per line, 132 hammers will be positioned to strike the carbon ribbon which is placed between the chain, paper and the hammer. In this printer also the hammer movement and chain movement should be accurately synchronized. Bad synchronization leads to blurred lines. Wavy lines do not appear in such printers as the characters are moved horizontally by the chain.

The main advantage of chain or band printers is the ease with which chains may be changed. Thus different fonts and different scripts may be used with the same printer. Line printers are normally designed for heavy printing applications and can print continuously for a few hours. Figure 3.11 is a photograph of a line printer.

3.3.3 Serial Printers

Serial printers print one character at a time, with the print head moving across a line. They are similar to typewriters. Serial printers are normally slow (30 to 300 characters per second). The most popular serial printer is called a "dot matrix" printer. In such a printer the print head consists of an array of pins.

Characters to be printed are sent one character at a time from the memory to the printer. The character code is decoded by the printer electronics and activates the appropriate pins in the print head.

These pins are moved forward to form a character and they hit the carbon ribbon in front of the paper thereby printing that character. Many dot matrix printers are bidirectional, that is, they print from left to right as well as print from right to left on return. This speeds up printing.

Fig. 3.11 Photograph of a line printer. (*Courtesy* : Digital Equipment Corporation)

An advantage of dot matrix printers is the possibility of converting them to print alphabets other than English. It is possible to adopt them to print Devanagari script, Tamil script etc.

Currently dot matrix printers which have a print head with 24 pins in a vertical line are available. In such printers the head is moved horizontally in small increments to print characters. These printers give very high quality printed outputs and are called "near letter quality" printers. They are quieter compared to older dot matrix printers.

Character printers are less expensive compared to line printers. But they cannot be used continuously for more than an hour or so and are thus called "light duty" printers. Figure 3.12 depicts a dot matrix print head.

3.3.4 Letter Quality Printers

As a character produced by a dot matrix printer is made up of a finite number of dots, the appearance of the printed output is not very good. For better looking output where characters are represented by sharp continuous lines, a character printer known as the *inkjet* printer is used. An inkjet printer consists of a print head which has a number of small holes or nozzles. Individual holes can be heated very rapidly (in a few micro seconds) by an integrated

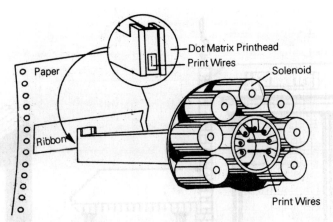

Fig. 3.12 A dot matrix print head.

circuit resistor. When the resistor heats up the ink near it vapourizes and is ejected through the nozzle and makes a dot on paper placed near the head. A high resolution inkjet printer has around 50 nozzles within a height of 7 mm and can print with a resolution of 300 dots per inch. A fairly complex electronic system selects the holes to be heated based on the character to be printed. The head is also moved rapidly across the paper. The printer has enough memory to print an entire page accommodating different fonts. Latest inkjet printers have multiple heads, one per colour which allows colour printing. The printing speed of inkjet printers is around 120 characters per second. Inkjet printers can also be used to draw figures besides printing text. Colour inkjet printers are now commonly available.

3.3.5 Printer Plotters

Apart from printed outputs, in many applications, a graphical output is very useful. For example, pie charts, bar charts and graphs with annotations are useful representations of information. Dot matrix character printers are now manufactured in which the print head can move from left to right and right to left and the paper movement is also controllable and it can move up or down. This enables the printer to draw graphs, pie charts etc. Some printers come with multiple colour ribbons. The ribbon movement is controllable and ribbons of the appropriate colour can be positioned in front of the print head at appropriate times. This allows printing of multicolour graphs and charts. Figure 3.13 illustrates the output obtained from a printer plotter. The drawings obtained by using inkjet printers, however, have much better resolution.

3.3.6 Plotters

Besides printer plotters special plotters to produce good quality drawings and graphs have been designed and are available in the market. There are two types of plotters. One is called a *drum plotter* and the other a *flat bed plotter*.

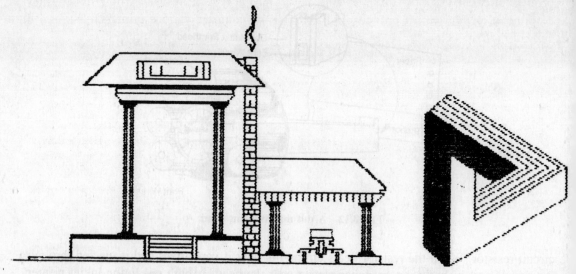

Fig. 3.13   Photograph of outputs obtained from a printer plotter.
(*Courtesy* : Ultra Business Machines, Bangalore)

In a drum plotter, the paper on which the graph is to be drawn is mounted on a rotating drum. A pen which can move linearly, i.e. perpendicular to the direction of drum rotation, is mounted on a carriage. The drum can rotate in either clockwise or anti-clockwise direction under the control of the plotting instructions sent by the computer. The pen can move left to right or right to left. The pen can also move up or down. The movements of the pen and drum are controlled by the graph plotting program. The program can thus draw various graphs and also annotate them by using the pen to draw characters.

A flat bed plotter has a stationary horizontal plotting surface on which paper is fixed. The pen is mounted on a carriage which can move in either *X* or *Y* direction. The pen can also be moved up or down. A graph plotting computer program is used to move the pen to trace the desired graph.

3.3.7   Laser Printers

The basic limitation of line and serial printers is the need for a head to move and impinge on a ribbon to print characters. This mechanical movement is relatively slow due to the high inertia of mechanical elements. Intensive research and development with the goal to eliminate mechanical motion in printers has been conducted by computer manufacturers. One such effort has led to the development of laser printers. In these printers, an electronically controlled laser beam traces out the desired character to be printed on a photoconductive drum. The drum attracts an ink toner on to the exposed areas. This image is transferred to the paper which comes in contact with the drum. Low speed laser printers which print 4 to 8 pages per minute are now very popular and cost around Rs 0.5 lakh. Very fast printers are also available which print over 10,000 lines per minute. At present they are very expensive and cost around Rs 5 lakhs. These printers give excellent (graphic arts quality) outputs and can print a variety of fonts. As these printers do not have a type head striking on a ribbon, they are known as *non impact* printers. In Table 3.1 we compare various printers.

Table 3.1 Comparison of printers

Printer type	Speed	Resolution	Capital cost	Running cost (per page)	Drawing capability	Capacity
Drum and Chain printer	100 lines/minute 132 char/line	Average	High	Low	No	Heavy duty. Can take multiple carbon copies
Dot matrix printer	100 char/sec	Average	Low	Low	Poor	Average. Can take 2 or 3 carbon copies
Inkjet printer	100 char/sec	Good 100 dots/cm	Low	Higher than dot matrix	Good	Light duty. Single copy
Laser printer (Low speed)	10 pages/min.	Good 120 dots/cm	Higher than inkjet	Lower than inkjet	Good	Light duty. Single copy
Laser printer (High speed)	10000 lines/min.	Very good 600 dots/cm	High	Low	Good	Heavy duty. Single copy

3.3.8 Computer Output on Microfilm and Microfiche

This is often used to store massive data in a compact form. The output from the computer, instead of being printed on a line printer, is displayed on a high resolution cathode ray tube. This is photographed on a 35 mm film. A camera is controlled to film successive output pages on the screen of the cathode ray tube. A special microfilm reader is used to read the output. Some microfilm readers also produce a hard copy using Xerographic process.

In some systems, the microfilm is converted to a *microfiche* form. A microfiche is a 4" × 6" sheet of film that holds 98 frames of $8\frac{1}{2}$" × 11" page images reduced 24 times. It is easier to read a microfiche with a microfiche reader than it is to read a microfilm. Besides this, microfiche is easier to mail between locations and hence its popularity.

3.3.9 Graphic Display Device

Video terminals capable of displaying graphs and pictorial data are very popular with computer users. Monochrome as well as multicolour terminals are available. Such terminals are particularly useful since pictorial information enhances one's understanding of solutions to problems. Figure 3.14 illustrates a graphic terminal. Details of such terminals are discussed in Chapter 14.

Fig. 3.14 **Desktop graphics computer.** (*Courtesy* : Silicon Graphics)

Input devices to input graphical information such as drawings and maps, called graphics tablets, are useful. A digitizing tablet (Fig. 3.15) locates the coordinates on its surface by the tip of a stylus positioned by the user and feeds these coordinates to the computer. One method of locating coordinates is to feed to the tip of the stylus electrical pulses. These pulses are picked up by electrodes embedded on the tablet. The position of the electrode which picks up a particular pulse locates the *X-Y* coordinates of the stylus.

3.3.10   Flat Panel Displays

Cathode ray tube displays used by desktop computers are very bulky and not suitable for portable computers generally known as laptop or notebook computers. Laptop computers use flat panel displays which use liquid crystals (used by digital watches and calculators) for displaying output of a computer. Other flat panel displays which are emerging are called Plasma Display and Field emission display. As of now so called active matrix Liquid Crystal Displays are most commonly used in portable computers but products based on other technologies are being test marketed and may emerge in a year or two.

3.3.11   Speech Output Unit

A speech output unit is one which reads strings of characters stored in a computer's memory and converts them into spoken sentences. Combinations of letters form a unit of speech called a phoneme. Electronic chips have been designed which accept ASCII characters of a sentence, combine sequence of words into a phoneme, amplifies them and outputs them through a small loudspeaker unit. These speech units for English have been greatly refined and a near natural speech emerges out of such units. These units are useful in many applications. They are used to give voice commands to operators of plants based on results of computations. They are used as parts of a machine which can read out printed matter to

Fig. 3.15 Photograph of a graphics tablet. (*Courtesy*: Hewlett Packard, Inc.)

blind persons. Sentences input and stored in a floppy disk can be read out to the blind by using these units. New machines are being sold in which a printed text can be placed on a flat bed scanner, scanned and the text spoken out. This enables blind persons to read books as soon as they are printed, rather than wait for the book to appear in braille.

SUMMARY

1. Data to be processed by computers originate as written documents. It is necessary to convert these to a form readable by computer's input unit.

2. Documents are converted to a machine-readable form by entering data using the keyboard of a Personal Computer and storing it in a floppy disk.

3. The commonly used input units are floppy disk reader, and video terminals. Besides this, magnetic ink character reader, bar code reader and optical mark reader are used for specific applications.

4. The most common output units are line printers and character printers. These provide hard copies. Video display terminals may also be used to examine sample outputs. Inkjet and laser printers are used to get good quality outputs.

5. Graphical output may be obtained using drum plotters or laser printers. Graphs may also be obtained using dot matrix printers which will be poorer in quality. Video graphical display units are also useful to examine graphical outputs.

6. Graphical information may also be input using light-pens associated with video terminals or by using flat-bed graphics tablets.

7. Speech input and output units are used for special applications.

REVIEW QUESTIONS

3.1 Explain the term 'data in machine readable form'.

3.2 What is the purpose of a data entry machine?

3.3 Explain the method used to ensure that input data is free from data entry errors.

3.4 Explain how characters are recorded on a floppy disk.

3.5 How many pages of text (each page has 2000 characters) can be stored in a 3.5 inch floppy disk?

3.6 Describe the operation of a floppy disk reader.

3.7 What is the difference between a line printer and a character printer?

3.8 What is the difference between a drum printer and a chain printer?

3.9 What is the advantage of a chain printer as compared to a drum printer?

3.10 What is the difference between an impact printer and a non-impact printer? Which is capable of higher speed?

3.11 What is the advantage of an inkjet printer compared to a dot matrix printer?

3.12 What is the advantage of a microfilm output?

3.13 What is the difference between a video graphic terminal and a graph plotter?

3.14 What is the main application of magnetic ink character readers?

3.15 What is the main application of an optical character reader?

3.16 How can graphical information such as graphs be fed to a computer?

3.17 What devices are used to obtain a graphical output from a computer?

3.18 What is an optical scanner? Explain how it works.

3.19 A page has 2000 characters. How many bits are needed to store it in a bit mapped form. How many bits are needed if it is stored as ASCII?

3.20 What is a speech input unit? What are its uses? How many types of speech input units are available?

3.21 What is a speech output unit? What are its applications?

4

Computer Memory

A memory or store is required in a computer to store programs and the data processed by programs. A memory is made up of a large number of *cells,* with each cell capable of storing one bit. The cells may be organized as a set of addressable words, each word storing a sequence of bits. In one such organization, the time to store or retrieve a word is independent of the address of the word. This organization, called a *Random Access Memory* (RAM), is used as the main memory of computers. Another organization arranges cells in a linear sequence to form a serial access memory.

Cells used to fabricate a random access memory are made (in current technology) with semiconductor flip-flops. Cells used in serial access memories of large size (tens of megabytes) are magnetic dipoles on movable magnetizable surfaces. Magnetic surface recording itself may be organized in different configurations such as hard disks, floppy disks, and tapes. Optical recording techniques have been recently used to store data on the surface of a coated disk. Such a serial access memory is known as CDROM (Compact Disk Read Only Memory). Better optical recording method which records data on multiple layers on a disk surface has been recently introduced. This storage device is known as Digital Versatile Disk Read Only Memory (DVDROM).

Various memory organizations discussed in this chapter can be classified on the basis of their storage capacity, the method of storing and retrieving data, the time needed to store and retrieve data, and the cost per bit of storage. As the speed of data retrieval increases, the cost per cell also goes up. In a computer system, a hierarchy of storage systems is provided. At the top of the hierarchy is a very high-speed, high-cost, low-capacity memory and at the bottom a low-speed, low-cost, high-capacity memory. The speeds and capacities at various levels are chosen so that for a given budget one gets a well balanced system which meets application requirements.

4.1 MEMORY CELL

A memory cell may be defined as a device which can store a symbol selected from a set of symbols and may be characterized by the following properties:

(i) The number of stable states in which it can be placed.

(ii) Whether a cell can store a symbol indefinitely even when power is turned off.

(iii) Whether, after reading a symbol from a cell, the stored symbol is retained in the cell or disturbed.

(iv) The time taken to read a symbol from a cell and the time to write a new symbol in it.

(v) Whether a symbol, once written, can only be read and not changed.

The number of stable states in which a cell can be placed determines the number of distinct symbols it can store. Each stable state may be assigned to represent a symbol. Thus if a cell can be placed in 10 stable states, each state may be used to represent one symbol and so the cell can store a decimal digit. If a cell can be placed in only one out of two stable states, then it may be used to store a binary digit.

If a symbol can be stored in a cell indefinitely without continuous supply of energy, it is known as a *non-volatile* cell. On the other hand, if the symbol stored in a cell disappears when no energy is supplied, it is known as a *volatile* cell.

Normally, reading a symbol from a cell should leave it undisturbed. Such a cell is known as one where readout is *non-destructive*. If the symbol is erased, as a consequence of reading, the readout is said to be *destructive*. The time taken to read a symbol from a cell is called *read-time* and the time taken to write a symbol *write-time*.

If in a memory cell, information is permanently written and can only be read, then it is known as a *read-only cell*.

4.2 MEMORY ORGANIZATION

Memory cells fabricated using current technology can be placed in one out of two stable states. We call these cells binary cells and each cell can store a binary digit. One of the two stable states is used to represent the binary 0 and the other the binary 1. Figure 4.1 depicts

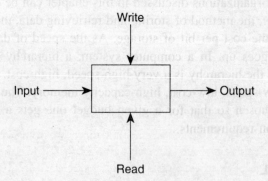

Fig. 4.1 A memory cell.

a storage cell. The cell has an *input data line* on which the symbol to be written is sent to the cell. In order to write this symbol in the cell, a *write-control signal* is sent to the cell via the write-line. If the content of a cell is to be read, a *read-control signal* is sent on the read-line and the content of the cell may be sensed on the *output data line*.

By appropriate variation in the interconnection of binary memory cells it is possible to organize different types of memories. We will assume that individual cells are non-volatile and reading is non-destructive. The simplest organization of a set of cells is shown in Fig. 4.2. In this organization, three cells are interconnected in such a way that the write-control lines of all the cells are connected together. The read-control lines are also connected together. The bits to be written in each cell is fed to the appropriate input data lines. When the write-signal is applied to the write-control line, these bits are written in the individual cells. The previous content in cells are automatically erased when the new information is written. In order to read the contents of the cells, a read signal is applied to the common read-line. The contents of the cells appear on the respective output data lines. The contents of individual cells are not erased by the read-operation as reading from these cells is .assumed to be non-destructive. This interconnection of cells is called a *register*. This register stores three bits.

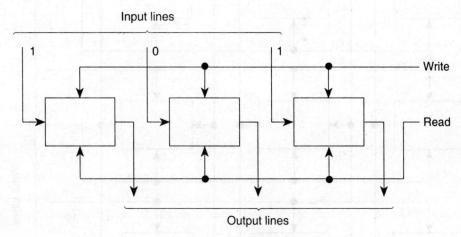

Fig. 4.2   A 3-bit register.

A group of registers may be interconnected as shown in Fig. 4.3 to form a memory. This memory is said to store four words of three bits each. In this organization, the input data lines of the first bit of all four registers are connected together. Similarly, the input data lines of the second bits are connected together and those of the third are also connected together as shown in Fig. 4.3. The output lines of each of the bits of the registers are also connected together. Observe that there are four write-lines, one for each 3-bit register and four read-lines. In order to write data in this memory, the register in which the data is to be written is specified. If data is to be written in the second register, a signal is sent on the write-line of this register. The data to be written is placed on the input lines. If the data in, say the third register, is to be read, a read-signal is sent on the read-line corresponding to this register. The contents of the third register appear on the output lines.

Each of the four registers has one read-line and one write-line. At a time we may either read from or write in a register. Each register in the memory should have a unique

identification so that the appropriate register may be selected for writing or reading. In
Fig. 4.3 each pair of read/write lines corresponding to a register are identified by the binary
code 00, 01, 10 and 11. The identification code of each register corresponding to a word
in the memory is known as its *address*. If a memory has eight words, the binary codes 000,
001, 010, 011, 100, 101, 110 and 111 will uniquely address these lines. In general with
n bits we can address 2^n words of a memory. In order to select an appropriate word in a

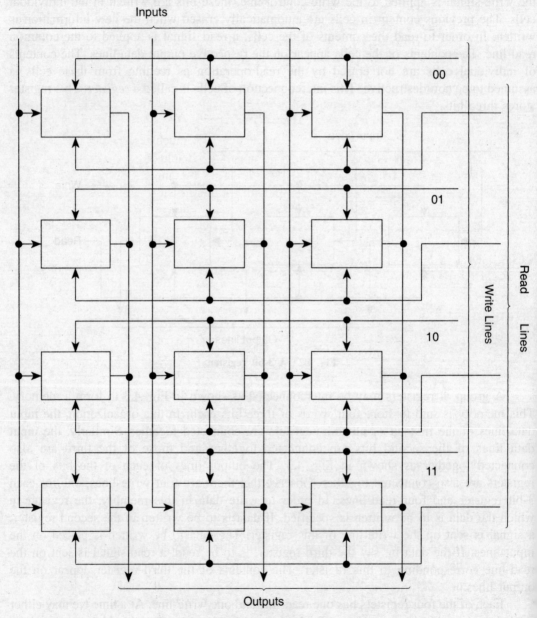

Fig. 4.3   A 3-bit per word 4 word memory.

memory, for either reading or writing, it is necessary to specify the address of the word. This address is usually specified as a binary number and is placed in a register called a memory address register (abbreviated MAR). A selector circuit is connected to MAR which selects the appropriate read or write-control line based on the contents of MAR and on whether read or write is specified. For the memory shown in Fig. 4.3 MAR will be a 2-bit register.

The data read from the memory or that to be written in the memory is placed in a register called a memory data register (abbreviated MDR). This register receives the outputs of memory cells during read operation. For write-operation, the data to be stored in the memory cells is placed in this register. In the example memory of Fig. 4.3, the MDR will be a 3-bit register.

Figure 4.4 is a block diagram of the memory of Fig. 4.3 including the registers used to specify the address for reading/writing and the register for storing the data read or to be written.

In practice the number of bits stored in memories is much larger than that shown in this example. The block diagram of a memory which is capable of storing 64K (K = 1024) bytes is shown in Fig. 4.5. Observe that $64K = 2^{16}$. Thus the number of bits in MAR is 16. The memory will be made up of 64K words with each word storing eight bits, that is, one byte. The MDR will be an 8-bit register. The selector block in Fig. 4.5 will select a read or write-line corresponding to the word to be read or written. Observe that the address of the word to be read or written will be placed in MAR. The data read from the memory or to be written in the memory will be placed in MDR.

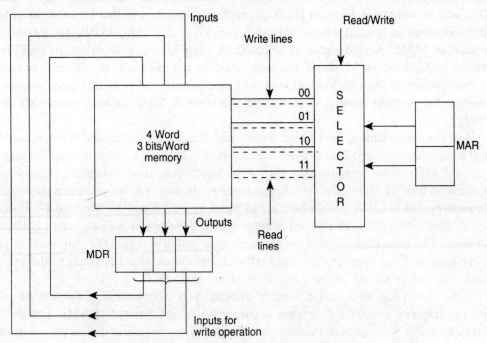

Fig. 4.4 Block diagram of a 4 word 3 bit per word memory.

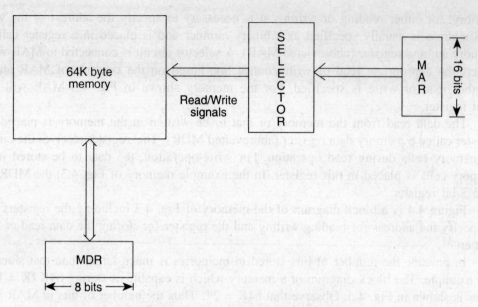

Fig. 4.5 Block diagram of a 64K byte memory.

If the number $173 = (10101101)_2 = (AD)_{16}$ is to be written in the memory in address $(1111110101011010)_2 = (FD5A)_{16}$ then the number $(AD)_{16}$ is entered in MDR and the address $(FD5A)_{16}$ in MAR. The write signal is initiated. The number in MDR, namely, $(AD)_{16}$ will be written in location $(FD5A)_{16}$ replacing the data in that location. In order to read the contents of a word whose address is $(AB34)_{16}$, this address $(1010101100110100)_2$ is placed in MAR. A read-signal is initiated. A copy of the data stored in $(AB34)_{16}$ is retrieved and placed in MDR. If the cells used in the memory are destructive-readout then the contents in the specified address will be cleared to zero. In this case, whatever is read from the memory would, however, be available in MDR to be written back in the memory.

Assume that at time t_0 the address from which data is to be retrieved is placed in MAR and at time t_1 the required data is available in MDR. The elapsed time $(t_1 - t_0)$ is known as the *access time* of the memory (see Fig. 4.6). The access time is usually slightly larger than the read-time of individual cells in the memory. If data is to be written in the memory, the data is placed in MDR and the address in MAR at time t_2 and a write-signal is initiated. If the writing operation is completed at time t_3 then the elapsed time $(t_3 - t_2)$ is called the *write time*. The time interval between the time t_0 at which a read/write command is given to a memory and the time t_4 when the next such instruction can be issued to the memory (namely, $t_4 - t_0$) is known as the *cycle time* of the memory.

If the time taken to access a word in a memory is independent of the address of the word, the memory is called a *random access memory* abbreviated (RAM). The memory illustrated in this section is a random access memory. The main memory used to store programs and data in a computer is a random access memory.

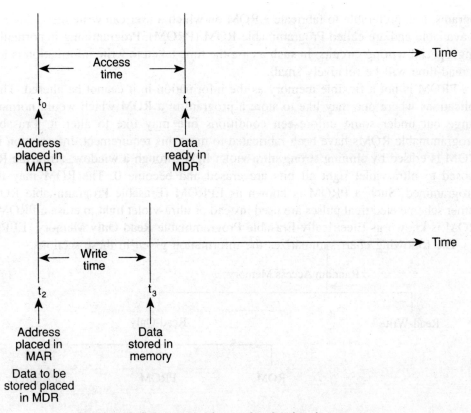

Fig. 4.6 Defining access time and write time in a memory.

4.3 READ ONLY MEMORY

There are random access memories in which data words are permanently written during fabrication. A word can later be read from the memory by specifying its address. The contents of the word cannot, however, be altered. Such a memory is called a *Read Only Memory (ROM)*. Reading from a ROM should be non-destructive. The memory should also be non-volatile. An important application of a ROM is to store tables which do not change, for example, tables of trigonometric functions. Suppose we want to store sin θ, then a ROM is fabricated to store the value of sin θ for various values of θ. To find sin ϕ for a given ϕ, the value of ϕ is placed in the address register of ROM and sin ϕ stored in a word of the ROM is retrieved and put in the MDR of ROM. Another application of ROM is for storing short programs for special applications. For example, a program to control the sequencing of operations of a washing machine may be stored in a ROM and interpreted by the processing unit. A ROM which has information written in it during manufacture in a factory is known as a factory programmed ROM. Such factory programming is feasible only in cases where the demand for such programmed ROMs is large. Examples cited above would be suitable for factory programming.

For more specialized uses where a user may like to store his own special functions or programs, it is preferable to fabricate a ROM on which a user can write these. Such ROMs are available and are called Programmable ROM (PROM). Programming is normally done using special writing circuits. In such a case the time taken to write information is long but the read-time will be relatively small.

PROM is not a flexible memory as the information in it cannot be altered. There are applications where one may like to store a program in a ROM which would normally not change but under some unforeseen conditions one may like to alter it. Erasable and reprogrammable ROMs have been fabricated to meet this requirement. Information in such a ROM is erased by shining strong ultra-violet light through a window. After the ROM is exposed to ultra-violet light all bits are erased and become 0. The ROM may then be reprogrammed. Such a PROM is known as EPROM (Erasable Programmable ROM). In another scheme electrical pulses are used instead of ultra-violet light to erase a PROM. Such a ROM is known as Electrically Erasable Programmable Read Only Memory (EEPROM).

The following chart summarizes the information given in these sections.

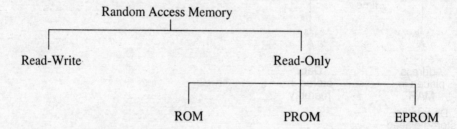

4.4 SERIAL ACCESS MEMORY

Consider the organization of memory cells shown in Fig. 4.7. In this organization the output of a cell is the input to the next cell. A read-signal places the contents of each of the cells on the respective output lines. A write-signal following this read-signal will store these bits in the respective "next" cells. One read-write pair of signals would thus "shift" the contents of the cells right by one cell position and the bit stored in the right-most cell will appear on the output line. A sequence of read-write signals will serially shift the contents of the register. After three read-write (namely, shift) signals the output will be 0. As the bits stored in the cells appear serially (that is, one after another) at the output, this memory is called a *serial access memory*. The structure shown in Fig. 4.7 is known as a *shift register*. If the output of the shift register is connected to its input, each shift-signal will circularly shift the contents of the memory. A series of shift-signals will keep the contents of the memory circulating.

Another model of memory cells is shown in Fig. 4.8(a). In this model, one bit is stored in each cell. The *Read-head* reads the content of the cell placed below it and places it on the output line. The cells are moved *physically* from left to right and as each cell appears below the read-head its content is placed on the output. The bits appear on the output as shown in Fig. 4.8(b).

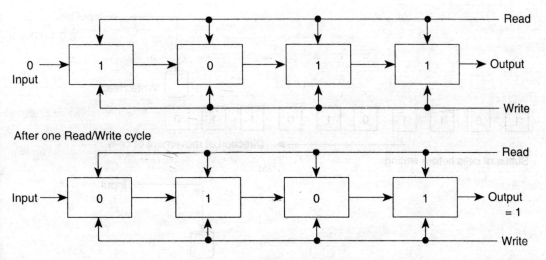

Fig. 4.7 A serial access memory.

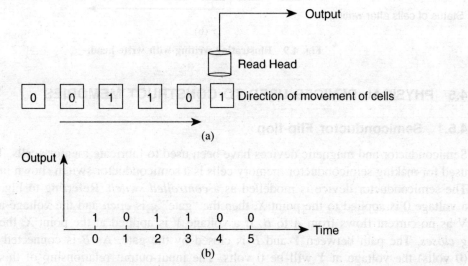

Fig. 4.8 Illustrating reading with read-head.

Writing in the cells is done using a *Write-head* as shown in Fig. 4.9(a). As the cells move below the write-head, the bits fed to the write-head are stored in the cells as shown in Fig. 4.9(b). This model of a serial access memory is appropriate to explain the operation of memories using magnetic surface recording.

A serial access memory is a non-addressable memory. In other words, sets of bits stored in the memory cannot be selectively retrieved by specifying their locations in the memory. The bits stored can be retrieved only in strict serial order.

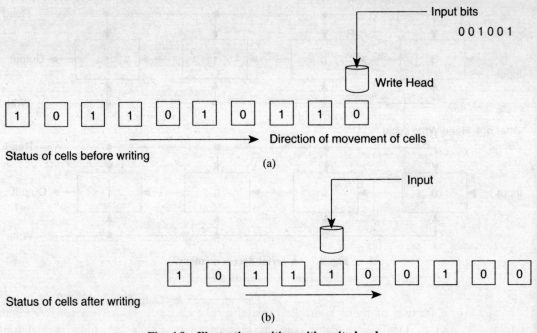

Fig. 4.9   Illustrating writing with write-head.

4.5   PHYSICAL DEVICES USED TO CONSTRUCT MEMORIES

4.5.1   Semiconductor Flip-flop

Semiconductor and magnetic devices have been used to fabricate memory cells. The device used for making semiconductor memory cells is a semiconductor switch shown in Fig. 4.10. The semiconductor device is modelled as a *controlled switch*. Referring to Fig. 4.10(a) if a voltage 0 is applied to the point X, then the "gate" g is *open* and the voltage at Y equals V as no current flows from A to B. If a voltage V is applied at the point X, then the gate g *closes*. The path between Y and B is closed by the gate. As B is connected to ground (0 volts) the voltage at Y will be 0 volts. The input-output relationship of this device is shown in Table 4.1(a). If we call the voltage V a binary 1 and 0 volts a binary 0, then Table 4.1(b) is obtained. This table completely defines the *logical* behaviour of the controlled switch.

Table 4.1   Describing the operation of the controlled switch

X	Y
0	V
V	0

X	Y
0	1
1	0

(a)   (b)

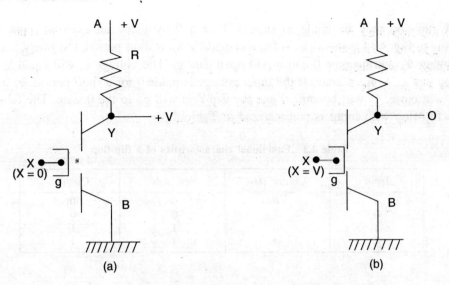

Fig. 4.10   A controlled switch.

In Fig. 4.11 two of these controlled switches are connected. The two switches are labelled T_1 and T_2. Observe that this configuration of switches can be in any one of four possible states. These states are shown in the first two columns of Table 4.2. Of these four states, g_1 and g_2 open together is not possible. For, if g_1 is open, the voltage at Y_1 will be V which will make X_2 also equal to V and thus close g_2. Similarly g_1 and g_2 closed together is not possible because if g_1 is closed Y_1 will be equal to 0 which will make X_2 also equal to 0 thus opening g_2. The state g_1 closed and g_2 open is possible. In this case Y_1 will be 0 as g_1 is closed and X_2 which is equal to Y_1 will also be 0 which will open g_2. This state is known as a *stable* state as the circuit will continue to remain in this state as long as it is not disturbed by an external voltage. The state g_1 open and g_2 closed is also stable. In this case g_1 open will make Y_1 equal to V, which in turn makes X_2 go to V which will close g_2. This circuit which has two stable states can be used as a memory cell. One of the stable states may be used to represent the storage of a binary 1 and the other a binary 0. This circuit is known as a *flip-flop*. Table 4.2 summarizes the above discussion.

Table 4.2   State of flip-flop of Fig. 4.11

g_1	g_2	State	Voltage Y_2	Bit stored
open	open	Not possible	—	—
open	closed	Stable	0	0
closed	open	Stable	V	1
closed	closed	Not possible	—	—

A flip-flop may be made to store a 1 or a 0 by using an external input voltage. Referring to Fig. 4.11 if the input voltage is made V for a short period, the gate g_1 will close. The voltage Y_1 will become 0 and it will open gate g_2. The voltage Y_2 will equal V and the flip-flop will go to the 1 state. If the input voltage is made 0 for a short period, g_1 will open and g_2 will close. Y_2 will become 0 and the flip-flop will go to the 0 state. The functioning of this flip-flop with input is summarized in Table 4.3.

Table 4.3   Functional characteristics of a flip-flop

Input	Current state	New state	Output
0	0	0	0
0	1	0	0
1	0	1	1
1	1	1	1

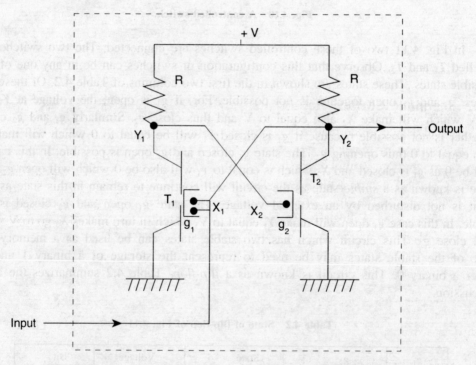

Fig. 4.11   Two controlled switches connected as a flip-flop memory cell.

Write and read controls may be introduced by two controlled switches which close the input and output paths as shown in Fig. 4.12(a). In Fig. 4.12(b), the memory cell with the controlled switches (shown within dotted lines in Fig. 4.12(a)) is shown as a memory cell of Fig. 4.1, which was used in the logical descriptions of Sec. 4.2.

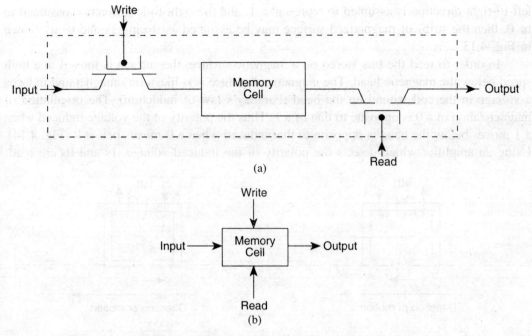

(a)

(b)

Fig. 4.12 A memory cell using controlled switches.

4.5.2 Magnetic Surface Recording

The physical device which realizes the logical memory cell model of Fig. 4.8 is a magnetic recording surface. A magnetic field is created in the gap in a magnetic-head by passing a current through a coil wound on the head. The field may be created in one of two directions. A plastic surface coated with a ferro-magnetic material is placed below the head. The surface is magnetized in either of two directions depending on the magnetic field across the recording-head. This is illustrated in Fig. 4.13. If a portion of a surface magnetized in the

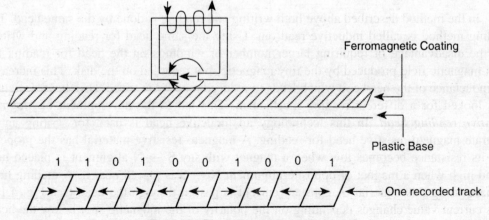

Fig. 4.13 Recording on a magnetic surface.

left-to-right direction is assumed to represent a 1, and the right-to-left direction assumed to be 0, then the strips of magnetized surface may be assumed as storing 1s and 0s as shown in Fig. 4.13.

In order to read the bits stored on a magnetic surface, the surface is moved at a high speed below the magnetic head. The magnetized surface acts like a tiny magnet and induces a voltage in the coil wound on the head (Faraday's law of induction). The orientation of magnetization of a 0 is opposite to that of a 1. Thus the polarity of the voltage induced when a 1 moves below the head is opposite to that induced when a 0 moves below it (Fig. 4.14). Using an amplifier which detects the polarity of the induced voltage, 1s and 0s are read.

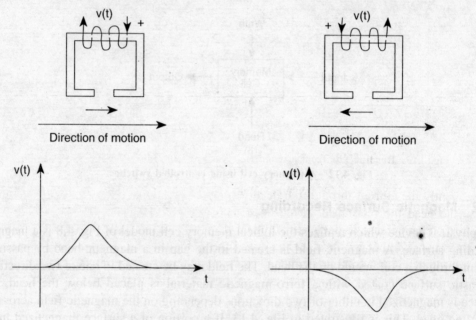

Fig. 4.14   **Reading bits from a magnetic recording.**

In the method described above both writing and reading is done by the same head. The reading method is called inductive read out. Using the same head for reading and writing has the disadvantage of requiring larger number of windings on the head for reading the faint magnetic field produced by the tiny magnetic spot recorded on the disk. This increases the inductance of the head coil which leads to reduced read/write speed. Disk head designers thus looked for a different reading mechanism. This led to the development of *Magneto resistive reading head*. In this technology an inductive head is used for writing and a separate magneto-resistive head for reading. A magneto-resistive material has the property that its resistance becomes low when a magnet with say S → N alignment is placed near it and high when a magnet of opposite alignment N ← S is placed near it. A reading head is made using this material. A constant current is passed through the head (see Fig. 4.15). This current value changes depending on the polarity of the magnetic spot below the head. When a 1 (S → N alignment) moves below the head the resistance of the head reduces and

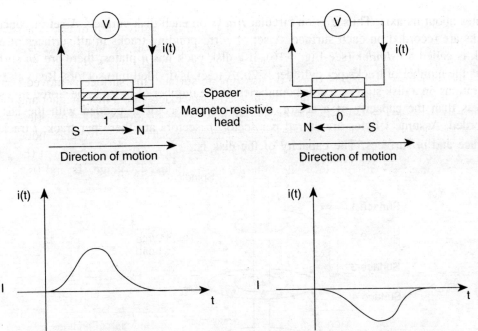

Fig. 4.15   Reading bits from a magnetic recording using a Magneto-Resistive head.

consequently the current through the head increases. When a 0 (N ← S alignment) moves below the head the resistance of the head increases and the head current decreases (see Fig. 4.15). The increase or decrease of the head current is detected by a sense amplifier and is interpreted as either a 1 or a 0. The magneto-resistive head (MR head) technology was first introduced by IBM in early nineties and is now being adopted by other manufacturers of disk drives. Both read and write heads use thin films of material on a tiny head. The MR head is very sensitive and has led to an increased density of packing bits on a magnetic surface. Bit density with MR heads is around 150 Mbits/sq.cm. compared to 30 Mbits/sq.cm with earlier inductive head. Recently (1998) IBM has announced Giant Magneto-resistive heads which gives a packing density of 400 Mbits/sq.cm.

The three most popular magnetic surface recording devices used currently are: (i) Hard disk, (ii) Floppy disk, and (iii) Magnetic tape.

4.6   MAGNETIC HARD DISK

Magnetic disks are smooth metal plates coated on both sides with a thin film of magnetic material. A set of such magnetic plates are fixed to a spindle one below the other to make up a disk pack (Fig. 4.16). The disk pack is sealed and mounted on a disk drive. Such a disk drive is known as a Winchester disk drive. The disk drive consists of a motor to rotate the disk pack about its axis at a speed of about 5400 revolutions per minute. The drive also has a set of magnetic heads mounted on arms. The arm assembly is capable of moving in and out in radial direction (Fig. 4.16). Information is recorded on the surface of a disk as it rotates about its axis. Thus it is on circular *tracks* on each disk surface. A set of concentric tracks are recorded on each surface. A set of corresponding tracks in all surfaces of a disk pack is called a *cylinder* (see Fig. 4.16). If a disk pack has n plates, there are $2n$ surfaces. Thus the number of tracks per cylinder is $2n$. A track is divided into sectors. Read and write operations on a disk start at sector boundaries. If the number of bytes to be stored in a sector is less than the capacity of a sector, the rest of the sector is padded with the last byte recorded. Assume s bytes are stored per sector, p sectors are there per track, t tracks per surface and m surfaces. The capacity of the disk is:

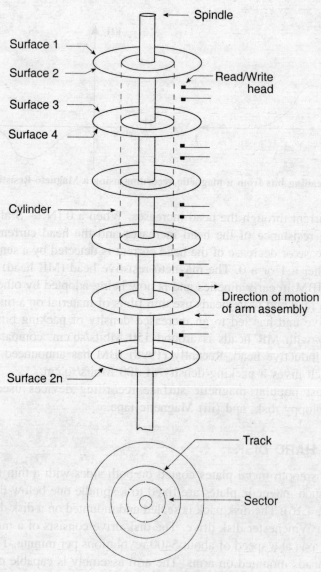

Fig. 4.16 A magnetic disk memory.

Capacity = $s \times p \times t \times m$ bytes

If d is the diameter of the disk, the density of recording is:

Density = $(s \times p)/(\pi \times d)$ bytes/inch

Example: A 2.5 inch diameter disk pack has 6 plates, 512 bytes per sector, 256 sectors, 5268 tracks per surface. The capacity of the disk is:

Capacity = $512 \times 256 \times 5268 \times 12 = 8.28$ Gigabytes

The recording density is:

Density = $(512 \times 256)/(\pi \times 2.5) = 16688$ bytes/inch

A set of disk drives are connected to a *disk controller*. The disk controller accepts commands from the computer and positions the read-write heads of the specified disk for reading or writing. In order to read from or write on a disk pack, the computer must specify the drive number, cylinder number, surface number and the sector number. Drive number should be specified, because a controller normally controls more than one drive. Table 4.4 shows the disk address format. Normally one or more tracks are reserved on a disk with permanent recording to provide timing pulses to aid the controller in positioning the heads at the specified address.

When a read-write command is received by the disk controller, the controller first positions the arm assembly so that the read-write head reaches the specified cylinder. The time taken to reach the specified cylinder is known as the *seek time* (T_s). The seek time varies depending upon the position of the arm assembly when the read-write command is

Table 4.4 **Disk address format for a disk controller of 8 drives, each disk pack having 5268 cylinders, 12 surfaces and 256 sectors**

Drive number	Cylinder number	Surface number	Sector number
3 bits	13 bits	4 bits	8 bits

received by the controller. The maximum seek time is the time taken by the head assembly to reach the innermost cylinder from the outermost cylinder or vice versa. The minimum seek time is 0 if the head assembly happens to be positioned on the selected cylinder. The average seek time is usually specified and it is of the order of 10 milliseconds.

Once the head assembly is positioned on the specified cylinder, the head corresponding to the specified surface is switched. This switching is electronic and is almost instantaneous. After the head is selected there is a further delay because the specified sector has to reach the read-write head. This rotation delay is variable. The average rotational delay equals half the time taken by the disk to rotate once. This time is known as the *latency time* (T_l). For a disk rotating at 7200 r.p.m., T_l is $\dfrac{0.5}{7200}$ min = 4.15 milliseconds. The sum of average latency and seek time is known as the average *access time*.

When a sector is reached, the data in it is read at a speed determined by the speed of rotation of the disk. One full revolution of a 7200 rpm disk takes 8.33 msec. In one revolution one track with 256 sectors, 512 bytes/sector is read. Thus in 8.33 msec 256×512 = 128 Kbytes are read giving a transfer rate of $128/8.33 \times 10^{-3}$ = 15.36 MB/sec. Observe that the time to access a sector = Average seek time + Average latency time = $(10 + 4.16)$ = 14.16 msec which is about 400 times the time required to read a sector. The main point is that the time to reach a sector dominates the time to read information. It is thus advantageous to read a number of consecutive sectors into a buffer store once a sector is reached assuming that consecutive sectors will be required in an application. This is called *disk caching*.

All disk drives nowadays have a built-in controller which is normally a microprocessor. The processing power is used to compress data before storing it in a sector. The compression method is called Run Length Encoding (RLE). The idea is to avoid storing long sequences of 1s or 0s if they occur in the data. For example, if a data is : 111111111111001. Observe a sequence of twelve 1s. Instead of storing these we can compress it to 11001 (12 followed by 1) before storing it, and expand it after retrieval. A long sequence of 0s can also be similarly compressed. We have given the basic idea without giving details. In actual practice we have to have an indication whether the data is compressed or not and also decide when RLE will be effective. It has been found statistically that RLE compression by a factor of 3 is often possible. Compression besides increasing the capacity of disk also increases the transfer rate of disks.

Besides moving the head to the correct sector for read-write and initiating read-write, the disk controller also checks whether the data sent from the main memory of the computer is correctly written on the disk. It is done by reading back through a read-head, which is physically located next to the write-head, the information written in the sector. Each byte so read is compared with the contents of a buffer register in the controller which contains the byte sent from the main memory for writing. The controller also appends a cyclic redundancy code (CRC) byte to the information written in a sector. The CRC byte is obtained by adding all the bytes in a sector and appending the least significant byte of the sum to the information bytes. When information is read back from a sector the individual bytes read are added and the least significant byte of the sum compared with CRC byte read. If they do not match an error is signalled.

The specifications of some common commercially available disk drives are shown in Table 4.5. Figure 4.17 is a photograph of the inside view of a disk drive.

Winchester disks come in many sizes and capacities and also with many types of controllers. Nowadays (1998) 4 GB is the smallest capacity for desk top PCs using a Pentium Processor. Normally an interface called ATA is used to connect it to the computer. A 3.5 in. diameter disk of 1 inch height is the preferred disk for this application. Servers with Pentium-Pro and workstations normally use a 9 GB disk with an interface known as a Small Computer System Interface (SCSI is normally pronounced SCUZZY). Larger disks of capacity over 18 GB are used in high end servers such as those which store video data or large organizational databases. They normally use fast SCSI interface and 5.25 inch diameter disks. Larger computers such as mainframes use an array of 9 GB disks in a configuration called RAID (Redundant Array of Inexpensive Disks). They use extra disk to do automatic error detection and (sometimes) correction during read operation.

Disk storage technology is progressing rapidly. Capacities go up each year (almost doubling every two years) and cost is going down. The specifications given in Table 4.5 are indicative of the present (1998) state-of-the-art. They will change (improve) every year.

Table 4.5   Specifications of some Winchester Disk Drives (1998)

Model	IBM Ultrastar 9ES	Seagate Medalist Pro	Mextor Diamond Max 1280	IBM Ultrastar 18 × P	Seagate Elite 23
Formatted Capacity GB	4.5	9.1	5.1	18.2	23.2
No. of heads	5	8	8	20	28
Interface controller	SCSI-3	ULTRA ATA	ATA – 4	SCSI – 3	Ultrawide SCSI
Average seek time (msec)	7.5	9.5	9.7	7.5	13
Track-to-Track seek time (msec)	0.8	2	1	0.7	1.1
Rotation speed (rpm)	7200	7200	5400	7200	5400
Buffer size KB	512	512	256	1024	2048
Transfer rate to host (MB/s)	40	33.3	33.3	40	40
Disk Diameter (inches)	3.5	3.5	3.5	3.5	5.25

Fig. 4.17   2.1 GB disk drive (5.25").   (*Courtsey*: Digital Equipment Corporation)

4.7 FLOPPY DISK DRIVES

The growing market of low-cost microcomputers created the need for low-cost high-capacity storage. This led to the development of floppy disk drives. Floppy disks are made of magnetic oxide-coated Mylar computer tape material. The flexible tape material is cut into circular pieces 3.5 inches in diameter. As the material used is not a hard plate but a flexible tape, it is called a "floppy disk". The floppy disk is packaged in a 3.5-inch square hard plastic envelope with a long slit for read-write head access, and a hole in the centre for mounting the disk drive hub (Fig. 4.18). The floppy disk, along with the envelope, is slipped into the drive mechanism. The mechanism holds the envelope and the flexible disk

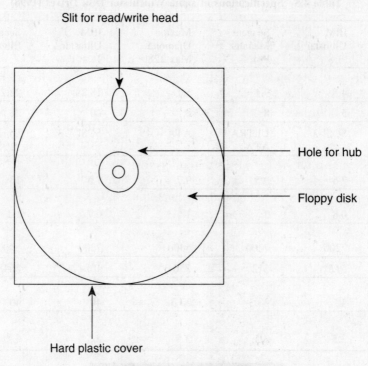

Fig. 4.18   A floppy disk.

is rotated inside the envelope by the drive mechanism. The inner side of the envelope is smooth and permits free rotation. The read-write head is held in physical contact with the floppy disk. The slit for read/write remains closed until the disk is inserted into the drive. The slit opens when the disk starts spinning. The head is moved radically along with slit. Track to track movement and positioning of the head is controlled by a servomechanism. A floppy disk has 192 tracks, 9 sectors per track, 512 bytes on one side of the disk. The gross capacity on both sides is 1.75 MB and the net capacity is 1.2 MB. The rotation speed of a floppy is of the order of 366 rpm with a transfer rate of 40 kilobytes/second. For reading and writing on the disk, the head has to be in contact with the disk surface. Thus disk and head wear take place. Manufacturers guarantee 2 million reads of a disk track.

Floppy disk technology is making rapid strides. Some of the technology used in hard disks such as non-contact recording, light weight heads driven by voice coils (similar to the ones used in loudspeakers) and effective sealing of the disk are being used in the design of floppy disk drives. Sony and Fuji films have just announced (1998) a new recording format called HiFD for storing data on a floppy disk. With this technology one can store 200 MB on a 3.5 inch floppy and it is backward compatible with standard floppies.

4.8 COMPACT DISK READ ONLY MEMORY (CDROM)

The latest and the most promising technology for high capacity secondary storage is known as Laser Disk Technology. This technology has evolved out of the entertainment electronics market where cassette tapes and long playing records are being replaced by CDs. The terminology CD used for audio records stands for Compact Disks. For use in digital computers similar technology is used. The disks used for data storage are known as Compact Disk Read Only Memory (CDROM). The CDROM disk, also known as a laser disk, is a shiny metal like disk whose diameter is 5.25 inches (12 cm). It can store around 650 Mega bytes (equivalent to 2,50,000 pages of printed text).

Information in CDROM is written by creating pits on the disk surface by shining a laser beam. As the disk rotates the laser beam traces out a continuous spiral. The sharply focused beam creates a circular pit of around 0.8 micrometre diameter wherever a 1 is to be written and no pit (also called a land) if a zero is to be written. From a master disk many copies can be reproduced by a process called stamping a disk (see Fig. 4.19).

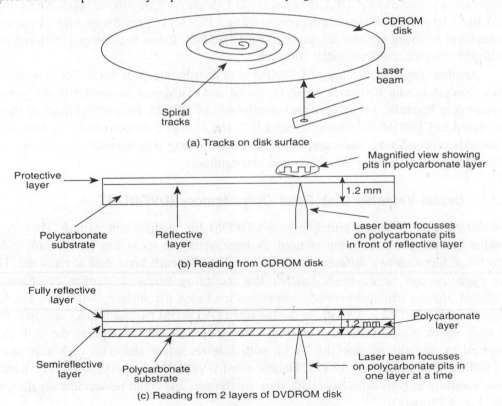

Fig. 4.19   CDROM and DVDROM.

The CDROM with pre-recorded information is read by a CDROM reader which uses a laser beam for reading. As in a magnetic floppy disk the CDROM disk is inserted in a slot. It is rotated by a motor at a speed of 360 revolutions per minute. A laser head moves in and out to the specified position. As the disk rotates the head senses pits and land. This is converted to 1s and 0s by the electronic interface and sent to the computer.

In recent models (1998) of CDROM, the rate of reading data is 4.8 MB/s. CDROM disk speeds as indicated by the notation nx, where n is an integer indicating the factor by which the original nominal speed of 150 KB/s is to be multiplied. Thus a 32x CDROM reading speed is 32×150 KB/s = 4800 KB/s. It has a buffer to keep the data temporarily. The buffer size is 256 kilobytes. It is connected to a computer by a Small Computer System Interface (SCSI) adapter.

A standard has been evolved for recording information on CDROM. This is essential to allow CDROMs to be widely distributed and read by different computers. The standard used is called ISO 9660, standardized by the International Standards Organization. It is accepted by all CDROM vendors. This standard defines a Volume Table of Contents (VTOC) which allows opening any one of 140,000 files with a single seek using directories in the CDROM. Recording in ISO 9660 format is facilitated by a software developed by Microsoft Corporation known as MSCDEX (Microsoft CD Extension). This software makes a CDROM look like a large hard disk to a programmer using a PC. All large software such as operating system and software updates are supplied on CDROMs. It has become essential to have a CDROM drive on a PC to install software.

Another major application of CDROM is in distributing large texts. For example, the entire Encyclopaedia Brittanica could be stored and distributed in one CDROM. Articles appearing in scientific journals are also distributed in CDROM. Recently bitmaps of images are stored in CDROM for display using a PC. The current booming market is multimedia CDROMs in which text, audio and video are stored. Along with appropriate software these CDROMs can be used for education and entertainment.

4.8.1 Digital Versatile Disk Read Only Memory (DVDROM)

DVDROM uses the same principle as a CDROM for reading and writing. However, a smaller wavelength laser beam is used. A lens system to focus the laser beam is used which can focus on two different layers on the disk. On each layer data is recorded. Thus the capacity can be doubled. Further the recording beam is sharper compared to CDROM and the distance between successive tracks on the surface is smaller. The total capacity of DVDROM is 8.5 GB. In double sided DVDROM two such disks are stuck back to back which allows recording on both sides. This, of course, requires the disk to be reversed to read the reverse side. With both side recording and with each side storing 8.5 GB the total capacity is 17 GB. Double sided DVDROM, however, should be handled more carefully as both sides have data, they are thinner, and could be accidentally damaged (see Fig. 4.19(a)–(c)).

In both CDROMs and DVDROMs, the density of data stored (i.e., pits and lands per unit length) is constant throughout the spiral track. In order to obtain a constant read-out rate the disk must rotate faster, near the centre and slower at the outer tracks to maintain a constant linear velocity (CLV) between the head and the CDROM/DVDROM platter. CLV scheme is used as data density is double that which is possible if a Constant Angular Velocity (CAV) is used as in Winchester Disks. In Winchester Disks which use CAV the density of data recording varies; it is more near the centre and less at the edges in order to maintain a constant read-out rate. CLV recording complicates the design of drive motor as it should readjust the speed of rotation of the disk every time the head moves. CLV has been used in CDROM/DVDROM as volume of data stored is the major criterion in design (Remember that CDROM uses spiral tracks, whereas Hard Disks use concentric circular tracks). The 1x speed of DVDROM is 1.38 MB/s as opposed to 150 KB/s of CDROMs. In Table 4.6 we give a comparison of CDROM and DVDROM. DVDROM of

Table 4.6 CDROM and DVDROM comparison

	CDROM	DVDROM
Pit length (micron)	0.834	0.4
Track pitch (micron)	1.6	0.74
Laser beam wavelength (nanometre)	635	780
capacity 1 layer/1 side	650 KB	4.7 GB
2 layers/1 side	No	8.5 GB
1 layer/2 sides	No	9.4 GB
2 layers/2 sides	No	17 GB
Speed 1x	150 KB/s	1.38 MB/s

80mm diameter (3.5 inch) are also being standardized to correspond to the smaller size floppy disks and Winchesters which are there in the market. Even though physical format of DVDROMs are different the *logical format* for storing and retrieving data uses a format called Universal Disk Format (UDF) which is standardized by the International Standards Organization.

4.8.2 CDROM-R (Recordable CDROM or Write Once CDROM—WOROM)

The primary method of producing and distributing CDROM is to create tape in ISO 9660 format and send it to a CDROM producer who creates a CDROM master using expensive equipment. The master is used to stamp multiple copies which are tested and labelled. This is economical for reproducing a large number of copies. For producing a few copies or for a single copy it is necessary to have a writable CDROM. Such a technology is available and allows CDROMs to be produced in-house. This CDROM can be read by any standard CDROM player.

The medium used is a 12 cm writable disk. Such a disk made of polycarbonate already has a groove cut in it. It is covered by a photosensitive dye. This layer is covered with a thin layer of gold (called reflecting layer). The final layer is a protective layer. A laser beam is used to write data. The disk is rotated by a motor. For writing a 1 the laser beam is turned on. The laser beam fuses the dye to the substrate forming a pit which can be read by any CDROM reader. The entire image of the files to be recorded is first stored in a hard disk in ISO 9660 format. It is streamed at 300 Kbytes/sec to the CDROM which continuously records the data in one shot. Writing cannot be done in multiple sessions. The recorded CD can be read on any ordinary CDROM drive.

Writable DVDROMs called DVD-R are also being introduced and getting standardized.

4.9 MAGNETIC TAPE DRIVES

Magnetic tape memories are similar to the commonly used audio tape recorders. A magnetic tape drive consists of a spool on which a magnetic tape is wound. The tape is transported across a set of magnetic heads and is taken up on another spool. Between the two spools, a set of nine heads are mounted to write and read information on the tape. Each head operates independently and stores information along one track on the tape. The nine heads record information on nine parallel tracks, parallel to the edge of the tape (Fig. 4.20). Out of the nine tracks, eight tracks are used to record a byte of data and the ninth track is used to record a parity bit for each byte. (In older tape drives, characters were coded using 6 bits and a seventh parity bit was used. Such tapes are known as seven track tapes.) The width of the tape is standardized as half an inch. The recording density, namely, the number of bits per inch (bpi) from a single track (along its length) is 1600, 3200, 6250 or 12500 bits. Notice that on one inch of a 9-track tape for a 1600 bpi recording the total number of bits stored will be $1600 \times 9 = 14400$ bits.

The speed of tape travel is of the order of 100 inches per second. The information can be read or written at the rate of 8×10^4 bits/second after the tape is brought on to full speed. During the time the tape is accelerated to its full speed, no recording can be performed. The distance traversed by the tape during this time is about 0.6 inches. This distance is called the *inter-block gap* (IBG). Normally a block of data is recorded, a gap is left and another block is recorded (Fig. 4.20(d)). The block should be at least 10 times as long as the IBG to reduce wastage of tape. The data are arranged as blocks because recording and retrieval are serial. There is no addressing. We find a record by knowing in which block it is and reaching it by skipping earlier blocks.

A tape is wound on a spool and its other end is threaded manually on a take-up spool and it positions itself ready to write. The beginning of the tape (BOT) is indicated by a metal foil called a marker. When a write-command is given, a block of data is written on the tape and it waits for the next block. The next block is written after the IBG. A series of blocks are written in this manner. The end of tape (EOT) is indicated by an end-of-tape marker which is a metal foil stuck in the tape. After the data is written, the tape is rewound and kept ready for reading. This operation is called "rewind and reload". The tape is read sequentially, that is, the data is read one after the other in the order in which the data has

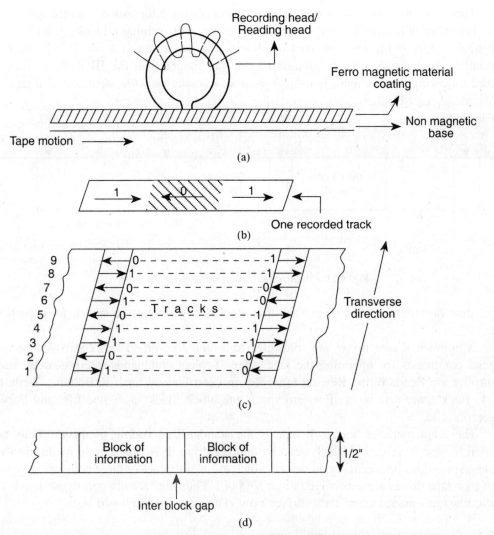

Fig. 4.20   **Magnetic tape recording.**

been written. When read-operation is over, the tape is rewound and unloaded. The tape spool may then be manually removed and stored.

The data recorded on a tape cannot be addressed. They can be retrieved sequentially in the order in which they were written. Thus if a desired record is at the end of a tape, all the earlier records have to be read before it is reached. The access time of information stored on tape is very high compared to that stored on a disk. Tapes are primarily used to save old information for long periods of time (archival store). Tapes are less expensive than disks and can be stored away conveniently. Thus tapes are used as back-up storage to store data from disks periodically. Standard coding is used in the recording of tapes. Thus a tape recorded on a drive may be read using another drive without difficulty. Besides, tapes are easily transported by mail from one place to another.

These factors make tapes the preferred medium for information interchange.

Information is stored on tapes as a group of *records* forming a block. A set of blocks constitute a *file*. A *file mark* is used to identify the beginning of a file. A file mark is a specially coded record usually preceded by a gap longer than the IBG (Fig. 4.21). The record following the file mark is usually used as a header or a *file identifier*. If a tape has

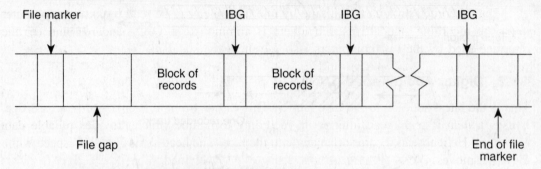

Fig. 4.21   Data organization on a magnetic tape.

more than one file recorded on it, then this identifier facilitates the search for a particular file.

A number of tape drives are connected to a *tape controller*. This controller interprets special commands for operating the tape drive. Typical commands interpreted by such a controller are Read, Write, Rewind tape, Rewind and Unload tape, Erase tape, Write tape mark, Back space one block, Forward space one block, Back space one file, and Forward space one file.

The main merit of half inch tape is the standardized coding of drives. Thus tapes written on one drive can be easily read by another drive. It is thus a good medium to send data and programs between organizations which use mainframes or large computing systems. Half inch tape drives are expensive (about $30000). Thus they are not commonly used. Very few companies manufacture these drives now. They are being phased out.

4.9.1   Quarter Inch Cartridge Tapes

These tapes are quarter inch wide and are sealed in a cartridge much like an audio cassette tape. Unlike a half inch tape, these tapes record information serially in a track with one head. When the end of the tape is reached the tape is rewound and data is recorded on the next track. There are 9 to 30 tracks and data is recorded in a *serpentine* fashion. Data bits are serial on a track and blocks of around 6000 bytes are written followed by error-correction code to enable correction of data on reading if any error occurs. The density of data is around 16000 bits per inch in modern tapes. The tapes store around 500 MB. The cassette size is 5.25 inch just like a floppy and mounted in a slot provided on the front panel of a computer (normally below the hard disk). Tape read/write speed is around 120 inch/second and data is transferred at the rate of 240 KB/second.

These tapes usually are interfaced to a computer using the SCSI standard. The data format used in these tapes is standardized by the industry and is called the *QIC standard*.

Cartridge tapes are also known as *streamer tapes* by vendors as they are usually used to copy and store data from disks. Such a copy can be used to restore data on a disk if they are lost accidentally. Ideally one would like to read data from a disk continuously and store it fast "as a stream on a tape". Hence the name.

Data recorded on a cartridge tape by one computer can be read by another computer if (i) the recording standard used by them is common (e.g. QIC standard), and (ii) the interface used by the two computers also use the same standard.

4.9.2 Digital Audio Tapes (DAT)

This is the latest addition to the tape family. This uses a 4 mm tape enclosed in a cartridge. It uses a *helical scan,* read after write recording technique which provides reliable data recording. Helical scan records at an angle to the tape. The head spins at a high speed while the tape moves. Very high recording densities are obtained. The tape length is either 60 metres or 90 metres. It uses a recording format called Digital Data Storage (DDS) which provides three levels of error correcting code to ensure excellent data integrity. The capacity is upto 4 GB with a data transfer speed of 366 KB/sec. This tape also uses SCSI interface. As in QIC if standard format and interface are used, data may be exchanged in this medium.

Magnetic tapes are used nowadays in computers for the following purposes:

(i) Backing up data stored in disks. It is necessary to regularly save data stored on disk in another medium so that if by accident the data on disk is overwritten or if data gets corrupted due to hardware failure the saved data may be written back on the disk.

(ii) Storing processed data (e.g., files of students' examination results) for future use. This is called *archiving*.

(iii) Interchanging programs and data between organizations. For example, a vendor may distribute changes in an operating system as an update tape. Such a use is called *software distribution* or data distribution.

The most appropriate tape for backing up data from a disk today is DAT. QIC tapes are also useful for this application. Archiving is best done on DAT or QIC. Software or data distribution is best done on QIC or half-inch tapes, as data interchange format for DATs is not standardized as of now. The best medium for storing individual files and retrieving them easily is the half inch tape. As of now it seems that QIC will take the place of half inch tape and the half inch tape drives will become extinct. In Table 4.7 we summarize the characteristics of various tapes discussed.

The advent of CDROM-R has broken the monopoly of tapes for backing up files from hard disks. DVD-Rs are also emerging with enormous storage capacities in Gbyte range. Thus in the near future optical disks will be an attractive alternative for backing up information from hard disk drives.

Table 4.7   Characteristics of some tape drives

Tape drive (Type and model)	Capacity MB	Transfer rate	Read/Write speed	Main application
Half inch DEC TSZ07	120	632	100	Software exchange, archiving
QIC DEC TZK 10	525	240	120	Back up, software exchange, archiving
QIC DEC TK50	95	62.5	75	Back up, software exchange, archiving
QIC* TS/1000 QUALSTAR	1000	300	66	Back up, software exchange, archiving
DAI DELTLZ06	4000	366	1GB/hour back up	Back up, archiving

* This drive has 30 tracks-serpentine recording. The recording density is 36,000 bits per inch.

So far we have discussed a number of devices used to store data in computer. In Table 4.8 we have summarized the average capacity of each of the devices, the access times of each and the relative cost per byte of storage of each. From the table it is seen that small semiconductor memories using high speed transistor flip-flops known as *cache memories* are the most expensive as well as the fastest in the set. At the other end we have CDROMs and DVDROMs with high capacity low speed serial access and a low cost per byte. In a computer system it is necessary to use a judicious combination of all these types of memories for best results. The situation is similar to the method used to store files in offices. The most urgent files will be kept for ready reference on the table of a manager. This is analogous to the information kept in a small high speed memory of a computer, called *cache* memory, which stores the instructions and data to be immediately used. Files which need to be examined on a given day would be normally kept in an in-tray on the side of the table and can be immediately accessed by the manager. The main semiconductor random access memory of a computer is similar to this. Files which do not have to be referred to immediately but which should be within easy reach of the manager are kept in an organized manner in a filing cabinet. The disk memory in a computer is similar to this. Files which require attention only rarely are kept in big index files in the main office away from the manager's room. The magnetic tape memory in a computer fulfils a similar purpose. Finally, legal and reference books are kept in a library. CDROM and DVDROM fulfils this purpose.

Table 4.8 Comparative characteristics of memories

Memory type	Average capacity in bytes	Technology	Average time to access a byte	Purpose in a computer system	Relative cost per byte in units
Cache	0.5 M	High speed integrated circuits	2 nsec	Instructions and data to be immediately used	10
Main memory	50 M	Integrated circuits	20 nsec	Program and data	1
Disk memory (hard disk)	50 G	Magnetic surfaces on hard disks	10 msec	Large data files and program overflow from main memory	1/100
Disk memory (floppy)	10 M	Magnetic surfaces on thin flexible disks	500 msec	Data entry. As input unit. Data and program files in microcomputers	1/1000
Magnetic Tape	5 G	Long 1/4" tape wound on cartridge	25 sec	Historical files. Back up for disk. Data and program exchange between installations	1/1000
CDROM	600 M	Laser disk	500 msec	Store large texts, pictures and audio. Software distribution	1/10000
DVDROM	8 G	Laser disk	500 msec	Video files	1/100000

SUMMARY

1. A memory or store of a computer is organized using a large number of cells. Each cell stores a binary digit.

2. A memory cell which does not lose the bit stored in it when no power is supplied to the cell is known as a non-volatile cell.

3. The time taken to store a bit in a cell and the time taken to read it are important parameters of a cell.

4. A number of cells, with each cell storing a bit, constitute a word. A word is a group of bits which are stored and retrieved as a unit. A memory system is organized to store a number of words. A word may store one or more bytes. The length of a word may be specified as "n bits per word". A storage capacity of a memory is specified as the number of bytes it can store.

5. Each word in a memory is stored in an addressable location. The address of the location from where a word is to be retrieved or where a word is to be stored is entered in a memory address register (MAR). The data retrieved from the memory or the data to be stored in memory are placed in a memory data register (MDR).

6. In order to store a word in memory, it is placed in MDR and the address where it is to be stored is entered in MAR. A write command stores the word. The time taken to write a word is known as the write time.

7. In order to retrieve a word from memory the address of the word is placed in MAR and a read command is issued. The retrieved data is placed in MDR by the memory. The time to retrieve information is called the access time of the memory.

8. In a random access memory, the write time and access time are independent of the address of the word.

9. A random access memory may be fabricated with permanently stored information which cannot be erased. Such a memory is called a Read Only Memory (ROM).

10. A ROM in which information can be written permanently in the field is known as a programmable ROM (PROM). If it can be erased and reprogrammed, it is known as an erasable programmable ROM (EPROM).

11. A serial access memory is organized by arranging memory cells in a linear sequence. Information is retrieved or stored in such a memory by using a read-write head. Data is presented serially for writing and is retrieved serially during read.

12. A flip-flop made of electronic semiconductor devices is used to fabricate a memory cell. These memory cells are organized as a random access memory.

13. A bit may be stored on a magnetic surface by magnetizing the surface in either one of two directions. The surface is magnetized using a write-head. A read-head is used to retrieve a stored bit.

14. Magnetic surface recording devices commonly used in computers are hard disks, floppy disks, and magnetic tapes.

15. A hard disk consists of a number of hard platters mounted on a spindle. The platters are coated with magnetic material. Data is organized along tracks on each platter. Each track is divided into sectors. Each sector on the disk has a unique address. Hard disks can store about 8 GB. Retrieval time is of the order of tens of milliseconds. Hard disks are used in computers to store user program files and data.

16. A floppy disk is a circular flexible disk made of magnetic tape material. Data are stored on a floppy disk along concentric tracks. Each track is divided into sectors. Tracks and sectors on a floppy disk may be assigned unique addresses. Floppy disks are used in data entry devices to store data to be processed by computers. Microcomputers employ floppy disks to store data and program files. The storage capacity of a floppy disk is about 1 Mbyte. Retrieval time is of the order of a fraction of a second.

17. CDROM uses a laser beam to record and read data along spiral tracks on a 5.25" disk. A disk can store around 650 Mbytes of information. CDROMs are normally used to store massive text data (such as encyclopaedias) which is permanently recorded and read many times. Recently CDROMs which can be written on in the user premises are appearing in the market.

18. DVDROMs are similar to CDROMs but allow storage of data on 2 layers on each side of a laser disk giving a maximum capacity of 17 GB. They can store full length video recording of upto 3 hours.

19. A magnetic tape is a serial access memory. It is a non-addressable memory. The time taken to store and retrieve information from tapes is of the order of seconds which is slow. Tapes are mostly used as a backup storage device. As tapes are compact, these units are also used to exchange data and programs between computer installations.

20. A computer system is organized with a balanced configuration of different types of memories. The main random access memory is used to store program being currently executed by the computer. Disks are used to store large data files and program files awaiting execution. Tapes are used to backup the files from disk. CDROMs and DVDROMs are used to store user manuals and large text, audio and video data.

REVIEW QUESTIONS

4.1 What is the purpose of memory in a computer?

4.2 What are the main characteristics of a memory cell?

4.3 What is a non-volatile memory?

4.4 What is destructive reading of a memory cell?

4.5 What is a register?

4.6 Draw a block diagram of a memory which has 8 words of 4 bits each.

4.7 What is the size of MAR of a 16K byte memory? Assume that the word size is 1 byte.

4.8 What are the sizes of MAR and MDR of 512K byte memory with 16 bit words?

4.9 Define the term "access time" of a memory.

4.10 What is the distinction between the write time of a memory and its access time?

4.11 Define the term "random access memory".

4.12 What is a read-only memory? Is a ROM a random access memory?

4.13 What is a serial access memory?

4.14 Explain the operation of a controlled switch.

4.15 Explain the operation of a flip-flop.

4.16 Explain how information is written on and read from magnetic surfaces.

4.17 Explain how data is organized on a floppy disk.

4.18 If 1600 bits may be stored per linear inch on a floppy disk surface, estimate the number of tracks on a 8-inch diameter floppy which can store 512K bytes on each surface.

4.19 If a floppy disk rotates at the rate of 300 rpm, what is the rate at which data will be read from a track? Assume recording density of 1600 bits per linear inch.

4.20   Explain how data is organized on a hard disk.

4.21   What are the main differences between a floppy disk and a hard disk?

4.22   Define the terms "seek time" and "latency time" of a hard disk.

4.23   If a hard disk has 10 surfaces, and each surface is 12 inch in diameter, and the density of recording is 60000 bits per linear inch, estimate the number of bits per cylinder of the disk.

4.24   If a hard disk rotates at 3600 rpm and surface recording density on it is 60000 bpi, what is the data transfer rate of the disk?

4.25   What is a sector in a hard disk?

4.26   Why do we have a variety of memories in a computer system?

4.27   How many tracks are recorded on a commercial disk pack?

4.28   What is a CDROM? In what way is it different from hard disk?

4.29   How is data recorded on a CDROM? How is it read?

4.30   How is high density of recording feasible in CDROM?

4.31   What is DVDROM? What are the differences between CDROM and DVDROM?

4.32   What is the difference between CLV recording and CAV recording? Do hard disks use CLV or CAV recording?

4.33   Does CDROM use CLV or CAV recording? Why does it use this recording?

4.34   What is CDROM-R? What is its application?

4.35   What is the major application of DVDROM?

4.36   What are the primary applications of a magnetic tape storage?

4.37   If a tape is recorded at 6250 bpi and there are 9 tracks on it, what is the capacity of a 2400 ft. tape?

4.38   When is a QIC tape used? What are its advantage over half inch tape?

4.39   What is a DAT? When is it used?

5

Processor

The processing unit in a computer interprets instructions given in a program and carries out the instructions. Processors are designed to interpret a specified number of instruction codes. Each instruction code is a string of binary digits. All processors have input/output instructions, arithmetic instructions, logic instructions, branch instructions and instructions to manipulate characters. The number and type of instructions available differ from processor to processor. In this chapter we will illustrate the general structure of a processor and show how instructions are interpreted and executed.

5.1 STRUCTURE OF INSTRUCTIONS

An instruction for a computer should specify the following:

1. The task to be carried out by the processor.

2. The address or addresses in memory where the operand or operands would be found.

3. The address in memory where the result is to be stored.

4. The address in memory where the next instruction to be carried out is stored.

For example, suppose an operand stored in address P in memory is to be added to one stored in Q and the result is to be stored in an address R, then an instruction would be of the type:

ADD	P	Q	R	S
What task? (operation code)	Address of first operand	Address of second operand	Address of result	Address where next instruction would be found

The instruction given above is known as a *four address instruction*. If a memory has 256K addresses then each address would be 18 bits long. Four addresses would require 72 bits and thus the storage required to store an instruction would be quite large. Many instructions, however, would not require all the addresses. Normally in an algorithm, instructions are carried out sequentially, i.e., one after another. If an instruction is stored in an address X, then the next instruction would be stored in the next consecutive address,

77

namely, $X + 1$. Only on rare occasions is the normal sequence violated and the program jumps to a specified address. Thus the fourth address, S, need not be explicitly specified in each instruction. If we remove the fourth address, we get a *three address instruction*. Three addresses will require 54 bits to specify if the memory has 256K addresses. This instruction length is also too long. Again, however, many instructions would not require all three addresses. For example, an instruction to change the sign of a number stored in memory would need only the address of the number. In order to simplify the design of processors, it would be preferable to have a uniform size for all instructions. If it is decided to use only one address in each instruction the processor design will be simplified. We would, however, need a register in the processor where an operand may be stored and whose address need not be explicitly specified but will be *implied* in various operations. One such register is known as accumulator register. If a processor has an accumulator, then an instruction to ADD given earlier may be reformulated as a series of three instructions:

1. Clear the accumulator register in the processor and place the first operand from address P in it.

2. Add to the accumulator register the operand stored in Q and leave the result in the accumulator.

3. Store the contents of the accumulator in address R of memory.

These instructions are summarized as the three single address instructions shown in Table 5.1. It should be clearly understood while writing a program that when we say ADD

Table 5.1 A sequence of single address instructions

What task? (operation)	Address of operand	Abbreviated instruction
Clear accumulator and place operand in it	P	CLA P
Add operand to accumulator	Q	ADD Q
Store contents of accumulator	R	STO R

Q we do not mean add the number Q. We mean add the number *stored in memory in address Q*. The availability of an accumulator in a processor allows intermediate results to be kept in it and subsequently used without unnecessary storing and retrieving from the memory. As an example, a series of instructions to read a set of numbers, add them and print the result is given in Table 5.2. Observe that the intermediate results remain in the accumulator and are used subsequently. Observe the column labelled 'instruction address' in the program of Table 5.2. Each instruction in a program is also stored in memory. The address where the first instruction of the above program is stored is X. The second instruction is stored in the next address $X + 1$. Succeeding instructions are stored in successive addresses.

The notation C(K) in Table 5.2 means contents of address K in memory. Contents of accumulator is abbreviated as ACC in this table.

In a processor, a string of bits is used to code the instructions. Addresses are also binary numbers. If a processor has 16 different operations, four bits would be needed to represent each operation. If the memory size is 4K words, then 12 bits are needed to represent each address. The format of a typical instruction is shown in Fig. 5.1. Using the operation codes given in Table 5.3, the program of Table 5.2 would be as shown in Table 5.4. The program is stored from address $(008)_{hex}$. Hexadecimal notation is used for conciseness. The term 'address' used in the preceding discussions refers to the address of

Table 5.2 A program to add a set of numbers

Address where instruction is stored in memory	Operation	Operand address	Remarks
X	READ	K	Read $n1$ and store in K
$X + 1$	READ	L	Read $n2$ and store in L
$X + 2$	READ	M	Read $n3$ and store in M
$X + 3$	READ	N	Read $n4$ and store in N
$X + 4$	CLA	K	Move C(K) = $n1$ to accumulator
$X + 5$	ADD	L	ACC ← ACC + C(L) = $n1 + n2$
$X + 6$	ADD	M	ACC ← ACC + C(M) = $n1 + n2 + n3$
$X + 7$	ADD	N	ACC ← ACC + C(N) = $n1 + n2 + n3 + n4$
$X + 8$	STO	W	C(W) ← ACC = $n1 + n2 + n3 + n4$
$X + 9$	PRINT	W	Print C(W) = $n1 + n2 + n3 + n4$
$X + 10$	HALT		

an operand. The length of the operand (number of bits in it) is not specified. If we assume that the length of an operand equals the length of an instruction, then the instruction and the operand are said to occupy one *word* in a computer's memory. If the smallest addressable unit in a computer is a word then such a computer is known as a *word addressable computer*. A computer in which each byte stored can be addressed individually is known as a *byte addressable* computer. The program given in Table 5.4 is known as a *machine language program*. Observe that the instructions are stored in the memory beginning from address 008 up to 012. Data to be processed is also stored in the same memory from address 200 up to 204. It is the responsibility of the machine language programmer to ensure that the program area and data area in memory are kept separate and data is not accidentally written over an instruction. In the next section we will examine the logical structure a processor must have to execute machine language programs.

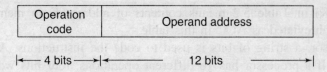

Fig. 5.1   Format of an instruction.

Table 5.3   Binary and hexadecimal codes for operations

Operation	Operation code (in binary)	Operation code (in hexadecimal)
READ	1010	A
CLA	0001	1
ADD	0010	2
STO	0110	6
PRINT	1011	B
HALT	1111	F

Table 5.4   Machine language program corresponding to the program of Table 5.2

Instruction address (Hexadecimal)	Instruction		Remarks
	Operation code	Operand address	
008	A	200	Read $n1$ and store in 200
009	A	201	Read $n2$ and store in 201
00A	A	202	Read $n3$ and store in 202
00B	A	203	Read $n4$ and store in 203
00C	1	200	Accumulator $\leftarrow$ C(200) = $n1$
00D	2	201	ACC $\leftarrow$ ACC + C(201) = $n1 + n2$
00E	2	202	ACC $\leftarrow$ ACC + C(202) = $n1 + n2 + n3$
00F	2	203	ACC $\leftarrow$ ACC + C(203) = $n1 + n2 + n3 + n4$
010	6	204	C(204) $\leftarrow$ ACC = $n1 + n2 + n3 + n4$
011	B	204	Print C(204) = $n1 + n2 + n3 + n4$
012	F		

5.2   DESCRIPTION OF A PROCESSOR

In this section we will describe the processor of a hypothetical computer which we will call HYPCOM. The processor of HYPCOM has an accumulator register (ACC). The other registers in its processor are an instruction register (IR) and a program counter register (PC). The instruction register is used to temporarily store the instruction being executed. It consists of two parts: an operation code part and an address part. The PC register stores the address of the next instruction to be executed. The block diagram of HYPCOM processor is shown in Fig. 5.2.

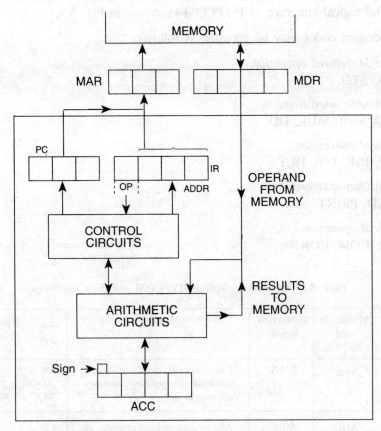

Fig. 5.2 Logical structure of HYPCOM processor.

The other specifications of HYPCOM are:

(i) It has a 4K word addressable memory.

(ii) A word of HYPCOM is 16 bits long.

(iii) A word of HYPCOM stores either an instruction or data to be processed.

(iv) It has 15 operation codes.

(v) The instructions are single address instructions. Four bits are needed to represent 15 operation codes. Twelve bits are needed to address a 4K memory. An instruction is thus 16 bits long.

(vi) It has an input unit which is used to feed both instructions and data. A 16-bit word is read via the input unit and stored in memory when a READ operation code is executed by the processor.

(vii) It has a printer as its output unit which is used to output a 16-bit word from the memory when a PRINT operation code is executed by the processor.

The operation codes of HYPCOM and what each one of them does are given in Table 5.5. The logical structure of HYPCOM is shown in Fig. 5.3.

The operation codes may be grouped as follows:

1. *Data Movement operations*
   CLA, STO

2. *Arithmetic operations*
   ADD, SUB, MUL, DIV

3. *Control operations*
   JMP, JNE, JZE, HLT

4. *Input/Output operations*
   READ, PRINT

5. *Logical operations*
   SHR, COM, EOR

Table 5.5   Operation codes of HYPCOM and their meanings

Operation code (Hexa-decimal)	Mnemonic used	Instruction format	Meaning	Status of registers
1	CLA	124A	Clear accumulator and place contents of specified memory address in it	OP = 1 ADDR = 24A ACC ← MEM(24A)
2	ADD	24BF	Add to accumulator contents of specified address	OP = 2 ADDR = 4BF ACC ← ACC + MEM(4BF)
3	SUB	3AFD	Subtract from accumulator contents of specified address	OP = 3 ADDR = AFD ACC ← ACC − MEM(AFD)
4	MUL	4BAF	Multiply contents of accumulator by contents of specified address	OP = 4 ADDR = BAF ACC ← ACC × MEM(BAF)
5	DIV	545D	Divide contents of accumulator by contents of specified address and leave integer quotient in accumulator	OP = 5 ADDR = 45D ACC ← ACC/ MEM(45D)

(Cont.)

Table 5.5 Operation codes of HYPCOM and their meaning (Cont.)

Operation code (Hexa-decimal)	Mnemonic used	Instruction format	Meaning	Status of registers
6	STO	6AFE	Store contents of accumulator in the specified address in memory	OP = 6 ADDR = AFE MEM(AFE) ← ACC
7	JMP	7653	Take next instruction from address 653 of memory	OP = 7 ADDR = 653 PC ← ADDR = 653
8	JNE	8446	Take next instruction from address 446 if ACC < 0 else next instruction from address given in PC	OP = 8 ADDR = 446 *if* ACC < 0 *then* PC ← ADDR
9	JZE	9648	Take next instruction from address 648 if ACC = 0 (ignore sign of ACC) else next instruction from address given in PC	OP = 9 ADDR = 648 *if* ACC = 0 *then* PC ← ADDR
A	READ	A798	Input into specified address in memory data read from input unit	OP = A ADDR = 798 MEM (ADDR) ← Input
B	PRINT	B547	Print data retrieved from the specified address in memory	OP = B ADDR = 547 Print MEM (ADDR)
C	SHR	C008	Shift contents of ACC (excluding sign) right by 8 bits	OP = C ADDR = 008. Shift ACC right by 8 bits
D	COM	D000	Complement contents of ACC. Each bit of ACC is replaced by its complement. If a bit is 1 it is made 0 and if it is 0 it is made 1	OP = D ADDR (None) ACC ← $\overline{\text{ACC}}$
E	EOR	EABF	Match each bit of ACC with each bit of contents of specified address. If bits are identical make the bit of ACC = 0	OP = E ADDR = ABF ACC ← ACC *EOR* MEM(ABF)
F	HLT	F000	Halt computation	OP = F ADDR (None)

Remarks: 1. MEM (Address) is interpreted as contents of memory in the specified address.
2. ACC ← MEM (address) is interpreted as "Move into ACC the contents of memory in the specified address".

The data movement group moves data from memory to accumulator and from accumulator to memory. The arithmetic group does addition, subtraction, multiplication and division.

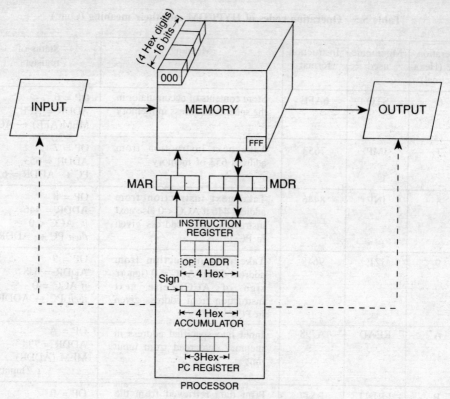

Fig. 5.3   Logical structure of HYPCOM.

The results of arithmetic operation are left in the accumulator and must not exceed the capacity of the accumulator. The control group is intended to implement decision boxes in flowcharts. Normal sequential execution of instructions are altered when jump instructions are executed. The input/output group's function is self-evident. The logical group is useful for operation on characters. The exclusive-or *(EOR)* operation is particularly useful to examine whether the contents of two words in memory are identical. Table 5.6 defines the

Table 5.6   Exclusive-or operator

A	B	A *EOR* B
0	0	0
0	1	1
1	0	1
1	1	0

Word 1	0 1 0 1 1 1 0 0 1 0 1 0 1 1 1 0
Word 2	0 1 0 1 1 1 0 0 1 0 1 0 1 1 1 0
Word 1 *EOR* Word 2	0 0 0 0 0 0 0 0 0 0 0 0 0 0 0 0

exclusive-or operation between bits. It is seen that if the exclusive-or of corresponding bits of two words give all zero, then the two words are identical.

5.3 A MACHINE LANGUAGE PROGRAM

We will now write a small machine language program for HYPCOM. The program is to compare two numbers X and Y and output the larger one. The program is given in Table 5.7. In this table columns 2 and 3 contain the machine instructions. Column 1 gives the address where the instruction itself is stored. This information is necessary to write the program. For example, in the program given in Table 5.7 the instruction 8007 stored in address 004 commands that the next instruction to be executed should be taken from memory address 007 if the contents of accumulator is less than zero. A programmer must know what instruction is stored in address 007.

Table 5.7 A machine language program to find larger of two numbers

| Address where the instruction is stored | Machine Instruction | | Explanation of instruction |
	Operation code	Operand address	
000	A	625	Read from input unit a number and store it in address 625 MEM(625) ← X
001	A	626	Read from input unit a number and store it in address 626 MEM(626) ← Y
002	1	625	ACC ← MEM(625) = X
003	3	626	ACC ← X-MEM(626) ∴ ACC ← X − Y
004	8	007	If $(X − Y) < 0$ then take next instruction from address 007; else continue
005	B	625	$(X − Y) \geq 0$ if control comes to this instruction. In this case output X
006	F	000	Halt
007	B	626	$(X − Y) < 0$ if control comes here. In this case output Y
008	F	000	Halt

The last column of Table 5.7 explains what each instruction in the machine language does. This explanation is essential to understand the program.

We will now examine step-by-step how this program is interpreted and executed by HYPCOM's processor.

Step 1: The program is read via the input unit and stored in successive addresses in memory. The first instruction is stored in address 000 of memory, the second in address 001 etc. The last instruction is stored in address 008. This step is known as *program loading* phase.

The status of memory of HYPCOM at the end of loading the program of Table 5.7 is shown in Table 5.8.

Table 5.8   Status of memory after the program is loaded

Memory address	Contents of address
000	A625
001	A626
002	1625
003	3626
004	8007
005	B625
006	F000
007	B626
008	F000

Step 2:   The address of the first instruction to be executed is entered in PC register in the processor. As the program has been stored starting at address 000, the initial number stored in PC register is 000.

PC ← 000

Step 3:   The instruction from memory, stored in address as given by PC, is fetched and placed in the Instruction register. This is done by the control circuits of the processor by copying the contents of PC into the memory address register MAR. The memory circuits then place the contents of the specified address in the memory data register MDR. The contents of MDR are then moved to the instruction register IR. This is summarized below:

MAR ← PC = 000;
MDR ← MEM(PC) = MEM(000) = A625;
IR ← MDR = A625

Step 4:   The contents of PC is incremented by 1 so that PC contains the address of the next instruction to be executed.

PC ← PC + 1 = 001

Step 5:   The OP code part of IR is decoded. Appropriate circuitry in the processor carries out the decoding operation. In the example, the operation code of the instruction in IR is A which is interpreted as "Read from the input unit a number and store it in memory at the address specified in the instruction". Suppose a number 285 is fed to the input unit, this number will be stored in address 625 specified in the instruction. The sequence of events which occur when this instruction is executed are sequentially:

MDR ← Input data
MAR ← 625
MEM(MAR) = MEM(625) = MDR = Input data = 285

Step 6: The processor will fetch from the memory the next instruction to be executed. The address in memory to be accessed is found in PC. Thus

$$MAR \leftarrow PC = 001$$
$$MDR \leftarrow MEM(PC) = MEM(001) = A626$$
$$IR \leftarrow MDR = A626$$

Step 7: PC is incremented by 1. Thus $PC \leftarrow PC + 1 = 002$.

Step 8: The OP code of the instruction is again A. Thus as in Step 5 a number from the input is read and stored in the specified memory address. If the number fed to the input unit is 899 then $MEM(626) = 899$.

Step 9: The next instruction is fetched from the memory address given in PC, namely, 002. Thus

$$MAR \leftarrow PC = 002$$
$$MDR \leftarrow MEM(MAR) = MEM(002) = 1625$$
$$IR \leftarrow MDR = 1625$$

Step 10: PC is incremented by 1. Thus $PC \leftarrow PC + 1 = 003$.

Step 11: The OP code is 1. When decoded the processor clears the Accumulator and moves into it the contents of memory address 625. Thus $ACC \leftarrow MEM(625) = 285$.

Step 12: The next instruction is fetched from Memory (PC), namely, MEM(003). Thus

$$IR \leftarrow MEM(003) = 3626$$

Step 13: PC is incremented by 1. Thus $PC \leftarrow PC + 1 = 004$.

Step 14: The OP code is 3. When decoded the processor subtracts from the Accumulator the contents of MEM(626). Thus

$$ACC \leftarrow ACC - MEM(626) = 285 - 899 = -614$$

Step 15: The next instruction is fetched from memory address given by PC, namely, 004. Thus

$$IR \leftarrow MEM(004) = 8007$$

Step 16: PC is incremented by 1. Thus $PC \leftarrow PC + 1 = 005$.

Step 17: The OP code is 8. When decoded the processor checks the contents of ACC. It finds that the number stored in ACC is less than 0. It thus replaces the contents of PC by the address part of the instruction in IR. Thus

$$PC \leftarrow 007$$

Step 18: The next instruction is fetched from memory address given by PC, namely, 007. Thus

$$IR \leftarrow MEM(007) = B626$$

Step 19:   PC is incremented by 1. Thus PC ← PC + 1 = 008.

Step 20:   The OP code in IR is B. The processor decodes this code. This code is to output the contents of specified address. Thus the contents of memory address 626 is sent to the output unit. As MEM(626) = 899, this number is given as output.

Step 21:   The next instruction is fetched from memory address given by PC, namely, 008. Thus

IR ← MEM(008) = F000

Step 22:   PC is incremented by 1. Thus PC ← PC + 1 = 009.

Step 23:   The OP code in IR is F. The processor decodes this code. This code is to halt execution of the program.

We see from the above example that a computer does the following in order to execute a program:

1. The program is stored in memory from a specified address. Instructions are stored in successive addresses.

2. The starting address of the program is placed in PC.

3. The instruction from the memory address as specified in PC is fetched and placed in IR.

4. PC is incremented by 1.

5. The operation code in IR is decoded by the control circuits of the processor.

6. If the specified operation requires an operand to be fetched from memory, it is done.

7. The operation is carried out.

8. Steps 3 to 7 are repeated until a halt instruction is executed.

5.4   AN ALGORITHM TO SIMULATE THE HYPOTHETICAL COMPUTER

In the last section we have shown how a machine language program for HYPCOM is executed step-by-step. We give as Algorithm 5.1 the entire operation of loading a program in memory and its execution. In this algorithm, we have used MAR to represent the memory address register and MDR to represent the memory data register.

Algorithm 5.1

Phase 1:   Loading program into memory.
{Initialize PC to the starting address of the program to be stored in memory}

PC ← 0; {The starting address is assumed to be 0.}

{The statements between *repeat* and *until* are repeated again and again until all instructions are stored in memory} *repeat*

> Read Instruction from the input unit and place it in MDR;
> {Store the contents of MDR in memory in address specified in PC.}
> MAR ← PC; MEM(PC) ← MDR;
> PC ← PC + 1

until end of program;

Phase 2: *In this phase, the program stored in memory is executed.*
{Initialize PC to the address of the first instruction in the program}

> PC ← 0;

{The statements between *repeat* and *until* are repeated again and again until a HALT instruction (OP code = F) is encountered}

repeat

> IR ← MEM(PC)

{The most significant 4 bits of IR is the OP code. The next 12 bits specify the operand address in memory}

OP = IR [16..13]; ADDR = IR [12..1];
PC ← PC + 1; {PC is incremented to specify the address from where the next instruction
　　　　　　is to be retrieved}
Decode OP code and perform actions specified.

OP = 1: ACC ← MEM(ADDR);

OP = 2: ACC ← ACC + MEM(ADDR);

OP = 3: ACC ← ACC − MEM(ADDR);

OP = 4: ACC ← ACC × MEM(ADDR);

OP = 5: ACC ← ACC/MEM(ADDR); {Division stores quotient in ACC}

OP = 6: MEM(ADDR) ← ACC;

OP = 7: PC ← ADDR;

OP = 8: *if* ACC < 0 *then* PC ← ADDR;

OP = 9: *if* ACC = 0 *then* PC ← ADDR;

OP = A: MEM(ADDR) ← Input;

OP = B: output ← MEM(ADDR);

OP = C: Shift ACC *right* by ADDR bits;

OP = D: ACC ← $\overline{ACC}$

OP = E: ACC ← ACC *Exclusive OR* MEM(ADDR);

OP = F: {HALT};

until (OP = F);

End of Algorithm 5.1.

We will now write another machine language program for HYPCOM. This program will illustrate the formation of a loop.

Example

Problem: A program is to be written to find the heaviest student in a class of students.

A procedure for solution:

Step 1:   Note down the weight of each student in the class on a slip.

Step 2:   When all the weights are noted down put a slip at the end which has an entry of 0. This slip will indicate the end of data on weights of students. As 0 cannot itself be a weight it is a logical number to choose as the end of data.

Step 3:   Read the weight written in the first slip and call it the Heaviest. This is logical because if there is only one student in the class, that student is the heaviest.

Step 4:   Read the next slip.

Step 5:   If the number in this slip = 0 it indicates that there are no more slips. Thus go to Step 8. Otherwise continue.

Step 6:   If weight read > Heaviest, then Heaviest ← weight read; otherwise retain Heaviest as it is.

Step 7:   Go back to Step 4.

Step 8:   Output weight stored in Heaviest.

The above procedure is formulated as the machine language program of Table 5.9.

Table 5.9   A HYPCOM machine language program to find the heaviest student in a class

Memory address where instruction is stored	Instruction		Remarks
	Operation code	Operand address	
000	A	501	Read first weight and store it in address 501 as heaviest
001	A	500	Read next weight and store it in address 500
002	1	500	ACC ← MEM(500) Move weight read to accumulator
003	9	009	ACC = 0 indicates end of weights. If ACC = 0 take next instruction from 009 which outputs heaviest stored in MEM(501)
004	3	501	ACC ← ACC − MEM(501)

(Cont.)

Table 5.9 A HYPCOM machine language program to find the heaviest student in a class (Cont.)

Memory address where instruction is stored	Instruction		Remarks
	Operation code	Operand address	
005	8	001	IF ACC < 0 then it means MEM(501) is larger than MEM(500). Thus MEM(501) is not disturbed. Program loops back to read next weight. Otherwise the next instruction is executed
006 007	1 6	500 501	If MEM(500) is larger then move it to MEM(501). This is done in two instructions
008	7	001	Program loops back to read the next weight
009	B	501	Output MEM(501) which has heaviest weight stored in it
00A	F	000	Halt

In this machine language we allocate address 500 to store the weight read and address 501 to store the heaviest. The comments in the remarks column of Table 5.9 explain the machine language program.

The reader is urged to go through this program using the HYPCOM simulation algorithm and understand in detail how HYPCOM would load and execute the instructions of the machine language program.

In this section we examined the logical structure of a hypothetical computer. Processors of real computers are more powerful. There are usually a large variety of operation codes. Operation codes are implemented to reduce programming effort and enable computers to perform a variety of jobs. For example, operation codes to facilitate implementing program loops, and to perform operations on arrays of numbers and strings of characters are usually implemented. Besides more operation codes, the processor is designed with more registers and a variety of methods of addressing the memory. Later in this book we will discuss this question again.

SUMMARY

1. A processing unit in a computer interprets instructions in a program and carries them out.

2. An instruction in general consists of a part which specifies the operation to be performed and other parts which specify the addresses of operands.

3. A single address instruction specifies the address of only one operand.

4. In a processor, a string of bits is used to code operations and another string of bits is used to specify the address.

5. In order to code n operations in binary, we need x bits such that $2^x = n$. Similarly, to specify W addresses in memory, we need y bits such that $2^y = W$. For example, to code 16 operations we need 4 bits such that $2^4 = 16$. Similarly to select one address out of 4K addresses in memory we need 12 bits such that $2^{12} = 4 \times 1024$.

6. An instruction consisting of an operation code and operand address or addresses designed for a specific computer is known as a machine language instruction of that computer.

7. A sequence of machine language instructions to solve a problem is known as a machine language program.

8. Machine language instructions for input/output, data movement, arithmetic, logic and controlling sequencing of operations are available in all computers.

9. A computer's processor has storage registers to store operands and results. It also has a register to store the instruction being executed and a register which stores the address of the next instruction to be executed.

10. Given a problem, it is possible to write a machine language program to solve it. In writing machine language programs, however, one has to pay attention to all details including status of all the processor registers, addresses of instructions and data in memory.

11. A machine language program is executed by a computer in two phases. In the first phase, it reads and stores the program in its memory. After storing the program, it initiates program execution. In the program execution phase, instructions are retrieved from memory one after another, decoded and executed.

12. The instruction set of a processor, namely, the group of instructions which it can interpret and execute is determined by the different application programs to be executed by it. The number and function of registers in the processor is also determined by the nature and size of application programs.

REVIEW QUESTIONS

5.1 What details are to be specified by an instruction to a computer?

5.2 Explain the term single-address instruction, two-address instruction, three-address instruction and four-address instruction.

5.3 Supposing that a computer has a two-address instruction, what is the most appropriate use of the two addresses?

5.4 Write a small machine language program for a two-address computer to add two numbers and output the sum.

5.5 If a computer has 128 operation codes and has a memory capacity of 512K addresses, how many bits would be required for a two-address instruction?

5.6 Repeat 5.5 for a computer with a single-address instruction.

5.7 Write a machine language program to add six numbers and output the answer. Assume single-address instructions. Use instruction codes given in Table 5.3.

5.8 Write a machine language program for HYPCOM to find the smallest of three numbers.

5.9 Explain how the operation code for jump (code 7) in HYPCOM is executed.

5.10 What is the purpose of PC register in HYPCOM?

5.11 If a computer is a single-address computer, word addressed, has 64 operation codes and 16K addresses, answer the following questions:

   (i) What is the length of the instruction register?
  (ii) How many bits are there in the PC register?
 (iii) What is the length of ACC register?

5.12 If the hexadecimal number AF64 is stored in address 456 of HYPCOM and the contents of ACC is FA64, what will be the contents of ACC after the HYPCOM instruction E456 is executed?

5.13 Repeat 5.12 assuming that the contents of address 456 in memory is FA64.

5.14 If the contents of address 847 of HYPCOM is AB76, what will be stored in 847 after the following HYPCOM instructions are executed:

             1847
            C008
            6847

5.15 If the contents of address FA3 of HYPCOM is A457, what will be stored in FA3 after the following instructions are carried out:

            1FA3
           D000
           6FA3

5.16 Explain step-by-step how the program written in Table 5.9 will be loaded in its memory and executed by HYPCOM.

5.17 Given a set of weights of students in a class (in hexadecimal) write a machine language program for HYPCOM to output the average weight of students in the class and the number of students in the class.

5.18 What is the largest positive decimal number which can be stored in the accumulator of HYPCOM?

5.19 Develop the logical structure of a computer we will call XYZ-COMP. This computer has the following specifications:

   (i) 8 operation codes which are: Load accumulator, store accumulator, add, subtract, halt, jump on negative, read and output.
  (ii) 32K word memory.
 (iii) Instruction and data length equal a word.
 (iv) Single address instruction format.

5.20 Write a simulation algorithm to simulate XYZ-COMP. Use octal numbers (numbers using base 8) in your simulation algorithm.

6

Binary Arithmetic

We saw in Chapter 2 that decimal numbers are converted to binary, because processors of computers perform arithmetic operations only on binary numbers. We should thus know how to do binary arithmetic in order to understand the working of processors. This is the main objective of this chapter.

6.1 BINARY ADDITION

We will see in this section how to add binary numbers. Counting is a form of addition since successive numbers, while counting, are obtained by adding 1. In the decimal system we start with 0 and by successively adding 1, we reach 9. As the base of the system is 10, there are no further symbols. Thus, after 9 we count 10. The 1 becomes a carry to the tens position in the positional system. In the binary system, the count progresses as follows:

$$0, 1, 1\,0, 1\,1, 1\,0\,0, 1\,0\,1 \ldots$$

When we add two binary numbers, we write the numbers one below the other with their least significant bits (LSBs) aligned. If the numbers have fractional parts, then the binary points must be aligned.

When we add, we start with the least significant bit. Depending upon the values 'a' and 'b' of the bits to be added, we will have a sum and may have a carry to the next stage of addition. There are four possible combinations in which 'a' and 'b' occur. The corresponding sum and carry are shown in Table 6.1.

Table 6.1 A half adder table

a	b	Sum	Carry
0	0	0	0
0	1	1	0
1	0	1	0
1	1	0	1

Example 6.1

We give three examples of binary addition.

SOLUTION:

Carry	11	01	111.0
Augend	11	101	11.10
Addend	01	001	01.11
	100	110	101.01

We see from these examples that, while adding two binary numbers, we may have to add a maximum of three bits. These are the carry bit, if any, from the previous stage of addition, and the bits of the augend and addend. An addition table for these three bits as inputs is given in Table 6.2, which is known as the "full adder table". Table 6.1 is known as a "half adder table".

Table 6.2 A binary addition table including carry

Augend bit	Addend bit	Carry from the previous stage	Sum	Carry to next stage
0	0	0	0	0
0	0	1	1	0
0	1	0	1	0
0	1	1	0	1
1	0	0	1	0
1	0	1	0	1
1	1	0	0	1
1	1	1	1	1

6.2 BINARY SUBTRACTION

In order to subtract, we use a subtractor table (Table 6.3) similar to the one used for addition. With reference to the second row of Table 6.3, note that when we have to subtract a '1' from a '0', we have to borrow a '1' from the adjacent higher bit position. The process of 'borrowing' as well as 'borrow propagation' is shown in Example 6.2.

Table 6.3 Half-subtractor table

A	B	Difference	Borrow
0	0	0	0
0	1	1	1
1	0	1	0
1	1	0	0

Example 6.2

We give four examples of binary subtraction.

SOLUTION:

Borrow	1	11.1	11	11
Minuend	101	10.00	100	110
Subtrahend	011	01.11	001	011
Difference	010	00.01	011	011

Thus, when we are performing subtraction of bits belonging to the nth stage, we have to know whether a '1' has been borrowed from that stage by the $(n-1)^{th}$ stage. Further, apart from finding the difference, we must also determine whether a '1' has to be borrowed from the $(n+1)^{th}$ stage. A full-subtractor table having the minuend, subtrahend and the bit borrowed from the nth stage as inputs and which gives the difference as well as the borrow to be taken from the $(n+1)^{th}$ stage, is shown in Table 6.4.

Table 6.4   Full-subtractor table

Inputs			Outputs	
A_n Minuend	B_n Subtrahend	Bit borrowed from the nth stage	Difference	Borrow to be taken to the $(n+1)^{th}$ stage
0	0	0	0	0
0	0	1	1	1
0	1	0	1	1
0	1	1	0	1
1	0	0	1	0
1	0	1	0	0
1	1	0	0	0
1	1	1	1	1

6.3   SIGNED NUMBERS

Hitherto we have been dealing with only positive numbers. In practice, we use both positive and negative numbers as operands. In the binary system, we represent the sign of a number using an extra bit at the extreme left of the number. By convention the symbol '0' is used to represent the '+' sign and '1' to represent the '−' sign. For instance, +5 is represented by 0,101 and −7 is represented by 1,111. The comma separates the sign bit from the number. This method of representation is known as sign magnitude representation.

When we have to subtract a number B from a number A, we look at the magnitudes as well as the signs of these numbers. When A and B have opposite signs, in effect we add their magnitudes and we know how to determine the sign of the result. On the other hand, if A and B have the same sign, we always subtract the smaller magnitude from the larger and once again, decide the sign independently. Similarly, when we have to add, depending upon the signs of the numbers, we may end up subtracting or adding their magnitudes, the procedures for which are different.

It would, of course, be more convenient if we could evolve another convention for representing positive and negative numbers which would allow us to use one basic procedure for both addition and subtraction. If the procedure was the same, we could use a single electronic circuit to implement both addition and subtraction. A convention for representing negative numbers which allows this is the 'complement representation' of numbers.

We will explain complement representation by first considering subtraction of decimal number. Consider the following examples of subtractions which are given in pairs.

Example 6.3

We give three examples of subtraction using 10's complement:

458	458	894	894	498	498
− 349	+ 650	− 648	+ 351	− 042	+ 957
109	+ 1	246	+ 1	456	+ 1
	1109		1246		1456
	− 1000		− 1000		− 1000
	109		246		456

The second method of subtraction in each of the above pairs is by addition of what is known as the 10's complement of the decimal number. The 10's complement of a digit x is defined as:

$$10\text{'s complement of } x = (10 - x) = (9 - x) + 1.$$

Suppose we want to find $y - x$. We can do the following:

$$y - x = y + (10 - x) - 10 = y + (9 - x) + 1 - 10$$

Finding $(9 - x)$ for any digit x is very simple as it can be done by table look up without subtracting as shown below:

x	0	1	2	3	4	5	6	7	8	9
$9-x$	9	8	7	6	5	4	3	2	1	0

The same idea is used in binary subtraction. In binary subtraction we use the addition of *2's complement* of a binary number.

6.4 TWO'S COMPLEMENT REPRESENTATION OF NUMBERS

The 2's complement of a binary number x, which has n bits, is given by $(2^n - x)$. Consider the number +3 whose binary representation is 011. It has three bits. Hence the 2's complement of +3 is $(2^3 - 3)$, which is 5. The binary representation of 5 is 101. Thus, 101 is the 2's complement of 011.

In a computer, all numbers are represented in a uniform fashion using a fixed number of bits. Thus, for an n-bit machine, the range of numbers it can handle is 0 to $2^n - 1$. For simplicity, consider a 4-bit machine. Sixteen numbers (0 to 15) can normally be represented using these four bits. Now we devise a new scheme of representing negative numbers as follows. We use the first seven combinations of bits for representing positive numbers one to seven. We reserve seven of the remaining combinations for representing negative numbers -1 to -7. Thus we have divided the total range into two parts, 0 and 8 being common to the two halves. Now we restrict ourselves to the use of numbers having a maximum magnitude of seven. In this way we can represent both positive and negative numbers as indicated in Fig. 6.1. With reference to the figure we see that the code 1111, which normally represents 15, is assigned to -1. Similarly the binary equivalent of 14 is assigned to -2. Since $15 = 2^4 - 1$, $14 = 2^4 - 2$, etc., this is called the 2's complement representation of 1,2, etc. In general the 2's complement of a n bit number x is $(2^n - x)$. Of the n bits of the complement representation $(n - 1)$ bits represent the magnitude.

There is a simple procedure to obtain the 2's complement of a binary number. We first complement each bit of the number (i.e., replace '1' by '0' and '0' by '1'). Now we add a '1' to the number. For example, consider the number 5 whose binary representation is 0101. Bit complementation yields 1010. Now adding a '1' to this number gives 1011 which is the 2's complement representation for -5.

Yet another method of obtaining the 2's complement of a binary number is to scan the number from right to left and complement all bits appearing after the first appearance of a '1'. For example the 2's complement of 0010 is 1110 and that of 0011 is 1101.

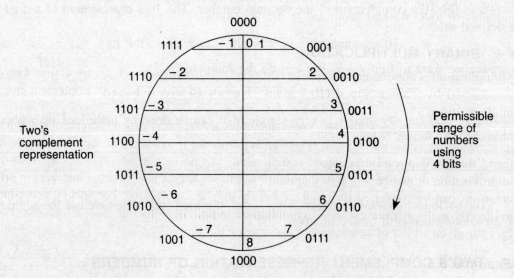

Fig. 6.1   Two's complement representation of numbers.

6.5   ADDITION/SUBTRACTION OF NUMBERS IN 2'S COMPLEMENT NOTATION

Represent all negative numbers in 2's complement form. Now we have the same procedure for addition and subtraction. Subtraction of a number is achieved by adding the 2's complement of the number. This is illustrated in the following example where the carry, if any, from the most significant bit, during addition, should be ignored. The result has to be interpreted appropriately using the same convention.

Example 6.4

Using 2's complement representation, (a) subtract 3 from 5; (b) subtract (− 3) from (− 5); (c) add (− 5) and (− 2); and (d) add 5 and 4.

SOLUTION:

(a) 5	0101	(b) − 5 1011
− 3	1101	+ 3 0011

$$
\begin{array}{rl}
\text{(a)} \quad 5 & 0101 \\
-3 & 1101 \\
\hline
& 10010 \\
& \text{ignore carry} \\
& \text{Answer} = +2
\end{array}
\qquad
\begin{array}{rl}
\text{(b)} \quad -5 & 1011 \\
+3 & 0011 \\
\hline
& 1110 \\
& \text{Answer} = -2
\end{array}
$$

$$
\begin{array}{rl}
\text{(c)} \quad -5 & 1011 \\
-2 & 1110 \\
\hline
& 11001 \\
& \text{ignore carry} \\
& \text{Answer} = -7
\end{array}
\qquad
\begin{array}{rl}
\text{(d)} \quad 5 & 0101 \\
4 & 0100 \\
\hline
& 1001 \\
& \text{incorrect answer}
\end{array}
$$

In the last example we get an incorrect answer because the sum 9 exceeds the range of numbers (0 to 7) we had stipulated in the beginning.

6.6 BINARY MULTIPLICATION

Multiplication is nothing but successive addition. Thus multiplication of 5 by 4, for example, is achieved by adding 5 to itself 4 times. This basic idea is used to implement binary multiplication.

The procedure for multiplying two signed binary numbers depends on the method used to represent negative numbers. If negative numbers are represented in the 2's complement form, then multiplication becomes complicated. In this section we will discuss only the multiplication of numbers in sign magnitude notation. This is justifiable as numbers in other notations can be converted to this form before they are multiplied. For special procedures to directly multiply numbers in 2's complement notation, the student may refer to the book by Chu given in list of references at the end of the book.

Example 6.5

Multiply 1101 by 1011.

SOLUTION:

Consider the following long-hand multiplication method:

Multiplicand	1101
Multiplier	1011
Partial product	1101
	1101
	0000
	1101
Product	10001111

The method used for multiplication is summarized as follows:

Step 1:   Examine the (least significant bit) LSB of the multiplier. If it is a 1, copy the multiplicand and call it the first partial product. If the LSB is a zero, then enter zero as the first partial product. Preserve (or store) the partial product.

Step 2:   Examine the bit which is to the left of the bit examined last. If it is a 1, go to Step 3. Else, go to Step 4.

Step 3:   Add the multiplicand to the previously stored partial product after shifting right the partial product by one bit. This sum becomes the new partial product. Go to Step 5.

Step 4:   Get new partial product by shifting to the right the previous partial product by one bit.

Step 5:   Repeat Steps 2 to 4 till all bits in the multiplier have been considered. The final value obtained for the partial product is the final product.

Observe from this "long-hand" or "paper and pencil" method of multiplying that we should

(i) preserve the multiplicand as it is added repeatedly to the partial products;

(ii) preserve the partial product and shift it;

(iii) note that, the number of bits in each new partial product is one bit more than the previous one. The number of bits in the final product can equal the sum of the number of bits in the multiplier and the multiplicand.

(iv) and also note that, after each bit of the multiplier has been used to develop a partial product, it is not used again. It may thus be erased or discarded.

These observations enable us to develop an algorithm for multiplication which is appropriate for implementation in a digital system.

In order to multiply we need three registers. Assuming an '*n* bit' multiplier and an '*n* bit' multiplicand, we need two '*n* bit' registers to store the multiplier and the multiplicand, and a '$2n$ bit' register to store the final product and the intermediate partial products. We reduce the length of the product register by remembering that, after each bit of the multiplier has been used to develop a partial product (and after its use) it may be discarded. Note that the length of partial products grows from n to $2n$.

We thus implement multiplication using three registers, namely, a multiplicand register which can store *n* bits, a multiplier-quotient (MQ) register of *n* bits to store the multiplier (or the quotient during division) and an accumulator in which partial products are added and stored. This register needs (*n* + 1) bits.

The configuration of the registers is shown in Fig. 6.2, for *n* = 4.

The accumulator and the MQ register are physically joined so that their contents can be shifted together either to the left or right.

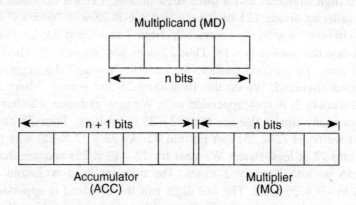

Fig. 6.2 Illustrating multiplication using registers.

Algorithm: Procedure for multiplying two *n* bit numbers. Keep the sign bits of all registers undisturbed.

Step 1:   Set count = *n*.

Step 2:   Check the least significant bit of MQ. If it is a 1, add the contents of the multiplicand register to the contents of the accumulator. If it is a zero, do not add.

Step 3:   Shift right contents of accumulator and MQ register together by one bit.

Step 4:   Replace count by (count − 1).

Step 5:   If count = 0 go to Step 6, Else go to Step 2.

Step 6:   The product will be contained in the accumulator and the MQ register. The most significant bits will be in the accumulator.

Step 7:   Set the sign of the product (sign of accumulator contents) negative, if either the sign of the multiplier or the sign of the multiplicand (but not both) is negative. Else, set the sign positive.

6.7 BINARY DIVISION

Binary division may also be implemented by following a procedure similar to that used in long-hand division with appropriate modifications. We will discuss in this section a method for dividing numbers represented by the sign magnitude notation. The method is called the 'restoring method' for division. Another method, called the 'non-restoring method', is also popular but we do not discuss it in this book.

We will illustrate division by the long-hand method used for decimal numbers, which can then be extended to binary numbers.

Example 6.6   Long-hand division of decimal integers

Consider a three digit dividend and a three digit divisor. Let the dividend be 721 and the divisor 025. In order to divide 721 by 25 we first see if 25 will "go into" the first digit 7 of the dividend. In other words, we subtract 25 from 7 and see if the answer is negative or positive. In this case the answer is -18. Thus 25 does not "go into" 7. The first digit of the quotient is thus zero. To proceed further, we have to "restore" the negative answer -18 back to the original dividend. We do this by adding 25 and getting 7 back. The next digit of the dividend, namely 2, is now appended to 7. We now examine whether 25 can go into 72 and if so how many times: We see that $72 - 25$ is positive. Thus 25 can go into 72 at least once. Next we try if (2×25) can go into 72. As $72 - (2 \times 25) =$ is positive we see that 25 can go into 72 at least twice. We next try $72 - (3 \times 25)$ and see that the answer is -3. Thus 25 can go into 72 only 2 times. The quotient digit is 2, and we restore the remainder back to $-3 + 25 = 22$. The last digit 1 of the dividend is appended to 22 giving 221. Repeating the same step, namely, finding out how many times 25 will go into 221, we see that it can go 8 times. Thus the quotient digit is 8. As no more digits are left in the dividend, the division process ends. The quotient is thus 028 and the remainder is 21. The division process is illustrated below. See (a).

Divisor	Dividend	Quotient		Divisor	Dividend	Quotient
025)	721	(028		11)	1011	(0011
	25				11	
	-18			Borrow →	110	
	25	→ Restoring step		Restore	11	
	72				010	
	75				11	
	-03			Borrow →	111	
	25	→ Restoring step		Restore	11	
	221				101	
	225				11	
	-004			No Borrow	101	
	25	→ Restoring step			11	
	21	→ Remainder		No Borrow	10 ← Remainder	

(a)   (b)

Binary division is similar and, in fact, simpler. It is simpler as we have to only check whether the divisor will go into, the dividend or not. The question of how many times the divisor will go into the dividend is irrelevant as the quotient bit can be either 1 or 0. Binary division is illustrated with an example below.

Example 6.7 Long-hand division of binary integers

We illustrate long-hand division of 1011 by 11 (see page 102 bottom).

The method used in Example 6.6 is expressed as the following step-by-step procedure.

Step 1: Let y be the most significant bit of the dividend

Repeat Steps 2, 3 and 4 four times as the dividend is 4 bits long.

Step 2: Subtract the divisor from y.

Step 3: If a borrow is generated in subtraction

   then set quotient bit to 0 and add divisor to the remainder

   else set quotient bit to 1

Step 4: Append the next significant bit of the dividend to the remainder and call it y.

For the long-hand division presented above we see that

(i) the divisor is to be preserved as it is to be successively subtracted from the dividend;

(ii) the dividend bits are used starting from the most significant bit. Once a bit is used to develop a quotient, it is not needed again. The bit to its right is appended to the remainder for developing the next quotient bit;

(iii) as each quotient bit is developed, a corresponding most significant bit of the dividend may be discarded.

We may thus use the same three registers used for multiplication. The three registers used are again a n bit register to store the divisor, a $(n + 1)$ bit accumulator in which the dividend is originally stored and from which the divisor is subtracted in each step and an n-bit quotient register (see Fig. 6.2). The accumulator and the MQ register may be again physically joined so that their contents can be shifted together.

6.8 FLOATING POINT REPRESENTATION OF NUMBERS

There are two types of arithmetic operations which are required in computers. These are:

   (i) Integer arithmetic,

   (ii) Real or floating point arithmetic.

Integer arithmetic, as the name implies, deals with integer operands, that is, operands without fractional parts. Real arithmetic, on the other hand, uses numbers with fractional parts and is used in most computations.

We saw, in the last chapter, that the memory of computers is organized as an array of words with each word capable of storing a finite number of bits. In HYPCOM we had a memory with each word storing 16 bits. One method of representing real numbers in HYPCOM would be by assuming a fixed position for the binary point and storing numbers (after appropriate shifting) with an assumed decimal point, as shown in Fig. 6.3.

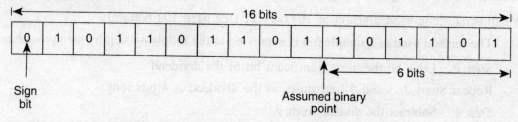

Fig. 6.3   A memory location storing + 101101101.101101

If such a convention is used, the maximum and minimum (in magnitude) numbers that may be stored are:

$$111111111.111111 = (2^9 - 1) \cdot (1 - 2^{-6}) \quad \text{(Maximum)}$$
$$= (511.984375)$$

$$000000000.000001 = 2^{-6} = 0.015625 \quad \text{(Minimum)}$$

This range is quite inadequate in practice and therefore a different convention for representing real numbers is adopted. This convention aims at preserving the maximum number of significant digits in a real number and increasing the range of values of real numbers stored. This representation is called the *normalized floating point mode* of representing and storing real numbers. In this mode, a real number is expressed as a combination of a *mantissa* and an *exponent*. The mantissa is made less than 1 and greater than or equal to 0.1, and the exponent is the power of 2 which multiplies the mantissa. For example, the number

$$1011.0101 \times 2^7$$

is represented in this notation as

$$0.10110101 \times 2^{11} = 0.10110101E01011$$

The mantissa is 0.10110101 and the exponent 1011. The number is stored as shown in Fig. 6.4.

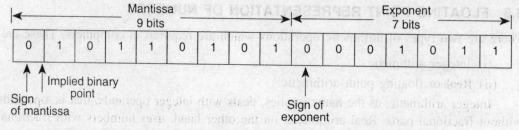

Fig. 6.4   Representation of a binary number in normalized floating point mode.

In the representation of Fig. 6.4, the 16 bits available in a memory word are arbitrarily divided into two parts. 9 bits are used for the mantissa and 7 bits for the exponent. The mantissa and exponent have their own independent signs. While storing numbers, the leading bit in the mantissa is always made non-zero by appropriately shifting it and adjusting the value of the exponent. Thus the number 0.000010101 would be stored as shown in Fig. 6.5. The shifting of the mantissa to the left till its most significant bit is non-zero is called *normalization.* The normalization is done to preserve the maximum number of useful (information carrying) bits. The leading zeros in 0.000010101 serve only to locate the binary point. The information may thus be transferred to the exponent part of the number and the number is stored as 0.10101×2^{-4}. In the memory word, it will have the representation shown in Fig. 6.5.

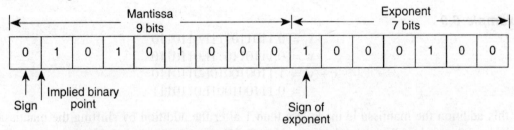

Fig. 6.5 Representation of 0.000010101 in normalized floating point mode.

When numbers are stored using this notation, the range of numbers (magnitude) that may be stored will be:

$$\text{(Maximum) } 0.11111111\text{E}0111111 = (1 - 2^{-8}) \times 2^{(2^6-1)}$$
$$\cong 2^{63}$$
$$\text{(Minimum) } 0.10000000\text{E}1111111 = (2^{-1}) \times 2^{-(2^6 - 1)}$$
$$= 2^{-64}$$

This range is much larger than the range 2^9 to 2^{-6} obtained with the fixed point representation. This increase in range has been obtained by sacrificing seven significant bits.

If a 16 bit word is used to store a real number, the number of significant mantissa bits is only 8, which is equivalent to approximately three decimal digits. This is not at all sufficient in practical computation. Thus, if we want to store and compute with real numbers in HYPCOM, we should allot at least two words (32 bits) to each real number. In this case, one possible way of dividing the 32 bits into mantissa and exponent is to allocate 24 bits to the mantissa (including sign) and 8 bits to the exponent and its sign. This will give about 7 decimal digits in the mantissa and an exponent range of $2^{\pm(2^7 - 1)} = 2^{\pm127} = 10^{\pm38}$. Incidentally this is the format used for floating point numbers in the IBM Personal Computer.

6.9 ARITHMETIC OPERATIONS WITH NORMALIZED FLOATING POINT NUMBERS

6.9.1 Addition

If two numbers represented in normalized floating point notation are to be added, the exponents of the two numbers must be made equal, and the mantissa of the smaller number shifted right by the difference in exponents. This is clarified by the following examples.

Example 6.8

Add $x = 0.111010010E0101010$ to $y = 0.110101101E0100101$

The difference between the exponents of x and y is 5. The number y is smaller. Thus y is shifted by 5 bit positions to the right and the mantissas added as shown below:

$$x = 0.111010010E0101010$$
$$y = 0.000001101E0101010$$
$$x + y = 0.111011111E0101010$$

Example 6.9

$$x = 0.110110111E0110110$$
$$y = 0.111011011E0110110$$
$$x + y = 1.110010010E0110110$$
$$= 0.111001001E0110111$$

In this addition the mantissa is made less than 1 after the addition by shifting the mantissa right by 1 bit and adding 1 to the exponent.

6.9.2 Subtraction

Subtraction is performed using complement representation. Once again the exponents of the two numbers are compared. The number with the smaller exponent is shifted right by the difference in exponents.

Example 6.10

$$x = 0.101010101E0001010$$
$$y = 0.100010110E0000110$$

To find $x - y$.

As the exponent of x is greater than that of y by 4, the mantissa of y is shifted by 4 bit positions to the right before adding its complement to x.

$$y \text{ shifted by 4 bits is} \quad 0.000010001E0001010$$
$$2\text{'s complement of } y \text{ is} \quad 0.111101111E0001010$$

$$x = 0.101010101E0001010$$
$$+ 2\text{'s complement of } y = 0.111101111E0001010$$
$$x - y = 0.101000100E0001010 \text{ (Discard overflow bit)}$$

6.9.3 Multiplication

Two numbers represented in the normalized floating point mode are multiplied by multiplying the mantissas and adding the exponents. After multiplication of the mantissas the result mantissa is normalized and exponents adjusted.

Example 6.11

$$x = 0.110101010E0010110$$
$$y = 0.110000000E0000101$$
$$x \times y = 0.100111111E0011011$$

Example 6.12

$$x = 0.101011001E01101101$$
$$y = 0.101000000E01111100$$
$$x \times y = 0.110101111E11101001$$
$$\downarrow$$

$$\text{overflow bit}$$

The exponent is larger than the largest positive exponent that can be stored. This is known as an *overflow condition*.

6.9.4 Division

Two numbers x and y represented in the normalized floating point mode are divided by dividing the mantissa of x by that of y. The exponent of y is subtracted from the exponent of x.

Example 6.13

$$x = 0.100110101E0110010$$
$$y = 0.110011100E0100010$$
$$(x/y) = 0.110000000E0010000$$

SUMMARY

1. Addition of binary numbers is simple as there are only two symbols 0 and 1 in the binary system. Addition uses the addition table: $0 + 0 = 0$, $0 + 1 = 1$, $1 + 0 = 1$ and $1 + 1 = 0$ with a carry of 1.

2. Binary subtraction uses the subtraction table:

$$0 - 0 = 0, \; 1 - 0 = 1, \; 1 - 1 = 0 \text{ and } 0 - 1 = 1 \text{ with a borrow of 1 to the next bit}$$
position.

3. Negative numbers may be represented using either a sign magnitude representation or a complement representation. In the sign magnitude representation, 0 is used to represent + sign and 1 the − sign.

4. The complement representation of negative numbers is useful primarily because it simplifies subtraction. The 2's complement of an n-bit binary number x is $(2^n - x)$. To subtract a number y from a number x, the 2's complement of y is added to x and the overflow bit is ignored.

5. Binary multiplication is similar to decimal multiplication. The multiplication table is extremely simple. $0 \times 0 = 0$, $0 \times 1 = 0$, $1 \times 0 = 0$ and $1 \times 1 = 1$.

6. Multiplication of two binary numbers is achieved by successive addition of multiplicand to itself after shifting it.

7. Binary division is achieved by successive subtraction of the divisor from the dividend and developing the quotient bits.

8. The number of bits in the operands stored and manipulated in computers is finite. To represent numbers with a fractional part (real numbers), we may use a representation with the decimal point at a fixed position, or use a mantissa and exponent representation. The representation using a mantissa and an exponent allows wider range of magnitudes for real numbers and is known as floating point representation.

9. To preserve the maximum number of significant digits, the mantissa is normalized with its leading bit as a 1.

10. Addition and subtraction of floating point numbers are performed by first making the exponents of the two operands equal. The mantissa is appropriately shifted. The mantissas are then added or subtracted.

11. In the multiplication of two floating point numbers, the mantissas are multiplied and the exponents are added.

12. In the division of two floating point numbers, the mantissas are divided and the exponent of the divisor is subtracted from that of the dividend.

REVIEW QUESTIONS

6.1 Add the following binary numbers:

    (i) 1110.1101 + 110101.01101

    (ii) 1011011.111 + 1010110.1010

    (iii) 110111.11 + 11011101.0101

6.2 Subtract the following binary numbers. Assume that the numbers are represented in sign magnitude notation:

    (i) 10101.1010 − 10001.0011

    (ii) 11011.011 − 11110.101

    (iii) 1001000.001 − 1000011.011

6.3 Subtract the following decimal numbers using 10's complement representation for negative numbers:

    (i) 485 − 128

    (ii) 684 − 35

    (iii) 964 − 988

6.4 Subtract the following binary numbers using 2's complement representation of negative numbers:

    (i) 10101 − 10001

    (ii) 11011 − 1110

    (iii) 100100 − 100011

6.5 Subtract the following binary numbers using 2's complement representation of negative numbers:

  (i) 101101.0011 – 100101.0001
  (ii) 11011.110 – 101.001
  (iii) 10111.1001 – 11000.1101

6.6 Multiply the following binary numbers using long-hand multiplication:

  (i) 10011 × 1101
  (ii) 110.101 × 1011.001
  (iii) 1101.101 × 110101.11

6.7 Divide the following binary numbers long-hand:

  (i) 1011/011
  (ii) 110111/1011
  (iii) 110001.110/111.110

6.8 Represent the following numbers using floating point notation. Assume 16-bit word:

  (i) 10110.1101
  (ii) 1101100.10
  (iii) 0.000011011011

6.9 If a word has 32 bits, how many bits would you allocate for mantissa and exponent? Explain your choice.

6.10 Add the following binary numbers using 16-bit floating point representation:

  (i) 1011011.110101 + 110101.0101
  (ii) 11011.1101 + 1011.10110
  (iii) 0.000111 + 111.00111

6.11 Subtract the following binary numbers using a 16-bit floating point representation:

  (i) 1011011.1101 – 01110.1101
  (ii) 101110.110 – 1110.0011
  (iii) 100110.101 – 011.110011

6.12 Multiply the following numbers using a 16-bit floating point representation:

  (i) 1011.110 × 1010.110
  (ii) 0.11011 × 0.111011
  (iii) 1110111.111 × 11011.1101

6.13 Divide the following numbers using a 16-bit floating point representation:

  (i) 1011.110/1010.110
  (ii) 0.11011/0.111011
  (iii) 110111.111/11011.1101

6.14 Repeat Exercise 6.11 using 2's complement representation for negative numbers.

7

Logic Circuits

In this chapter we will first introduce an algebra which is useful in designing logic circuits of processors. Subsequently we will use this algebra to design simple logic circuits for logical and arithmetic operations performed by processors.

7.1 INTRODUCTION

George Boole (1815–1864) a logician, developed an algebra, known as Boolean algebra to examine a given set of propositions (statements) with a view to checking their logical consistency and simplifying them by removing redundant statements or clauses. He used symbols to represent simple propositions. Compound propositions were expressed in terms of these symbols and connectives. For example 'Ram is intelligent *and* he does well in examinations' is a compound proposition consisting of two simple ones connected by the connective 'AND'.

Let the proposition 'Ram is intelligent' be represented by the symbol *A* and let the symbol *B* represent the proposition 'Ram does well in examinations'. A symbolic way of representing the whole statement will be *A* and *B*. Similarly the proposition, 'My friend gives me a box of sweets *or* a greeting card for my birthday' contains the connective 'OR'. Once again, representing the individual propositions by the symbols *C* and *D* we can write *C or D* to refer to the whole statement.

The use of symbols to represent propositions, connectives, and their truth and falsity led to the name *Symbolic Logic* for this area of enquiry.

In 1938 Shannon discovered that a simplified version of Boolean algebra can be used in the analysis and synthesis of telephone switching networks where a large number of electro-mechanical relays and switches are used. The one-to-one correspondence between logic on one hand and switching circuits on the other comes about as follows.

7.2 SWITCHING CIRCUITS

Consider a switch which is either 'closed' or 'open'. This is similar to the situation in Propositional Calculus where a proposition is either 'true' or 'false'. In Fig. 7.1(a) we have two switches *A* and *B* which are normally open. They are connected in series with a battery and a bulb. The bulb will light only when both *A* and *B* are closed. Notice the similarity between this and a compound proposition in which an AND connective is used.

Now consider the arrangement of switches shown in Fig. 7.1(b) where two switches *C* and *D* are connected in parallel. The bulb will light when either *C* or *D*, or both, are closed. We recognize the similarity between this and the truth of a compound proposition

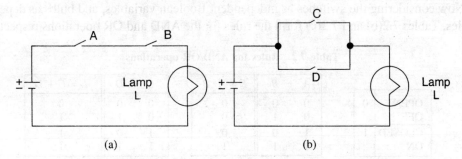

Fig. 7.1 **(a) Switches in series; (b) Switches in parallel.**

when the OR connective is used. We can now see a one-to-one correspondence between 'closed' and 'true'. Similarly 'open' corresponds to 'false'. Because of this analogy, we call these switching circuits as logic circuits.

Thus we have switches which can be only open or closed and similarly propositions which are either true or false. In other words, these can be considered as variables which can only assume either of two values at one time. For convenience we use the symbols '0' or '1' to represent these values. Remember that '0' and '1' have no arithmetic significance at all. They only have a logical significance because they are symbolic representations of falsehood and truth respectively. Such variables which can only have two values are called *Boolean variables*. Thus, a Boolean variable *x* is either '1' or '0', i.e., either true or false.

We have already observed a one-to-one correspondence between series and parallel connections of switches on the one hand and the connectives AND and OR of propositional calculus on the other. We can consider these connectives as performing operations on Boolean variables. Let us further represent AND by the symbol ' · ' and OR by the symbol '+' so that the condition for lighting the bulb in Fig. 7.1(a) can be written as $A \cdot B$, and for Fig. 7.1(b) the condition can be expressed as $C + D$.

7.3 AND/OR OPERATIONS

The behaviour of the switching circuits shown in Figs. 7.1(a) and 7.1(b) is summarized in Table 7.1.

Table 7.1 **Logical nature of switching circuit operation**

Switch *A*	Switch *B*	Lamp *L*	Switch *C*	Switch *D*	Lamp *L*
open	open	OFF	open	open	OFF
open	closed	OFF	open	closed	ON
closed	open	OFF	closed	open	ON
closed	closed	ON	closed	closed	ON

| (a) Series connected switches (AND) | (b) Parallel connected switches (OR) |

Table 7.2(a) shows the use of symbols '0' and '1' for representing the states of switches and bulbs. Using this symbol assignment, we construct the Tables 7.2(b) and 7.2(c) from 7.1(a) and 7.1(b) respectively.

Now considering the switches as independent Boolean variables, and bulbs as dependent variables, Tables 7.2(b) and 7.2(c) form the rules for the AND and OR operations respectively.

Table 7.2   Rules for AND/OR operations

		A	B	$L = A \cdot B$		C	D	$L = C + D$
OPEN	0	0	0	0		0	0	0
OFF		0	1	0		0	1	1
CLOSED	1	1	0	0		1	0	1
ON		1	1	1		1	1	1

(a) Symbol assignment to   (b) Rule for AND operation   (c) Rule for OR operation
states of switch and bulb

With reference to Table 7.2(b), we note that the rule for AND operation is exactly the same as that of ordinary multiplication. This is a happy coincidence. Although the logical AND operation has nothing to do with the arithmetic operation of multiplication, it enables us to remember the rule without any additional effort. Thus we refer to $A \cdot B$ as 'product' of A and B.

Referring to Table 7.2(c), the coincidence of this table with an addition table is limited only to the first three rows. The last row gives $1 + 1 = 1$ which obviously is not valid for addition in arithmetic. We have to specially remember this and, in spite of this, for convenience, we refer to $C + D$ as the 'sum' of C and D.

Note that the AND and OR operations involve at least two variables and hence these are called *binary operators*. Obviously, by their repeated use, we can perform these operations on many variables.

With reference to Fig. 7.1(a) we note that the order in which the switches A and B are connected in series is not important from the point of view of the circuit operation. In other words, we could interchange the switches A and B and still obtain the same performance. This idea is expressed as $A \cdot B = B \cdot A$. Similarly we see from Fig. 7.1(b), $C + D = D + C$. Thus, we recognize that commutative law holds good for the '+' and '·' operations. Figure 7.2 illustrates the basis for the distributive law of 'AND' operation in Boolean algebra which gives

$$A \cdot (B + C) = A \cdot B + A \cdot C \qquad (7.1)$$

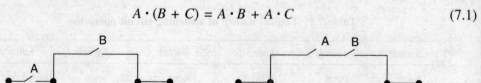

Fig. 7.2   Equivalent switch connections illustrating distributive law for AND operation.

Similarly Fig. 7.3 shows how, in Boolean algebra, distributive law holds good for 'OR' operation as well. This gives us the interesting equality $A + (B \cdot C) = (A + B) \cdot (A + C)$ which does not apply in the algebra of real numbers we are used to. Boolean algebra does not have operations equivalent to subtraction and division.

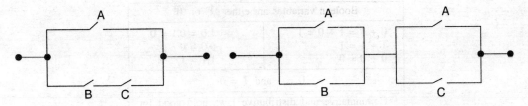

Fig. 7.3   Equivalent switch connections illustrating distributive law for OR operation.

7.4   NOT OPERATION

When the proposition 'Ram is intelligent' is *true*, the *negated* proposition 'Ram is *not* intelligent' is *false* and vice versa. There is an analogous situation in switching circuits. There are some electromechanical relays which have normally-closed contacts. These contacts open when the relays operate. Thus the normally-closed contact represents a negation of the normally-open contact of the *same relay*.

Again using symbol assignment, we define the NOT operation as follows. If $A = 0$ 'NOT A' (written as $\bar{A}$ and read as 'A bar') = 1. Or when $B = 1$, $\bar{B} = 0$. In other words, the process of negation, which is also called complementation, converts the symbolic '0' to a '1' and vice versa, i.e., $\bar{0} = 1$ and $\bar{1} = 0$. Note that the 'NOT' operation is performed on a single variable and hence it is called a *unary operation*. There is no equivalent operation in the algebra of real numbers.

7.5   BOOLEAN FUNCTIONS

We have seen that the AND, OR and NOT operations performed on Boolean variables, in turn, result in Boolean variables. This gives the 'closure' property. As in ordinary algebra, we have the concept of a function of Boolean variables or an expression containing Boolean variables. For example, consider the equation

$$X = A \cdot B + \bar{C} \cdot D + E \cdot F \qquad (7.2)$$

Here the variable X is a function of A, B, C, D, E and F. This is written as $X = f(A, B, C, D, E, F)$ and the right hand side of the equation is called an *expression*. The symbols A, B, C, D, etc. are referred to as *literals*.

7.6   POSTULATES

With these ideas we now introduce the postulates of a simplified Boolean algebra which, strictly speaking, should be called *switching algebra*. However, in practice this distinction is not often made and switching algebra is referred to as Boolean algebra itself. The postulates are summarized in Table 7.3. Using these we will now prove some theorems.

Table 7.3 Postulates of switching algebra

Boolean variables are either '1' or '0'	
$0 + 1 = 1 + 0 = 1$ $1 + 1 = 1$ $0 + 0 = 0$	$1.0 = 0.1 = 0$ $0.0 = 0$ $1.1 = 1$
$\bar{0} = 1$ and $\bar{1} = 0$	
Commutative and distributive laws hold good for AND and OR operations	

7.7 DUALITY PRINCIPLE

Observe that we have listed some of the postulates in two parts. One part may be obtained from the other if '+' is interchanged with '·' and '0' is interchanged with '1'. This important property is known as the *duality principle*. This principle ensures that if a theorem is proved using the postulates, then a dual theorem obtained interchanging '+' with '·' and '0' with '1' automatically holds and need not be proved separately. Thus in the following section, along with each theorem, the dual theorem is stated without proof.

7.8 THEOREMS

As Boolean algebra deals with variables which can have only two values, it is, in principle, possible to prove every theorem by considering all possible cases. This method of proving theorem is called exhaustive enumeration or perfect induction. We will first present some simple theorems. Using the postulates and these simple theorems, we will prove some more theorems which are not so obvious.

SIMPLE THEOREMS

These are directly implied in the postulates. Thus these are often considered as postulates themselves.

$$0 + X = X \qquad\qquad 1 \cdot X = X \qquad\qquad (7.3)$$

$$X + \bar{X} = 1 \qquad\qquad X \cdot \bar{X} = 0 \qquad\qquad (7.4)$$

Theorem 1(a) $A + A = A$ *1(b)* $A \cdot A = A$

Proof :

When $A = 0$, $0 + 0 = 0 = A$.   When $A = 1$, $1 + 1 = 1 = A$.

For both $A = 0$ and 1, $A + A = A$.   Thus the theorem holds.

Theorem 2(a) $A + 1 = 1$ *2(b)* $A \cdot 0 = 0$

Proof :

When $A = 0$, $0 + 1 = 1$.   When $A = 1$, $1 + 1 = 1$.
Thus $A + 1 = 1$.

Theorem 3(a) $A + A \cdot B = A$ *3(b)* $A \cdot (A + B) = A$

Proof :

$A + A \cdot B = A \cdot 1 + A \cdot B = A \cdot (1 + B) = A \cdot 1 = A.$

Theorem 4 $\bar{\bar{A}} = A$

Proof :

When $A = 0$, $\bar{A} = 1$, $\bar{\bar{A}} = \bar{1} = 0 = A$.   When $A = 1$, $\bar{A} = 0$, $\bar{\bar{A}} = \bar{0} = 1 = A$.
       Thus $\bar{\bar{A}} = A$.

Theorem 5(a) $A + (\bar{A} \cdot B) = A + B$,   *5(b)* $A \cdot (\bar{A} + B) = A \cdot B$

Proof :

$A + (\bar{A} \cdot B) = (A + \bar{A}) \cdot (A + B)$ (Distributive law)
            $= 1 \cdot (A + B) = (A + B)$

Theorem 6(a) $\overline{A + B} = \bar{A} \cdot \bar{B}$ *6(b)* $\overline{A \cdot B} = \bar{A} + \bar{B}$

Proof :   Table 7.4 is used to show that the left hand side is equal to the right hand side for all values of A and B.

Table 7.4   Proof of Theorem 6(a)

A	B	$A + B$	$\overline{A + B}$	$\bar{A}$	$\bar{B}$	$\bar{A} \cdot \bar{B}$
0	0	0	1	1	1	1
0	1	1	0	1	0	0
1	0	1	0	0	1	0
1	1	1	0	0	0	0

The columns 4 and 7 are identical and hence the theorem is proved. Theorems 6(a) and 6(b) are important and useful. They are known as *De Morgan's Laws*. They can be extended to n variables as given below.

$$\overline{A_1 + A_2 + A_3 + \dots + A_n} = \bar{A}_1 \cdot \bar{A}_2 \cdot \bar{A}_3 \dots \bar{A}_n \tag{7.5}$$

$$\overline{A_1 \cdot A_2 \cdot A_3 + \dots \dots + A_n} = \bar{A}_1 + \bar{A}_2 + \bar{A}_3 \dots \bar{A}_n \tag{7.6}$$

Some important identities of Boolean algebra are collected in Table 7.5. The student should become thoroughly conversant with this table in order to use the algebra effectively.

Table 7.5 Summary of important identities

THEOREMS	DUAL THEOREMS
$A + 0 = A$	$A \cdot 1 = A$
$A + B = B + A$	$A \cdot B = B \cdot A$
$A \cdot (B + C) = A \cdot B + A \cdot C$	$A + (B \cdot C) = (A + B) \cdot (A + C)$
$A + \bar{A} = 1$	$A \cdot \bar{A} = 0$
$A + A = A$	$A \cdot A = A$
$A + 1 = 1$	$A \cdot 0 = 0$
$A + A \cdot B = A$	$A \cdot (A + B) = A$
$\bar{\bar{A}} = A$	
$A + \bar{A} \cdot B = A + B$	$A \cdot (\bar{A} + B) = A \cdot B$
$\overline{A + B} = \bar{A} \cdot \bar{B}$	$\overline{A \cdot B} = \bar{A} + \bar{B}$

7.9 PRECEDENCE OF OPERATORS

In order to evaluate Boolean expressions it is necessary to define the precedence of operators. The precedence is as follows:

1. Scan the expression from left to right.
2. First evaluate expressions enclosed in parentheses.
3. Perform all the complement (NOT) operations.
4. Perform all '$\cdot$' (AND) operations next in the order in which they appear.
5. Perform all '+' (OR) operations last.

Example 7.1

Indicate the precedence of operations in the Boolean expression $X \cdot \bar{X} + Y \cdot (\overline{X + Z}) + (X \cdot Z)$.

SOLUTION:

$$X \cdot \bar{X} + Y \cdot (\overline{X + Z}) + (X \cdot Z)$$

$$\overline{X + Z} \qquad X \cdot Z \qquad \qquad \text{First scan}$$

$$\bar{X} \cdot \bar{Z} \qquad X \cdot Z \qquad \qquad \text{Second scan}$$

$$0 + Y \cdot \bar{X} \cdot \bar{Z} + X \cdot Z \qquad \qquad \text{Third scan}$$

7.10 VENN DIAGRAM

To fix our ideas of Boolean algebra, a pictorial model known as the Venn diagram is useful. This diagram consists of a rectangle inside which a number of circles are drawn, one circle for each variable. The region inside the circle belongs to the variable and the region outside belongs to its complement. Figure 7.4 shows a Venn diagram for two variables X, Y. Region inside the circle named X, represents X and that outside, $\overline{X}$. With two intersecting circles X and Y we have 4 regions corresponding to $X \cdot Y$, $X \cdot \overline{Y}$, $\overline{X} \cdot Y$, $\overline{X} \cdot \overline{Y}$ respectively as shown in the figure.

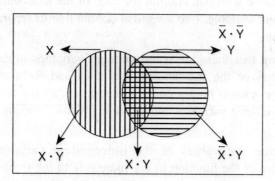

Fig. 7.4   Venn diagram for two variables.

Venn diagrams may be used to illustrate postulates and theorems of Boolean algebra. Figure 7.5 illustrates the identity $a + b \cdot c = (a + b) \cdot (a + c)$. In Fig. 7.5(a), the area covered

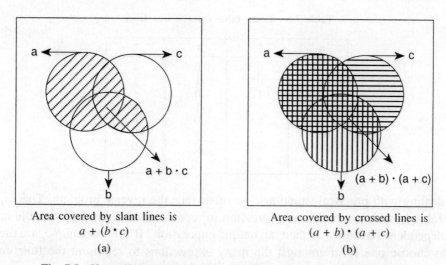

Area covered by slant lines is
$a + (b \cdot c)$
(a)

Area covered by crossed lines is
$(a + b) \cdot (a + c)$
(b)

Fig. 7.5   Venn diagram illustrating distributive law for OR operations.

by the slanted lines corresponds to the expression $a + (b \cdot c)$. In Fig. 7.5(b) area $(a + b)$ is marked by horizontal lines and area $(a + c)$ by vertical lines. The area intersected by the horizontal and the vertical lines corresponds to the expression $(a + b) \cdot (a + c)$ and this is identical to the area in Fig. 7.5(a). Venn diagrams thus provide an aid to remember or prove the theorems of Boolean algebra.

7.11   TRUTH TABLE

Consider a Boolean function $z = f(a, b, c)$. A table which lists the value of the dependent variable z for each set of values of the independent variables a, b and c is known as a Truth Table. We will now obtain a Truth Table for $z = \bar{a} + b \cdot c$. To obtain the table we follow the steps enumerated below.

Step 1:   Form a table with one column for each of the independent variables and one column for the dependent variable. Use a vertical double line to separate the dependent and the independent variables.

Step 2:   Assuming that there are n independent variables in the function, start with 00. .0 (n bits) as values of the independent variables and form successive rows (each containing n bits) in the natural binary counting sequence till the count becomes $(2^n - 1)$. In our example there are three variables and hence eight rows starting from 000 and ending with 111.

Step 3:   Substitute the values of the independent variables in each row and enter the evaluated value of the function in the same row to the right of the double vertical line.

Following this procedure the truth table for $z = \bar{a} + b \cdot c$ is developed in Table 7.6. Given a Boolean function, it is thus easy to obtain the Truth Table.

Table 7.6   Truth table for $z = \bar{a} + b \cdot c$

a	b	c	z
0	0	0	1
0	0	1	1
0	1	0	1
0	1	1	1
1	0	0	0
1	0	1	0
1	1	0	0
1	1	1	1

In dealing with practical situations, we often face the reverse problem. That is, given a Truth Table how do we obtain an expression to represent the dependent variable in terms of the independent variables? Is there an unique expression? If it is not unique, are there any criteria to choose one from amongst the many expressions to represent the function? We will devote the rest of this chapter to answer these questions.

7.12   CANONICAL FORMS FOR BOOLEAN FUNCTIONS

Table 7.7(a) is the table for $z_1 = \bar{x} \cdot \bar{y}$ and Table 7.7(b) is the table for $z_2 = x \cdot \bar{y}$. Let a third variable z be defined as

$$z = z_1 + z_2 = \bar{x} \cdot \bar{y} + x \cdot \bar{y} \tag{7.7}$$

Let us form the truth table for z which is given in Table 7.7(c). Note that the column corresponding to z could have been formed by 'ORing' the columns corresponding to z_1 and

z_2. Thus there are two entries of 1 for z (corresponding to the rows $xy = 00$ and 10) one contributed by z_1 and the other contributed by z_2 respectively.

Table 7.7   Illustrating canonical form of Boolean function

x	y	$z_1 = \bar{x} \cdot \bar{y}$	x	y	$z_2 = x \cdot \bar{y}$	z_1	z_2	$z = z_1 + z_2$
0	0	1	0	0	0	1	0	1
0	1	0	0	1	0	0	0	0
1	0	0	1	0	1	0	1	1
1	1	0	1	1	0	0	0	0
		(a)			(b)			(c)

With reference to Eq. 7.7, we note the same fact namely that z becomes 1 when z_1 becomes 1 or z_2 becomes 1. z_1 assumes the value 1 only when $x = 0$, $y = 0$ for which $z_2 = 0$. Similarly, z_2 becomes 1 only when $x = 1$, $y = 0$ for which $z_1 = 0$. Thus each term on the right hand side of Eq. 7.7 assumes a value 1 for one and only one set of values of x and y. Each such set leads to a value 1 in the corresponding row of the truth table for z. Thus by concentrating on the 1 entries in the truth table we can form a Boolean expression corresponding to any truth table. The systematic procedure for this is as follows:

Step 1:   Inspect the column corresponding to z starting with the top row. Pick the row with an entry 1 for z.

Step 2:   One term in the Boolean expression for z is obtained by 'ANDing' all the independent variables in the truth table; the independent variables with 0 entry appear in the complement form and those with 1 entry appear as they are.

Step 3:   Repeat Steps 1 and 2 till all the 1 entries in z column are exhausted. Obtain the final expression for z by 'ORing' the terms corresponding to the 1 entries in the z column.

We will now apply this procedure to the Truth Table 7.8.

Table 7.8   Truth table of a Boolean function

a	b	c	z
0	0	0	0
0	0	1	1
0	1	0	0
0	1	1	0
1	0	0	1
1	0	1	1
1	1	0	1
1	1	1	1

Step 1:   Row 2 of the column corresponding to z is a 1.

Step 2:   The term corresponding to this '1' in the Boolean expression for z, is $\bar{a} \cdot \bar{b} \cdot c$.

Step 3:   Rows 5, 6, 7, 8 have 1 entries for z. The corresponding terms are: $a \cdot \bar{b} \cdot \bar{c}$, $a \cdot \bar{b} \cdot c$, $a \cdot b \cdot \bar{c}$ and $a \cdot b \cdot c$. Thus

$$z = \bar{a} \cdot \bar{b} \cdot c + a \cdot \bar{b} \cdot \bar{c} + a \cdot \bar{b} \cdot c + a \cdot b \cdot \bar{c} + a \cdot b \cdot c \qquad (7.8)$$

We will take another example of obtaining a Boolean expression corresponding to a truth table. The example is the table for the full adder discussed in the last chapter. The table is reproduced as Table 7.9. In this table a_n and b_n are the augend and addend bits and c_n is the carry bit to be added. These are the input variables. The outputs are the sum bit s_n and

Table 7.9   Truth table for a full adder

a_n	b_n	c_n	s_n	c_{n+1}
0	0	0	0	0
0	0	1	1	0
0	1	0	1	0
0	1	1	0	1
1	0	0	1	0
1	0	1	0	1
1	1	0	0	1
1	1	1	1	1

the carry bit c_{n+1} which is to be taken to the $(n + 1)$th bit position before addition. The Boolean expression for s_n is obtained by inspecting the rows in which $s_n = 1$ and obtaining a Boolean term corresponding to those rows and "ORing" them. Thus

$$s_n = \bar{a}_n \cdot \bar{b}_n \cdot c_n + \bar{a}_n \cdot b_n \cdot \bar{c}_n + a_n \cdot \bar{b}_n \cdot \bar{c}_n + a_n \cdot b_n \cdot c_n \qquad (7.9)$$

$$c_{n+1} = \bar{a}_n \cdot b_n \cdot c_n + a_n \cdot \bar{b}_n \cdot c_n + a_n \cdot b_n \cdot \bar{c}_n + a_n \cdot b_n \cdot c_n \qquad (7.10)$$

7.13   LOGIC CIRCUITS

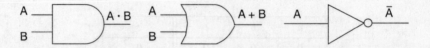

Fig. 7.6   Standard symbols for logic gates.

The three logical operations AND, OR and NOT are said to be logically complete, as any Boolean function may be realized using these three operations. The standard symbols given in Fig. 7.6 are used to represent the Boolean operations AND, OR, and NOT respectively. Using these gates we can realize the expressions for s_n and c_{n+1} given as Eq. (7.9) and Eq. (7.10) as shown in Fig. 7.7. This circuit is called a *full adder* circuit. If the three bits to be added are fed to the inputs a_n, b_n and c_n of the full adder, the sum s_n and carry c_{n+1}, appear as output.

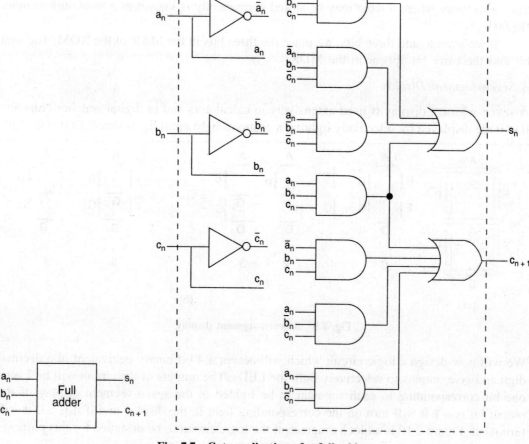

Fig. 7.7   Gate realization of a full adder.

The truth table of Table 7.9 may also be realized using a memory. Suppose we permanently store in a memory, which has 8 words, the values of s_n and c_{n+1} of Table 7.9 as shown in Fig. 7.8. The information from the memory may be retrieved by placing the

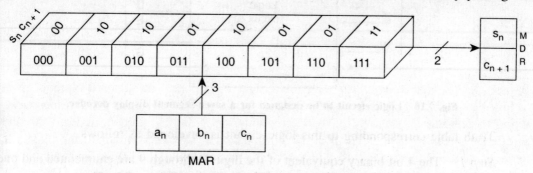

Fig. 7.8   A ROM (read only memory) realization of a full adder.

bits corresponding to a_n, b_n, c_n in the MAR of the memory (see Chapter 4, Sec. 4.2). The contents of the specified location would appear in MDR and are the values of s_n and c_{n+1}. Such a memory where a table may be stored permanently is known as a *read only memory* (ROM).

If we want to add three bits, we place the three bits in the MAR of the ROM. The sum bit and the carry bit appear in the MDR.

A Seven-segment Display

A seven-segment display is used extensively in calculators and in digital watches Numbers 0 to 9 are displayed by selectively lighting a group of light emitting diodes (LED) (Fig. 7.9).

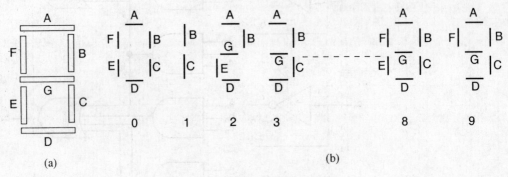

Fig. 7.9   A seven-segment display.

We will now design a logic circuit which will accept a 4 bit binary equivalent of a decimal digit and give outputs to selectively light the LEDs. The outputs of the circuit will be 7 bits, one bit corresponding to each segment to be lighted in the seven-segment display. If the output bit is a 1 it will turn on the corresponding light in the display and if it is a 0 it will turn it off. Figure 7.10 is a block diagram of the logic circuit to be designed for this purpose.

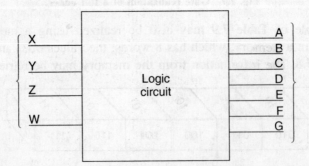

Fig. 7.10   Logic circuit to be designed for a seven-segment display decoder.

Truth table corresponding to this logic circuit is developed as follows:

Step 1:   The 4 bit binary equivalent of the digits 0 through 9 are enumerated and one row of the truth table is formed for each of these.

Step 2: For each row of the truth table the values of 7 output bits necessary to light the segments of the display corresponding to the input digit are entered. For example, to display the digit 0 the lights *A*, *B*, *C*, *D*, *E* and *F* of the seven-segment display should light up. Thus the bits for *A*, *B*, *C*, *D*, *E* and *F* should be 1 and the bit corresponding to *G* should be 0. Similarly to display a 1 the bits *B* and *C* of the output should be 1 and *A*, *D*, *E*, *F*, *G* should be 0.

Step 3: The combinations of input bits 1010, 1011, 1100, 1101, 1110 and 1111 should not occur, as the input is expected to be a single digit. If these inputs occur by mistake, an error indication should be displayed. We will use the letter *E* as an error indication and display it by lighting up segments *A*, *F*, *G*, *E* and *D*.

The truth table developed is given as Table 7.10.

Table 7.10   Truth table to design seven-segment display

		INPUTS				OUTPUTS						
		X	Y	Z	W	A	B	C	D	E	F	G
L	0	0	0	0	0	1	1	1	1	1	1	0
E	1	0	0	0	1	0	1	1	0	0	0	0
G	2	0	0	1	0	1	1	0	1	1	0	1
A	3	0	0	1	1	1	1	1	1	0	0	1
L	4	0	1	0	0	0	1	1	0	0	1	1
D	5	0	1	0	1	1	0	1	1	0	1	1
I	6	0	1	1	0	1	0	1	1	1	1	1
G	7	0	1	1	1	1	1	1	0	0	0	0
I	8	1	0	0	0	1	1	1	1	1	1	1
T	9	1	0	0	1	1	1	1	1	0	1	1
S												
E		1	0	1	0	1	0	0	1	1	1	1
R		1	0	1	1	1	0	0	1	1	1	1
R		1	1	0	0	1	0	0	1	1	1	1
O		1	1	0	1	1	0	0	1	1	1	1
R		1	1	1	0	1	0	0	1	1	1	1
		1	1	1	1	1	0	0	1	1	1	1

We can realize a logic circuit using AND, OR, NOT gates by writing Boolean expressions for *A*, *B*, *C*, *D*, *E*, *F*, *G* in terms of *X*, *Y*, *Z*, *W*. For example, the expression for *B* is

$$B = \bar{X} \cdot \bar{Y} \cdot \bar{Z} \cdot \bar{W} + \bar{X} \cdot \bar{Y} \cdot \bar{Z} \cdot W + \bar{X} \cdot \bar{Y} \cdot Z \cdot \bar{W} + \bar{X} \cdot \bar{Y} \cdot Z \cdot W +$$

$$X \cdot Y \cdot \bar{Z} \cdot \bar{W} + \bar{X} \cdot Y \cdot Z \cdot W + X \cdot \bar{Y} \cdot \bar{Z} \cdot \bar{W} + X \cdot \bar{Y} \cdot \bar{Z} \cdot W$$

Similar expressions may be obtained for *A*, *C*, *D*, *E*, *F* and *G*.

Another method of realizing the seven segment display is to store the outputs *A*, *B*, *C*, *D*, *E*, *F*, *G* in a 16-word ROM. The 16 words of the ROM are the 16 rows of the truth table (Table 7.10). The address bits are *X*, *Y*, *Z*, *W* and the contents are the corresponding values of *A*, *B*, *C*, *D*, *E*, *F*, *G* in the truth table. For example, address 0111 corresponding to $X = 0$, $Y = 1$, $Z = 1$, $W = 1$ will store the bits $A = 1$, $B = 1$, $C = 1$, $D = 0$, $E = 0$, $F = 0$ and $G = 0$. In order to display a digit its binary values X, Y, Z, W are fed to the MAR of the ROM. The output of the ROM, which appears in a 7-bit MDR lights up the display LEDs.

7.14 PARALLEL AND SERIAL ADDERS

In the last section we obtained a logic circuit for a full adder. The full adder adds three bits fed to it and produces a sum bit and a carry bit. If we want to add two 15-bit integers, we can use fifteen full adders and get a sixteen-bit answer as shown in Fig. 7.11. Such an adder is called a *parallel adder*. As this uses one full adder per bit to be added, it is expensive. It is, however, very fast.

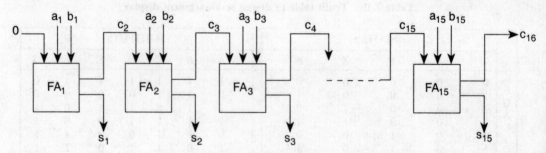

Fig. 7.11 A parallel adder to add two fifteen-bit numbers.

Another method of addition is by using a single full adder and feeding bits to be added one after another to it. Such an adder is called a *serial adder*. A serial adder for 15-bit operands is shown in Fig. 7.12. The two operands are stored in two 15-bit shift registers. At time t_1 the two least significant bits are shifted and the full adder adds the two bits. Carry,

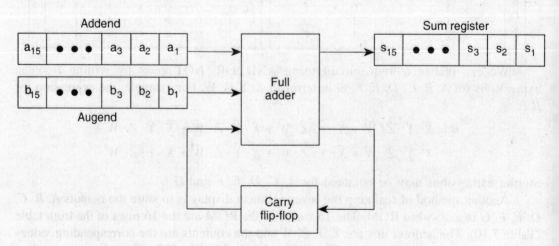

Fig. 7.12 A serial adder to add two fifteen-bit numbers.

if any, is stored in the carry flip-flop (see Chapter 4 Sec. 4.4 for a description of a shift register). At time t_2, the two bits a_2 and b_2 of the two operands and the carry bit c_2 (if any) which resulted from adding a_1 and b_1 are shifted to the full adder and added. This sequence is continued, and at interval t_{15} the two bits a_{15} and b_{15} along with carry bit c_{15} are added producing the sum bit s_{15} and carry bit c_{16}. The sum bits are stored in the sum register. Carry bit c_{16}, if any, will be stored in the carry flip-flop.

7.15 PHYSICAL DEVICES USED TO CONSTRUCT GATES

In Sec. 4.5.1 we presented a model of a controlled semiconductor switch. We showed how such a switch may be used to construct a storage cell. In this section we will see how the controlled switch may be used to construct NOT, AND and OR gates.

For ready reference we give, in Fig. 7.13, the model of a controlled switch. If a voltage 0 is applied to the point A, then the "gate" g opens and the voltage at W equals V as no current will flow from P to Q. If a voltage V is applied at the point A then g closes, the path PQ closes and the voltage at W becomes 0. The input-output relationship of this device is shown in Table 7.11(a). If we call V a binary 1, and 0 a binary 0, then Table 7.11(b) is

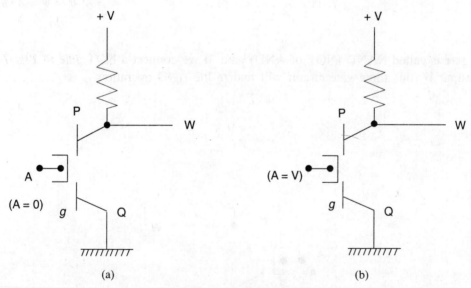

(a)   (b)

Fig. 7.13 A controlled switch.

Table 7.11   Truth table for a controlled switch

A	g	Path PQ	W	A	W
0	open	open	V	0	1
V	closed	closed	0	1	0

$$W = \bar{A}$$

(a)   (b)

obtained. It is clear from this table that the output W is the NOT of A ($W = \bar{A}$). Thus the controlled switch is a NOT gate.

If we connect two controlled switches in series, as shown in Fig. 7.14, we obtain Table 7.12(a) which gives the output voltage as a function of the input voltages at A and B. The truth table describing the operation of the switches is given as Table 7.12(b). We see from it that the output W of the gates is given by

$$W = \overline{A \cdot B}$$

Table 7.12   Truth table for series connected switches

A	B	g_1	g_2	Path PQ	W
0	0	Open	Open	Open	V
V	0	Closed	Open	Open	V
0	V	Open	Closed	Open	V
V	V	Closed	Closed	Closed	0

(a)

A	B	W	$\bar{W}$
0	0	1	0
1	0	1	0
0	1	1	0
1	1	0	1

$\bar{W} = A \cdot B$ or $W = \overline{A \cdot B}$

(b)

This gate is called NAND (NOT of AND) gate. If we connect a NOT gate of Fig. 7.13 to the output W, this three gate circuit will realize the AND operation.

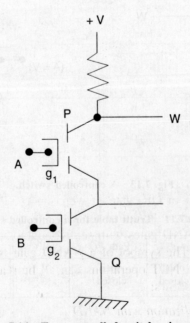

Fig. 7.14   Two controlled switches in series.

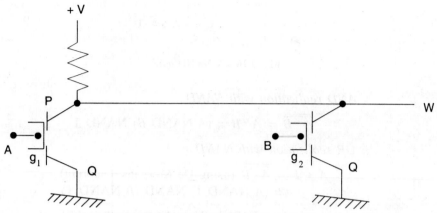

Fig. 7.15   Two controlled switches in parallel.

Two controlled switches connected in parallel is shown in Fig. 7.15. The operation of this configuration is explained with reference to Table 7.13(a). The truth table corresponding to Table 7.13(a) is given as Table 7.13(b). The output W of this gate is given by

$$W = \overline{A + B}$$

Table 7.13   Truth table for parallel connection of switches

A	B	g_1	g_2	Path *PQ*	W
0	0	Open	Open	Open	V
0	V	Open	Closed	Closed	0
V	0	Closed	Open	Closed	0
V	V	Closed	Closed	Closed	0

(a)

A	B	W	$\overline{W}$
0	0	1	0
0	1	0	1
1	0	0	1
1	1	0	1

$$\overline{W} = A + B$$
$$W = \overline{A + B}$$

(b)

This gate is called NOR (NOT of OR) gate. If we connect a NOT gate of Fig. 7.13 to the output W, this three-gate circuit will realize the OR operation.

It is simple to realize NAND gates with semiconductor devices. It is thus commonly used to design logic circuits. The symbol of a NAND gate is shown in Fig. 7.16. It is a "universal" gate as AND, OR, NOT operations can all be realized using only the NAND operation. This is shown as follows:

NOT realization with NAND

$$\overline{A} = \overline{A \cdot 1} = A \text{ NAND } 1 \text{ (1 is a constant)}$$

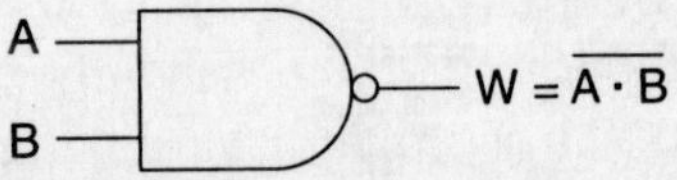

$$W = \overline{A \cdot B}$$

Fig. 7.16   A NAND gate.

AND realization with NAND

$$\overline{\overline{A \cdot B}} = A \cdot B = (A \text{ NAND } B) \text{ NAND } 1$$

OR realization with NAND

$$A + B = \overline{\overline{A} \cdot \overline{B}} \text{ (using De Morgans Theorem)}$$
$$= (A \text{ NAND } 1) \text{ NAND } (B \text{ NAND } 1)$$

These realizations are shown in Fig. 7.17(a), (b) and (c) respectively.

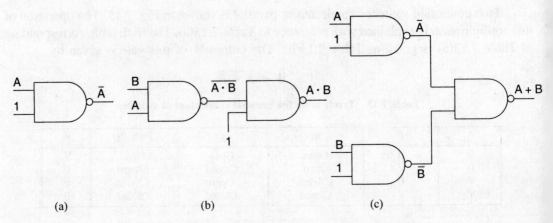

Fig. 7.17   NOT, AND, OR realization with NAND gates.

NOR gates are also universal gates. A number of NAND or NOR gates are packaged into an integrated circuit chip and are used for designing logic circuits.

7.16 TRANSISTORS

The controlled switch is constructed using an electronic device called a *transistor*. The raw material used in making transistors is *silicon*, a semiconductor. In order to understand how transistors can be made from silicon, we must first understand the electrical properties of silicon. Metals like copper are good conductors of electricity and they have a large number of free electrons which are free to wander around the material. Insulators such as glass, on the other hand, are poor conductors of electricity as all the electrons in the material are tightly bound to their parent atoms. A large voltage is required to release them from their parents. Semiconductors such as germanium and silicon are neither good conductors nor insulators. They do not have many free electrons but are capable of releasing electrons bound to the atoms with a modest amount of energy.

An atom of silicon has four electrons in its valence or outermost shell. In pure silicon crystal, pairs of these electrons are shared with neighbouring atoms so that each atom is surrounded by eight shared electrons in a tight bond. Thus pure silicon is a poor conductor (see Fig. 7.18). Semiconductor devices are made by introducing 'minute' amounts of

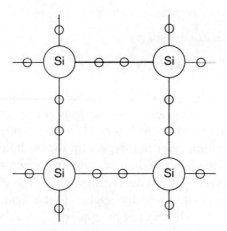

Fig. 7.18 Pure silicon crystal.

controlled impurity atoms in the crystal (about one in a million atoms). This process is called *doping*. For example, we may dope silicon with phosphorus atoms which have five electrons in their outermost shell. A phosphorous atom can displace a silicon atom in the crystal without disrupting the crystal structure. The extra electron gets detached from its parent in the crystal structure and can be moved around by applying a small voltage. Silicon doped with phosphorous (or any other pentavalent atom) is called an *n-type* semiconductor as it has mobile electrons. If we dope silicon with boron, an element with three electrons in its outermost shell, the resulting crystal structure will have a missing electron in the bonds between neighbours. This deficiency is said to create a *hole*. The hole which arises due to the impurity atom can also be released and it becomes mobile when a small voltage is applied to the material. The hole is not a real particle, but only the absence of an electron. However, a hole can move through the crystal lattice and behave like a positive charge. Silicon doped with boron (or a trivalent atom) is known as a *p-type* semiconductor as it has mobile positive electric charge.

One type of transistor widely used in digital computers is called Metal-Oxide-Semiconductor-Field-Effect Transistor or MOSFET for short. These terms refer to the three elements employed in its construction. In a typical MOSFET two areas of *n*-type silicon are embedded on a *p*-type silicon substrate. The two *n*-type areas are connected to metal terminals called the *source* and the *drain*. The surface of the *p*-type substrate is oxidized. The silicon dioxide layer formed on the surface is an insulator and isolates the source and the drain. A layer of metal is deposited on the silicon dioxide layer betwen the source and the drain. This layer is called the *gate* (see Fig. 7.19).

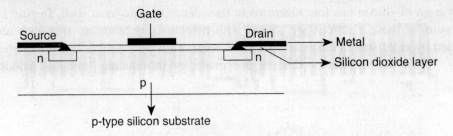

Fig. 7.19   A MOSFET.

The transistor is operated by grounding the source and the substrate. A positive voltage is applied to the drain. As the substrate is *p*-type with excess holes (positive charge), no current flows between substrate and drain. If the gate is grounded, no current can flow from source to drain as the intervening layer is *p*-type with excess holes. If a positive voltage is applied to the gate, it repels the holes and attracts the free electrons. Thus a small layer of electrons forms near the surface. This layer is called an *n*-type channel (Fig. 7.20). These electrons are attracted by the positive voltage applied to the drain and thus a current flows from the source to the drain. In other words by applying a positive voltage to the gate we 'close' the electrical path between the source and drain. Thus the MOSFET is a controlled switch.

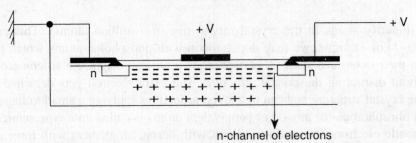

Fig. 7.20   Illustrating transistor action.

Dimensions are critical in fabricating MOSFET. The critical dimensions are the thickness of the oxide layer under the gate electrode, and the distance separating source from drain. The sensitivity of the transistor's response to a gate voltage is inversely related to the thickness of the oxide layer.

7.17 INTEGRATED CIRCUITS

Electronic circuits may be fabricated by using discrete components such as transistors, resistors and capacitors and connecting them with wires. Such circuits are called *discrete circuits*. The invention of *printed circuit boards* (PCB) represents a major advance in circuit fabrication. In order to make a PCB, the interconnections among the components are laid out as strips of black lines (see Fig. 7.21). This design is photographed and a negative is taken and reduced to a size determined by the size of the PCB. A raw PCB is a sheet of

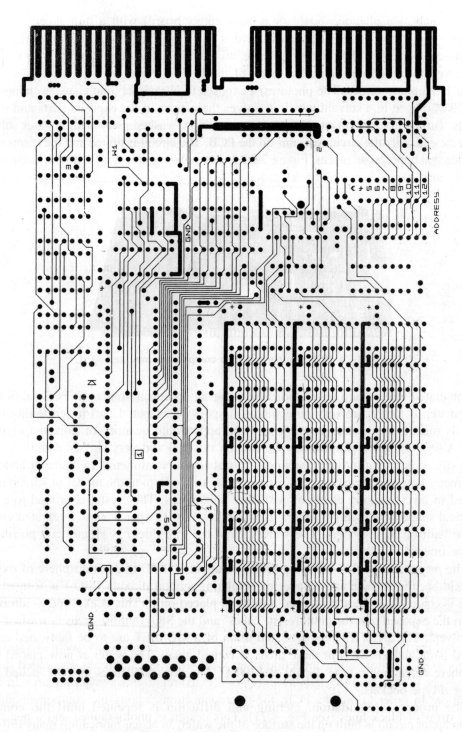

Fig. 7.21   Photograph—A portion of a PCB.

insulator (such as a phenolic board or a glass epoxy board) with a thin sheet of copper bonded on one or both of its sides. This board is taken and coated with a *photoresist*. After the photoresist dries up, the photographic negative is placed in close contact with the PCB and exposed to ultraviolet light. The parts of the PCB covered with the dark part of the negative remain unchanged. The photoresist exposed to ultraviolet light changes chemically. The PCB is dipped in a solvent which dissolves the copper in the exposed parts and leaves the parts with photoresist intact. The photoresist is now washed away with another solvent. Thus at the end, only the circuit remains on the PCB. The circuit is tinned and the components are soldered at appropriate places. Figure 7.22 shows a photograph of a PCB with components mounted on it.

Fig. 7.22   A PCB photograph with components mounted on it.

Integrated circuits are also fabricated using an approach similar to PCB fabrication. The first step is to prepare very pure silicon (impurity less than 1 part in ten million). The silicon is melted in a quartz crucible and the appropriate quantity of dopant (*p*-type) is added. A seed crystal is dipped into the molten material and very slowly withdrawn. The molten silicon is drawn into a giant single crystal several centimetres in diameter and more than a metre long. A single crystal is used in order to conform to the model of silicon atoms arranged in layers sharing electrons with four neighbours. The crystal is ground to a truly cylindrical shape. It is then cut with a diamond saw into circular wafers. Integrated circuits (IC) are built on these wafers. The wafer (about 0.5 mm thick) is ground and polished to a mirror finish.

The *p*-type silicon wafer is next heated to about 1000°C in an atmosphere of oxygen. This oxidizes the surface and a layer of insulating silicon dioxide (SiO_2) is formed. The surface is coated with photoresist and a mask is placed on it. This is exposed to ultraviolet light. In the exposed part the photoresist 'cakes' and the SiO_2 in those areas is washed away by a solvent. The areas where source and drain of a MOSFET are to be fabricated are the exposed parts and the SiO_2 in these areas is etched away. The wafer is now placed in an atmosphere containing *n*-type dopant at 1200°C. The dopant diffuses into the etched areas forming *n*-type pockets.

The process of oxidation, etching and diffusion is repeated until the complete semiconductor circuit is built on the surface of the wafer. In actual fabrication many diffusion steps and as many as six to ten photographic masking steps may be required. The final step is the interconnection of the semiconductor circuit elements. This is done by exposing the surface to a metallic vapour such as aluminium. This forms an aluminium layer over the whole layer. This is etched using masking, photoresist coating, and exposure steps leaving the desired conductor connections intact. Figure 7.23 illustrates the steps for a small section of an IC.

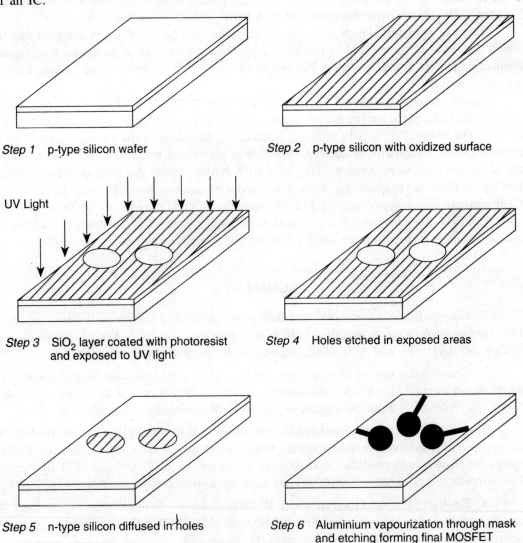

Step 1   p-type silicon wafer

Step 2   p-type silicon with oxidized surface

UV Light

Step 3   SiO₂ layer coated with photoresist and exposed to UV light

Step 4   Holes etched in exposed areas

Step 5   n-type silicon diffused in holes

Step 6   Aluminium vapourization through mask and etching forming final MOSFET

Fig. 7.23 Steps in fabricating an integrated circuit.

All the above processes are applied to the entire wafer which may contain 100 individual ICs. Each wafer may contain a million transistors. The wafer is now probed and each chip is tested electrically for insulation, etc. The chip is then tested for its functional characteristics using automatic electronic test equipment. Circuits which fail any of the tests are marked with a spot of ink. Many circuits do fail. As much as 50% may fail but production is automatic and in large quantities low yields are acceptable.

The wafer is scribed with a diamond tool and broken like glass, separating the individual ICs. Each good chip is mounted on a package base and glued down. Connections are made to the external leads in the package by bonding gold wires to the metal 'islands' on the chip boundary. The chip is now encapsulated in a metal, plastic or ceramic can.

The most critical and expensive operation in the fabrication of ICs is the final step in which the leads are connected to the terminals. Thus the number of terminals for outside connection is kept small. Even for ICs incorporating 10000 transistors, the terminals used are only around 30.

ICs are classified as Small Scale Integrated circuits (SSI), Medium Scale Integrated circuits (MSI), Large Scale Integrated circuits (LSI) and Very Large Scale Integrated circuits (VLSI). The classification is in terms of number of transistors in the circuit which in turn determines the complexity of the logical function performed by the IC. An SSI normally has about 20 transistors corresponding to 4 to 8 NAND gates. An MSI may have about 100 transistors corresponding to a 4-bit parallel adder. An LSI may have about 1000 transistors corresponding to a 512-bit memory. A VLSI may have 100000 transistors corresponding to the complete central processing unit of a computer. Currently microcomputers in a chip containing a few million transistors are being fabricated.

SUMMARY

1. George Boole a mathematician developed an algebra known as Boolean algebra. This algebra deals with propositions which are either *true* or *false*. The operators in this algebra are *AND, OR* and *NOT*. These operators are used to combine propositions.

2. Shannon discovered that Boolean algebra can be used to design switching circuits. As computer circuits also use a combination of switches which can be in one of two states *"open"* or *"closed"*, Boolean algebra is useful in designing these circuits.

3. A set of axioms or postulates is first stated in Boolean algebra. These postulates define the valid symbols in this algebra, which are 0 and 1. The valid operators which operate on these two symbols are next defined. These are the AND, OR and NOT operators. The symbols '·', '+' and '−' (overbar) are used to represent these operators (Table 7.3).

4. Boolean variables connected with Boolean operators form Boolean expressions. A set of theorems is derived using postulates of Boolean algebra. These are useful to manipulate Boolean expressions (Table 7.4 summarizes the theorems).

5. In order to design a logic circuit we first list all the "input" or independent variables. We then make a table whose rows are all possible combinations of values of input variables. As each input variable can have only one out of two values (0 or 1), the number of distinct combinations of n variables is 2^n. Thus if there are 3 independent variables there will be 8 rows in this table. For each input combination, the appropriate values of the dependent or output variables are entered in the table. Such a table is called a *truth table*.

6. Given a truth table, it is possible to obtain closed form Boolean expressions which relate the output variables to the input variables.

7. Examples of truth tables to describe a full adder and a display decoder are derived in Sec. 7.12.

8. Boolean expressions corresponding to truth tables may be implemented as logic circuits using AND, OR and NOT gates.

9. Truth Tables may also be implemented using read only memories (ROM). In this implementation the independent variables in the truth table are the addresses in a ROM. The output bits are stored in the ROM in the corresponding addresses.

10. Controlled semiconductor switches may be used to realize AND, OR and NOT operations. Thus these switches may be used to construct logic circuits in processors.

11. A commonly used controlled switch is a transistor which is fabricated using silicon. One useful component is the Metal Oxide Silicon Field Effect Transistor (MOSFET) used as a switch.

12. A MOSFET consists of a p-type silicon substrate on which a source and drain of n-type silicon are diffused. The surface of the p-type substrate is oxidized forming an insulator. Over this a metallized strip is fabricated between the source and the drain forming a gate. A small voltage applied to the gate creates an electrical path between source and drain (Figs. 7.19 and 7.20).

13. An integrated circuit is fabricated on a chip of doped silicon using processes of oxidation, coating with photoresist chemical, etching, diffusion, metal vapourization, gold bonding of leads and finally encapsulation.

14. Integrated circuits may be classified as SSI, MSI, LSI and VLSI depending on the number of transistors in the chip and complexity of the logical function performed by it.

REVIEW QUESTIONS

7.1 Why is Boolean algebra relevant in the design of logic circuits of computers?

7.2 State the postulates of Boolean algebra.

7.3 Realize the following Boolean expressions using switches,
   (i) $L = A + B \cdot C$
   (ii) $M = A \cdot D + B \cdot D + A \cdot C$.

7.4 Obtain truth tables for L and M defined in Exercise 7.3.

7.5 Show that
$$X \cdot Y + X \cdot Z + X \cdot Y \cdot Z = X \cdot Y + X \cdot Z$$
by method of perfect induction.

7.6 Show that $(A + B) \cdot (A + C) = A + B \cdot C$.

7.7 Prove De Morgan's laws for three variables.

7.8 Using theorems of Boolean algebra prove the following:

(i) $X \cdot Y + X \cdot Z + Y \cdot Z = X \cdot Y + \bar{X} \cdot Y \cdot Z + X \cdot Z$

(ii) $(\dot{X} \cdot Y) \cdot (\bar{X} \cdot \bar{Z} + Z) \cdot (X \cdot \overline{Z + Y}) = 0$

(iii) $X \cdot \bar{Y} + Y \cdot \bar{Z} + \bar{X} \cdot \bar{Z} = X \cdot \bar{Y} \cdot Z + \bar{Y} \cdot \bar{Z} + Y \cdot \bar{Z}$

7.9 Obtain the truth table for the exclusive OR *(EOR)* operation described by the equation $A \ EOR \ B = A \cdot \bar{B} + \bar{A} \cdot B$.

7.10 Prove that $(A \ EOR \ B) \ EOR \ C = A \ EOR \ (B \ EOR \ C)$.

7.11 Obtain a truth table to design a 3-bit subtractor. The input bits are the subtrahend, minuend and borrow. The output bits are the difference and borrow to next bit. Obtain Boolean expressions for the truth table.

7.12 Realize the 3-bit subtractor using AND, OR, NOT gates.

7.13 Realize the 3-bit subtractor using a ROM.

7.14 Design a logic circuit to multiply two positive numbers each 2-bits long.

7.15 A comparator is a circuit which compares two numbers A and B and gives an output 1 if $A \geq B$. Assume A and B are two-bit positive numbers. Obtain a logic circuit for the comparator. Use NAND gates for realization.

7.16 Design a logic circuit to generate an odd parity bit for hexadecimal digits. Use NOR gates for realization.

7.17 What element is used to fabricate a transistor?

7.18 What is the difference between a conductor, a semiconductor and an insulator?

7.19 What is an *n*-type silicon and a *p*-type silicon?

7.20 What do you understand by the acronym MOSFET?

7.21 What is the purpose of gate in MOSFET?

7.22 How is MOSFET useful as a controlled switch?

7.23 What dimensions are critical in MOSFET fabrication?

7.24 Define a discrete circuit.

7.25 What is a PCB?

7.26 Explain how PCB is fabricated.

7.27 Describe the steps followed in fabricating ICs.

7.28 Why is the circuit called IC?

7.29 What are the most critical operations in IC fabrication?

7.30 Differentiate between SSI, MSI, LSI and VLSI.

8

Computer Architecture

In the previous chapters we described how each of the main units of a computer works. In this chapter we will discuss how the units are interconnected physically and their functioning coordinated by appropriate communication.

The main difficulty in coordinating the functioning of the units is the inherent speed mismatch between the units. For example, a processor can process data at a rate of about 5 nsec/byte, the rate of fetching data from memory is around 50 nsec/byte. Thus the processor will be forced to wait for data and will not be able to work at its full speed. The speed mismatch between processor and I/O units is much worse. Even a fast floppy disk reader could read data only at a speed of around 5 microsecond/byte. But within this time, the processor could process 1000 bytes. The magnitude of this speed mismatch can be appreciated by the following analogy. Suppose an officer takes 10 minutes to process a file. If a clerk takes 10 × 1000 minutes = 20 working days to give each file to the officer, the highly paid officer is forced to be idle most of the time! Carrying this analogy further, assume that a data stored in memory is equivalent to the officer's file being stored in his "in-tray". The processor being 10 times faster than the time taken to fetch data from memory would be equivalent to the clerk taking 100 minutes to take a file out of the tray and placing it before the officer who would take only 10 minutes to process the file.

Another complication which arises when interconnecting I/O units to a computer is the variety of I/O units. Manual inputs through terminals would be at a rate of about 1 byte/second, whereas input from a disk would be at the rate of around 1 byte per microsecond. A manual input sends 1 byte at a time whereas a disk would send a stream of more than 1000 bytes. Thus the I/O unit-memory-processor coordination is quite complicated.

One may reduce the speed mismatch problem through system solutions. A very important idea is that of buffering. Buffer storage is introduced between units to increase the overall system speed and to ease coordination. Ideally one would like each unit to work at its full potential speed and all the units to work simultaneously. This ideal cannot be achieved by hardware only. A software-hardware-system solution is needed.

8.1 INTERCONNECTION OF UNITS

We saw in Chapter 4 that the main memory of a computer stores a set of addressed words. Words are retrieved from memory by specifying the address. As all data to be processed by a computer has to be stored in memory, the characteristics of the interconnection paths are determined by the memory structure. In order to achieve reasonable speed, all the bits in a word are transmitted simultaneously. A set of wires which carries a group of bits in parallel and has an associated control scheme is known as a *bus*. A bus which carries a word to or from memory is known as a *data bus*. Its width will equal the word length (in bits) of the memory. In order to retrieve a word from memory it is necessary to specify its address. The address is carried by a *Memory address bus* whose width equals the number of bits in the MAR of the memory. Thus if a computer's memory has 64K, 32-bit words, then the data bus will be 32 bits wide and the address bus 16 bits wide. Besides buses to carry address and data, we also need control signals between the units of a computer. For instance, if the processor has to send READ and WRITE commands to memory, START command to I/O units, etc., such signals are carried by a *control bus*. A system bus will thus consist of a data bus, a memory address bus and a control bus. Figure 8.1 shows the processor—memory interconnection.

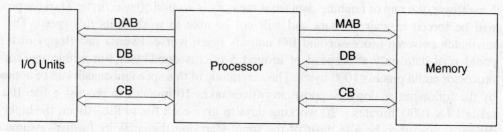

DAB – Device address bus, DB – Data bus, CB – Control bus, MAB – Memory address bus

Fig. 8.1 Illustrating interconnection of computer units via two system buses.

One method of connecting I/O units to the computer is to connect them to the processor via a bus. This bus will consist of a bus specifying the addresses of the I/O units to be accessed by the processor, a data bus carrying a word from the addressed input unit to the processor or carrying a word from the processor to the addressed output unit. Besides these two buses, a control bus carries commands such as READ, WRITE, START, SEEK, STOP, etc., from the processor to I/O units. It also carries the I/O units' status information to the processor. The I/O to processor system bus will thus encompass I/O device address lines, data lines and control lines. In Fig. 8.1 the I/O to processor bus interconnection is also shown. This method of interconnection will require the processor to completely supervise and participate in the transfer of information from and to I/O units. All information will be first taken to a processor register from the input unit and from there to the memory. Such data transfer is known as *program controlled transfer*.

The interconnection of I/O units, processor and memory using two independent system buses in known as a *two bus* interconnection structure.

As was pointed out in the previous para, this interconnection structure requires the processor to share its resources during I/O transfer. As I/O units are much slower than the processor, this is not desirable. Thus another interconnection method which minimizes processor participation in I/O transfer is often used. This is also a two bus structure. One bus interconnects the processor to the memory. The other bus, instead of connecting I/O units to the processor, connects them directly to memory. In this structure, the I/O devices are connected to a special interface logic known as *Direct Memory Access* logic (DMA) or a *Channel* or a *Peripheral Processor Unit* (PPU). The processor issues a READ or WRITE command giving the device address, the address in memory where data read from the input unit is to be stored (or from where data is to be taken to output), and the number of data words to be transferred. This command is accepted by the PPU which now assumes the responsibility of data transfer. This interconnection structure is shown in Fig. 8.2.

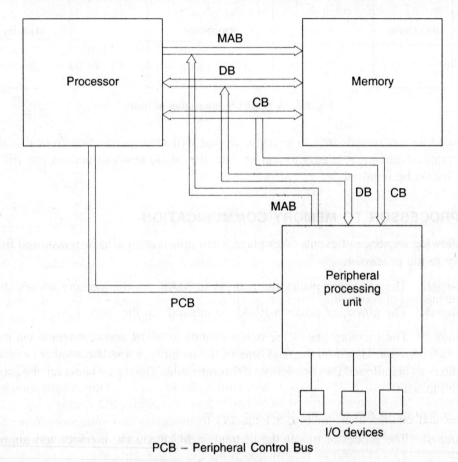

PCB – Peripheral Control Bus

Fig. 8.2   Illustrating direct PPU-Memory connection.

Another popular method of interconnecting units (mostly used in small computers) is through the use of a single bus as shown in Fig. 8.3. This is called a *unibus* system. In this case, the bus is shared by the three units and thus transfer of information can take place at a time only between two of the three units. The main advantage of this system is the addressing of I/O units. These units use the same memory address space. This simplifies programming of I/O units as no special I/O instructions are needed. A READ instruction

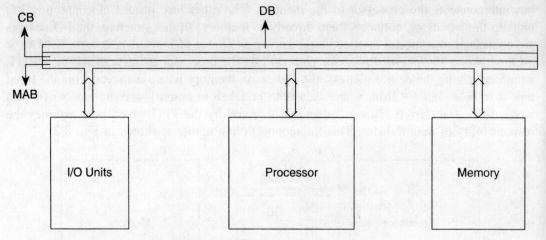

Fig. 8.3   A UNIBUS connection of units.

with an address corresponding to an input device will read information from that device. Besides this advantage, it is easy to add new devices as no new instructions specific to the device would be required.

8.2   PROCESSOR TO MEMORY COMMUNICATION

The following sequence of events takes place when information is to be transferred from the memory to the processor.

Step 1:   The processor places the address in MAR via the memory address bus.

Step 2:   The processor issues a READ command via the control bus.

Step 3:   The memory places the retrieved data in MDR and transfers it via the data bus to the processor. Based on the read time of the memory, a specific number of processor clock intervals are allotted for completion of this operation. During this interval, the processor is forced to wait.

For writing in memory, the steps are similar.

Step 1:   The processor places the address in MAR via the memory address bus.

Step 2:   The processor transmits the data to be written in memory via the data bus to MDR.

Step 3:   The processor issues a WRITE command to memory via the control bus.

Step 4:   The data in MDR is written in memory in the address specified in MAR.

The main problem is the 1 to 10 speed mismatch between the processor and the memory. Thus the processor is forced to wait for data or instructions from memory. This speed mismatch is alleviated by using a small fast memory as an intermediate buffer between the main memory and the processor (see Fig. 8.4). This memory is known as a *cache memory*. It is fabricated using high speed semiconductor devices. The effective cycle time of cache would be about a tenth of the main memory cycle time and its cost about 10 times the cost per byte of main memory.

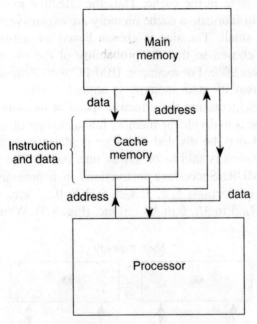

Fig. 8.4   Illustrating use of a cache memory.

Most programs execute instructions in the order in which they are written. This is called *spatial locality* of reference of instructions in a program. We also find *temporal locality* in programs. In other words if an instruction is executed there is a likelihood of the same instruction being executed again soon. This is true as most programs have a number of *while* and *for* loops and the instructions in a loop are executed again and again. Locality of reference to instructions is upset when branch instructions are encountered but such instructions do not occur frequently in well written programs. Locality of reference is true not only for instructions in a program but also for data referred by a program (For example, arrays, records in a file etc.).

Locality of reference is the main feature which makes the use of a cache effective in alleviating the speed mismatch between the main memory and the processor. Many computers are designed with two cache memories one is called an *instruction cache* and the other a *data cache*. They are normally of equal size and small compared to main memory; of the order of 64KB whereas main memory sizes are of the order of 64MB.

A series of instructions are copied in the cache from the main memory. Data to be processed by these instructions are copied into the data cache. The processor fetches instructions and data from the caches. Thus fetch time is considerably reduced. When instructions in the caches are exhausted, the next series of instructions/data are copied into them from the main memory. This is done automatically by the hardware without any programmer intervention. If at any time there is a jump and the required instruction is not in the cache, the program fetches the instruction from the main memory. The probability of this occurring is not very high. It is found in practice that more than 90% of time, the needed instruction and data would be available in the cache. Thus the effective memory speed is increased.

The devices used to fabricate a cache memory are expensive. Therefore the size of the cache memory is kept small. The size is chosen based on statistical studies of program behaviour. The size is chosen so that the probability of the required instruction and data being in the cache is over 90%. For example, IBM PC with Pentium Processor has a cache memory of 64KB whereas its main memory is around 32MB.

Another method of increasing the effective speed of memory is achieved by *memory interleaving*. The method is to divide the memory into a number of submodules. For example, a memory of 8M word may be divided into four modules with each module having 2M words. Such an organization is said to be 4 way interleaved. The four modules each have their own MAR and MDR. Successive instructions in a program are put in successive modules. For example, instructions 1, 2, 3, 4, 5, 6, 7, 8, 9, ... etc., are placed with 1 in M_1, 2 in M_2, 3 in M_3, 4 in M_4, 5 in M_1, 6 in M_2 . . . etc. (Fig. 8.5). When an instruction FETCH

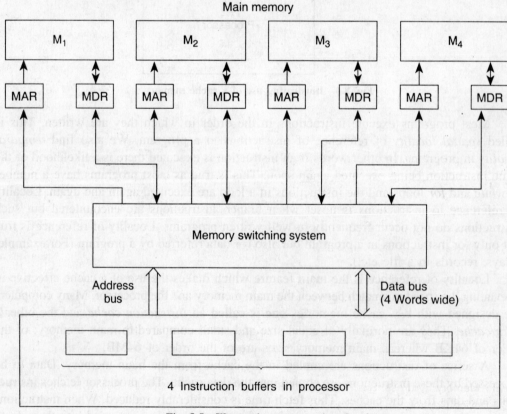

Fig. 8.5 Illustrating memory interleaving.

is issued by the processor, a memory access circuit creates four consecutive addresses and places them in the four MARs. A memory read command reads all the 4 modules *simultaneously* and retrieves four instructions. These are sent to the processor. Thus each FETCH instruction fetches 4 consecutive instructions. As instructions are normally executed in the sequence in which they are written having four successive instructions readily available in the processor speeds up execution time. Only when a branch instruction is encountered does the fetched instruction not prove useful. As the percentage of branch instructions in a program is small, this method is effective in minimizing memory-processor speed mismatch.

One may combine interleaving and a cache to reduce the speed mismatch between the cache memory and the main memory.

8.3 I/O TO PROCESSOR COMMUNICATION

We saw in Sec. 8.1 that one way of connecting I/O units to the computer is to connect them to the processor using a device address bus, a data bus and a control bus. Each device in a computer has a *controller* which controls the operation of the device. For example, a floppy disk controller controls the movement of the reading head, positioning of the head, and detection of errors. The controller is connected to the buses via an *interface logic* unit. The interface logic decodes the control commands received from the processor and sends them to the controller. It also buffers the flow of data from the device to the processor and vice versa. Figure 8.6 illustrates the details of one interface unit. With this connection of

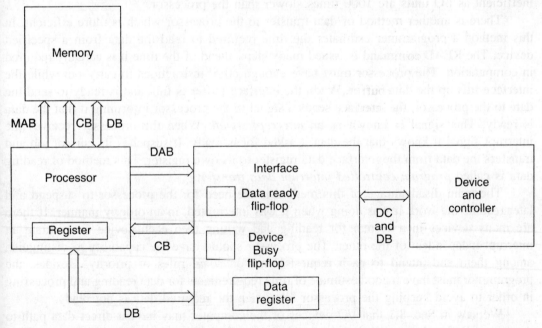

MAB – Memory Address Bus, DB – Data Bus, DAB – Device Address Bus, CB – Control Bus, DC – Device Control

Fig. 8.6 Details of processor to I/O communication.

I/O device to the processor, data from a device is transmitted to the memory through a register in the processor. The sequence of steps followed to transmit data is given below:

Step 1:   Processor sends the address of the device from which data is to be read via the device address bus and issues a READ command.

Step 2:   The device interface logic acknowledges the signal and turns on a "device busy" flip-flop. No further requests are entertained by the device as long as the busy flip-flop is set.

Step 3:   The I/O device reads the data and places it in the data register of the interface. It also sets the data ready flip-flop.

Step 4:   The processor continually interrogates the data ready flip-flop and waits until this flip-flop is set.

Step 5:   When the data ready flip-flop is set, the processor reads the data from the interface data register and places it in the appropriate processor register. It sends data received acknowledgement signal to the device interface and resets the device busy flip-flop.

This method of transfer of information is called *program controlled transfer*. This method forces the processor to wait till the device is able to read data and is thus very inefficient as I/O units are 1000 times slower than the processor.

There is another method of data transfer to the processor which is more efficient. In this method a programmer estimates the time required to read the data from a specified device. The READ command is issued many steps ahead of the time it is actually required in computation. The processor must have enough other instructions to carry out while the interface fills up the data buffer. When the interface buffer is full, and is ready to send the data to the processor, the interface sends a signal to the processor informing it that the data is ready. This signal is known as an *interrupt signal*. When the processor receives the interrupt signal it knows that the data it asked for is ready. It suspends its current job and transfers the data from the interface data register to its own register. This method of reading data is called *program controlled interrupt data transfer*.

The main disadvantage of this method is the need for the processor to suspend and later resume the work it was doing when it was interrupted, in an orderly manner. If there are many devices in a system for reading and writing then each device can initiate an interrupt independent of the other. The processor should have the capability to distinguish among them and attend to each request based on some rules of priority. Besides, the programmer must have a good estimate of time requirements for data reading and processing in order to avoid keeping the processor idle when the required data is not ready.

We saw in Sec. 8.1 that I/O devices of the computer may have a direct data path to the memory. If such a connection exists, another method of data transfer will be appropriate. This method uses the logic in the direct memory access interface (DMA interface) and eliminates the participation of the processor in data transfer.

The configuration of the computer system with this interconnection structure is shown in Fig. 8.7. The DMA interface, in addition to a data buffer register, DMA busy flip-flop and data ready flip-flop, has a memory address register which gives the location in memory where the data is to be stored. If a number of words are to be transferred from the device to memory the count of the words is also stored in a counter in the DMA.

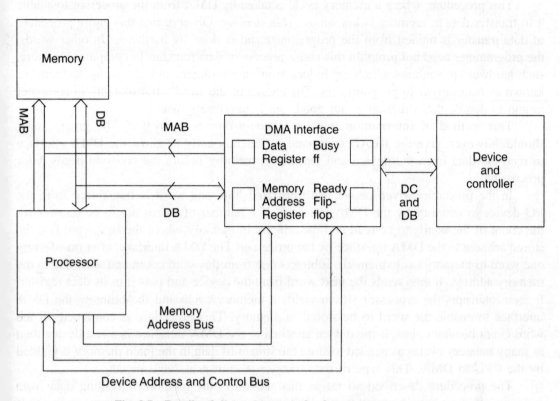

Fig. 8.7 Details of direct data transfer from input to memory.

The procedure used to transfer data via DMA is as follows:

Step 1: When a READ instruction is encountered, the processor sends the device address via the I/O device address bus. This is decoded by the I/O controller, and the DMA interface of the appropriate device is selected. The processor also sends the address in main memory where the data is to be stored and the command to read.

Step 2: The processor continues with the next instruction in the program. It has no further direct role in data transfer.

Step 3: The DMA sets its busy flip-flop, reads the data from the device and puts it in the data register.

Step 4: When the data has been entered in the data register the data ready flip-flop is set and an interrupt signal is sent to the processor.

Step 5:   The processor completes the current instruction which is being executed by it. It then yields the memory address and memory data buses to the DMA interface for one memory cycle. The DMA transfers the data in its data register to the address specified in its address register.

This procedure, where a memory cycle is taken by DMA from the processor to enable it to transfer data to memory is known as *cycle stealing*. Observe that this entire procedure of data transfer is hidden from the programmer and is done by hardware. In other words, the programmer need not program this entire process of data transfer. In computer literature, such hardware procedures which are hidden from programmers and *not visible* to them are known as *transparent* to programmers. The choice of the word, "transparent" in computer jargon to denote this situation is not good, but is universally used.

This method of information transfer is *non-program controlled*. The programmer, should, however, give the READ command sufficiently early to allow the DMA interface to read the data from the device and place it in memory before the program needs it for processing.

In the procedure given above, we illustrated how one word is transferred from the I/O device to memory by the DMA interface. If a number of words are to be transferred, the count of the words to be read and the address in memory where the first word is to be stored are sent to the DMA interface by the processor. The DMA interface, after transferring one word to memory (as explained), subtracts one from the word count and adds one to the memory address. It then reads the next word from the device and puts it in its data register. It then interrupts the processor which yields a memory cycle and the buses to the DMA interface to enable the word to be stored in memory. This procedure is continued till the word count becomes zero. If the device attached to the DMA interface is a fast device then as many memory cycles as needed to store the stream of data in the main memory is yielded by the CPU to DMA. This type of data transfer is known as *burst mode*.

The procedure described so far in this section is the method of reading data from a device. If data is to be written on an output unit from memory, the processor sends the device address to the I/O controller which selects the device. The beginning address and output word count are sent to DMA. The DMA now reads a word from memory by cycle stealing and sends it to the device. After the device writes the data, DMA reduces word count by one, adds one to memory address, and reads the next word from memory in a memory cycle stolen from the processor. This continues until all words are written. Observe that in this case also, the processor proceeds with its work after giving a WRITE command and the DMA writes out data without further direct participation of the processor.

To summarize, we see that DMA transfer is faster and more convenient to use than program controlled data transfer via a processor register. Processor's valuable time is not wasted in DMA transfer. This advantage is gained by providing extra hardware in DMA and by introducing additional buses. The new buses are data and address buses connecting DMA with memory and an address bus connecting processor to DMA.

At this stage one may wonder why the Memory Address Bus and Data Bus are shared by the DMA interface and the Processor which forces the Processor to yield these buses whenever data is to be transferred by DMA to memory. Why should one not provide two separate set of buses to memory, one set for the processor and second set for the DMA so that the two can work independently? The reason is cost. Memory with two independent paths (called ports) is expensive as it has to resolve contention if both ports try to write at the same location. Further as Input/Output is slow the number of times the Processor has to yield the buses to DMA may be once in 100 memory cycles, which will not slow down the Processor. Thus it is not cost effective to provide two independent ports to main memory.

8.4 INTERRUPT STRUCTURES

In the last section we introduced the idea of transferring data from I/O devices to the memory by program controlled interrupt transfer. We will expand on this idea in this section.

An interrupt signal is a signal sent by an I/O interface to the processor when the I/O is ready to send or receive data to or from memory. The processor completes the instruction it is processing, and acknowledges the interrupt signal. It then preserves the information needed to resume the program it was executing and jumps to another program called an *interrupt service routine* to cater to the I/O read/write requirement.

The interrupt servicing may be compared to what a house-wife does when she hears the telephone ring while boiling milk in the kitchen. She turns off the flame, closes the pan with a lid, and rushes to the phone. After attending to the call, she returns to the kitchen, removes the lid on the pan and turns on the flame to resume what she was doing.

An interrupt servicing procedure consists of the following steps:

Step 1: An interrupt signal is received by the processor.

Step 2: The processor completes the present instruction being executed.

Step 3: The processor stores the contents of the program counter and other registers in the processor in a reserved area in memory. This information is required to enable the processor to resume the program it was executing. It suspends the current program it is executing.

Step 4: The processor sends an interrupt acknowledge signal to the interrupting I/O interface and jumps to another program already stored in memory to service the interrupt.

Step 5: The interrupt servicing program carries out the required transfer of information from or to the specified I/O device. The last instruction in the interrupt servicing program restores the contents of all the processor registers including the program counter which was stored in the memory by the suspended program.

Step 6: The suspended program is resumed.

In practice a processor should handle a variety of interrupts from many I/O devices. The order of importance or priority of these interrupts will differ. Besides interrupts to transfer data from or to devices, other interrupts are also generated in a computer. An example is the occurrence of an emergency condition such as power failure. When a sensor detects impending power failure, it sends an interrupt signal to the processor. The processor initiates a power failure service routine which stores the contents of all important registers in the memory so that the program may be resumed when the power is restored. Interrupts caused by events occurring outside the processor such as I/O, power failure, high voltage, etc., are called *external interrupts*.

There is another class of interrupts known as *internal interrupts* or *traps* which occur when there is a mistake in a user's program. Common mistakes which lead to traps are: attempt to divide by zero, accumulator overflow or underflow, and illegal operation code. When such an error is detected by the processor, it interrupts a user's program and branches to a trap routine which usually prints out the value of PC and other registers when the trap occurred and a message giving the possible reason for the trap. The processor may continue executing the program if the error is not serious. If the mistake is serious and continuing the program is meaningless, then the program is aborted

Another type of interrupt is caused if the hardware of a computer develops a fault. When the error detecting circuitry detects a fault, the processor is informed of the location and nature of the fault. The processor then jumps to a fault servicing routine which determines if it is a correctable fault (such as when error correcting codes are used) and carries out the correction and resumes the user's program. If it is a non-correctable fault, operation is stopped after printing an appropriate message.

Interrupts are also generated by the real-time hardware clock in a computer. Such a clock is used to regulate the allocation of processor time to users. Such interrupts are necessary to ration out time to users and to throw out programs stuck in endless loops.

Multiple interrupts from I/O devices may be handled in several ways. In the simplest method, when an interrupt occurs, an interrupt servicing routine interrogates each I/O interface in turn, normally starting with the device which has the highest priority. After finding out which device interrupted it, it jumps to the I/O device handling program appropriate to that device. This method is called *programmed device polling*. While a device handling program is being run, the interrupt line is disabled so that during this time no further interruptions can take place. This solution is a software solution. It is inexpensive but slow.

In the most sophisticated method using special hardware, the processor has an interrupt register which has one bit corresponding to each source which can interrupt the processor. Each interrupting source sets its "private" bit in this register. In Fig. 8.8, we illustrate such a register for four sources. The processor has a register called an "interrupt masking register" which has one bit corresponding to each interrupting source. The bits in this register may be set by a programmer. When an interrupt is received the bit corresponding to the interrupting source is set to 1. If a particular interrupt i is to be ignored, the corresponding bit in the mask register is set to 0 by the programmer (see Fig. 8.8). The corresponding bits of the interrupt register and the mask register are ANDed giving bits M_1, M_2, M_3, M_4. If more than one interrupt is set and admitted by the mask register, the priority logic circuit enables only the highest priority interrupt line. These lines P_1, P_2, P_3, P_4 are fed to an encoder which gives the beginning address of the interrupt servicing program of the interrupting device.

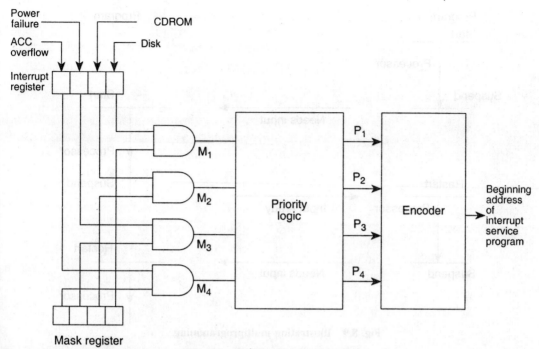

Fig. 8.8 Priority interrupt logic.

8.5 MULTIPROGRAMMING

In Sec. 8.3 we saw that by introducing DMA interface with some processing capability, it is possible for the processor to delegate I/O transfer responsibility to the DMA and proceed with arithmetic processing. If an arithmetic operation needs data and if it has not yet been transferred to the memory by DMA, then the processor has to wait. In order to eliminate this processor waiting time, programmers are required to do careful timing estimation which is difficult and impractical. On the other hand, if two independent programs are stored in memory, when one program cannot proceed due to lack of data, the other may be started by the processor. When the input for the first (suspended) program is available in memory, the processor may be interrupted and the original program resumed after suspending the second program. This is illustrated in Fig. 8.9. This method of utilizing the processor's resources is known as *multiprogramming*.

For multiprogramming to effectively overlap processor and I/O operations, it is necessary that, when one of the programs is waiting for I/O, the other must have enough computation to keep the processor busy. If both programs need input data at the same time, the processor will be idle again. As the speed mismatch between I/O and processor is very large, it is necessary to be able to work simultaneously on many programs (about four to eight) to keep the processor always busy. With a large number of programs, the probability of all programs being suspended for lack of input is very small.

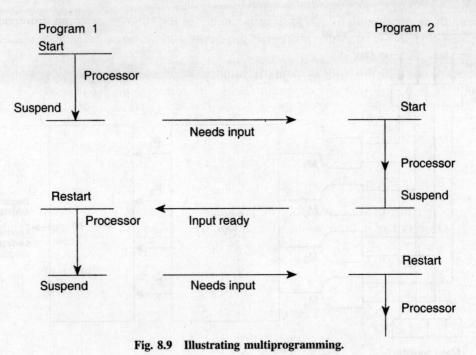

Fig. 8.9   Illustrating multiprogramming.

For a computer to work simultaneously on many programs, a number of special hardware and software features are required. First, the main memory of the computer should be large enough to accommodate all the programs. When a program is suspended, all information required to restart it should be saved in the memory. Besides this, it is necessary to prevent one program from overwriting the memory occupied by another program. In order to do this one may allocate specific areas in main memory to each program and protect it with a "lock". A program is allowed to write in an area only if it has a "key" which fits the protection "lock". This is usually a hardware feature and is called *memory allocation and protection* feature.

In order to perform all the above functions, namely, scheduling programs, attending to interrupts, storing information regarding suspended programs to enable them to be restarted, attending to I/O errors, etc., it is necessary to write a program called the *supervisor* or the *executive*. The supervisor has to permanently reside in the main memory in a reserved area and it should receive top priority. The supervisor is a part of what is known as the *operating system* of a computer. We will discuss this again in the Chapter 10 on operating systems.

8.6 PROCESSOR FEATURES

In Chapter 5, we discussed the functioning of the processor of a hypothetical computer. The main objective there was to explain in simple terms how a processor works. Real processors have many more features. The features are introduced with two basic objectives. The first is to simplify programming by introducing a number of well chosen machine instructions. The second objective is to reduce processor to memory and I/O to memory communication delays.

We will illustrate this with an example. Suppose it is required to add nine components of a vector a_i and print the sum. A simple algorithm to do this is given below:

$$S \leftarrow 0$$
$$for\ i = 1\ to\ 9\ do$$
$$begin\ Read\ a_i;\ S \leftarrow S + a_i\ end;$$
$$Write\ S;$$
$$Stop.$$

Using the instructions available in HYPCOM a program to do this is given in Table 8.1. Observe that in order to store 0 in S, we have to read and store in a given address in memory the number 0 fed from the input unit. Similarly the *for* loop indices 1 and 9 also

Table 8.1   A machine language program for HYPCOM to add the components of a vector

Address where the instruction is stored	Machine instruction		Explanation of instruction
	Operation code	Operand address	
000	A	090	Mem(90) ← 0. S Stored in 90
001	A	091	Mem(91) ← 9. Final index in 91
002	A	092	Mem(92) ← 1. Decrement in 92
003	A	109	Read into Mem(109) a_1
004	1	090	ACC ← Mem(90) = S
005	2	109	ACC ← S + Mem(109) = S + a_1
006	6	090	Mem(090) = S ← S + a_1
007	1	003	ACC ← A109
008	3	092	ACC ← ACC – 1 = A108 (Address modified)
009	6	003	Mem(003) ← A108 (Instruction in 003 changed)
00A	1	005	ACC ← 2109
00B	3	092	ACC ← ACC – 1 = 2108
00C	6	005	Mem(005) ← 2108 (Instruction in 005 changed)
00D	1	091	ACC ← Mem(91)
00E	3	092	ACC ← ACC – 1 = 9 – 1 = 8
00F	6	091	Mem(091) ← ACC = 8 (Index decremented)
010	9	012	If ACC = 0 go to 012
011	7	003	go to 003 (003 now has A108)
012	B	090	Print Mem(90) = S
013	F	000	Stop

have to be read from input. As input is slow, it would be desirable to directly store constants in registers in the processor. In the program of Table 8.1 instructions in memory addresses 003 to 011 implement the *for* loop. Observe instructions in 007, 008 and 009. Instruction in 007 takes into the accumulator the contents of 003 which is itself an *instruction*. Instruction 008 subtracts one from it, and the new value is stored back in 003 by instruction 009. Thus, the next time the instruction in 003 is retrieved, it will be A108, which will be interpreted as "read a number and store it in 108". Observe that the *address* of the instruction in 003 and 005 have been *modified*. Such *address modification* is essential in operations with vectors. In fact the *for* loop index has been used to modify the address. Exit from the *for* loop is implemented by instructions in 00D, 00E, 00F, and 010. This is done explicitly by taking the final value of the index, namely, 9 into the accumulator, subtracting 1, storing it back and checking if it has become 0. Two memory-processor data transfers have taken place, which it would be desirable to avoid, keeping in view memory-processor speed mismatch. Besides this, the method used to explicitly modify address is tricky and prone to error.

We will now look at a modification of HYPCOM which meets the twin objectives of easing programming and reducing unnecessary transfer of data between I/O and memory, and between processor and memory. First we introduce registers in the processor which are useful in storing intermediate results during processing without having to store them in memory. They can also be used to store indices and modification of indices required in setting up *for* loops and for use as subscripts of vectors. The instruction structure is changed to include, besides memory address, addresses of two registers—one acting as an operand register and the other as an *index register*. Besides this, some additional instructions are needed to make good use of these registers.

The new instruction structure is:

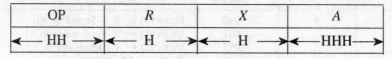

OP	R	X	A
← HH →	← H →	← H →	← HHH →

(H is a Hexadecimal digit)

The operation code has been expanded to two hexadecimal digits. We can now code up to 256 instructions. The *R*-field is the address of a register where operands may be stored and manipulated. The *X*-field is the address of a register which would be used as an index register. *A* is the address in memory.

The new instructions we introduce are:

1. Store a number given in *A* field in the specified register

Example:

OP	R	X	A
21	2	0	009

The new Op-code 21 means: store the *number* in the address field in the specified register, namely, Reg. 2. This instruction thus stores 9 in Reg. 2. Observe that the address field of the instruction is used as an *operand*. Such an instruction is known as an *immediate* instruction. Instead of reading a number via the input unit, storing it in memory, and then bringing it into a register in the processor, this instruction puts a number directly in a register and thus saves time.

2. The immediate instruction may be extended to all arithmetic operations. For example, the instruction

OP	R	X	A
22	2	0	004

may be used to add the operand 4 to the contents of register 2. Instruction 2330005 may be interpreted as subtract 005 from contents of register 3. Similar instructions may be used for multiplying and dividing.

3. It would be useful to move the contents of register to memory and vice versa. For example, the instruction

OP	R	X	A
06	2	0	345

may be interpreted as: "store the contents of register 2 in address 345 of memory". Observe that we are using a register instead of the accumulator in this modified new instruction. The instruction

OP	R	X	A
01	2	0	468

may be interpreted as: "clear register 2 and load contents of address 468 in memory to it". Moving data between registers would also be useful. Thus the instruction

OP	R	X	A
26	2	4	000

may be interpreted as: "move contents of register 4 to register 2".

4. An instruction using an index register is primarily used to modify the address and use an *effective address*. For example, the instruction

OP	R	X	A
01	2	3	468

would be interpreted as follows:

Add the contents of the register 3 specified in the X field (index register field) in the instruction to the address. The sum is the effective address to be used. Move the contents of this effective address in memory, to register 2. Thus if the contents of register 3 is 11 then the effective address would be 468 + 11 = 479. Thus the contents of address 479 will be moved to register 2 by this instruction.

Indexing may be used with the instructions add, subtract, multiply and divide. Thus the instruction

OP	R	X	A
02	3	4	643

would mean: "Add to contents of register 3 the contents of memory address (643 + contents of register 4). If register 4 has 5 in it then the contents of memory address 648 will be added to register 3".

5. One of the main uses of an index register is to facilitate setting up *for* loops and for subscript manipulation of vectors and matrices. Thus decrementing (subtracting 1) and incrementing (adding 1) to index register coupled with a test to see if the index has reached a preset value of zero is very useful. For example, the instruction

OP	R	X	A
19	0	2	008

may be interpreted as: "decrement index register 2 by 1 and jump to 008 if the index register value is zero, else go to next instruction in sequence". The instruction

OP	R	X	A
20	3	2	120

may be interpreted as: "increment index register 2 by 1 and jump to 120 if the index register value equals the contents of register 3".

Using some of these new features, we have rewritten the program of Table 8.1 and given it in Table 8.2. Observe that the program has become shorter and easier to understand and will also be executed faster.

Table 8.2 A machine language program for enhanced HYPCOM to add components of a vector

Address of instruction	Machine instruction				Explanation of instruction
	OP	R	X	Address	
000	21	2	0	009	C(Reg 2) ← 009. Index i in Reg 2
001	21	3	0	000	C(Reg 3) ← 0. Reg 3 used for S
002	A	0	2	100	Mem(100 + Reg (2)) ← input $= a_1$
003	2	3	2	100	C(Reg 3) ← Mem(100 + Reg (2)) + C(Reg 3) $= a_1 + S$
004	19	0	2	006	C(Reg 2) ← C(Reg 2) − 1 If C(Reg (2)) = 0 go to 006
005	7	0	0	002	go to 2. (Repeat loop)
006	6	3	0	099	Mem(99) ← C(Reg 3) = S
007	B	0	0	099	Print S
008	F	0	0	000	Stop

Other important features introduced in processors are the use of a *base register* in an instruction, and a feature known as *indirect addressing*.

Base register: The three hexadecimal digits in the address field of HYPCOM may be used to address 4096 locations. A larger memory may be addressed by increasing the length of the A-field. However, it is not an acceptable solution as each instruction will become longer. In an instruction using an index register, the contents of the index register are added to the address field in the instruction to create an effective address. If the index register stores 8 hexadigits (32 bits) then the effective address can be as large as 32 bits giving an addressable space (number of addressable locations) of $2^{32} = 4$ Gigawords (1 Giga = 10^9)! This is an enormous address space. Index registers are introduced for mainly subscript manipulation. For the purpose of address-space expansion, another register called a *base register* is introduced in some computers. For example, the HYPCOM instruction structure may be modified as

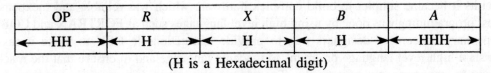

(H is a Hexadecimal digit)

where the *B*-field refers to a register address to be taken as a base register. The effective address is calculated as $A + C$ (Reg X) + C (Reg B).

Besides this use in expanding the addressable memory space, base registers are useful in *program relocation* also. Suppose a program occupies addresses 008 to 103 in memory, and at a different time it is to be located from 408 to 503. This type of relocation is inevitable when more than one program is simultaneously stored in memory in multi-programming. Assume that a program is written using Reg 8 as the base register with its contents 0. If a program changes the contents of Reg 8 to 400, the program will have all its memory references relocated between 408 and 503.

Indirect addressing: In direct addressing, the address of an operand is given in the A-field. In indirect addressing, the A field specifies the address where one should look to get the address of an operand. It is somewhat like going to find a "treasure" in an address but getting at that address not the treasure but another address where you would find the treasure. Thus if we have an instruction (whose OP code is 31): "move contents of memory to register indirect" its effect will be as shown below:

	OP	R	X	A
Instruction:	31	2	0	468

Reg 2 ← MEM (MEM(468))
If MEM(468) = 862 then Reg 2 ← MEM(862).

Indirect addressing is very useful in programming access to a table which may be relocated in memory. It is also useful in passing the parameters to a subroutine when a subroutine is called.

8.7 REDUCED INSTRUCTION SET COMPUTERS (RISC)

In the last section we saw how new instructions are added to the instruction set of CPU to make it simpler to program a computer. We saw how new addressing modes such as indirect addressing and relative addressing using a base register are designed. Apart from the motivation of making it simpler to program in machine language, another reason for introducing some of the instructions was to reduce CPU to memory traffic. As CPU is atleast 10 times faster than memory it is desirable to keep as many operands in CPU as possible and reduce references to memory.

In the evolution of CPU architecture early machines had small instruction sets as complex hardware was expensive and difficult to build. With the advent of integrated circuits it became simpler to build complex hardware which was reliable and inexpensive. Most programming was done by using high level languages such as FORTRAN and COBOL. A primary concern of designers was to provide instructions in CPU to make it easy to translate high level language programs to machine language and to ensure that the machine language programs run effectively. To achieve this more and more instructions were introduced. For example, one found 100 to 200 instructions in some computers. Besides this, as main memory was expensive, designers tried to pack more instructions in memory by introducing variable length instructions such as half word, one and half word etc. For example, an operand in an immediate instruction needs fewer bits and can be designed as a half word instruction. A variety of addressing modes were also provided. Computers with large number of instructions, complex addressing modes and variable length instructions are now called *Complex Instruction Set Computers* or CISC.

In early 80s, CPU designers saw that using too many instructions was counterproductive as the frequency of use of some of the instructions was very small. Further, it was felt that if a small number of instructions with uniform length are used, decoding and execution becomes simple and fast. If the instructions are designed in such a way that they retrieve operands stored in registers in CPU rather than from memory it will speed up computation. These ideas have been used in designing *Reduced Instruction Set Computers* (abbreviated RISC).

The general philosophy of designing instruction sets and CPU structure of RISC machines are:

1. Reduce the number of instructions and make them of equal length. Reduce addressing modes. These make decoding instructions easy. The decoding circuits can be integrated as part of the CPU chip. This will enable instructions to be decoded fast.

2. Reduce references to memory to retrieve operands. This is achieved by increasing the general purpose registers in CPU. Operands and intermediate results are stored in these registers. Usually 32 to 256 registers are provided in the CPU of RISC machines. The only references to memory are to load an operand from memory into a register in CPU and store

a result from a CPU register to a location in memory. Thus RISC architecture computers are sometimes called *Load-store architecture* computers.

3. When an instruction is to be executed, the following sequence of steps are carried out:

(i) Fetch instruction from memory.

(ii) Decode the instruction to determine what is to be done.

(iii) Fetch the operand from a register.

(iv) Execute the instruction.

(v) Store the result in a register.

If operands and results are stored in CPU and decoding circuit is simple, then each step takes about the same time. This allows overlapping of various stages of instruction fetching and execution as shown in Fig. 8.10 when a series of instructions are retrieved from memory. This is called *pipelining*. One instruction can thus be executed in one CPU clock cycle. One of the distinguishing features of RISC architecture is *Single cycle execution* of most instructions.

There are complications which arise if there is a branch instruction. Details of RISC

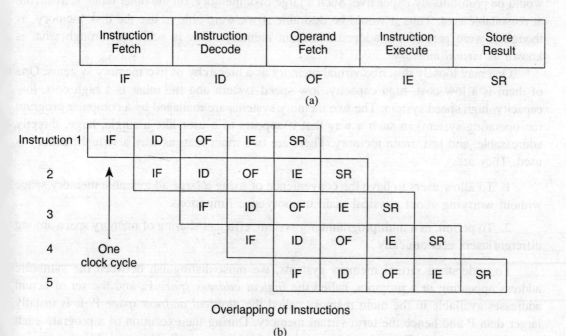

Fig. 8.10 **Illustrating instruction pipelining in RISC machines.**

CPU design is outside the scope of book and the interested student can refer to the book by Stallings given in the references at the end of the book.

Recently RISC machines have been further improved leading to CPUs which are known as *superscalar RISC*. The term superscalar means that in one CPU clock cycle more than one instruction can be carried out. This is achieved by having on CPU chip multiple arithmetic execution units so that two or more instructions can be executed simultaneously.

8.8 VIRTUAL MEMORY

In Chapter 4, we saw that there are many types of memories used in computers differing in speeds. In descending speeds they are: registers, cache, main MOS memory, hard disk, floppy disk and CDROM. In a computer configuration, there would be, besides the main random access memory, disk memory and CDROM. The disk memory would be, in today's computers, much larger than the main memory. For example, a small computer configuration may have a 32 Mbyte main memory and disk memory of 2 GB. The disk is normally used for storing program and data files of users.

We saw in the last section that the use of a base register allows a large addressable memory space. For example, we saw that with a 32-bit address, it would be possible to address 4 Gigawords. Such a large random access physical memory using CMOS technology would be prohibitively expensive. Such a large disk memory, on the other hand, is available at reasonable cost. Thus it would be desirable if we were able to use the disk memory, as though it were part of the addressable main memory. This is achieved through what is known as *virtual memory*.

One may loosely describe virtual memory as a hierarchy of two memory systems. One of them is a low cost, high capacity, low speed system and the other is a high cost, low capacity, high speed system. The two memory systems are managed by a computer program (an operating system) in such a way that it appears to a user like a single, large, directly addressable, and fast, main memory. There are two main reasons why a virtual memory is used. They are:

1. To allow users to have the convenience of using a large addressable memory space without worrying about physical main memory size limitations.

2. To permit, in a multiprogramming system, efficient sharing of memory space among different users economically.

To understand virtual memory systems, we must distinguish between the symbolic address appearing in a program, called the *logical address space* L, and the set of actual addresses available in the main memory called the *physical address space* P. L is usually larger than P and hence the term virtual memory. During the execution of a program each logical address l in L is translated into a physical address p in P. Thus an *address mapping* mechanism is needed which will give: $f(l) \rightarrow p$.

If it is found that the specified item is not in the main memory, the execution of the program is suspended while the relevant item is transferred to the main memory from the disk memory.

In order to implement a virtual memory system, memory is divided into fixed size contiguous areas, called *page frames.* Programs are also divided into pieces of the same size, called *pages.*

At any given time the processor uses the logical address to retrieve the item from the memory. A page address table is maintained by the system which has information on which pages of each program are in main memory at a given time. Before retrieving a word, the algorithm checks the page table to see if the required word is in a page in the main memory. If it is not in the main memory a *page fault* is said to occur. The program is then suspended till the required page is brought to the main memory from the disk memory. The page table is simultaneously updated. In a multiprogrammed system, the processor will switch to another program while a page is being swapped from the disk to the main memory. Page swapping is an I/O operation between disk and main memory and is independently controlled by a DMA channel.

An algorithm called a *demand paging* algorithm is used to swap programs between the main memory and secondary disk memory. It uses the method explained so far in this section as is given below:

Algorithm for demand paging

Step 1: Compute physical address *l* of the next word to be retrieved by the program;

Step 2: Look up page table to see if *l* is in the main memory M;

Step 3: *if l* is in M
    then begin Fetch required word;
             Process fetched word;
             go to Step 1 *end*
    else Suspend normal execution of program and continue with next step;

Step 4: *if* there is a free page frame in M
    then go to Step 5
    else begin
    Select page frame F in M to replace and mark it as free.
    if F is altered
       then Transfer page in F to disk
       else go to Step 5 *end*;

Step 5: Transfer page containing *l* from disk to free page frame F in M;

Step 6: Update page address tables and go to Step 1.

A base register is used for dynamic memory management in such a system. The operating system adds the contents of the base register which is a *page address,* to every memory address generated by a program thereby translating it to the right page. A page address table for each program is maintained by the operating system.

SUMMARY

1. Computer architecture is concerned with designing and coordinating the operation of different units in a computer, namely, I/O units, Memory and Processor in order to optimally use the system to run programs.

2. The processor is about 10 times faster than the main memory and about 1000 times faster than I/O units. The challenge in computer design is to invent hardware and software solutions with the aim of keeping all the units of the computer simultaneously active performing useful tasks.

3. The individual units of a computer are interconnected with *buses*. A set of wires which carries a group of bits in parallel and has an associated control scheme is known as a *bus*.

4. In one scheme, I/O units are connected to the processor by means of a device address bus, a data bus and a control bus. In this case information to and from the memory is sent via a processor register to I/O units. As I/O units are 1000 times slower than the processor this is not a desirable interconnection.

5. In another scheme the I/O units are connected to the memory via a DMA logic interface using a data bus and memory address bus. The processor is also connected to I/O via a memory address bus, I/O device address bus, and control bus. When an I/O command is sent to a device, data is directly transferred from the I/O unit to memory via DMA without using any processor register.

6. In a unibus system, the I/O units, Processor and Memory share a common system bus. This allows I/O devices to be addressed in the same way as memory addresses. Due to sharing of the bus, transfer of data can take place at any given time only between two of the three units.

7. In order to alleviate speed mismatch between processor and memory, a cache memory is interposed between the main memory and processor. A cache is a small fast memory. As most programs are sequential, most references will be restricted to small contiguous words in memory. This locality of memory reference is used in designing a cache. The part of a program currently being executed is automatically brought to the cache by the hardware. Thus most of the required instructions will be in the cache and thus the effective speed of the memory will be increased.

Besides a cache to store instructions (called an instruction cache), another cache is provided to store the data to be processed by the instructions. This is called a *data cache*.

8. Memory interleaving is used to retrieve simultaneously a number of words from a set of memory modules. This decreases the effective access time per word.

9. Data from I/O devices may be transferred to memory via a processor register using program controlled interrupt data transfer. In this scheme, an I/O command is issued by the processor well before a data is needed. When the data is assembled by the I/O interface logic, it sends an interrupt signal to the processor. The processor suspends the current task and receives the data and puts it in memory.

10. In DMA transfer, an interrupt is sent by the I/O interface to the processor when data is ready to be transferred. The processor yields a memory cycle and the data and address buses to the DMA interface to enable it to transfer the data to memory. DMA transfer of data is faster and more convenient to use than program controlled transfer.

11. As there are many I/O devices in a system there could be a number of interrupts. A system should be established to recognize the interrupting source and take appropriate action based on the priority of the device. A combined software-hardware solution is normally used.

12. A trap is an internal interrupt generated by mistakes in a user program such as an attempt to divide by 0. Unrecoverable hardware errors also lead to traps.

13. Multiprogramming is an architectural solution using both software and hardware to solve the problem of processor—I/O speed mismatch. In this method, a number of programs are simultaneously kept in memory. They are scheduled in such a way that when one program is busy performing I/O another program uses the processor. Thus both I/O and processor are kept simultaneously active. A good mix of I/O-intensive and processor-intensive programs is needed to successfully implement this idea. Besides this, a large physical main memory, a large disk and a protected memory area for the multiprogramming supervisor are essential.

14. Processors are designed with the twin objectives of easing programming, and preventing processor-to-memory communication delays.

15. Specific features introduced in a processor to reduce communication with memory include a number of general purpose registers, and immediate addressing. In the latter, data is used in the address field of an instruction.

16. Index registers coupled with special instructions facilitate setting up program loops and operation on vectors.

17. Base registers are used to enhance addressable memory space and to facilitate program relocation (required in multiprogramming).

18. In 70s the trend was to introduce large number of instructions, a variety of addressing modes and variable length instructions to build powerful CPUs. Such processors are known as Complex Instruction Set Computers (CISC).

19. In the 80s with the advancement in integrated circuit technology memory became cheap and the art of writing compilers to translate high level languages to machine language matured. This led to a newer CPU architecture called RISC (Reduced Instruction Set Computers). RISC machines use large number of registers in CPU, reduce references to memory except to load registers and store results, use simple addressing modes and uniform instruction length. This simplifies instruction decoding and allow instructions to be carried out fast (one instruction per clock cycle). Currently RISC CPUs are very popular among computer designers.

20. Virtual memory is a hierarchy of two memory systems; a main memory of size S1 and a secondary, slower and cheaper memory of a much larger size S2. The two systems

are managed by a software system in such a way that it appears to a user that a main memory of size S1 + S2 and speed nearly equal to that of main memory is available.

21. Virtual memory is implemented by dividing the logical memory space into a group of page frames. Programs are also divided into small pieces each requiring one *page*. A demand paging algorithm is used to place a page required by a user automatically in the main memory from the secondary disk memory.

REVIEW QUESTIONS

8.1   What is the nature of the speed mismatch between different units of a computer?

8.2   What is the fastest unit in a computer and which is the slowest? What is the order of magnitude of the difference in speed between them?

8.3   Define a 'bus'.

8.4   What buses are used to connect I/O devices to the processor?

8.5   What is the function of each of the buses used to connect I/O devices to the processor?

8.6   What buses are used to connect a memory to a processor?

8.7   What bus systems are used to interconnect I/O devices to the memory?

8.8   What is a DMA? What is its function?

8.9   What is a 'unibus system'? What are the advantages and disadvantages of using a unibus system?

8.10 Give the detailed steps used in memory-processor communication.

8.11 What is a 'cache memory'?

8.12 What important idea is used in introducing a cache memory?

8.13 Explain how a cache memory reduces the effective memory access time.

8.14 What is 'memory interleaving'?

8.15 Explain how instructions are distributed in different modules in an interleaved memory.

8.16 A memory module has an access time of 1 microsecond. Eight such modules are interleaved. What is the effective access time of the interleaved memory?

8.17 What is an I/O device controller? Explain its functions.

8.18 What is an I/O device interface logic? Explain its functions.

8.19 Give the algorithm used in program controlled I/O transfer.

8.20 If a data is to be written from memory to an output device, how will it be done by a program-controlled transfer via a processor register?

8.21 What is an interrupt signal? Explain how a processor can take advantage of an interrupt signal to reduce its waiting period to read input data.

8.22 Explain how data is read into memory from an input device with DMA interface logic.

8.23 What is cycle stealing?

8.24 How is data written on an output device using DMA interface?

8.25 What is the advantage of DMA data transfer as opposed to program-controlled data transfer?

8.26 What is an interrupt service routine?

8.27 Explain how a processor services an interrupt.

8.28 What is the difference between external and internal interrupts?

8.29 What is a trap? What are the different trap conditions which may occur in a computer?

8.30 Explain how multiple interrupts could be handled by a software routine.

8.31 What is programmed device polling? When is it used?

8.32 Explain how multiple interrupts can be handled by special hardware. How is the priority of different interrupts handled in this method?

8.33 How is device interrupt priority handled in software interrupt servicing?

8.34 What is multiprogramming? What are the objectives of multiprogramming?

8.35 What are the special hardware features needed to support multiprogramming in a computer system?

8.36 What conditions should be satisfied to meet the objectives of multiprogramming?

8.37 What is the function of a multiprogramming supervisor?

8.38 Write a machine language program for HYPCOM to add two vectors each having 8-components.

8.39 Explain the necessity of address modification in a machine language program.

8.40 Rewrite the program of Exercise 8.38 using modified HYPCOM presented in Sec. 8.6.

8.41 Write a machine language program for modified HYPCOM to find the scalar product of two 8-component vectors.

8.42 What is the purpose of immediate addressing?

8.43 What is the purpose of index registers in a processor?

8.44 What is the objective of introducing several general purpose registers in a processor?

8.45 What instructions are useful in implementing *for* loops?

8.46 What is a base register?

8.47 What is the difference between an index register and a base register?

8.48 What is the primary use of a base register?

8.49 What is 'program relocation'? How is a base register useful in achieving this?

8.50 What is 'indirect addressing'? What is the use of such addressing?

8.51 What do you understand by the term RISC architecture?

8.52 Enumerate the important characteristics of a RISC CPU.

8.53 What are the main differences between a RISC CPU and a CISC CPU?

8.54 What do you understand by the term superscalar RISC?

8.55 Define 'virtual memory'.

8.56 What is the objective of a virtual memory feature in a computer?

8.57 What is the difference between logical address space and physical address space?

8.58 What do you understand by the term 'page frames'?

8.59 What is a 'page' of a program?

8.60 What is 'demand paging'?

8.61 Explain how a demand paging algorithm works.

8.62 In what way is a base register useful in implementing a virtual memory system?

8.63 What is a 'page address table'? How is it used in implementing a virtual memory system?

8.64 What are the similarities and differences between a cache memory and a virtual memory?

9

Computer Languages

Programs, namely, the list of instructions to be executed by a computer are known as the *software* of a computer. The electronic circuits used in building the computer that executes the software is known as the *hardware* of a computer. To take an analogy, a home television set bought from a shop is hardware; the various entertainment programs transmitted from the television station are its software. It is immediately evident that hardware is necessary but software is vital. What is the use of a home television set if the programs shown on it are all boring! Another important point brought out by this analogy is that software production is difficult and expensive. Hardware is a one-time expense whereas software is a continuing expense.

Computer software may be classified into two broad categories: *application software* and *system software*. Application software is the set of programs necessary to carry out operations for a specified application. For example, programs to solve a set of equations, process examination results, etc., constitute application software. System software, on the other hand, are general programs written for the system which provide the environment to facilitate the writing of application software.

Programming language translators are examples of system software. In this chapter we will discuss the evolution of programming languages and associated translators. In the next chapter we will discuss another important system software known as *operating systems*.

9.1 WHY PROGRAMMING LANGUAGE?

In Chapter 5, we examined the logical structure of the processing unit of computers. We examined in some detail the structure of a hypothetical machine HYPCOM. An instruction for HYPCOM consisted of an operation code which specified the operation to be performed and an operand address which specified the address in memory where the operand would be stored. A sequence of such machine instructions, called a *machine language program*, was used to solve problems.

In order to write a machine language program, a programmer has to remember all the operation codes of the computer and know in detail what each code does and how it affects various registers in the processor. He also has to keep track of all the operands and know exactly where they are stored in memory. Writing a machine language program requires meticulous attention to detail and deep knowledge of the internal structure of the computer. Writing long machine language programs and testing them take a lot of time. Thus it is necessary to look at better methods of writing programs for a computer.

The main purpose of using computers is to solve problems which would otherwise be difficult to solve. It must thus be possible for a computer user to concentrate on the development of good algorithms for solving problems rather than be concerned with the details of the internal structure of the computer. This situation is analogous to that which confronts the user of a motor car. From the user's point of view a motor car is meant to take him from one place to another. If one has to know all about how the engine of the motor car works before one can drive it, not many persons will be able to drive a car. Driving must be made as simple as possible with minimum number of controls so that it would be easy for anyone to drive and fulfil the objective of owning a car. A general knowledge of how the motor car works is useful if a person wants to be a good driver and reduce wear and tear and petrol consumption. It is, however, not essential for a driver to be a good mechanic. Similarly, it is desirable, but not essential, for a programmer to know in detail how a computer works.

Computer programming languages are developed with the primary objective of facilitating a large number of people to use computers without the need to know in detail the internal structure of the computer. Languages are matched to the type of operations to be performed in algorithms for various applications. Languages are also designed to be *machine-independent*. In other words, the structure of a programming language would not depend upon the internal structure of a specified computer. Ideally, one should be able to execute a program on any computer regardless of who manufactured it or what model it is.

9.2 ASSEMBLY LANGUAGE

The first step in the evolution of programming languages was the development of what is known as an *assembly language*. In an assembly language, mnemonics are used to represent operation codes, and strings of characters to represent addresses. We give in Table 9.1 a machine language program and the corresponding assembly language program. It may be observed from this table that there is a one-to-one correspondence between the assembly

Table 9.1 An assembly program and a machine language equivalent

Assembly code		Machine code	
Operation	Operand address	Operation	Operand address
READ	K	A	200
READ	L	A	201
READ	M	A	202
READ	N	A	203
CLA	K	1	200
ADD	L	2	201
ADD	M	2	202
ADD	N	2	203
STO	W	6	204
PRT	W	B	204
HLT		F	

language program and the equivalent machine language program. As an assembly language is designed mainly to replace each machine code with an understandable mnemonic and each address with a simple alphanumeric string, it is matched to a particular computer's processor structure. It is thus *machine dependent*. It is necessary for an assembly language programmer to know all details of a computer's logical structure in order to write a program. It thus suffers from many of the disadvantages of machine language.

In order to execute an assembly language program on a computer, it should first be translated to its equivalent machine language program. This is necessary because the computer's circuitry is designed to execute only the operation codes of the machine. The mnemonic operation codes should be converted to absolute numeric operation codes. The symbolic addresses of operands used in assembly language should also be converted to absolute numeric addresses. The translator which does this is known as an *assembler* (see Fig. 9.1). The input to an assembler is the assembly language program and is known as the *source program*. Its output is the equivalent machine language program and is known as the *object program*. The assembler is a system program which is supplied by the computer manufacturer. It is written by system programmers with great care.

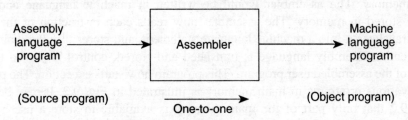

Fig. 9.1 Depicting an assembler.

The main advantage of using an assembly language for programming is the efficiency of the machine language program resulting from it. As all hardware features available in the processor of the computer, such as registers, stacks, etc., are available to the assembly language programmer, he has great flexibility in writing programs well-matched to the computer.

The main disadvantages of an assembly language are:

(i) It is machine-dependent. Thus programs written for one model of a computer cannot be executed on another model. In other words it is *not portable* from one machine to another.

(ii) An assembly language programmer must be an expert who knows all about the logical structure of the computer.

(iii) Writing assembly language programs is difficult and time-consuming.

The trend is thus to avoid using an assembly language. It is used only when efficiency is of paramount importance or when there is a need to control input/output devices. Efficiency is important, for instance, if a command to control an aircraft is to be given in a specified time. In cost-sensitive applications for instance, when a microprocessor based controller is used as a consumer item such as a washing machine, the program is stored in a Read Only Memory and the size of ROM determines the cost. The control program has to be concise and Assembly Language ensures this.

9.2.1 Executing Assembly Language Program

Before a machine language program can be executed it must be stored in the memory of the computer. The program itself may be stored in a floppy disk. This program is to be read into memory by another program called a *loader* which is already stored in the memory. The loader, or initial program load (IPL) is automatically stored in the memory by the hardware of the computer when the computer is switched on. In cheaper computers this program (in binary form) is loaded manually by the operator using console switches.

The loader program should be kept small. Thus a procedure is used whereby the first few instructions of the loader load the rest of the loader program. This is called *bootstrap loading*.

In order to execute an assembly language program, we must first store the loader. The loader then reads the assembler from a peripheral memory (such as a disk) and stores it in the main memory. The assembler would be written in machine language and can thus directly be stored in memory. The assembler now reads each instruction of the assembly language, translates it into a machine language statement, and stores it in the main memory. When the entire assembly language is translated and stored, control is passed to the first instruction of the assembled user program. This program now starts execution. The progression of storing various programs in main memory is illustrated in Fig. 9.2. It may be observed from Fig. 9.2 that only part of the main memory is available to store a user's program. The available free memory for user programs is usually specified by the manufacturer.

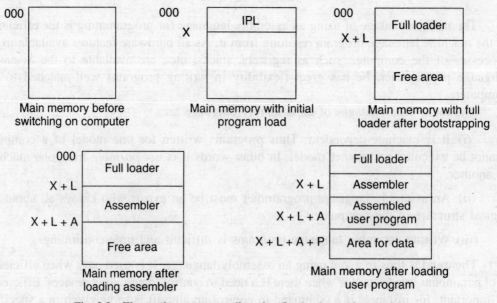

Fig. 9.2   Illustrating memory allocation for loader and assembler.

The assembler is a machine language program. Since machine language programs are difficult to write, it would be preferable to keep them small. One method of doing it would be to define an assembly language with minimal features and write an assembler for this language. A higher level assembly language may then be defined (for example one which allows expressions for addresses). A program in this higher level assembly language may be translated by a program written in the rudimentary assembly language for which a translator already exists. This is a very powerful method and is called *bootstrap method*. Figure 9.3 illustrates this.

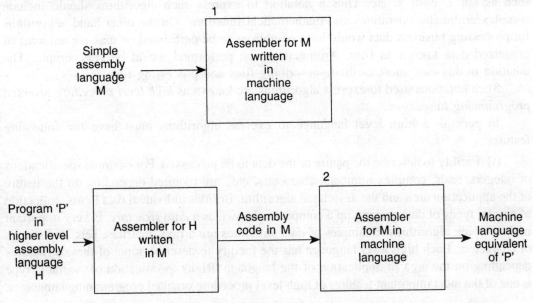

Fig. 9.3 Illustrating bootstrap method of writing translators. (Boxes 1 and 2 are identical.)

9.3 HIGHER LEVEL PROGRAMMING LANGUAGES

During the evolution of computers, till about 1955, computers were slow, and had a small memory. Thus programming efficiency was very important and assembly language was dominant. The use of computers was also limited to a small group of scientists. With improvements in technology, computers were designed with larger memory capacity, higher speed and improved reliability. The tremendous potential of computer applications in diverse areas was foreseen. It was evident that this potential could be realized only if a non-expert user could effectively use the computer to solve problems. It was thus clear that a user should be concerned primarily with the development of appropriate algorithms to solve problems of interest to him and not with the details of the internal logical structure of a computer. Consequently a good notation to express algorithms became an essential requirement. It would be ideal if an algorithm written in a natural (spoken) language such as English were translated to machine language automatically by the computer and executed. This is not possible because natural languages are not precise or unambiguous. The interpretation of the meaning of a natural language sentence depends on the context also. For example, the sentence "Give me a ring" may mean either give me a ring to wear or a ring on the telephone depending on the context. In fact the whole profession of lawyers would be redundant if sentences had unique interpretation!

Thus if algorithms are to be executed by computers, it is necessary to develop a simple, concise, precise and unambiguous notation to express them. The notation should also match the type of algorithm. For example, algorithms to solve science and engineering problems would have complex arithmetic operations and would use mathematical functions such as tan x, cosh x, etc. Thus a notation to express such algorithms should include complex arithmetic operations and mathematical functions. On the other hand, algorithms for processing business data would have operations to be performed on massive amounts of organized data known as files. Arithmetic to be performed would be very simple. The notation in this case must facilitate describing files and processing files.

Such notations used to express algorithms are known as *high level procedure oriented programming languages.*

In general, a high level language to express algorithms must have the following features:

(i) Facility to describe the nature of the data to be processed. For example specifications of integers, reals, complex numbers, characters, etc., are required depending on the nature of the application area and the associated algorithm. Besides individual data items, collection of similar types of data making up a composite, known as a *data structure,* is very important in developing algorithms. Examples of data structures are arrays, matrices, sets, and strings of characters. Each high level language has the facility to describe some of these structures depending on the area of application of the language. Rigid specification of variable type is one of the most important features of high level procedure oriented programming languages.

(ii) Operators which are appropriate to the data items and data structures in the language. For example, if we have a facility to represent complex numbers, then, complex addition, subtraction, multiplication and division operations would be useful.

(iii) A set of characters using which symbols in the language are constructed. These symbols have a precise meaning in the context of the language. For example, the symbol ** is used to represent the exponentiation operation in FORTRAN. Thus A**B would mean raising A to the power B.

(iv) Control structures to sequence the operations to be performed are important. In most algorithms one would find alternate set of statements to be performed on the basis of testing a condition. Repetition of groups of statements is also necessary in many algorithms. Thus a high level language should provide control structures appropriate to express algorithms. For example, a common control structure found in a high level language is:

if A > B *then* X:= Y + Z *else* X:= P + Q;

which means "compare the numbers stored in A and B. If the number stored in A is larger than that stored in B then add the number stored in Y to that stored in Z and place it in X, otherwise add the number stored in P with that stored in Q and place it in X".

A repetition structure, for example, is

      I:= 0;

repeat

      I:= I + 1;

      SUM:= SUM + N;

      N:= N + 5;

until   (I = 10);

(v) A set of words each with a precise and unambiguous meaning and a role to play in creating the program. For example the words READ, WRITE, DO have specific meanings in the context of a programming language.

(vi) A set of syntax rules which precisely specify the combination of words and operators permissible in the language. For example, a language may specify that A * B is a legal combination in a language whereas A*/B may be illegal. The syntax rules are rules of grammar valid for the language. These rules are derived systematically and their number is kept small to enable users to memorize them.

(vii) A set of semantic rules which assign a single precise and unambiguous meaning to each legal syntactic structure in the language. For example, the statement: C = B/D would have the meaning "Divide the number stored in B by the one stored in D and store the result in C" in a particular high level language.

A syntactically correct statement is not necessarily semantically meaningful. In natural language (English) for instance the sentences:

"Ram plays football"

"Football plays Ram"

are both syntactically correct. The second sentence, however, is semantically meaningless. Similarly the statement C = B/D would be semantically incorrect if D happens to be zero. In high level languages for computers, there should be no semantic ambiguity. Each syntactically correct structure should have one and only one semantic interpretation. This is in contrast with natural languages.

(viii) The syntax and semantic rules of the language, besides being concise and precise, should aid in understanding the program. An understandable program is self-documenting and thus easily maintainable. One chooses words in the language which have meanings similar to their meanings in English usage.

Besides this, the facility to intersperse the program with comments (which are not part of the program) should be provided to aid program understanding.

High level languages are designed independent of the structure of a specific computer. This facilitates executing a program written in such a language on different computers. Associated with each high level language is an elaborate computer program which translates it into the machine language of the computer in which it is to be executed. The translator program is normally written in the assembly language of that computer. Figure 9.4 explains various terms used in high level language translation. Figure 9.5 illustrates how machine-independence is achieved by using different translators to translate a high level language program to machine languages of different computers.

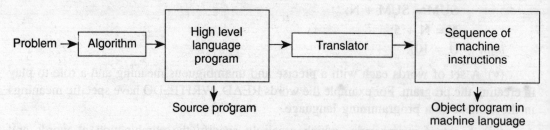

Fig. 9.4   Illustrating terminology used in High level language translation.

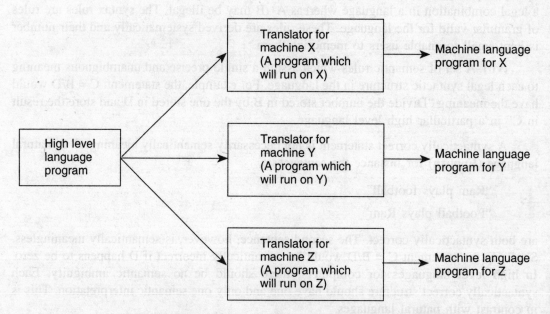

Fig. 9.5   Illustrating machine independence of High level language.

In Table 9.2 we illustrate a small program written in a high level language called BASIC and the equivalent machine language program of HYPCOM. Observe that one high level language statement is translated into *many* machine language statements. This is *one-to-many translation*. The terminology, high level language, arises due to this. An assembly language is a low level language as its translation to machine language is one-to-one. It is possible to translate a high level language to one at a lower level, but the reverse is not always possible.

There are two approaches to writing language translators. One method is to take one statement of a high level language at a time and translate it into a machine instruction which is immediately executed. This is called an *interpreter*. Interpreters are easy to write and they do not require large memory space in the computer. The main disadvantage of interpreters is that they require more time to execute on a computer.

The other approach to translation is to store the high level language program, scan it and translate the whole program into an equivalent machine language program. Such a translator is known as a *compiler*. A compiler is a complex program compared to an interpreter. It takes more time to compile than to interpret. However, a compiled machine language program runs much faster than an interpreted program.

Table 9.2   A basic program and its HYPCOM machine language equivalent

BASIC PROGRAM		MACHINE LANGUAGE	
10 READ K, L, M, N		A	200
20 LET W = K + L + M + N		A	201
		A	202
		A	203
30 PRINT W			
40 END		1	200
		2	201
		2	202
		2	203
		6	204
		B	204
		F	

The difference between an interpreter and a compiler may be understood with the help of the following analogy. Suppose we want to translate a speech from Russian to English. There are two approaches one can use. The translator can listen to a sentence in Russian and immediately translate it to English. Alternatively, the translator can listen to the whole passage in Russian and then give the equivalent English passage. If the speaker repeats the same or a similar sentence, then, in the first case, the equivalent English sentence will also be repeated. In the second case, the translation will be more concise as the English equivalent of a whole passage will be given and there will be no repetitions. A person who can translate a whole passage has to be a better translator and must remember more information than one who translates sentence-by-sentence. An interpreter is similar to sentence-by-sentence translation whereas a compiler is similar to translation of the whole passage.

High level languages which have the power to express a general class of algorithms are known as *procedure oriented languages*. These languages express in detail the procedure used to solve a problem. In other words, a programmer gives details of *how* to solve a problem. Another class of high level languages is called *problem oriented languages*. These languages are designed to solve a narrower class of problems. A user of such a language need not express in detail the procedure used to solve the problem. Ready-made procedures are preprogrammed. The user merely presents the input data to the program in a flexible "language". For example, a problem oriented language called STRESS (STRuctural Equation System Solver) accepts a description of a set of equations to be solved in a simple format of the type:

$$\text{NODE 5 IS AT X} = 25.5, \text{ Y} = 20.7, \text{ Z} = 10.5$$
$$\text{BEAM BETWEEN NODES 5 AND 15}$$

. . . .

. . . .

It then generates the equations to be solved, invokes built-in algebraic equation solution program and solves the problem. The user need not specify how to solve the problem. He merely has to state *what* problem is to be solved using the appropriate language.

Recent popular problem oriented languages are MATLAB and MATHEMATICA. MATLAB is popular among scientists and engineers to solve a wide class of problems modelled by differential equations, and matrices. MATHEMATICA is used to simplify complex algebraic expressions, find expressions resulting from indefinite integration and similar symbol manipulation problems.

9.4 COMPILING HIGH LEVEL LANGUAGE PROGRAM

In this section we will discuss briefly the steps in compiling a high level language program to an executable machine language program. Broadly the compilation process consists of two steps. The first step is the analysis of the source program and the second is the synthesis of the object program in the machine language of the specified machine (Fig. 9.6). The analysis step uses the precise description of the source programming language. A source language is described using *Lexical rules, Syntax rules* and *Semantic rules*.

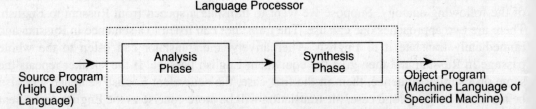

Fig. 9.6   Block diagram of a language processor.

Lexical rules specify the valid syntactic elements or words of the language. *Syntax rules* specify how the valid syntactic elements are combined to form statements of the language. *Semantic rules* assign meanings to valid statements of the language.

Consider, for example, the following statement in a high level language.

```
principal := principal * ( 1 + rate/100)
```

The syntactic elements of the statement are:

```
principal, := , *, ( , 1, +, rate, /, 100, and )
```

The syntactic elements `principal` and `rate` are called *identifiers*. The symbols `:=`, `+`, and `/` are *operators*. The numbers `1` and `100` are *integer constants* and the symbols `(`, `)` and `;` are called *delimiters*. Each syntactic element is defined using the syntax rules of the language. The syntax rules are given using a notation called *Backus Naur Form* abbreviated BNF in honour of Backus and Naur who invented this notation to describe computer languages. Each syntactic unit is given a name and shown as <name>. For example the syntactic unit digit is defined as:

$$<\text{digit}> \rightarrow 0\,|\,1\,|\,2\,|\,3\,|\,4\,|\,5\,|\,6\,|\,7\,|\,8\,|\,9\,|$$

The arrow $\rightarrow$ represents "defined as" and the vertical bar | is used to represent "or". The above definition is thus read as: <digit> is defined as 0 or 1 or 2 or 3 or 4 or 5 or 6 or 7 or 8 or 9. We define letter as:

$$<\text{letter}> \rightarrow a\,|\,b\,|\,c \,......\, x\,|\,y\,|\,z$$

In other words a <letter> is any one of the lower case English letters. These characters are combined to form a syntactic unit called <identifier> which is defined as:

<identifier> := <letter> | <identifier><letter>|<identifier><digit>.

Observe that the above definition is defined in terms of itself. This is called a *recursive definition*. Using this rule the following are valid identifiers:

`p,    pr,    pr2,    principal`

as `p` is an <identifier> and `pr` is an <identifier> followed by a <letter> r which is also an <identifier>. Following this argument `pr` followed by a <digit>, namely, 2 is also an <identifier>. The reader can verify that `principal` is a valid identifier as it conforms to these rules. On the other hand the following are not valid identifiers as they violate syntax rules.

`2p,  2 + p,  p - 2,  ?  x,  x;  y`

Some other rules are:

$$<\text{a.o.}> \rightarrow +\,|\,-\,|\,*\,|/$$

where <a.o.> is abbreviation for <arithmetic operator>
<delimiters> $\rightarrow$) | (| ;
<assignment operator> $\rightarrow$:=

Having defined the "words" of the language, we next define how "sentences" of the language are formed using syntax rules. Some of the rules are given below:

<arithmetic expression> $\rightarrow$ <identifier><a.o.><identifier> where <a.e.> is abbreviation for arithmetic expression <a.e.> $\rightarrow$ <(a.e.)>
<a.e.> $\rightarrow$ <a.e.> <a.o.> <a.e.>

An arithmetic statement is defined as:

<arithmetic statement> → <identifier> := < a.e.>. Using the above rule and the rules given earlier defining <a.e.> it can be verified that

```
principal := principal * (1 + rate/100)
```

is a syntactically correct arithmetic statement. Next we have to assign meanings to syntactically correct units. In the above example the semantic interpretation of the computation is:

Compute the value of the expression on the right hand side of := and replace the value stored in the variable name `principal` by this value. The rules on how to compute the arithmetic expression should also be specified as semantic rules.

The steps used in the process of translating a high level language source program to executable code is given in Fig. 9.7. The first block is a lexical analyzer (or scanner). It reads successive lines of a program and breaks them into individual lexical items, namely,

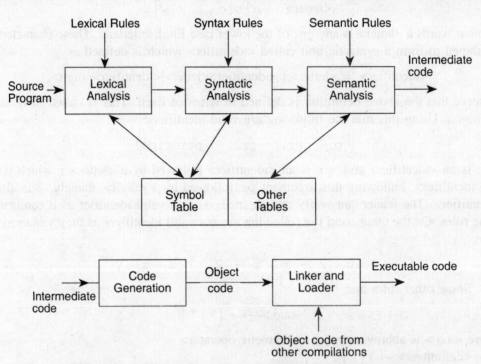

Fig. 9.7 Steps in translation of high level language to machine language.

identifier, operator, delimiter etc., and attaches a type tag to each of these. Besides this it constructs a *symbol table* for each identifier and finds the internal representation of each constant. The symbol table is used later to allocate memory to each variable.

The second stage of translation is called *syntax analysis* or *parsing*. In this phase expressions, statements, declarations etc., are identified by using the results of lexical analysis. Syntax analysis is aided by using techniques based on formal grammar of the programming language.

In the semantic analysis phase the syntactic units recognized by the syntax analyzer are processed. An intermediate representation of the final machine language code is produced. This phase bridges the analysis and synthesis phases of translation (see Fig. 9.6).

The last phase of translation is code generation. A number of optimizations to reduce the length of machine language program are carried out during this phase. The output of the code generator is the machine language program of the specified computer. If a subprogram library is used or if some subroutines are separately translated and compiled a final linking and loading step is needed to produce the complete machine language program ready for execution. If subroutines are separately compiled the addresses of the resulting machine language instructions will not be their final address when all the routines are placed together in main memory. The linker's job is to find the correct locations of the final executable program. The loader will then place them in the memory at their right addresses.

9.4.1 Tools to Build Compilers

We saw that the analysis phase of all high level language translators have three distinct phases; lexical analysis, syntax analysis and semantic analysis. The output of the analysis phase is an intermediate representation (see Fig. 9.7). As the methodology of analysis is well understood and applicable to a variety of language processors, tools have been developed to automatically generate programs for scanning the source code to identify syntactic units, parsing the programs and generating the intermediate code. Two of these tools which are popular are called LEX (lexical analyzer) and YACC (Yet Another Compiler Compiler). LEX accepts an input specification of strings representing lexical units of a high level language and semantic actions necessary to build the intermediate code and generates a scanner. YACC generates a parser of the language given the grammar of the language. The scanner produced by LEX can be called by a parser generated by YACC. LEX and YACC normally generate C code which is machine independent. The code generator for specific computers are written using the intermediate code as input. Some tools have also been developed to obtain code generators if a formal specification of the processor of the target computers are given but they are not as popular as LEX and YACC.

9.5 SOME HIGH LEVEL LANGUAGES

In this section, we will briefly describe some popular high level languages and the areas of their applicability.

FORTRAN: FORTRAN stands for *FOR*mula *TRAN*slation. This language is the oldest high level language. In a pioneering effort John Backus and his team at IBM (International Business Machine Corporation) developed this language and its translator in 1956-57. The language was designed to solve scientific and engineering problems and is currently the most popular language among scientists and engineers. With the evolution of better computers and with increasing maturity of users, FORTRAN has also evolved. The first version which was extensively used in late 50's and early 60's was known as FORTRAN II. The next popular version was FORTRAN IV. This version was standardized by the American National

Standards Institute (ANSI) in 1966. In 1977 an updated version of FORTRAN IV incorporating widely adopted good features and improvements was announced and standardized by ANSI. This version is known as FORTRAN 77.

More recently a version of FORTRAN known as FORTRAN 90 has been standardized to supersede FORTRAN 77. Special features incorporated in FORTRAN 90 include provision to store and manipulate characters, operations for vector operands and better constructs for expressing program loops. Recently FORTRAN 95 has been standardized which has incorporated features to write programs for parallel computers.

The *computational instructions* in FORTRAN resemble ordinary algebra. For example, $X = (A + B + C)/(D + E)$ is a computational instruction. *Control* and *input/output* instructions resemble English language imperative statements. For Example, IF (A .GT. B) GO TO 10 is a control instruction. READ*, A, B and WRITE (3, 35) X, Y, Z are input and output instructions. Storage instructions resemble English declarative sentences. For example, NUMBER = PREVNO is interpreted to mean "store in memory address with name NUMBER, the contents of memory address with name PREVNO".

We give below a FORTRAN program to calculate the average height of boys in a class.

```
C   FORTRAN PROGRAM TO FIND AVERAGE HEIGHT OF BOYS
C   IN A CLASS
    NSTUD = 0
    SUMHT = 0
C   NSTUD IS NUMBER OF STUDENTS
C   SUMHT IS SUM OF HEIGHTS
C   BOTH ARE INITIALIZED TO 0
10  READ*, HEIGHT
    IF (HEIGHT .EQ. 0) GO TO 20
C   A DATA HEIGHT = 0 IS USED TO INDICATE END OF DATA
    SUMHT = SUMHT + HEIGHT
    NSTUD = NSTUD + 1
    GO TO 10
20  AVHT = SUMHT/NSTUD
    PRINT*, NSTUD, AVHT
    STOP
    END
```

COBOL: COBOL stands for *CO*mmon *B*usiness *O*riented *L*anguage. This language grew out of the desire of the data processing professionals for a high level, machine independent language for business data processing which would be accepted by any computer which has a COBOL compiler. The work on the language began in 1959 with strong support from the United States department of defence under the guidance of Commander Grace Murray Hopper. The maintenance and further orderly growth of the language was handed over to a group called *CO*nference on *DA*ta *SY*stems *L*anguages (abbreviated to CODASYL).

The first formal COBOL report was published in 1960 and revised in 1965. The version was gradually improved. ANSI standardized COBOL in 1968, 1974 and 1984. Object oriented version of COBOL has recently (1997) appeared in the market. COBOL is a widely used programming language for business data processing.

A COBOL program is divided into four parts or divisions. These divisions describe four main aspects of a program and are called IDENTIFICATION DIVISION, ENVIRONMENT DIVISION, DATA DIVISION and PROCEDURE DIVISION. The Identification Division is used to establish the identification of the program and its author. The Environment Division specifies the computer and the peripherals which are used to compile the program and execute the program. The Data Division describes in detail the format of the input and output data and describes the structure of the files used by the system. The Procedure Division describes the sequence of operations to be performed on the files declared in the Data Division.

The main objective of COBOL designers was to develop a truly machine independent language which is as close to English as possible. Further, COBOL is intended to be easily readable and understandable. Thus instructions written in COBOL are verbose.

For example, a COBOL statement to add is:

> ADD PAY TO ALLOWANCES GIVING GROSS_PAY

An input statement is:

> READ STUDENT_FILE AT END CLOSE STUDENT_FILE.

A storage statement is:

> MOVE GROSS_PAY TO OUTPUT_PAY

The major reasons for the popularity of COBOL for business data processing are:

1. Clear specification of data used by the program.

2. Very good methods of specifying different types of files used in data processing and manipulating them.

3. Excellent method available to generate reports as output of program.

4. Self-documentation of the program if a programming team adheres to standard coding practices.

We give below a COBOL program to find the average height of boys in a class. The program is given to illustrate the nature of COBOL program.

```
*PROGRAM TO FIND AVERAGE HEIGHT OF BOYS IN A CLASS.
IDENTIFICATION DIVISION.
PROGRAM_ID. SAMPLE.
AUTHOR. V RAJARAMAN.
DATE WRITTEN. 2-FEB-98.
DATE_COMPILED.
ENVIRONMENT DIVISION.
```

```
        CONFIGURATION SECTION.
        SOURCE_COMPUTER. DECSYSTEM_1090.
        OBJECT_COMPUTER. DECSYSTEM_1090.
        INPUT_OUTPUT SECTION.
        FILE_CONTROL.
              SELECT IN_STUD_FILE ASSIGN TO DSK
              RECORDING MODE IS ASCII.
        DATA DIVISION.
        FILE SECTION.
        FD    IN_STUD_FILE
              RECORD CONTAINS 80 CHARACTERS
              VALUE OF ID IS 'INSTUDDAT'
              DATA RECORD IS IN_STUD_RECORD.
              01    IN_STUD_RECORD
              02    IN_SER_NO PICTURE 9(5).
              02    IN_STUD_HEIGHT PICTURE 999V9.
              02    FILLER X (71).
        WORKING_STORAGE SECTION.
        77    NO_OF_STUDENTS PICTURE 999 VALUE 0.
        77    AVERAGE_HEIGHT PICTURE 999V9 VALUE 0.
        77    SUM_OF_HEIGHT PICTURE 9(5)V9 VALUE 0.
        PROCEDURE DIVISION.
        OPEN_FILE.
              OPEN INPUT IN_STUD_FILE.
        READ_INPUT.
              READ IN_STUD_FILE AT END GO TO END_OF_JOB.
              ADD IN_STUD_HEIGHT TO SUM_OF_HEIGHT.
              ADD 1 TO NO_OF_STUDENTS.
        END_OF_JOB.
              DIVIDE SUM_OF_HEIGHTS BY NO_OF_STUDENTS
                 GIVING AVERAGE_HEIGHT ROUNDED.
              DISPLAY NO_OF_STUDENTS.
              DISPLAY AVERAGE_HEIGHT.
              STOP RUN.
```

COBOL has been the dominant language for business data processing in the 70s and 80s. In the 90s we have seen the emergence of languages known as 4GLs (Fourth Generation Languages) which provide query languages (known as SQL – Structured Query Languages) to access data from data bases and manipulate them. 4GLs also have special features like "fill in the blanks" to obtain answers to queries and elegant form generation.

BASIC stands for *B*eginners' *A*ll purpose *S*ymbolic *I*nstruction *C*ode. BASIC was developed at Dartmouth College, U.S.A. in 1963 by Dr. John G. Kemeny and Thomas E.

Kurtz. The language is designed for a beginner and can be learnt quickly. A beginner is expected to develop a BASIC program while sitting at a computer terminal. As the program is entered, it is checked for syntax errors which can be immediately corrected. The translator for BASIC is thus an interpreter. BASIC is available on all personal (home) computers and even in some pocket calculators. BASIC as a language has not been standardized and that is probably its greatest drawback.

A program in BASIC to find the average height of students is given below:

```
5    REMARK: PROGRAM TO FIND AVERAGE HEIGHT
10   LET S = 0
20   LET N = 0
30   READ H
35   REMARK: H IS THE HEIGHT OF STUDENT
40   REMARK: N IS NUMBER OF STUDENTS
45   REMARK: S IS THE SUM OF HEIGHTS
50   LET S = S + H
60   LET N = N + 1
70   IF H = 0 THEN 90
80   GO TO 30
90   LET A = S/N
100  PRINT "AVERAGE HEIGHT", A
110  DATA 20, 30, 45, 50, 55, 60, 0
120  END
```

PASCAL is a programming language named after Blaise Pascal, the famous French mathematician who built one of the early calculating devices in 1642. This language was designed by Niklaus Wirth in 1971 with the primary aim of providing a language which allows beginners to learn good problem solving and programming methods. Pedagogical opinion is of the view that a simple and logical language is essential to teach programming to a beginner and to instil in him good programming habits. Pascal is widely recognized as such a language. Pascal has been standardized by International Standards Organization (ISO) and ANSI. Pascal has facilities to manipulate, not only numbers, but also vectors, matrices, strings of characters, sets, records, files and lists. Thus it is a very good language for "non-numeric" programming in which data are not numbers but are strings of characters, etc. Professional computer scientists find this language very attractive.

A Pascal program which does the same job as the other programs in the earlier part of this section is given below:

```
PROGRAM AVEHEIGHT (INPUT, OUTPUT);
Var    SUM, HEIGHT, AVERAGE: real;
       NUMBER: integer;
begin
       SUM:= 0; NUMBER:= 0;
       While not EOF(INPUT) do
```

```
    begin
       READ(HEIGHT);
       SUM:= SUM + HEIGHT;
       NUMBER:= NUMBER + 1
    end;
       AVERAGE:= SUM/NUMBER;
       WRITE ('AVERAGE HEIGHT = ', AVERAGE)
 end.
```

Unlike BASIC, Pascal is more readable and thus self-documenting.

ADA: Most computer languages evolve from the work of a small group and take years to get standardized. Through an initiative from the United States Department of Defence in early 1970s a standard for a programming language called Ada was approved in 1983 before a working compiler was written. Ada was designed based on world wide competition; a French entry by Jean Ichbiah won in 1979. Initially the language was named DOD-1 but the name was changed later to ADA in honour of Lady Ada Augusta Lovelace who is reputed to have programmed an early mechanical computer designed by Charles Babbage in UK in the 1850s. ADA is a large complex language which includes the concept of tasks, concurrent execution, real-time execution of tasks and exception handling of abstract data types. Due to its complexity, compilers did not appear till 1987 in spite of support and funding of U.S. Department of Defence. It was revised in 1995 to include better object orientation and better tasking models for processes. It is, however, more or less dead today probably due to its complexity and strong competition from C and later C++ and Java.

C Language: C was developed by Dennis Ritchie in 1972 at the Bell Telephone Laboratories in U.S.A. C had been defined so that it has the advantages of a high level language, namely, machine independence. At the same time it is concise, providing only the bare essentials required in a language so that a translator can translate it into an efficient machine language code. The first major use of C was to write an operating system known as UNIX. The current popularity of C is due to its efficiency and its connection with UNIX. Many ready-made programs used by UNIX which are written in C can be easily borrowed by a C programmer in writing application programs.

An aspect of C which makes it a powerful programming language is the access it provides to the addresses in memory where variables are stored. These addresses are known as pointers. The access to pointers and the operations which can be performed with pointers is what distinguishes C from other high level languages such as FORTRAN and COBOL. Pascal does provide pointers but restricts their use. C has minimal restrictions on the use of pointers. C has been standardized by ANSI. The main disadvantage of C, particularly for a beginner, is its conciseness and extensive use of pointers. Brief programs may be written to carry out complex computation. This is a disadvantage as it is difficult to read C programs and understand what they do particularly when pointers are used extensively.

Inspite of these deficiencies why has C become popular? The reasons are:

1. It is flexible and can be used to program a variety of applications.

2. It is efficient in the sense that the object code produced is concise. This is due to the fact that C is closer to machine language semantics.

3. C compilers are widely available and inexpensive

4. It is reasonably easy to port applications written in C to a variety of computers.

A C program which does the same job as the PASCAL program given in the last section is given below:

```
/* Program to find average height */
# include <stdio.h>
main ( )
    {  int number = 0;
       float sum, height, average;
       sum = 0;
       while (scanf ("%d", & height)!= EOF)
          { sum += height;
            ++ number;
          } /* end of while */
       printf ( " average height = %f\n");
    } /* end of main */
```

C++ *Language:* Languages such as FORTRAN, COBOL and C are purely algorithmic. These languages provide a methodology to break up a large job into a number of tasks and programming the tasks independently as functions or subroutines. These functions or subroutines are then combined to form a program. The general idea is to simplify debugging a program and to reuse the procedures in other programs which may need them. Over the years it was realized that this was not sufficient to enable re-use of programs. Subroutines and functions are too rigid in requiring a specific data type to be used and data to be passed to them in a rigid order. As the cost of programming continually increased it was realized that building programs using a library of reusable "components" was imperative. This led to the emergence of the so-called *object-oriented languages*. In these languages the concept of subroutine/functions is extended to that of an *object*. An object models a complex real world or abstract object. A real world object, for example, is a student whereas an abstract object is a course taken by a student. In an Object Oriented Program (OOP) an object is modelled by a collection of data structures and a set of procedures that can be performed on this data structure. A program consists of a collection of objects, each object providing a service when it is invoked and all the objects cooperating to get the job done. Objects are invoked by sending messages to them and objects return messages when the job is done.

The action performed in response to a message can vary depending on the data type of parameters. This is called *polymorphism*. Objects form a class hierarchy with superclass (parent) and subclass (child) relationship. An object can use procedures and data defined on objects in its superclass through *inheritance*.

The advantages of object oriented programming (OOP) accrue only when a large software project is undertaken—also known as "programming in the large". The methodology of OOP enables a programmer to remain close to the conceptual higher level model of the real world problem. One of earliest OOP language which was developed was Smalltalk. It, however, did not become popular. An object oriented version of C called C++ is currently (1998) the most popular OOP language. C++ was designed by B. Stroustrup in the mid 80s at the Bell Telephone Laboratories. It was designed as an extension of C and its popularity is mostly due to the popularity of C.

JAVA: Another development which has taken place in the last few years is the *internet* — an international network of a very large number of national computer networks. The technology developed in creating the internet has been adapted for networking computers within an organization. A computer network within an organization using protocols and providing services similar to an internet is called an *intranet*. In both inter and intranet small application programs (agents or objects to perform some services—known as *applets)* may be developed at any one of the computers connected to the network. One would like to create a new application by using these applets by either importing them to one's own computer or using them via the network. This is achieved by a language known as JAVA which is an object oriented language. This language achieves machine independence by defining a JAVA *virtual machine* for which the compiler is written. By a virtual machine we mean a non-existent machine. In other words it is a hypothetical machine which can be simulated by software similar to HYPCOM defined by us in Chapter 8. The JAVA code compiled for the virtual machine is then executed on any machine by an interpreter which generates machine code from the compiled code for that specific machine. This technique makes it easy to port JAVA language to any machine quickly (see Fig. 9.8). JAVA is getting wide acceptance now as a programming language to write applications for a network of heterogeneous computers.

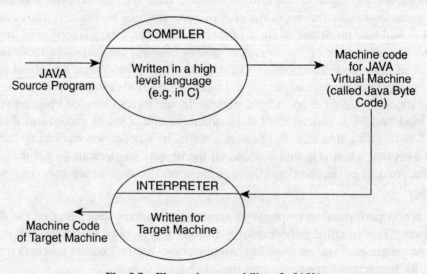

Fig. 9.8   Illustrating portability of JAVA.

Scripting Languages: Programming languages such as C and JAVA are also known as system programming languages as they have been used to develop large systems. For example C has been used to write the Unix operating system. System programming languages use strongly typing, that is, each variable must be declared as a particular type — real, integer, pointer etc. Typing is used both for easy readability and enabling more efficient compilation and error detection. Another class of languages which is gaining wide acceptance is called *scripting languages*. Scripting languages assume that a collection of useful programs, each performing a task, already exist. It has facilities to combine these components to perform a complex task. A scripting language may be thus thought of as a *gluing language* which glues together components. One of the earliest scripting language is *Unix Shell*. In Unix shell, filter programs read a stream of bytes from an input and write a stream of bytes to an output. Any two programs can be connected by attaching the output of one program to the input of the other. The following shell commands stacks three filters to count the number of lines in the selection that contains the word "language".

```
select | grep language | wc
```

The program `select` reads the given text that is currently on the display and prints the text on its output; the `grep` program reads this and prints as its output the lines containing the word "language"; the `wc` program counts the number of lines on its input. Each of these programs `select`, `grep` and `wc` are independent programs which could be combined with other programs also in many ways. Another popular scripting language is Visual Basic which is used to develop Graphical User Interfaces (GUIs) on the screen of a Visual Display Unit. It is expected that with increasing complexity of applications it will be more cost effective to glue together existing "program components" using scripting languages. In Table 9.3 we give a comparison of some of the languages.

Table 9.3 Comparison of Languages

	Assembly	System Programming (e.g. C)	Scripting (e.g. PERL)
No. of instructions/ statement of language	1	5	100
Specification of data types	None	Strong	Weak
Applications	Time Critical, Cost Critical	Routine applications	GUI, Gluing components

Non-Procedural Languages: In Procedural languages (also known as imperative languages) each statement causes the values stored in one or more memory locations to change. Program design consists of writing a sequence of statements which transform the "state" of the memory from an initial state to a final state which is the solution to the problem. In non-procedural languages, on the other hand, variables are not synonymous to locations in memory. They are treated as arguments of functions. One class of non-procedural languages are known as *applicative* or *functional languages*. These functional languages solve a problem by applying a set of functions to the initial variables in specific ways to get the answer. The syntax of such languages is similar to

$$f_n\ (f_{n-1}\ (f_{n-2}\ ....f_1\ (data))......)$$

where f's are the successive function applications which transform their arguments which, at the start, is the initial data. LISP and ML are two languages in use which support this model. LISP has been widely used to program Artificial Intelligence applications.

Another non-procedural class of languages are called *rule based languages* or *logic programming languages*. A logic program is expressed as a set of atomic sentences (known as facts) and Horn clauses (*if then* rules). A query is then posed. Execution of the program now begins and the system tries to find out if the answer to the query is *true* or *false* for the given facts and rules. PROLOG is the best known language of this type. PROLOG has also been extensively used in Artificial Intelligence applications.

We give in Fig. 9.9 a classification of programming languages.

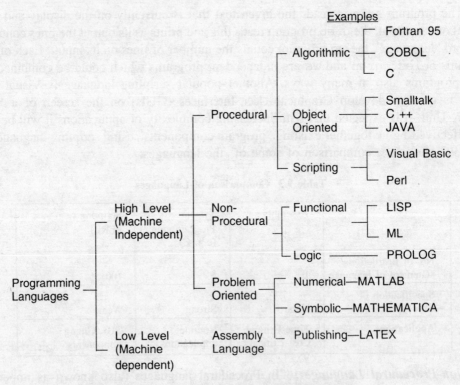

Fig. 9.9   Classification of Programming Languages.

9.6   CONCLUSIONS

The area of programming languages is dynamic even somewhat chaotic. As more sophisticated hardware systems appear in the market new computer applications emerge. These applications spawn new languages to solve such applications. Another trend is the continuous increase in complexity of applications as hardware become more sophisticated and cheaper. The increase in size of programs needs new methods of tackling complexity while keeping the cost of program development low and ensuring correctness of programs.

SUMMARY

1. The set of programs which provides the environment to write application programs is known as the system software of the computer.

2. A program written using the binary codes specified for the processor's operations and absolute binary memory addresses is known as the machine language of the computer.

3. Writing a machine language program involves clerical chores. To alleviate this, assembly languages were developed. The assembly language for a computer uses mnemonics to represent operation codes and symbolic addresses instead of absolute numerical addresses.

4. An assembly language has a one-to-one correspondence with the machine language of a computer and is thus machine dependent.

5. High level languages were developed to allow application programs to be run on a variety of computers. These languages are machine independent and procedure oriented. One statement in a high level language would be translated into many statements in its machine language equivalent.

6. A program written in a high level language is converted to a machine language program by a translator program. Translators are of two types: interpreter and compiler. An interpreter translates a program, one statement at a time, and immediately executes it. A compiler on the other hand translates the entire program into the lower level language and then executes it.

7. High level languages express algorithms using a concise, precise and unambiguous notation. These languages have facilities to describe data structures of relevance to the application area of the corresponding algorithm and operations appropriate to the data. They are often designed to be self-documenting.

8. High level programming languages are described precisely using lexical rule, syntax rules and semantic rules. Lexical rules specify the valid syntactic elements or "words" of a language. Syntax rules describe how these words are combined to form statements of the language and semantic rules assign meanings to valid statement of the language.

9. Syntax rules of a language are often described using a notation known as BNF notation.

10. Writing compilers for high level languages has been simplified using well known tools known as LEX and YACC which are used for lexical analysis and parsing of statements respectively.

11. The most commonly used high level languages are FORTRAN, COBOL, BASIC, PASCAL, C, C++ and JAVA.

12. FORTRAN is the most popular language for Engineering and Scientific work. COBOL is used mostly in business data processing.

13. BASIC is a simple high level language which can be learnt quickly by beginners and is popular among users of small computers.

14. Pascal is a language whose main use is in teaching computer programming to beginners. It has a rich data structure representation and is thus useful for system programs.

15. C is now a popular language. It is similar to Pascal but is more concise and efficient. It allows extensive use of pointers and has instructions for bit manipulation.

16. Object oriented programming is becoming popular as it allows reuse of old code and program generalization. C++ is an object oriented language.

17. The emergence of large computer networks gave an impetus to develop languages which can be executed on a variety of computers connected to the network. If application programs can be "imported" from different machines new applications can be developed using these. JAVA is an object oriented language which has been designed to enable easy application development using a network of computers.

18. Scripting languages assume that a collection of useful programs, each performing a task, already exist. It has facilities to combine these to perform a complex task. A scripting language can be thought of as a gluing language which glues together components. Some scripting languages are Unix Shell, Perl and Visual Basic.

19. Non-procedural languages concentrate on precisely defining specifications rather than detailed procedure to realize specifications. One class of non-procedural languages is known as Applicative or Functional language. LISP and ML are two languages of this type. Another class of non-procedural languages are rule-based languages. PROLOG is the best known language of this type.

REVIEW QUESTIONS

9.1 What do you understand by the term software of computers?

9.2 Define the terms systems software and application software.

9.3 What do you understand by the term machine language?

9.4 What is an assembly language for a computer?

9.5 What is an assembler?

9.6 Is assembly language to machine language translation one-to-one or one-to-many?

9.7 What do you understand by the term machine independent language?

9.8 What do you understand by the terms source code and object code?

9.9 What is a high level language?

9.10 What features are necessary in a high level language?

9.11 What do you understand by the term data structure?

9.12 What is the difference between syntax and semantics of a language?

9.13 What is the main difference between a procedure oriented language and a problem oriented language?

9.14 What are the major application areas of MATLAB?

9.15 What are the major application areas of MATHEMATICA?

9.16 What do you understand by lexical analysis?

9.17 An integer constant is a sequence of digits without a decimal point. It may have + or − sign. Give BNF definition of integer constant.

9.18 A real constant is a sequence of digits with one decimal point anywhere in it. It may have either sign + or −. Give BNF definition of a real constant.

9.19 What is a linker?

9.20 What is a loader?

9.21 What is LEX?

9.22 What is YACC?

9.23 What does the term FORTRAN stand for?

9.24 What are the most important application areas of FORTRAN?

9.25 What does the term COBOL mean?

9.26 In what applications is COBOL used?

9.27 What are various divisions in COBOL and what is the purpose of each division?

9.28 What are the distinctive advantages of COBOL?

9.29 What does the term BASIC stand for?

9.30 What is the major application area of BASIC?

9.31 What does the term Pascal stand for?

9.32 What are the main merits of Pascal?

9.33 What is ADA?

9.34 What is the main area of application of ADA?

9.35 In what way is C language different from Pascal?

9.36 What is C++ language? Why is it popular?

9.37 What is the difference between a procedure oriented language and a non-procedural language?

9.38 What are the major reasons for the popularity of C?

9.39 What do you understand by object oriented language? Give the names of three object oriented languages.

9.40 What is JAVA?

9.41 What is an applet?

9.42 What is a scripting language?

9.43 What is an applicative language? In what way is it different from a procedural language?

9.44 What is a logic programming language? Where is it used?

9.45 What are the main differences between scripting languages and procedure oriented languages?

10

Operating Systems

In this chapter we will first discuss the need for a system program called an *operating system*. We will then look at the evolution of operating systems during the last two decades and discuss their features.

10.1 WHY DO WE NEED AN OPERATING SYSTEM?

We saw in the last chapter that high level languages were developed to enable computer users to concentrate on designing appropriate algorithms for solving problems instead of being concerned with the details of a computer's internal structure. Operating systems were also developed with a similar objective. When a program written in a high level language is executed by a computer, the following steps are followed:

(i) The compiler to translate the program is loaded in the memory.

(ii) The source program is read and loaded in the memory.

(iii) The source program is compiled into the object code. While compiling, if any syntax errors are detected in the program, appropriate messages are printed.

(iv) During compilation, machine language routines for reading and writing required by the program are brought in from a library of routines stored in a peripheral store and linked to the object program.

(v) The compiler may now be taken out of the memory as its job is over and the space made available for the data of the program. The object program is now executed. If any errors are detected during execution, the contents of various registers in CPU at that time are communicated to the user to aid him in correcting the program.

When a computer has many languages, many compilers would be available. Therefore the appropriate compiler should be selected and loaded at Step 1. The input-output routines for different devices should include monitoring their status and detecting errors. These are programmed by experts with great care to relieve users of this chore. As all programs need these, they are kept in the disk storage with appropriate identification for easy retrieval.

In effect, a computer must provide, besides the hardware and high level language translators, many other routines which enable a user to effectively use the system. An *operating system* provides these routines. The user of a computer does not merely interact with the physical hardware of the machine. He interacts with a machine + compilers + an operating system. In Fig. 10.1 we have illustrated this fact. Thus a user of a modern computer uses a *virtual* (or non-existent) *machine* with features which include, besides those provided by its processor (arithmetic and logic operations), a number of functions provided by the operating system.

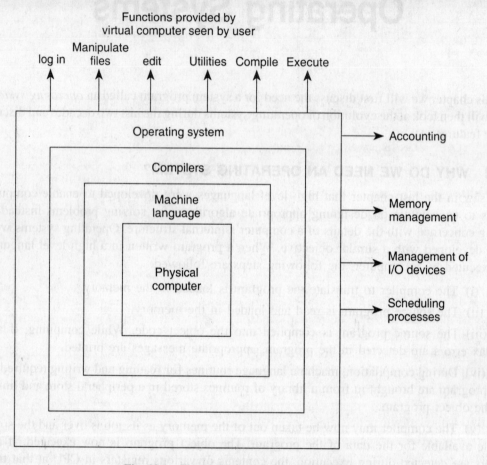

Fig. 10.1   Illustrating user's virtual machine.

An operating system may thus be defined as a set of system programs that control and coordinate the operation of a computer system. Some of the major facilities provided by a modern operating system are:

- Easy interaction between humans and computers
- Starting computer operation automatically when power is turned on
- Loading and scheduling users' programs along with necessary compilers
- Controlling input and output
- Controlling program execution
- Scheduling processes

- Managing use of main memory
- Managing and manipulating (e.g. editing) files
- Providing security to users' jobs and files
- Accounting resource usage

Every operating system has a *kernel* or a *nucleus* which permanently resides in the main memory of a computer to perform some of the basic functions of OS and to access other portions as and when they are needed. The remaining parts of an OS are normally stored in a disk ready to be loaded into the main memory when required and ordered to do so by the kernel.

10.2 BATCH OPERATING SYSTEM

The earliest operating systems, also called *control programs,* were a collection of commonly required utility programs stored in the main memory to provide the following simple services:

(i) Elementary I/O routines to ease a programmer's task.

(ii) Dumping of the contents of the memory on a line printer to facilitate detecting errors in programs.

(iii) A control supervisor that facilitated passing controls between subroutines.

While using such a control program a user fed his program and data and watched the progress of his job using the computer's console. Contents of the instruction register and the program counter value were displayed on the console.

When the job stalled for some reason, the user manipulated switches and restarted the program after 'fixing' the error. If the mistake was difficult to find, the contents of memory were printed and examined. After one job was completed, the memory was cleared and then the next program was loaded. These manual operations took time and the processor was made to wait between jobs.

The next step in the evolution of operating systems was to design a system to minimize the time wasted between jobs. A number of jobs were batched and kept ready. A *batch monitor* program was written which facilitated the transition from one program in the batch to the next without manual intervention. The algorithm of a batch monitor was:

While there are jobs in the input queue *do*
 begin
   Read program;
   compile program;
   if no error *then* execute object code
       else give error message and quit;
   if error during execution then give error message;
 end

Each job was identified by a distinctive "program-begin" statement and a "program-end" statement. The batch monitor used these statements to separate one job from the next.

Whenever a computer accepts a batch of programs for processing, some means should be available to separate each job, provide to it the appropriate compiler, detect errors and provide I/O routines. For this purpose each program has, besides the program itself, a set of instructions called *job control language* instructions which instruct the *batch operating system* on the identity and the requirements of the job. A typical job would have the structure shown in Table 10.1. All the job control language statements start with $ in first column to distinguish them from regular program statements (This implies that no program or data should have $ in its first column).

Table 10.1   Illustrating job control language statements

Job control statements

$ JOB IDENTITY, PASSWORD
$ Pages to be printed, memory needed, time needed, etc.
$ Files needed
$ Name of compiler to be used
$ Program beginning

Program statements

$ Start of data

Data

$ End of job

The $JOB statement signals the beginning of a new job to the batch operating system. It checks the identification number given by the user with the file of valid numbers. Most systems also have a password besides the user identity number to provide added protection. This password is checked to see if it is valid for the given programmer and then the batch operating system proceeds to the next step of the job. The batch operating system also keeps track of the resources used by the programmer. This information is also used to prematurely terminate a job if resources used exceed what was requested by the user in his job control statement. Paths for accessing files specified by the programmer are opened. The compiler specified by the user is fetched from the back-up memory and placed in the main memory to facilitate translation of his program. The program is then translated and executed. Devices required by the user are activated and all the input/output operations are performed. A log of all activities, particularly errors detected, are listed along with the output of the program and spooled on the back-up memory. When $END of job statement is encountered, the batch operating system closes access paths to files used by the job, clears the memory, and gets ready to read the next job. A good batch operating system ensures that any errors made by a program do not affect other jobs in the queue.

10.3 MULTIPROGRAMMING OPERATING SYSTEM

In a batch operating system, programs are taken from the queue and executed one after the other in the order in which they appear in the queue. The program currently being executed will be the primary occupant of the memory and it will have the CPU exclusively available to itself. If the program needs data or has to output a result, it will read from, or write on the secondary memory (normally disk). Even though disks are faster compared to the I/O units they are slower than the CPU by a factor of 20 to 100. If a program has a large amount of data to be read or results to be printed (as often happens in commercial data processing), the expensive CPU will be idle most of the time waiting for I/O. Such programs are called *I/O-bound programs.* Programs used for science and engineering computations, on the other hand, need very little I/O but require high speed processing. These programs are known as *processor-bound programs.* In early computers, I/O was performed under CPU's control and thus I/O and CPU could not work simultaneously.

With improvements in computer technology two major developments took place. Very large, random access, high-speed main memories (about 2M bytes) became available at low cost. Magnetic disk memory capacity also increased to about 100 Megabytes and its cost also came down. Thus it became feasible to store many users' programs simultaneously in the main memory. I/O could be directed to disks, which, being direct-access memories, allowed fast and convenient storage of information. Small specialized processors were associated with disks which could monitor direct information transfer between main memory and disk without using the CPU. In effect, I/O operations between disk and memory could go on while CPU was busy processing another program.

These developments in hardware led to the advent of multiprogramming operating systems. In a multiprogramming operating system, a number of programs belonging to different users are kept simultaneously in distinct areas in the main memory. A program called a monitor is also permanently kept in a portion of the memory. Each program is said to occupy a *partition* in memory. For example, the programs A, B, C, D, E, each occupies a partition in the memory in Fig. 10.2. The monitor will have the job of scheduling the computers' resources to these programs. In Table 10.2 we show the various states the program can be in. Observe that at time t_1 the status of the job is as shown in the first row of the table. Suppose at time t_2, program A needs some input. The monitor would then stop executing it and schedule program B to the CPU. In the meanwhile, if C completes its input, then it will wait for CPU. If D's output is completed then it will be taken out of memory and a program waiting in the disk will be brought into the main memory.

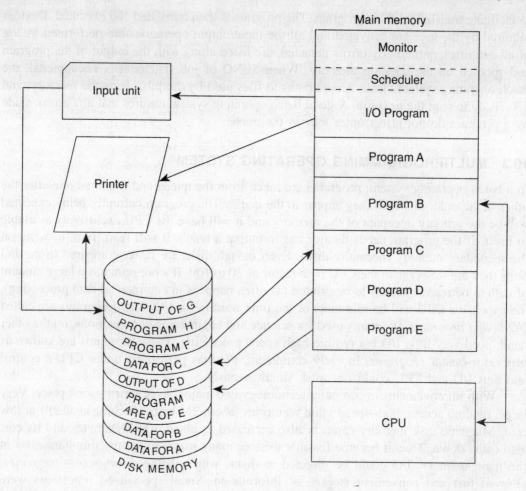

Fig. 10.2   Illustrating a multiprogramming operating system.

Table 10.2   Illustrating the various states of programs in a multiprogramming system

Time	PROGRAM A	PROGRAM B	PROGRAM C	PROGRAM D	PROGRAM E	PROGRAM F
t_1	Being executed using CPU.	Waiting in memory for CPU.	Reading input data from disk	Writing output data on disk	Being taken out of memory and stored on disk as it is completed.	Ready and waiting in disk for space in main memory.
t_2	Wants data and starts reading from disk	Starts execution using CPU	Waits for CPU if input over	If program over then being taken out of memory and stored on disk	Results being printed on printer from disk	Being read into area vacated by Program E

For multiprogramming to effectively overlap the operations of the processor and I/O devices, it is necessary that when a program is waiting for I/O, another program must have enough computation to keep the processor busy. If all programs need I/O at the same time, the processor will again be idle. As the speed mismatch between I/O and processor is quite large (100 to 1), it is necessary to have a suitable mix of programs—some processor-bound and others I/O-bound (4 to 8 programs)—so that at least one of the programs which does not need I/O is available to the processor.

For a computer to work simultaneously on many programs, a number of special hardware and software features are required. First, the main memory of the computer should be large enough to accommodate all the programs. It should be possible to stop executing a program and restart it on the basis of signals received from I/O devices. In order to restart a program, all the values that were stored in memory and the CPU registers that were being used at the time of its stopping should be restored. The information stored in memory allocated to one program should not be disturbed by another program. A new program would however need all CPU registers for its use and would clear them. Thus, before a program is suspended, the values of all CPU registers (namely PC, accumulator, etc.) should be stored in the memory area of that program.

Besides this, it is necessary to prevent a program from writing in areas of memory occupied by another program. In order to achieve this, specific areas in memory are reserved for each program. Along with this reservation, the program is provided with a *protection lock* by the hardware. A program is allowed to write in an area of memory only if its key fits the protection lock. This hardware feature is called the *memory protect feature.*

The monitor has the functions of scheduling programs to CPU based on their priority, supervising I/O of all the programs in main memory, bringing in new programs from disk to main memory and taking out completed programs from the memory to the disk.

10.4 TIME SHARING OPERATING SYSTEM

If a computer is used in a batch mode, a user submits his program along with a number of other users and all the jobs are put in a job-queue and fed to the computer. A number of jobs in the queue are kept in the computer's memory and a multiprogramming operating system is invoked which schedules the execution of individual jobs with the main objective of keeping all the units of the computer simultaneously busy. Using this method the total number of jobs processed by the computer in a given period is maximized. This is known as maximizing the computer's *throughput.* It is more desirable for an individual user to minimize the time elapsed between the submission of his job and obtaining the results. This time is known as the *turnaround* time. If the user is able to use the computer to only execute his job and no other jobs, this turnaround time will be minimum. During program development it is very desirable for a programmer to observe the effect of changes in his program on results. A multiprogrammed batch system will not allow such an interaction to an individual programmer because its aim is to increase the throughput of a computer system. *Time sharing operating systems* were evolved to give rapid turnaround to an individual user while catering to many users.

It is not economically feasible to allow a single user to use a large computer interactively as his speed of thinking and typing is much slower than the processing speed of a computer. Thus the computer would be idle most of the time if a single user used it interactively. It is therefore necessary to allow a large number of users, each using the computer interactively, to time-share the computer. This is achieved by using a time sharing operating system. In such a time sharing system, many video terminals are attached to the computer. Each user has a terminal available to him. A user can initiate a program from his terminal and interact with it during its execution. Typically, a user enters a program from a terminal and corrects any typing errors during program entry. The program is then stored as a file on disk. The user then compiles his program by invoking a compiler through a command from the terminal. If any syntax errors are found in the program by the compiler, they are displayed on the video screen. The user corrects his program with an editing system and recompiles it from the terminal. When all the syntax errors are corrected, the program is submitted to the processor for execution. The requisite data is fed from the terminal during program execution. The data may also be stored in a data file on disk and fed to the program when needed. Errors encountered during execution of the program are displayed on the terminal. If no errors are found, the answers may either be displayed on the terminal or stored in a file on disk.

In a time shared computer a number of terminals (around 50) are used simultaneously and each terminal is provided access to the computer's resources. The time sharing operating system allocates about 20 milliseconds to each terminal during which a program belonging to this terminal user is executed. In 20 milliseconds, about $20 \times 10^{-3} \times 10^6$ (= 20,000) instructions can be carried out by a processor whose speed is of the order of 1 million instructions per second. If there are 50 terminals working simultaneously and if 20 milliseconds is allocated to each terminal, a given terminal will get the processor's attention once in every 20×50 milliseconds = 1 second. As human reaction times are a few seconds, a terminal user will not notice any delay in carrying out his commands and may feel that the machine is working solely for himself! As the total memory available in a computer is limited, it is not possible to keep the entire programs of all the users of a time sharing system simultaneously in the main memory. The time sharing operating system would keep only that portion of a program which is being executed currently in the main memory. The remaining part is kept in the disk storage. As and when a segment of a program is to be executed, it is brought back to the main memory from the disk and the inactive segment sent to the disk. The operation of transferring programs from the main memory to the disk storage and back is known as *swapping*.

Multiprogramming is necessary in a time sharing system because a number of programs are kept in the disk memory. Thus one may view a time sharing operating system as a multiprogramming operating system with a job scheduling algorithm to aid simultaneous interactive use of a computer by many users.

10.5 PERSONAL COMPUTER OPERATING SYSTEM

The advent of Personal Computers (PCs) has brought about a revolution in computer use.

The main mode of use of a PC (as its name implies) is by a single user. Thus OS for PCs were designed as a single user single task operating system, that is, it is assumed that only one user uses the machine and runs only one program at a time.

The operating system of PCs consists of two parts. One part is called the BIOS (Basic Input Output System) which is stored in a non-erasable memory called ROM (Read Only Memory). The other part called the DOS (Disk Operating System) is stored in a floppy disk or a hard disk. A DOS called MS-DOS (Microsoft Disk Operating System) is widely used.

When power is turned on BIOS takes control. It does what is known as power-on-self-test. The test sees whether memory is OK and all other relevant units function. Having done this, it reads from the disk a small portion of OS known as the *boot* and loads it into the main memory. This boot program then "pulls" the rest of the OS from the disk and stores it in the main memory. This is known as *booting the system*. Among other programs contained in BIOS are:

- system configuration analysis
- time-of-day
- I/O support programs for
  - keyboard
  - disk
  - floppy
  - printer
  - display

One of the main features of BIOS is that it provides hardware-independent access to the physical devices of PC ensuring that programs are simple and portable to other PCs.

BIOS provides basic low-level services whereas DOS provides many user-level services. The major services provided by DOS are:

- File management which allows users to create, edit, read, write and delete files.
- Directory management which allows creation, change, search and deletion of directories.
- Memory management which allows allocation and deallocation of memory.
- Command interpreter which interprets commands issued by the user and executes DOS functions, utility programs or application programs.
- Executive functions which provide programs to load and execute user programs, retrieve error codes, correct and rerun programs.
- Utility programs that do housekeeping chores such as COPY, ERASE, DIR etc.

The interfaces and levels of functionality of MS-DOS are not well separated (Fig. 10.3). Application programs can access I/O routines to write directly on disk, VDU etc. This allows programs to corrupt users' systems without their knowledge.

Earlier versions of MS-DOS were written for smaller IBM systems which used Intel

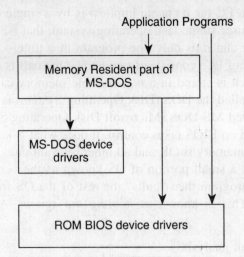

Fig. 10.3   Structure of MS-DOS operating system.

8088 microprocessor. They limited program addressability to 640 Kbytes. Further, MS-DOS does not allow two programs stored in memory to run concurrently protected from one another.

Currently microprocessors have become very powerful. They use fast processors such as Intel Pentium and have main memories of 32 MB and hard disk of 2 GB. MS-DOS due to its limitation cannot use this power. Thus newer OS have been developed and are currently being used. The important ones are MS-WINDOWS, and WINDOWS-NT designed by Microsoft Corporation, OS2 designed by IBM, and UNIX designed by AT&T. We will discuss first MS-WINDOWS and OS2. UNIX is described in the next section. WINDOWS-NT is briefly described in Section 10.7.1.

The main objectives of MS-WINDOWS are to provide an easier way for a user to work with a PC, to use the full memory available in a PC and use other advanced features available in the latest PCs. The major new facility provided by MS-WINDOWS is a Graphical User Interface. Instead of typing in commands a user can point at a graphical icon presented on the VDU and click a mouse button. For example to delete a file one can point a trash appearing on the screen to the file and click the button on the mouse. MS-WINDOWS also allows *multitasking*. By multitasking we mean the possibility of running one out of a number of programs stored in the main memory using the CPU without in any way disturbing the individual programs. As a PC is used by an individual and human response is much slower than computer speed, a multitasking system will look to a user as though it is running many programs concurrently in the CPU. A user may thus be running more than one program when such an OS is available. For example, while editing a file in the foreground a sorting job can be given in the background. The status of each of the programs can be viewed on the screen of the VDU by partitioning the screen into a number of windows. The progress of programs can be viewed on different windows. IBM's OS2 provides facilities such as multitasking, good graphical user interface and multiple windows which is comparable to that provided by MS-WINDOWS.

10.6 THE UNIX OPERATING SYSTEM

UNIX is a multiuser, time sharing operating system which was written in 1973 by Ritchie and Thomson at the Bell Telephone laboratories, U.S.A. It was not conceived as a commercial system but was written for the convenience of a group of programmers at Bell Laboratories. It was written for a small computer—the PDP 11 manufactured by the Digital Equipment Corporation (DEC). Unlike all operating systems in the 70s, UNIX was written in a high level language—C which was a revolutionary step. By writing the Operating System in C both storage and running time increased by 30% to 40% but as events have shown, this loss in efficiency did not affect the spread of UNIX as a Operating System because computers became larger, faster and cheaper every year. It became a very popular operating system which has been implemented on a wide variety of computers. The variety of UNIX systems implemented use the general philosophy advocated by UNIX designers but differ in implementation details. The version of UNIX implemented by IBM on their workstations is called AIX. Hewlett Packard's version of UNIX is known as HP-UX, Sun's version is called SOLARIS and DEC's version ULTRIX. A version available in the open domain (by open domain we mean that the source code is available free of cost for non commercial use and can be copied from a computer connected to the internet) is called LINUX. One may wonder why UNIX is popular? The major reasons for its popularity are:

- UNIX is written in C, a high level language, and is thus portable to a variety of computers.
- The interface provided to users is simple but yet powerful. It provides most of the services which a user normally wants.
- The file system used by UNIX is hierarchical which allows efficient implementation and easy maintenance.
- UNIX considers all files to be a continuous sequence of characters, known as a *byte stream*. Application programs thus have the flexibility to format the files as per their requirements.
- UNIX treats peripheral devices as if they are files. Peripherals are given device file names and thus programs can access devices with the same syntax they use when accessing regular files. Thus UNIX provides a simple, consistent interface to peripheral devices.
- UNIX is a multi-user multiprogrammed operating system. Individual users can, execute several processes simultaneously. It can also be time shared by several users and this is a multitasking system.
- UNIX supports a scripting language (see Chapter 9) called *shell* which allows complex jobs to be performed using several built-in programs provided by UNIX. The output of a shell command can be fed as input to another command, without the need to store the output in a file, by a mechanism known as a *pipe*.
- UNIX assumes no knowledge of machine architecture from the user. Thus programs written using UNIX can be run on a variety of architectures.

- UNIX can support any programming language that has a compiler or an interpreter provided it has an interface that maps user requests for Operating system services to the standard set of requests used by UNIX.

As we can see from the above, the philosophy of design of UNIX emphasises uniformity and simplicity.

10.6.1 UNIX System Layers

The UNIX OS can be thought of as a layered system. The innermost core is called the *kernel*. Kernel is a set of programs which perform various primitive operations requested by user processes. The following services are provided by the UNIX kernel.

- Controlling the creation, suspension and termination of processes. Inter-process communication is also controlled by the kernel.

- Scheduling processes on the CPU. In a time shared mode the CPU is shared by several processes. Thus (to be fair) each process is given a time slice. When the time slice expires the process is suspended and one of the waiting processes is scheduled. The suspended process is scheduled again when its turn comes.

- Main memory is allocated to an executing process as requested by the process. If sufficient memory is not available a waiting process is written on a disk and memory occupied by it is temporarily allocated to the executing process. Processes may have private and public address space. Kernel protects the private address space from accidental tampering.

- It manages users' files by providing them space in secondary storage, protecting them from illegal access and ensuring efficient storage and retrieval.

- It provides processes controlled access to peripheral devices such a terminals, disk drives, network devices etc.

All these services are provided by hiding all low level details from user processes.

The next layer has programs supported by the OS. The most interesting of these is one called *shell* which is a command interpreter.

There are a large number of very useful commands provided by shell. Users can create a series of shell commands and store it in a file. This file can be made an executable file and when invoked will act like a new shell command. UNIX also provides a very interesting idea called a *pipe*. A pipe is a way to send the output of one program as the input of another program without storing the output of the first program in a temporary file. A *pipeline* is a connection of two or more programs through pipes.

There are a large family of UNIX shell programs that read an input, perform a single transformation, and write an output. For example there is a command called *grep* which searches a file for lines that match a given pattern and outputs them. A command *sort* sorts a file as per some specification. A command that accepts its standard input, processes it and sends the result to its standard output is called a *filter*. Apart from filters provided by the system, a user can create his own filter by combining shell commands.

The outermost layer of UNIX has language compilers for C, Fortran 90 etc. A unique feature of the language compilers in UNIX is that it provides a common object code format which allows easy mixing of high level languages.

UNIX has some good text processing programs. Many additional utilities such as calendar, games, graphics etc., are available. In Fig. 10.4 we show the structure of the layers in UNIX.

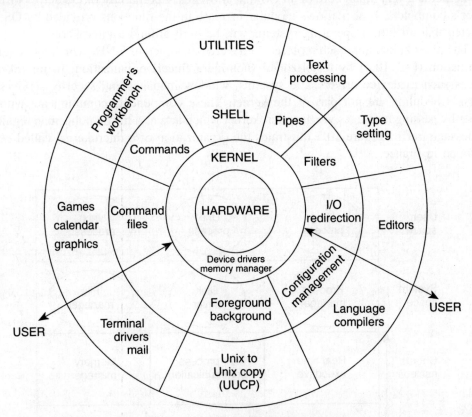

Fig. 10.4 Layers of UNIX operating system.

Execution of user processes on UNIX systems is divided into two modes known as *user mode* and *kernel mode*. When a user process requests services provided by the UNIX kernel the execution mode changes from the user mode to the kernel mode. In user mode the user process can access their own instructions and data and not those belonging to the kernel. The kernel process can however access addresses of user processes. Further, there are some special hardware instructions which can be executed only in kernel mode. It should be remembered that the kernel runs on behalf of a user process and does not function independently. Processing interrupts and exceptions and management of memory are all delegated to the kernel.

10.7 MICROKERNEL BASED OPERATING SYSTEM

Operating systems continuously evolve and adapt to newer requirements imposed by the technology and the market. UNIX was the first major attempt towards portable OS. Portability was achieved by using C as the language for writing UNIX. However UNIX is not easily portable as the kernel of UNIX provides, besides low-level machine dependent functions, device management, interprocess communication etc., and is quite large. In order to make an OS portable it is necessary to make the machine dependent part as small as possible. A microkernel is a very small core of an OS that allows easy portability of OS across different vendor's computers. It also allows modular increase in the functions provided by OS. It is predicted that all future operating systems will be built around a microkernel.

The microkernel approach replaces the layered approach of UNIX which has a vertical stratification (Fig. 10.4) by a horizontal (non-hierarchical) organization. In microkernels services such as device drivers, file systems, window management, security services and process scheduling are not part of the kernel. These components communicate with one another by passing messages via the microkernel which acts as a traffic policeman regulating the message traffic. Figure 10.5 illustrates the organization of a microkernel called *chorus* developed in France.

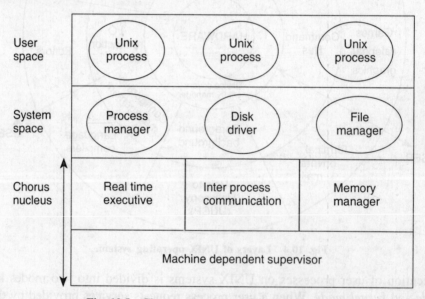

Fig. 10.5 Chorus microkernel OS organization.

Many computer software vendors are developing their new operating system based on microkernels. For example Microsoft has now developed an OS called WINDOWS-NT which has features similar to WINDOWS but is portable to non IBM PC platforms. Microkernel based OS have also been announced by Sun Microsystems (Spring OS) by IBM (Workplace OS), Taligent OS (by a cooperating group of vendors), and Novell's UNIX Systems (chorus). We will describe Windows NT now.

10.7.1 Windows NT Operating System

The Microsoft Windows NT Operating System is the latest offering of Microsoft primarily intended as a portable OS for the new generation of powerful microprocessors. Versions of NT have been ported to DEC Alpha workstations, Power PC and MIPS R4000 based workstations. The two versions of NT are Windows NT Workstation and Windows NT Server. They use the same kernel and OS code but the server is configured for client-server application. NT uses a micro-kernel architecture which facilitates selective enhancement of parts of the OS. Windows NT is a multi-user, multitasking system. The major goals in NT design are:

- Portability with compliance to Portable Operating System Interface (POSIX) standard
- Compatibility with applications written in MS-DOS or MS Windows
- Security against virus attacks
- Multiprocessor support
- Easy enhancement capability
- Support for international use with multi-lingual and multi-currency features. For supporting a variety of languages (e.g., Chinese and Japanese) it uses UNICODE for characters which is a 16 bit character code.

10.8 ON-LINE AND REAL TIME SYSTEMS

A time shared operating system allows a user to interact with the computer and it facilitates program development. The *response time* of a good computer system to users' requests is of the order of 1 or 2 seconds. Delays in response are irritating to a user but are not catastrophic. Files of users are available "on-line" in a disk and may be retrieved quickly.

The availability of large disk storage in such systems makes it feasible to store large volumes of data and to retrieve them fast. This facility is very useful in implementing systems such as an airline reservation system. In such a system, the response time should be very short because a customer's reservation is to be done while he waits. A short delay, however, would not be disastrous. Files should, however, be updated immediately after a transaction is completed. As soon as a seat is reserved for a flight, the available seats should be reduced by one. Such systems are called *on-line systems.*

There are applications in which a computer is expected to control the operation of a physical system. For example, a satellite in orbit may be controlled by a computer. The position, velocity, acceleration and spin information of the satellite may be fed to a computer which may be programmed to compute the orbit and give instructions to rocket motors to correct the orbit. In such an application the operation is in *"real time"*, that is, the control has to be exercised during the actual functioning of the system. Any delay beyond that specified for control would be disastrous. Real time operating systems have to work within strict time limits for critical jobs. Critical jobs are locked in memory and receive the highest priority.

Real time systems are required to be highly reliable. Any failure of a system which controls a space vehicle in motion may result in a fatal accident. In such cases, duplicate systems are used so that if one system fails, the other will take over.

SUMMARY

1. An operating system of a computer is a set of system programs which provides a number of facilities to a user to allow easy use of the computer. Among the facilities provided are (a) programs to control input/output devices, (b) programs to select appropriate translators requested by a user, (c) allocation of resources of a computer, (d) program to manage user files, and (e) provides a good interface for human-computer interaction.

2. To reduce the time wasted between jobs when a number of jobs are to be processed by a machine, and to reduce the manual operations of loading each job, a batch monitor system is used. In this system, jobs are made into a batch and fed to the computer. The monitor loads the appropriate compiler for each job, compiles the program, keeps track of error messages and facilitates smooth transition from job to job.

3. To alleviate the speed mismatch between I/O devices and CPU in a high speed computer, a batch operating system spools all programs and results in a secondary memory (disk). The spooling is done by a slower, inexpensive computer. The faster computer takes the programs from disk, computes the results and places the results on the disk. The I/O computer prints the results from this secondary memory.

4. A multiprogrammed operating system keeps in a computer's memory a set of jobs belonging to different users, schedules them on CPU, provides I/O facilities requested by each user and optimizes the use of the computer's resources. The primary objective of a multiprogrammed operating system is to maximize the number of programs executed by a computer in a specified period and keep all the units of the computer simultaneously busy. In other words, it maximizes the throughput of a computer.

5. A time shared operating system allows a number of users to simultaneously use a computer. The primary objective of a time shared operating system is to provide fast response to each user of the computer. Programmer productivity is considerably improved through access to a time shared computer.

6. Personal Computers are now widely used. The majority of PC users use a single user OS called MS-DOS along with a Basic Input Output System (BIOS). BIOS is stored in a ROM supplied by the hardware vendor. BIOS provides the device drivers and initial program to load the MS-DOS into memory. MS-DOS provides services such as editing, file management and other utility programs.

7. MS-Windows is an improved OS for more powerful PCs which have a large memory (16 to 32 MB) and disk (2 to 4 GB). This provides a very good Graphical User Interface (GUI) which simplifies the use of the computer. It also allows multiple programs to be simultaneously stored in memory and executed. A user can see the progress of computation in multiple windows.

8. UNIX is a very popular multiuser, time sharing OS implemented in a large class of machines from PCs to supercomputers. It is popular as it provides a very simple yet powerful command interpreter. UNIX is written in C, thus making it portable. UNIX is organized as a layered OS. The innermost part is called the kernel. It provides low level services such as device drivers and memory management. The next level is called the shell and is a command interpreter. The outermost level provides miscellaneous services. The user interacts with the kernel using commands and utilities.

9. A new development in the design of Operating Systems is the emergence of microkernel based OS. A microkernel is a very small machine dependent part of the OS which coordinates the activities of other servers within OS providing services such as memory management, device management, process scheduling and file management. Microkernel based OS are easily portable across computers.

10. An on-line system has files which are updated as soon as a transaction is completed. Response time should be short but a delay would not be fatal. Airline reservation systems fall in this category.

11. A real time system is used in the control of physical systems. The response time of such systems should match the needs of the physical system. A delay in response may lead to fatal failures.

REVIEW QUESTIONS

10.1 What is an operating system of a computer?

10.2 Why is an operating system required for a computer?

10.3 What facilities are provided by an operating system to a user?

10.4 What do you understand by the term "users' virtual machine"?

10.5 What do you understand by the term batch operating system?

10.6 What facilities are provided by a batch operating system?

10.7 What do you understand by the term multiprogramming?

10.8 Why is multiprogramming used in a computer?

10.9 What special hardware features are required in a computer to implement multi-programming?

10.10 What do you understand by the term "throughput" of a computer system?

10.11 What do you understand by the term "turnaround time"?

10.12 What do you understand by the term "time sharing operating system"?

10.13 Why is a time sharing operating system used?

10.14 What hardware facilities are required to implement time sharing in a computer system?

10.15 Is time sharing and multiprogramming mutually exclusive?

10.16 What do you understand by the term response time of a time sharing system?

10.17 What are the functions of a BIOS in PCs?

10.18 Why is BIOS stored in a ROM?

10.19 What are the functions of MS-DOS?

10.20 How is MS-DOS loaded into main memory?

10.21 What do you understand by booting?

10.22 What does the boot sector in a DOS disk contain?

10.23 Is MS-DOS a multiuser OS?

10.24 How does MS-WINDOWS differ from MS-DOS?

10.25 What facilities are provided by MS-WINDOWS?

10.26 Why has UNIX become a popular OS?

10.27 Is UNIX a multiuser OS?

10.28 What are the functions of the kernel of UNIX?

10.29 What is a shell in UNIX?

10.30 What do you understand by shell programming?

10.31 What facilities are provided by the outermost layer of UNIX OS?

10.32 What do you understand by UNIX pipes?

10.33 What do you understand by a UNIX filter?

10.34 What is multitasking?

10.35 In what way is multitasking different from multiprogramming?

10.36 What is a microkernel?

10.37 What are the advantages of designing a microkernel based OS?

10.38 Distinguish between a real-time system and an on-line system.

10.39 Give an example of a real-time system.

10.40 Why is response time critical in a real-time system?

10.41 Give the most important requirement of an on-line system?

10.42 What are objectives of Windows NT OS?

10.43 What is LINUX?

10.44 Why does Windows NT use microkernel based design?

10.45 Is Windows NT multitasking?

10.46 What is UNICODE?

10.47 Can MS-DOS applications be run on Windows NT?

10.48 Is Windows NT prone to virus attacks?

10.49 Is UNIX a multitasking OS?

10.50 Does Windows NT provide multiprocessor support?

11

Microcomputers

In the previous chapters we had an overview of the logical organization of computers and the software systems necessary to use a computer. In this chapter we will take an example of a specific 'real life'. computer. We have chosen to discuss microcomputers first as they have ushered in a revolution in computer usage by making computers inexpensive and widely available.

The first microprocessor chip, which is the main component of a microcomputer, was invented by Dr. Ted Hoff of Intel Corpn. (USA) in 1969 and it became a commercial product in 1971. Since then technology has progressed rapidly and we now see what has been called the 'fourth generation' microprocessors. There is also a multitude of manufacturers with a bewildering array of products. It would be counter-productive to concentrate on a specific processor in an introductory presentation. We will thus give a general picture.

11.1 AN IDEAL MICROCOMPUTER

The ideal microcomputer is a self-contained computer fabricated as an *integrated circuit* (IC) on a single chip of silicon. The microcomputer (Fig. 11.1) has N input lines feeding it and M output lines coming from it. Within the microcomputer a program is stored to

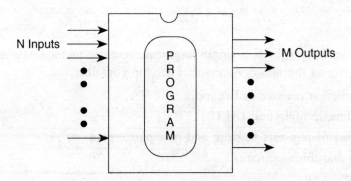

Fig. 11.1 An ideal microcomputer.

process the data presented to it through the N input lines. The data processed by the program is put on the M output lines which may be connected to displays, actuators, printers, digital to analog convertors or any one of a host of output devices. Both the input and the output are constrained to be binary digits. The outputs at any instant of time are thus dependent on the complete history of past inputs and the stored program.

11.2   AN ACTUAL MICROCOMPUTER

Even though the ideal microcomputer would have enough memory within it to store a program, in actual practice (with the current state-of-the-art), sufficient storage cannot be provided within a single IC chip for programs and data. Besides this, the number of input and output lines is constrained by the technology. A typical microcomputer would thus consist of the following units (Fig. 11.2):

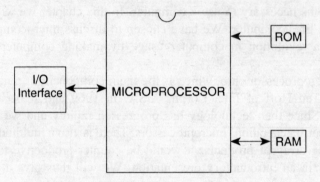

Fig. 11.2   A typical microcomputer.

1. A microprocessor on a single IC chip which is the CPU.
2. A Random Access Memory (RAM) used normally to store program and data.
3. A Read Only Memory (ROM) used normally to store invariant programs.
4. Input/Output (I/O) interface units.

11.2.1   CPU

The Central Processing Unit is a single largescale semiconductor integrated circuit (LSI) chip and is known as the *microprocessor*. The chip contains:

- An instruction register and decoder
- An arithmetic logic unit (ALU)
- A number of registers to store and manipulate data
- Control and timing circuits
- Cache memory

The microprocessor is connected to the other units in the system by means of an *address bus,* a *data bus* and a *control bus.* The functions of the various units are described below:

(i) *Instruction register and decoder:* The instruction register holds the instruction read from memory. The decoder sends the control signals appropriate to the decoded instruction to the ALU.

(ii) *Arithmetic logic unit*: The ALU has circuits to perform the basic arithmetic operations (add, subtract), logical operations (and, or, complement, exclusive or), register operations (clear, shift, load, move, etc.), memory operations (store, read), program sequencing control operations (such as jump, conditional jump, jump to subroutine) and input/output operations.

In addition, it usually has two registers known as the accumulator and temporary register. It also has a status register which typically has bits which are set to 1 to indicate the results of ALU operation. The status bits are:

Negative result
Zero result
Overflow of result
Carry
Parity
Interrupt mask bits to enable interrupts from I/O devices.

Figure 11.3 gives the structure of CPU and its connection.

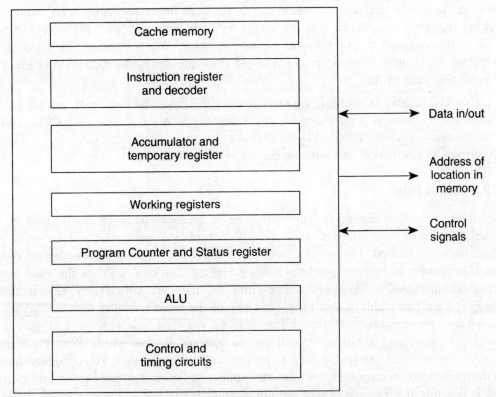

Fig. 11.3   The internal structure of a microprocessor.

(iii) *Working registers:* The time required to retrieve data from registers and to store results in them is at least four times faster than that required to retrieve and store data in the RAM. Thus some working registers are provided in the CPU to store temporarily intermediate results obtained during computation. Besides these, there are two other registers known as PC (Program Counter) and SP (Stack Pointer). The PC register holds the address of the instruction to be executed next. A stack is a sequence of locations in the RAM which is reserved for a specific purpose. The stack pointer is a register which holds the address of the first location (also known as the top location) of the stack.

When a program is to be written for carrying out a task, it is advisable to break it up into a number of subtasks. Each subtask can then be programmed as a small program called a *subprogram*. The subprograms are then linked up with a main program to perform the task. This method facilitates rapid program development.

When a subprogram is to be called while executing a program the contents of PC should be stored so that control can return to the (calling) program. The PC value is stored in RAM, and the address of the location in RAM where PC is stored, is stored in SP. Another type of a call by a program is a call to an interrupt service routine to input or output data from peripheral units. Normally, important I/O ports are allowed to interrupt the CPU during normal program execution. Such an interrupt is initiated by hardware. When an interrupt is encountered, the contents of all the important registers (Accumulator, working registers) are pushed into the stack. As each byte is pushed the address stored in SP is decremented to point to the top of the stack. When the interrupt servicing is completed, the values in registers are restored from the stack. As each byte is restored, SP is incremented by 1.

(iv) The number of working registers in the CPU has to be kept small as they should be addressable. As was pointed out the main memory is much slower than CPU. Thus a cache memory is used in the CPU to alleviate the speed mismatch (see Sec. 8.2). The normal size of instruction and data caches are around 32 KB each.

11.2.2   Data Bus

One of the important limitations in fabricating a microcomputer on an IC chip is the limited number of pins allowed on it. Thus the number of pins allocated for input and output lines are limited. Usually the number of input lines equals the number of output lines. The number of input/output lines is known as the *data path width* or the *word length* of the microprocessor. The lines which carry the data are collectively known as the *data bus*. Data bus width or word length is one of the most common parameters used to characterize a microprocessor. In 8-bit processors, the data bus width is 8. Figure 11.4 illustrates a shorthand notation we will use to indicate the bus width. With eight input and eight output lines, one would need 16 pins on the microprocessor. To economize further on the pins most microprocessors use the same eight pins for both input and output. This is possible if input and output are not done simultaneously. Physically the mode of transfer of information—input or output—is indicated by a control output. When the control output is 1, the mode is input mode and switches inside the microprocessor will route the signals as input, otherwise the direction of transmission of data will be reversed. This is shown in Fig. 11.5. Such a data bus is known as a *bidirectional data bus*. Technology has improved over the years and currently 32- and even 64-bit data buses are available in some microprocessors.

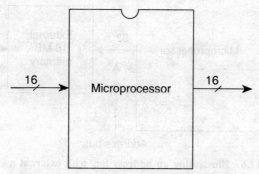

Fig. 11.4   Notation to indicate bus widths.

11.2.3   Address Bus

In the ideal microcomputer (Fig. 11.1) we had indicated the presence of a program storage within the chip. As was pointed out earlier in this section, technology does not permit a

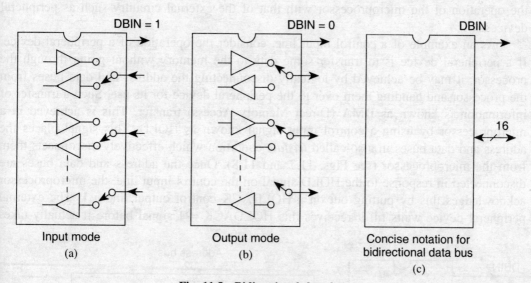

Input mode
(a)

Output mode
(b)

Concise notation for
bidirectional data bus
(c)

Fig. 11.5   Bidirectional data bus.

large storage within the chip. Thus one is constrained to use a memory external to the chip. If we want to address 4 GB of memory, we will need 32 addressing bits. These bits are transmitted via 32 lines which constitute the *address bus* of the microprocessor. Some microprocessors time-share data bus as part of the address. Figure 11.6 illustrates the use of the address bus. Observe that data may be either written into or read from memory using the bidirectional data bus.

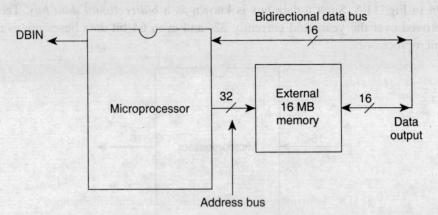

Fig. 11.6   Illustrating an address bus with external memory.

11.2.4   Control Bus

In addition to data and address buses, microprocessors also require a set of control lines. We have already encountered one such control output line which indicates whether the data bus is in input or output mode. Control lines are required to synchronize the operation of the microprocessor with that of the external circuitry such as peripheral devices.

As an example of a control input line, consider the operation of a peripheral device. If a peripheral device is to transfer some data to the memory without going through the processor, it may be achieved by logically disconnecting the address and data buses from the processor and handing them over to the peripheral device for its use. Such a transfer of information is known as DMA (Direct Memory Access) transfer. This is achieved in a microprocessor by using a control input signal known as HOLD. This signal places the address and data buses in a so-called *tristate* condition which effectively disconnects them from the microprocessor (see Figs. 11.7 and 11.8). Once the address and data buses are disconnected in response to the HOLD signal on the control input line, the microprocessor acknowledges this by putting out on a HOLDACK control output line a 1. The external peripheral device waits till it receives this HOLDACK = 1 signal before it actually takes

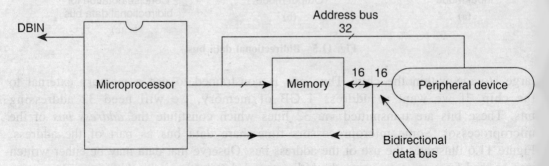

Fig. 11.7   Illustrating DMA transfer.

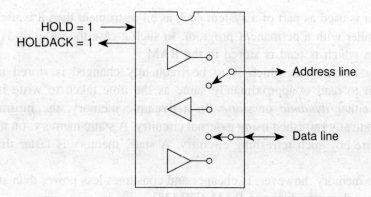

HOLD = 1

HOLDACK = 1

Address line

Data line

Fig. 11.8 Illustrating tristate condition of data and address lines.

control over the data and address buses for information transfer to memory. This communication protocol of sending a request and waiting till it is acknowledged before acting is called *handshaking protocol*.

We may now consolidate the picture of a microprocessor indicated in Fig. 11.9. Besides data, address and control buses, a microprocessor also has lines for power supply and ground connections.

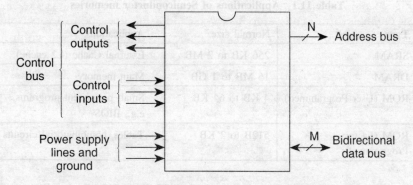

Control outputs

Control bus

Control inputs

Power supply lines and ground

N Address bus

M Bidirectional data bus

Fig. 11.9 A generalized microprocessor.

11.3 MEMORY SYSTEMS FOR MICROCOMPUTERS

Two distinct types of memory may be used in a microcomputer. These are (i) volatile memory, and (ii) non-volatile memory. The information in a volatile memory is lost when power is switched off, whereas the contents of non-volatile memory is stored permanently. A semiconductor random access memory (RAM) is a volatile memory. A semiconductor read only memory (ROM) is a non-volatile memory. A ROM is thus used to store programs which should not be lost when power is turned off. When microprocessors are used as CPU of general purpose computers then ROM contains programs to control the peripherals and program to load the operating system into the main memory which is a RAM. If the microprocessor is used as part of a system such as an instrument then it is used as a special purpose controller with a permanent program. In such a case the program is stored in the ROM and data which is read is stored in the RAM.

Normally information which is to be frequently changed is stored in a RAM as the time taken to read is approximately same as the time taken to write in it. RAM is classified as either *dynamic* or *static*. In a dynamic memory, the information stored has to be periodically refreshed using external circuitry. A static memory, on the other hand, does not require any such refreshing circuitry. A static memory is faster than a dynamic memory.

Dynamic memory, however, is cheaper and consumes less power than static memory. Large memories thus use dynamic RAM (DRAM).

Many microcomputer systems use a static RAM as an external cache in addition to the cache built-in to the chip. Such a cache is called a Level2 (or L2) cache to distinguish it from the on-chip cache which is known as Level1 (or L1) cache. The L2 cache being outside the chip can be of larger size. It is normally of the order of 1 MB in some recent systems. The main memory is normally a DRAM as it is large (greater than 16 MB) and it will be expensive to use SRAM of this size. In Table 11.1 we list the normal sizes and applications of the semiconductor memories discussed in this chapter

Table 11.1   Applications of Semiconductor memories

Type	Normal size	Applications
SRAM	256 KB to 2 MB	External Cache (L2 cache)
DRAM	16 MB to 1 GB	Main memory
ROM (User Programmed)	4 KB to 64 KB	Small permanent programs, e.g., BIOS
ROM (Factory Programmed)	512B to 2 KB	Tables, combinatorial circuits

The diagram given below classifies various RAM and ROM memory systems. ROM memories may be classified as *factory-programmed* or *user-programmed*. The factory-programmed ROMs are manufactured using appropriate masks. They are thus the most reliable and also the least expensive. User-programmed ROMs (PROMs) are divided into erasable and non-erasable. The non-erasable PROM is programmed using fuse-links. Once a fuse-link is burnt it is permanent. Erasable programmable ROMs (EPROMs) can be erased and reprogrammed by a user. There are two varieties of EPROMs. One variety can be erased by shining intense ultraviolet light on it. Such an EPROM is called UVEPROM. The other variety is electrically erasable using high voltage pulses, and is known as EEPROM. UVEPROM is the most popular variety used in the development of microcomputer applications.

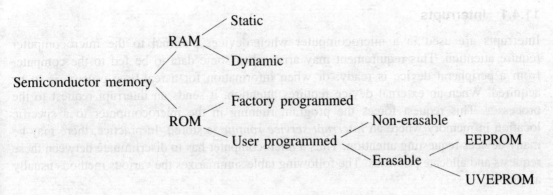

11.4 A MINIMUM MICROCOMPUTER CONFIGURATION

Along with a microprocessor chip, other support chips are required to configure a microcomputer system. At the very minimum it is necessary to have the following chips:

(i) A voltage regulator chip used along with a full wave rectifier connected to the mains. This provides a power supply regulated to ± 5%.

(ii) A clock signal which is a square wave is required to synchronize the operations of a microprocessor. A special clock chip is used along with a quartz crystal of appropriate type to generate this clock.

(iii) Integrated circuit chips to buffer and control the information from memory to the processor and from input/output devices to the processor.

(iv) Memory chips and associated controllers to interface them to the processor.

Figure 11.10 depicts a microcomputer using support chips. The trend is to reduce the need for support chips and build controllers within the processor.

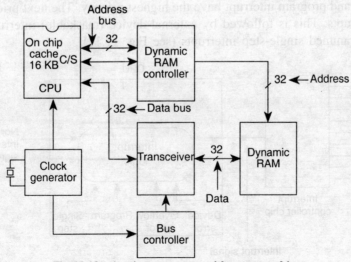

Fig 11.10   A microprocessor with support chips.

11.4.1 Interrupts

Interrupts are used in a microcomputer when devices external to the microcomputer require attention. This requirement may arise when some data to be fed to the computer from a peripheral device is ready, or when information for a real-time process is to be acquired. When an external device requires attention, it sends an interrupt request to the processor. This request forces the program running in the microcomputer to a specific location in memory where an *interrupt service routine* is stored. In practice, there may be many devices requesting attention. Thus a microcomputer has to discriminate between these requests and allocate priorities. The following table summarizes the various methods usually available.

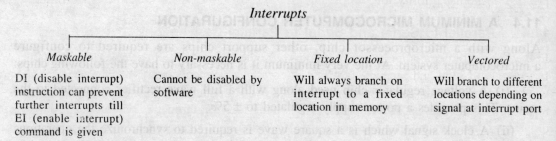

Maskable	Non-maskable	Fixed location	Vectored
DI (disable interrupt) instruction can prevent further interrupts till EI (enable interrupt) command is given	Cannot be disabled by software	Will always branch on interrupt to a fixed location in memory	Will branch to different locations depending on signal at interrupt port

Consider, for example, an IBM PC. Four classes of interrupts are possible. They are:

 (i) CPU internal interrupt,
 (ii) Non-maskable interrupt,
 (iii) External interrupt,
 (iv) Single-step interrupt.

These interrupts have a priority determined by the CPU. Internal interrupts, namely, divide error, overflow and program interrupt have the highest priority. The next priority is for non-maskable interrupts. This is followed by external-device (maskable) interrupts and finally internally programmed single-step interrupts (see Fig. 11.11).

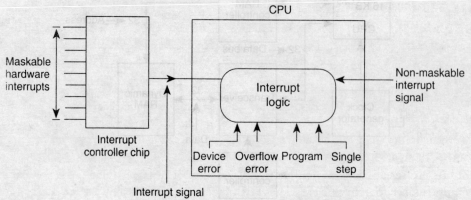

Fig. 11.11 Interrupt sources of IBM PC.

The CPU recognizes an interrupt when appropriate interrupt signals are sensed by the CPU chip. When an interrupt is recognized CPU transfers control to a new program location. Locations 000 (Hex) to 3FF (Hex) (total of 1024 locations) are dedicated to store upto 256 four-byte interrupt vectors. Each vector is the starting address of interrupt routines stored elsewhere in the main memory.

When an interrupt occurs the CPU completes its current instruction and then services the interrupt based on its priority. The delay between the recognition of an interrupt by the CPU and the execution of the interrupt service routine varies between 50 to 60 clock cycles. The delay includes the time taken to save CPU status and register contents. When an interrupt is being serviced other interrupts can occur. They are serviced based on their priority. A higher priority interrupt cannot be interrupted by a lower priority interrupt.

11.4.2 Parallel to Serial and Serial to Parallel Conversion

In the minimal microcomputer configuration presented in Section 11.4, we assumed that all I/O ports will send and receive eight bits in parallel. In practice there are many situations where information can be transmitted only serially as a sequence of bits. In particular, when information is to be sent or received from a remote location through a communication line, only serial data transmission is economical. Most peripheral devices such as video terminals and teletypes accept and transmit bits serially. As serial to parallel and parallel to serial conversion is frequently needed, a special IC chip called UART (universal asynchronous receiver transmitter) is available. Figure 11.12 illustrates the function of a UART. Logically, UART may be divided into a receiver part and a transmitter part. The receiver receives a series of bits at a predetermined rate called *baud rate* (bits per second). A clock at a frequency equal to the baud rate synchronizes the received bits. A UART assembles eight serial bits and puts them out as a parallel set of eight bits. When the bits are assembled and ready to be transmitted, a ready bit (RDA) is put out on an output port.

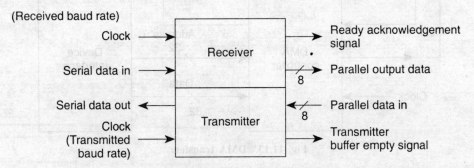

Fig. 11.12 UART functional diagram.

The transmitter part of UART accepts eight bits in parallel, serializes them, and synchronizes them with another baud rate clock and transmits the bits serially. As soon as the eight bits are serialized, and the buffer in UART is emptied, a signal TBE (Transmitter buffer empty) is set to 1 by UART. The TBE and RDA signals may be used as interrupt signals to the microprocessor.

11.4.3 Direct Memory Access (DMA)

The fastest way an external device can store and retrieve information from memory (RAM) is by taking over the data and address buses from the microprocessor and using them to transfer information. This is known as direct memory access (DMA). In the simplest method, the external device sends a bus request signal to the microprocessor. This is acknowledged by the microprocessor after completing the current machine cycle (i) by disconnecting itself from the address and data buses (by placing bus buffers in a tristate condition) and (ii) by sending an acknowledge signal after yielding the buses to the DMA chip. The DMA chip has internal circuitry to receive from the peripheral device the starting address in memory where data is to be transferred, and the number of bytes to be transferred. Having taken control of the bus, the DMA chip proceeds to transfer the requisite number of bytes from or to the memory. After completing the transfer it is acknowledged and the processor takes back the control of the buses. Figure 11.13 illustrates DMA transfer.

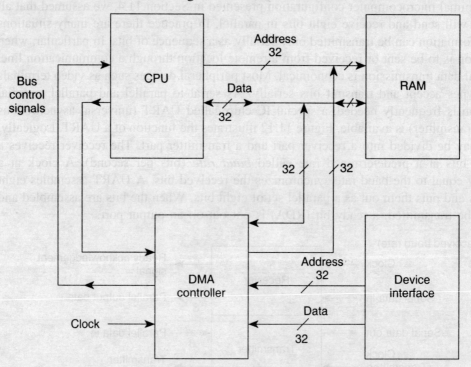

Fig. 11.13 DMA transfer.

11.5 EVOLUTION OF MICROCOMPUTERS

Ever since the introduction of microprocessors, there have been rapid improvements in integrated circuit technology. Early microprocessors had only a 4-bit data path and could address only small memories. Now microprocessors are available with 32-bit data paths and addressing capability to address 4G byte memories. The developments in technology and the evolution of microprocessors are tabulated in Table 11.2. This table gives details of some popular commercially available microprocessors. It has been observed that a new generation microprocessor appears once every 44 months.

Table 11.2   Evolution of microprocessors

Characteristics	MICROPROCESSOR							
	8008	8080	8748	8086	68020	80386	Power PC 603	Pentium celeron
Year of introduction	1972	1973	1977	1978	1984	1985	1993	1998
Data path width (in bits)	8	8	8	16	32	32	64	64
Internal register width (bits)	8	8	8	16	32	32	32/64	64
Number of internal registers		8	8	14	16	16	64	32
Directly addressable memory (Bytes)	16K	64K	4K	1M	4G	4G	4G	4G
Estimate of throughput	1	10	20	100	1000	1000	5000	50000
Clock speed MHz	0.75	3	5	5	16	20	80	300
Manufacturer	Intel	Intel	Intel	Intel	Motorola	Intel	IBM/Apple	Intel
No. of transistors in chip (in 1000s)	4	6	20	29	120	200	1600	4000

11.6   SPECIAL PURPOSE MICROPROCESSORS

We have discussed so far general purpose microprocessors. With the lowering of cost of designing and fabricating Very large Scale Integrated Circuits special purpose microprocessors for specialised but growing applications, particularly in consumer products such as washing machines, CD players, television and automobiles are being designed. These are very large and growing markets and computer engineers will be required to design systems with these specialised microprocessors. In this section we will describe two important class of microprocessors known respectively as Digital Signal Processors (DSP) and microcontrollers.

11.6.1   Digital Signal Processors

Digital signal processors are special purpose microprocessors which are optimized to process real-time audio and video signals. As they are widely used in cost-sensitive consumer products their cost must be much lower than that of a general purpose microprocessor such as Pentium. Whereas the cost of general purpose microprocessors are in the hundreds of dollars range, that of DSP is in the tens of dollars range. In Fig. 11.14 we show how a DSP is connected to external input/output. The input signal to DSP is analog, that is, it is a

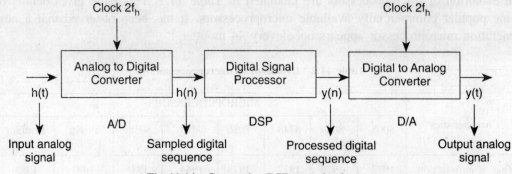

Fig. 11.14   Connecting DSP to analog input.

continuously varying signal such as speech, music, video or an electro-cardiogram. A typical analog signal is shown in Fig. 11.15 as a function of time. This signal can be represented

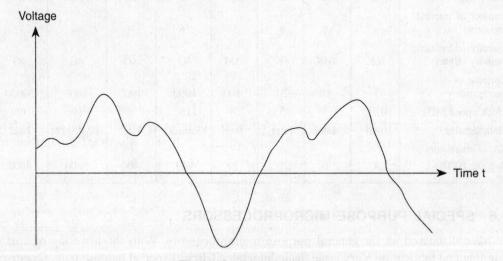

Fig. 11.15   An analog signal.

as a sum of sine waves (using Fourier analysis) as shown in Eq. 11.1.

$$h(t) = V_1 \sin 2\pi f_1 t + V_2 \sin 2\pi f_2 t + \ldots + V_n \sin 2\pi f_n t \tag{11.1}$$

In order to understand this representation it is necessary to understand the characteristics of a sine wave signal. A sine wave signal is shown in Fig. 11.16. The amplitude of the signal is defined as V and its frequency is defined as f. The amplitude of electrical signal is measured in volts and its frequency in Hertz and is abbreviated Hz. If the frequency is low the number of times sine wave crosses the t axis will be low. If $f = 0$ it is called dc voltage. For large values of f the sine wave will cross t axis very frequently. We can plot the signal $h(t)$'s characteristics as a function of frequency by plotting the values of $(V/V_m)^2$ along the y-axis and the values of f along the x-axis. V_m is highest value of V in the representation of Eq. 11.1. Such a characterization of a signal is known as its frequency

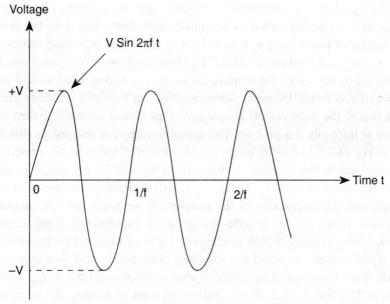

Fig. 11.16 A sine wave.

domain or power spectrum representation. In Fig. 11.17 we give the spectrum of $h(t)$. In the frequency domain the analog signal is characterized by its spectrum. From the spectrum we can find the bandwidth of the signal. Observe that $V(f)$ is zero when $f = 0$ for our sample signal and also zero for $f > f_m$. $V(f)$ is flat over a range of values of f. The lowest frequency where $(V_f/V_m)^2$ is 50% of the value in the "flat" portion of the curve is called its low cut off frequency f_l. The highest frequency where $(V_f/V_m)^2$ is again 50% of the value in the flat portion of the curve is called high cut off frequency f_h of the signal. The difference between these two frequencies is known as the bandwidth of the signal. The physical significance of the bandwidth is that most of the energy in the signal is within this frequency range.

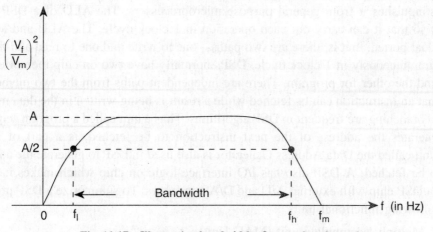

Fig. 11.17 Illustrating bandwidth of an analog channel.

The analog signal $h(t)$ is converted to a digital equivalent before it is fed to the DSP. How do we represent an analog signal by its digital equivalent? It is done by taking samples of the analog signal at times t_1, $t_1 + \tau$, $t_1 + 2\tau$, $t_1 + 3\tau$, ..., $t_1 + n\tau$ and representing their amplitudes x_1, x_2, x_3, ..., x_n by binary values. The two questions which arise are: How many bits should be used to represent the amplitudes x_1, x_2, ..., x_n and what should be the value of τ? The value of τ is found by using sampling theorem proved by Claude Shannon. The theorem states that if the high cut off frequency of an analog signal is f_h then the samples should be taken at intervals $\tau \leq (1/2\,f_h)$. The sampling theorem guarantees that if a sample is taken once every $(1/2\,f_h)$ seconds no peaks of the signal $h(t)$ will be missed and all the information contained in the original continuous signal will be preserved in the samples. The number of bits used to store x_1, x_2, x_3, ..., x_n will depend on the precision with which we want to represent the amplitudes of the samples. If we use n bits $2n$ amplitude levels can be represented. If $n = 12$, $2^{12} = 4096$ levels can be represented. 4096 levels represent a precision of $1/4096 = 0.024\%$ which is adequate for most practical purposes. Thus we see that an analog signal can be converted to a sequence of binary number, one number appearing every τ seconds. This sequence of numbers is what is input to a DSP. If $f_{max} = 20$ kHz then $\tau = 1/40 \times 10^3 = 25$ microsecond. If the DSP is required to process the input in real time then it should process each sample of 12 bits appearing every 25 microseconds. This is equivalent to a processing rate of $12/25 \times 10^{-6}$ bits/second $= 480$ Kbps for a single channel audio. For video signals the processing rate will be at least 1000 times higher. It is thus necessary for a DSP to have fast processing capability.

Most DSP applications such as speech synthesis and signal filtering multiply digitized sample values and accumulate the products as shown in Equation 11.2

$$y_n = \sum_{k=1}^{m} x_k h_{n-k} \tag{11.2}$$

for $n = 1, 2, ..., p$ with m between 8 and 16.

Thus fast multiply and accumulate unit, called MAC, is an important unit of a DSP which distinguishes it from general purpose microprocessors. The ALU of a DSP is also made fast so that it can carry out each operation in 1 clock cycle. The ALU and MAC of DSP are dual ported, that is, there are two paths—one to write and one to read and they can be used simultaneously in 1 clock cycle. DSPs normally have two on-chip memories—one for data and the other for program. There are independent paths from the two memories to CPU so that an instruction can be fetched while a result is being written in the data memory. Loops and branching are frequent in DSP algorithms. Thus a unit called a program sequencer, which generates the address of the next instruction to be fetched, is a part of a DSP. Another unit called the Data Address Generator is also used in DSP to generate the addresses of data to be fetched. A DSP also has I/O interface logic on chip which makes it easy to integrate a DSP chip with external A/D and D/A converters. To summarize a DSP processor has the following functional units:

- A Multiply accumulate unit (MAC Unit)

- A fast ALU
- An on-chip data memory
- An on-chip program memory
- A program sequencer
- A data address generator
- On-chip I/O interface logic

Figure 11.18 is a block diagram of a typical DSP chip. In this figure we have shown only the essential parts of the chip.

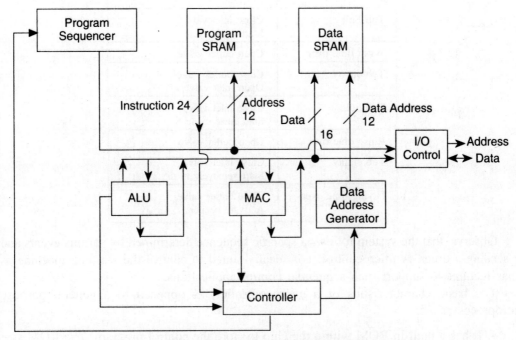

Fig. 11.18 Block diagram of a Digital Signal Processor chip.

11.6.2 Microcontrollers

Microcontrollers are special purpose microprocessors whose architecture is tuned to cater to control applications. Many consumer products such as washing machines, VCRs, microwave ovens and high-end audio systems have built-in microcontrollers to obey commands from a remote control or are programmed to follow a cycle through some states based on the occurrence of some events. For instance, a washing machine senses the level of water in the wash tub and when it reaches a preset level, starts the wash cycle. A timer is set by the user for a specified time and a timer starts. When the specified time is over, the controller automatically opens a drain valve to drain out the soapy water. A sensor determines the empty state and the controller opens the water inlet valve to let in water for the rinse cycle. A timer set by the user determines the duration of this cycle after which, the drain valve is again opened by the controller to drain out the water. When water is drained, a sensor sends a signal to the controller to start the spin cycle. After a preset time the spinner stops. A beeper is activated by the controller to indicate to the user that washing is over. We summarize the actions initiated by the washing machine controller in Table 11.3.

Table 11.3   Washing machine control

Event	Action
Start Pressed	Open inlet valve Fill tub
Tub Full	Close inlet valve Start wash cycle
Wash time over	Open outlet valve
Tub empty	Close outlet valve Open inlet valve
Tub Full	Close inlet valve Start rinse cycle
Rinse time over	Open outlet valve
Tub empty	Close inlet valve Start spincycle to dry cloth
Drying time over	Close outlet valve Activate beeper

Observe that the system follows a specific sequence determined by various events and by sensing a timer. A microcontroller is ideally suited to control the washing machine as it has features to support such sequential control applications.

The basic characteristics of a microcontroller, as opposed to a general purpose microprocessor are:

- It has a built-in ROM within the chip to store the control program. The ROM size is of the order of 4 Kbytes.

- It has a small built-in RAM for temporary data storage. The RAM size is of the order of 128 bytes.

- The CPU uses single byte instructions so that the limited program memory (ROM) is effectively used.

- Many microcontrollers have a Boolean co-processor along with the CPU to simplify implementing Boolean expressions occurring often in control applications.

- Microcontrollers have built-in counters and timers which can be set by users

- There are built-in I/O ports and control for easy interaction with external devices.

As can be seen, with very little external circuits, the microcontroller can carry out its function effectively. The cost of a microcontroller is a fraction of the cost of a general purpose microprocessor. In Fig.11.19 we give a block diagram of a typical microcontroller chip.

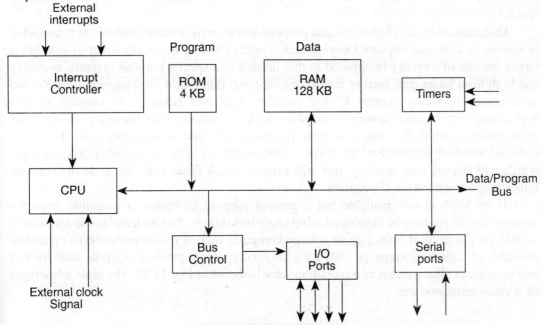

Fig. 11.19   Internal architecture of a single chip microcontroller.

Currently the most popular microcontroller is Intel's model 8051. The cheaper model has 128 bytes of RAM and 4 KB of ROM for program. The program is factory programmed for specific applications. Costlier model with UVEPROM is available which is normally used to build a prototype in the laboratory for testing the program. Low power versions are also being manufactured which are used in portable systems.

Development systems with necessary software are available for different models of microcontrollers. Such systems are necessary to create bug free application programs, before the microcontroller is incorporated in a product such as a washing machine.

11.7   SPECIAL PURPOSE MICROCOMPUTER SOFTWARE

There are two basically different classes of applications of microcomputers. One class is their use in general purpose computers. In this case, high level languages such as BASIC, FORTRAN, COBOL, Pascal, and C are available. Besides this, suitable operating systems are also supplied by the vendors.

The other class of use is in special purpose applications such as controllers of motors, lifts, traffic lights, data loggers, data processors in sophisticated instruments, communications controllers such as a small telephone exchange, etc. Only small 8-bit microcomputers such as 8085 or microcontrollers are used in such applications as cost is a very important criterion in consumer products. In these applications, the available memory will be small and only one dedicated, specially designed program will be running all the time. The software design philosophy in such applications is quite different. We will discuss first the development of special purpose software.

One method of developing special purpose software for microcomputers is to use what is known as a Microcomputer Development System (MDS). A development system has a larger amount of memory (compared to that needed in a special purpose system), assembly and high level languages, facility for debugging programs, facility to program a PROM and an adequate operating system. C is a popular high level language to program control applications with microcomputers. A translator for C is normally available in a microcomputer development system. It is easier to write programs in C than in assembly code. However, a skilled assembly language programmer would be able to write an assembly code for a job which will occupy less memory and will execute much faster than the code obtained by translating an equivalent C program.

If an MDS is not available but a general purpose computer is available, then the software for micros may be developed using *cross-translators*. A cross-translator is a translator written in a high level language on a large computer (called a *host computer*) to translate assembly or high level language code for a microcomputer to produce machine code for that microcomputer. The concept of a cross-translator is shown in Fig. 11.20. The main advantages of a cross-translator are:

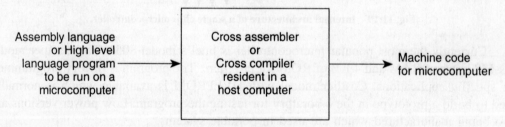

Fig. 11.20 **Illustrating a cross-translator.**

(i) The cross-translator is easier to develop because one can use all the resources of a large computer in developing it.

(ii) The cross-translator is usually written in a high level language such as C which expedites its development.

(iii) A cross-translator may be designed to produce the machine code for a variety of microcomputers/microcontrollers.

The main disadvantages of a cross-translator are:

(i) The machine code may not be efficient.

(ii) As the machine code is produced on another machine, it is necessary to run it on the microcomputer for which it is intended before it can be authenticated.

11.8 SPECIAL PURPOSE APPLICATIONS OF MICROCOMPUTERS

11.8.1 An Example Application

The versatility of the microprocessor stems from the fact that, by changing the program stored in it, we can use the same processor for a variety of jobs. As a specific example of a microcomputer application, consider the design of a controller for adjusting the input feeds to a furnace in a foundry which melts scrap iron. As the composition of the scrap is variable from batch to batch, it is necessary to control the 'quality' of the molten metal in real time in order to reduce rejections of castings. Quality may be measured in real time by means of a spectrum analyzer. The output of the spectrum analyzer is converted to a binary digital form and fed as an input to a microcomputer. The computer, using a stored program based on metallurgical theory, determines the amount of silica, carbon and manganese which need to be added to meet specifications. These are outputs which are communicated to a plant operator who adds the requisite quantities. In an automated system, the outputs will be used to operate feeders for silica, carbon and manganese. Load cells will measure the weights added and stop the feeders when appropriate quantities are charged into the furnace. The system is shown in Fig. 11.21.

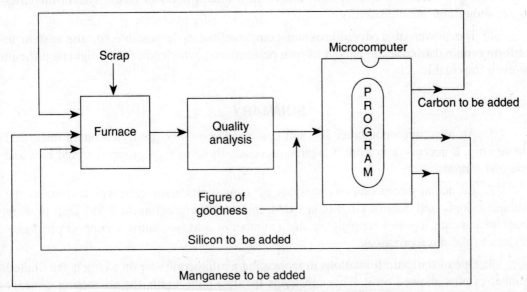

Fig. 11.21 A microcomputer application.

11.8.2 Typical Applications

Application areas for microprocessors are limited only by the limitation of the imagination of users. More than 60 percent of the current applications are in the replacement of hard-wired transistor circuitry. They are used in data collection terminals, office equipment, business machines, calculators, point-of-sale terminals, and data communications equipment. The programmability and flexibility of microprocessors make them popular in all types of instruments including those for electronics labs, medicine, and physical analysis. Even areas where electronics was not used previously find microprocessors quite useful. These include control of traffic lights, appliances, such as washing machines and microwave ovens and lifts. They are also used to assist handicapped persons, in automobiles, and in entertainment electronics like TV games.

There are a number of reasons for microprocessors becoming so popular. The most important reason is that they provide a good substitute for hard-wired logic and are programmable and flexible. It has been shown that a ROM can replace a large number of standard logic gates and a single 16K bit ROM is equivalent in logic power to 100 or more small scale integrated circuits. The following advantages of microprocessor-based systems are worth remembering.

(1) Designing with ROMs and programming microprocessors is very simple compared to designing with logic gates and hardware trouble-shooting. This simplicity brings down the development time and leads to a host of associated benefits.

(2) Their flexibility makes possible quick response to market needs and changes required by users.

(3) The smaller number of components in a microprocessor-based system increases its reliability and maintainability.

(4) The power of a stored-program computer makes it possible for the system to perform certain data collection about its own performance, which otherwise might be difficult or even impossible.

SUMMARY

1. An ideal microcomputer is a self-contained computer fabricated on an integrated circuit chip. It accepts data from N inputs, processes these using a program stored in it and gives M outputs.

2. An actual microcomputer consists of a microprocessor chip which contains the arithmetic logic and control circuits, a ROM chip to store program, a RAM chip to store program and data, a power supply chip and a number of interface chips to connect peripheral devices to the microprocessor.

3. One of the main limitations in fabricating a microcomputer on a chip is the limited number of pins allowed on it. This constrains the data path width, the addressing capacity and the number of control lines. Sometimes the same set of lines are used at different times for different purposes. Advances in semiconductor fabrication, however, is making this constraint less important. General purpose microprocessor such as Intel's Pentium had 273 pins and microprocessors with over 400 pins are emerging.

4. A data bus is used to send and receive data in a microprocessor; an address bus is used to specify address in memory from which data or instructions are to be sent or received; a control bus is used to send/receive signals to coordinate the functioning of the processor with the input/output devices and memory.

5. Interrupts are used in microcomputers whenever an external device wants data to be sent to or received from it. Interrupt halts the currently running program in the microprocessor and activates another program to service the appropriate I/O device.

6. A UART chip is used to serialize parallel information coming from a microcomputer and send it on a transmission line. Similarly, serial information coming on a transmission line is reformatted as a parallel set of bits and sent on the data bus.

7. A DMA chip is used to transfer data from a peripheral device to the memory without using CPU resources.

8. Microprocessors have evolved in twenty years from small 8-bit systems which could address 16 K byte memory to 64-bit systems with the capacity to address 4 G bytes of memory.

9. With lowering of cost of digital VLSI chips newer special purpose microprocessors have emerged. These are Digital Signal Processors and Microcontrollers.

10. Digital Signal Processors accept continuously varying signals, digitized with Analog to Digital Converters, process them, reconvert them to analog form with Digital to Analog Converters.

11. Special features of DSP are fast ALU and Multiply Accumulate unit, separate on-chip data and program memory and I/O controllers. Their main uses are in speech synthesis, video signal processing, CD players and many high quality consumer entertainment electronics systems.

12. Microcontrollers are special purpose microprocessors whose architecture is tuned to cater to control applications. They have built-in ROM for program and RAM for data. Besides these they have built-in I/O controllers and timers. The architecture is well suited to design programmed controllers for products such as washing machines, VCRs, automobiles etc. Programmed controllers are much more flexible and versatile compared to hard wired digital electronic systems. Many products incorporating microcontrollers are advertised as "intelligent systems".

13. Microcomputer applications fall into two distinct classes. One class is their use as general purpose computers and the other class is their use as special purpose systems. For programming special purpose applications, a microcomputer development system (MDS) is used. An MDS usually has a large memory, high level language translators, and a PROM programmer.

14. If an MDS is not available then special purpose applications are programmed using a larger general purpose computer. A cross-translator may be implemented in the large computer which accepts a high level language program intended for a microcomputer and produces a machine language program corresponding to it.

15. All general purpose computers, starting with laptop computers to high performance parallel computers, use microprocessors as their CPU. Latest microprocessors (1998) have a clock of 400 MHz and can carry out serveral billion operations per second.

16. Special purpose applications of microcomputers are as data entry units, office equipment, data communication equipment, controllers of lifts, traffic lights, washing machines etc. They are extensively used to replace large relay controllers and transistor digital circuits.

REVIEW QUESTIONS

11.1 Define an ideal microcomputer.

11.2 What is the difference between an ideal microcomputer and an actual microcomputer?

11.3 What are the main constraints in realizing an ideal microcomputer?

11.4 What is a microprocessor?

11.5 Describe the logical structure of a typical microprocessor.

11.6 What is the purpose of the data bus of a microprocessor?

11.7 Why is the width of the data bus an important parameter in microprocessors?

11.8 Define the word length of a microprocessor.

11.9 What is the purpose of the address bus in a microprocessor?

11.10 What is the maximum size of memory which can be addressed with an address bus width of 20 bits?

11.11 What is the purpose of a control bus in a microcomputer?

11.12 What do you understand by the term tristate condition?

11.13 What is the use of a ROM in a microcomputer?

11.14 Is ROM used to store programs or data?

11.15 Is ROM a volatile or non-volatile memory?

11.16 What is the difference between a RAM and a ROM?

11.17 What is a PROM?

11.18 What is the main use of a PROM?

11.19 What is an EPROM?

11.20 What is the main use of an EPROM?

11.21 Give a block diagram of a microcomputer.

11.22 What are the "support chips" in a microcomputer?

11.23 Define an interrupt.

11.24 Why are interrupts used in a microcomputer?

11.25 What is an interrupt service routine?

11.26 What is a UART?

11.27 What is the main function of UART?

11.28 What do you understand by the term 'baud rate'?

11.29 What is DMA?

11.30 How does a DMA chip work in cooperation with a microprocessor to transfer data from I/O device to memory?

11.31 Among the microprocessors listed in Table 11.2, which one is closest to the ideal microprocessor?

11.32 What is the significant difference between INTEL 80386 and Pentium?

11.33 Give the significant differences between a general purpose microprocessor and Digital Signal Processor.

11.34 What are the applications of DSP?

11.35 How many samples per second of an analog signal (with highest frequency 20 kHz) should be taken for converting it to its digital equivalent?

11.36 The required precision in A/D conversion is 0.05%. How many bits per sample of the analog signal should be taken?

11.37 What is the function of the MAC unit in DSP?

11.38 Give the significant differences between a general purpose microprocessor and a microcontroller.

11.39 What are the applications of a microcontroller?

11.40 Can a microprocessor be used in place of a microcontroller in applications? Justify your answer.

11.41 What is a Microcomputer Development System?

11.42 What facilities does MDS provide for microcomputer program development?

11.43 What is a cross-translator?

11.44 Why are cross-translators used in program development for microcomputers?

11.45 Why are microcomputers preferred over hard-wired logic in control applications?

12

Computer Generations and Classification

In this chapter we will present a historical perspective on the development of computers. The term "computer generation" is widely used particularly by the sales personnel of computer manufacturers. Most often it is used in relation to the hardware of computers. We will take a broader view and examine the developments in software and applications besides hardware. In the second part of the chapter we will explain the commonly used current classification of computers as Laptop computers, PCs, Workstations, Mainframes, Distributed computers and Parallel computers.

12.1 FIRST GENERATION OF COMPUTERS

The first electronic computer was completed in 1946 by a team led by Professors Eckert and Mauchly at the University of Pennsylvania in U.S.A. This computer called Electronic Numerical Integrator and Calculator (ENIAC) used high speed vacuum tube switching devices. It had a very small memory and was designed primarily to calculate the trajectories of missiles. The ENIAC took about 200 microseconds to add two digits and about 2800 microseconds to multiply.

A major breakthrough occurred in the logical design of computers when the concept of a *stored program* was proposed by Professor John Von Neumann in 1946. His idea was to store machine instructions in the memory of the computer along with data. These instructions could themselves be modified as required by other instructions. This allowed easy implementation of program loops. The first computer using this principle was designed and commissioned at Cambridge University, U.K. under the leadership of Professor Maurice Wilkes. This computer called EDSAC (Electronic Delay Storage Automatic Calculator) was completed in 1949 and used mercury delay lines for storage.

Commercial production of stored program electronic computers began in the early 50s. One of the early computers of this type was UNIVAC I built by Univac division of Remington Rand and delivered in 1951. This computer also used vacuum tubes. As vacuum tubes used filaments as a source of electrons, they had a limited life. Each tube consumed about half a watt power. Computers typically used about ten thousand tubes. Power dissipation was very high. As a large number of tubes, each with limited life, was used in fabricating these computers, their mean time between failures was low—of the order of an hour.

During this period, computer programming was mainly done in machine language. Assembly language was invented in the early fifties. Initial applications were in science and engineering. With the advent of UNIVAC, the prospects of commercial application were perceived. The concept of an operating system had not yet emerged. By and large during this period one had to be a good electronics engineer, and understand the logical structure of a computer in great detail, and also know how to program an application in order to use a computer. It was somewhat like the early days of motor cars when one had to be a good mechanic to be able to drive a car!

12.2 THE SECOND GENERATION

A big revolution in electronics took place with the invention of transistors by Bardeen, Brattain and Shockley in 1947. Transistors made of germanium semiconductor material were highly reliable compared to tubes since transistors had no filament to burn. They occupied less space and used only a tenth of the power required by tubes. They also could switch from a 0 to a 1 state in a few microseconds, about a tenth of the time needed by tubes. Thus switching circuits for computers made with transistors were about ten times more reliable, ten times faster, dissipated one tenth the power, occupied about one tenth the space and were ten times cheaper than those using tubes. Computer manufacturers thus changed over to transistors from tubes. The second generation computers emerged around 1955 with the use of transistors instead of vacuum tubes in computers. This generation lasted till 1965.

Another major event during this period was the invention of magnetic cores for storage. Magnetic cores are tiny rings (0.02 inch diameter) made of ferrite and can be magnetized in either clockwise or anti-clockwise direction. The two directions are used to represent a 0 and a 1. Magnetic cores were used to construct large random access memories. Memory capacity in the second generation was about 100 kilo bytes. Magnetic disk storage was also developed during this period.

The higher reliability of computers and large memory availability led to the development of high level languages. Fortran, COBOL, Algol and Snobol were developed during this generation. With higher speed CPUs and the advent of magnetic tape and disk storage, operating systems were developed. Good batch operating systems, particularly the ones on IBM 7000 series computers emerged during the second generation.

Commercial applications rapidly developed during this period and dominated computer use by mid 1960s. More than 80% of installed computers were used in business and industry. All systems were batch oriented. Payroll, inventory control, marketing, production planning and general ledger systems were developed. A number of applications of operations research such as Linear Programming, Critical Path Methods (CPM) and Simulation became popular. Engineering applications, particularly in process control, increased rapidly.

New professions in computing such as systems analysts and programmers emerged during the second generation. Academic programmes in computer science were also initiated.

12.3 THE THIRD GENERATION

The third generation began in 1965 with germanium transistors being replaced by silicon transistors. Integrated circuits, circuits consisting of transistors, resistors, and capacitors grown on a single chip of silicon eliminating wired interconnection between components, emerged. From small scale integrated circuits which had about 10 transistors per chip, technology developed to medium scale integrated circuits with 100 transistors per chip. Switching speed of transistors went up by a factor of 10, reliability increased by a factor of 10, power dissipation reduced by a factor of 10 and size was also reduced by a factor of 10. The cumulative effect of this was the emergence of extremely powerful CPUs with the capacity of carrying out 1 million instructions per second.

There were significant improvements in the design of magnetic core memories. The size of main memories reached about 4 Megabytes. Magnetic disk technology improved rapidly. 100 Megabytes/drive became feasible.

The combined effect of high capacity memory, powerful CPU and large disk memories led to the development of time shared operating systems. Time shared systems increased programmer productivity.

Many important on-line systems became feasible. In particular dynamic production control systems, airline reservation systems, interactive query systems, and real-time closed loop process control systems were implemented. Integrated data base management systems emerged.

High level languages improved. Fortran IV and optimizing Fortran compilers were developed. COBOL 68 was standardized by the American National Standards Institute. PL/1 of IBM emerged and was quite a powerful language.

The third generation probably ended by 1975. The improvements in the period 65–75 were substantial but no revolutionary new concept could be identified as heralding the end of third generation.

12.4 THE FOURTH GENERATION

First Decade (1976–85)

The fourth generation may be identified by the advent of the microprocessor chip. Medium scale integrated circuits yielded to Large and Very Large Scale Integrated circuits (VLSI) packing about 50000 transistors in a chip. Magnetic core memories were replaced by semiconductor memories. Semiconductor memory sizes of 16 Megabytes with a cycle time of 200 nsecs were in common use. The emergence of the microprocessor led to two directions in computer development. One direction was the emergence of extremely powerful personal computers. Computer cost came down so rapidly that professionals had their own computer to use in their office and home. Hard disks provided a low cost, high capacity secondary memory.

The other direction of development was the decentralization of computer organization. Individual microprocessor controls for terminals and peripheral devices allowed the CPU to concentrate on processing the main program. Networks of computers and distributed computer systems were developed. Disk memories became very large (1000 Mbytes/drive). A significant development in software was the development of concurrent programming languages. Such languages are important to program distributed systems and real time systems. The most ambitious language of this type was ADA. Another important development was interactive graphic devices and language interfaces to graphic systems. The emergence of graphics gave a great impetus to computer-aided engineering design.

Fourth generation saw the coming of age of UNIX OS and time shared interactive systems. These systems became user friendly and highly reliable. The effective cost of computing came down. Computers also became all pervading.

Second Phase (1986–1998)

The second phase of the fourth generation has seen a relentless increase in the speed of microprocessors and the size of main memory. The speed of microprocessors and the size of main memory and hard disk went up by a factor of 4 every 3 years. Many of the features originally found in CPUs of large expensive mainframe computers of the first decade of the fourth generation became part of the microprocessor architecture in the 90s. Thus the mainframe computer of early 80s died in mid 90s. The alpha microprocessor chip designed by DEC in 1994 packed 9.3 million transistors in a single chip, was driven by a 300 MHz clock and could carry out a billion operations per second. It had a built-in 64-bit floating point arithmetic unit, used 64-bit data and 64-bit address buses. It had a built-in cache memory of 64 KB and 32 registers to store temporary operands. Apart from this IBM, Apple computers and Motorola cooperated in designing a microprocessor called Power PC 600 series. Intel also designed a powerful chip in 90s called Pentium (1993) which sold in large numbers. The original Pentium was followed by Pentium with MMX (Multimedia Extension) and Pentium II with a clock speed of 466 MHz and a Celeron processor with a 300 MHz clock. In 1999 Intel is planning to introduce a 64bit processor called IA 64.

Microprocessors such as Pentium, Power PC, etc., are being used as the CPU of Personal Computers and portable laptop and palm held computers. Desk top workstations and powerful servers for numeric computing as well as file services use RISC microprocessors such as Alpha, MIPS and SUNSPARC.

The area of hard disk storage also saw vast improvements. 1 GB of disk on workstations became common in 1994. For larger disks RAID technology (Redundant Array of Inexpensive Disks) was used to give storage of 100 GB. Optical disks also emerged as mass storage particularly for read only files.

Optical storage sizes were of the order of 600 MB on a 5.25" disk. New optical disks known as Digital Versatile Disk ROMs, (DVD ROMs) with maximum storage capacity of around 17 GB emerged around 1998. Writable CDs were developed around the same time. The availability of optical disks at low cost saw the development of multimedia applications. Multimedia workstations were widely used.

Computer Networks came of age. The networks became very powerful with the advent of fibre optic Local Area Networks which could transmit 100 MB/sec to 1 GB/sec. Many mainframes were replaced by powerful workstations connected by fibre optic network. Another major event during this phase was the rapid increase in the number of computers connected to the internet. This led to the emergence of the World Wide Web which eased information retrieval. The Internet also brought out the need to execute programs on a variety of computers. This led to the emergence of a new object oriented language Java. Applications written in Java, called Java applets, could be glued together with a software called Java script to create large programs.

In the area of languages C language became popular. This was followed by a new method of design called object oriented design. The primary objectives of object oriented design are to generalize programs and to reuse objects. The C++ language emerged as the most popular object oriented language. One also saw a trend towards design of specification oriented languages. PROLOG was designed for logic oriented specification language and MIRANDA, FP etc., as functional specification oriented language. With the emergence of distributed computers connected by networks considerable effort has gone into programming distributed systems. A number of parallel computers were built but no commonly accepted standard parallel programming language emerged.

12.5   THE FIFTH GENERATION

It is not very clear now what direction the fifth generation will take. It is estimated that by 2000 we may see computers of this generation.

Even though computers in the last 40 years have become very fast, reliable and inexpensive, the basic logical structure proposed by Von Neumann has not changed. The basic block diagram of a CPU, memory and I/O is still valid today. With the improvements in integrated circuit technology, it is now possible to get specialized VLSI chips at a low cost. Thus an architecture which makes use of the changes in technology and allows an easier and more natural problem solving is being sought. In Table 12.1 we summarize and compare various generation of computers.

12.6   MOORE'S LAW

In 1965 Gordon E. Moore (one of the founders of Fairchild Semiconductors, U.S.A) predicted, based on data available at that time, that the density of transistors in integrated circuits will double at regular intervals of around 2 years. Based on the experience from 1965 to date, it has been found that his prediction has been surprisingly accurate. In fact the number of transistors per integrated circuit chip has approximately doubled every 18 months. The observation of Moore has been called "Moore's Law". In Fig.12.1 we have given two plots. One gives the number of transistors per chip in Dynamic Random Access Memory along the y-axis and years along x-axis. Observe that the y-axis is a logarithmic scale and the x-axis a linear scale. The second plot gives the number of transistors in microprocessor chips. Observe that in 1974 the largest DRAM chip had 16 Kbits whereas in 1998 it has 256 Mbits, an increase of 16000 times in 24 years. The increase in the number of components in microprocessors has been similar. It is indeed surprising that the growth has sustained

Table 12.1 Computer generations — A comparison

Generation	Years	Switching device	Storage device	Switching time	MTBF*	Software	Applications
First	1949–55	Vacuum tubes	Acoustic delay lines and later magnetic drum. 1 Kbyte memory	0.1 to 1 millisecond	30 mts. to 1 hour	Machine and assembly languages. Simple monitors	Mostly scientific. Later simple business systems
Second	1956–65	Transistors	Magnetic core main memory, tapes and disk peripheral memory. 100 K byte main memory	1 to 10 microseconds	About 10 hrs	High level languages. FORTRAN, COBOL, Algol, Batch operating systems	Extensive business applications. Engineering design optimization, scientific research
Third	1966–75	Integrated Circuits (IC)	High speed magnetic cores. Large disks (100 MB). 1 Mbyte main memory	0.1 to 1 microsecond	About 100 hrs	FORTRAN IV, COBOL 68, PL/1. Timeshared operating system	Data base management systems. On-line systems
Fourth — First phase	1975–84	Large scale integrated circuits. Microprocessors (LSI)	Semiconductor memory. Winchester disk. 10 Mbyte main memory. 1000 Mbyte disks	10 to 100 nanoseconds	About 1000 hrs	FORTRAN 77, Pascal, ADA, COBOL-74, Concurrent Pascal	Personal computers. Distributed systems. Integrated CAD/CAM Real time control. Graphics oriented systems
Fourth — Second phase	1985–present	Very large scale integrated circuits. Over 3 million transistors per chip	Semiconductor memory. 1 GB main memory. 100 GB disk	1 to 10 nanoseconds	About 10,000hrs	C, C++, JAVA, PROLOG, Miranda, FP	Simulation, Visualization, Parallel computing, Virtual reality, Multimedia

* MTBF — Mean time between failures of the processor.

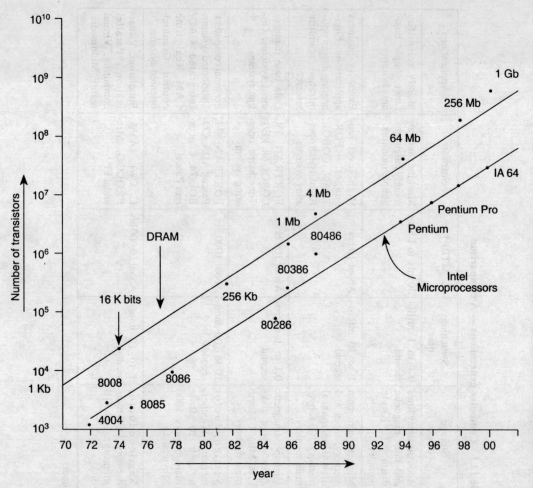

Fig. 12.1 **Moores law which shows the growth in the number of components in Integrated Circuits. Observe that the *y*-axis uses a logarithmic scale whereas the *x*-axis is linear. (Adapted from IEEE spectrum article—June 1997)**

over 30 years. By extrapolating Moores' law it is expected that by the year 2000, DRAMs will have nearly a billion bits which implies that PCs will have 256 MB of main memory. The next generation microprocessor will be 64 bit processors with clocks in the range of 1 GHz. Moore's law has other implications. The availability of large memory and fast processors has in turn increased the size and complexity of systems and applications software. It has been observed that software developers have always consumed the increased hardware capability faster than the growth in hardware. This has kept up the demand for hardware.

Another interesting point to be noted is the increase in disk capacity. In 1984 disk capacity in PCs was around 20 MB whereas it is 5 GB today — a 250 fold increase in about 14 years again doubling every 20 months which is similar to Moore's law. These improvements in capacity of computers has come about with hardly any increase in price. In fact the price of computers has been coming down!

The implication of Moore's law is that in the foreseeable future we will be getting more powerful computers at reasonable cost. It will be upto our ingenuity to use this increased power of computers effectively. It is clear that a number of applications such as speech recognition — voice and video user interfaces which require large amount of memory and computing power will be extensively used.

12.7 CLASSIFICATION OF COMPUTERS

Until recently computers were classified as microcomputers, minicomputers, supermini computers, mainframes, and supercomputers. Technology, however, has changed and this classification is no more relevant. Today all computers use microprocessors as their CPU. Thus classification is possible only through their mode of use. Based on mode of use we can classify computers as Palmtops, Laptop PCs, Desktop PCs and Workstations. Based on interconnected computers we can classify them as distributed computers and parallel computers.

Palmtop PCs

With miniaturization and high density packing of transistors on a chip, computers with capabilities nearly that of PCs which can be held in a palm have emerged. Palmtops accept handwritten inputs using an electronic pen which can be used to write on a Palmtop's screen (besides a tiny keyboard), have small disk storage and can be connected to a wireless network. One has to train the system on the user's handwriting before it can be used. A Palmtop computer has also facilities to be used as a mobile phone, Fax and email machine. A version of Microsoft operating system called Windows-CE is available for Palmtops.

Laptop PCs

Laptop PCs (also known as notebook computers) are portable computers weighing around 2 kg. They use a keyboard, flat screen liquid crystal display, and a Pentium or Power PC processor. Colour displays are available. They normally run WINDOWS OS. Laptops come with both hard disk (around 1 GB), CDROM and floppy disk. They should run with batteries and are thus designed to conserve energy. Many Laptops can be connected to a network. There is a trend towards providing wireless connectivity to Laptops so that they can read files from large stationary computers. The most common use of Laptop computers is for word processing, and spreadsheet computing while a person is travelling. As Laptops use miniature components which have to consume low power and have to be packaged in small volume they cost 3 to 4 times the cost of table top PCs of the same capacity.

Personal Computers (PCs)

The most popular PCs are desktop machines. Early PCs had intel 8088 microprocessors as their CPU. Currently (1998), intel Pentium II is the most popular processor. The machines made by IBM are called IBM PCs. Other manufacturers use IBM's specifications and design their own PCs. They are known as IBM compatible PCs. IBM PCs mostly use MS DOS or MS-Windows, WINDOWS-NT or UNIX as Operating System. An OS called OS/2 is available for IBM PCs, and is also widely used. IBM PCs, nowadays (1998) have 16 to 32 MB main memory, 2 to 4 GB of disk and a floppy disk. Besides these a 600 MB optical disk is also provided in PCs intended for multimedia use. PCs are also made by another company called Apple. Apple PCs are known as Apple Macintosh. They use Apple's proprietary OS which is designed for simplicity of use. Apple Macintosh machines used Motorola 68030 microprocessors but now use Power PC 603 processor. IBM PCs are today the most popular computers with millions of them in use throughout the world.

Workstations

Workstations are also desktop machines. They are, however, more powerful providing processor speeds about 10 times that of PCs. Most workstations have a large colour video display unit (19 inch monitors). Normally they have main memory of around 32 to 64 MB and disk of 1 to 5 GB. Workstations normally use RISC processors such as MIPS(SIG), ALPHA(DEC), RIOS (IBM), SPARC (SUN) or PA-RISC (HP). Some manufacturers of Workstations are Silicon Graphics (SIG), Digital Equipment Corporation (DEC), IBM, SUN Microsystems and Hewlett Packard (HP). The standard Operating System of Workstations is UNIX and its derivatives such as AIX(IBM), Solaris (SUN), and HP-UX (HP). Very good graphics facilities are provided by most workstations. A system called X Windows is provided by Workstations to display the status of multiple processes during their execution. Most workstations have built-in hardware to connect to a Local Area Network (LAN). Workstations are used for executing numeric and graphic intensive applications such as those which arise in Computer Aided Design, simulation of complex systems and visualizing the results of simulation.

Mainframe Computers

There are organizations such as banks and insurance companies which process large number of transactions on-line. They require computers with very large disks to store several Giga Bytes of data and transfer data from disk to main memory at several hundred Megabytes/sec. The processing power needed from such computers is several million transactions per second. These computers are much bigger and faster than workstations and several hundred times more expensive. They normally use proprietary operating systems which usually provide extensive services such as user accounting, file security and control. They are normally much more reliable when compared to operating systems on PCs. These types of computers are called mainframes. There are a few manufacturers of mainframes (e.g. IBM and Hitachi). The number of mainframe users has reduced as many organizations are rewriting their systems to use networks of powerful workstations.

Supercomputers

Supercomputers are the fastest computers available at any given time and are normally used to solve problem which require intensive numerical computations. Examples of such problems are numerical weather prediction, designing supersonic aircrafts, design of drugs and modelling complex molecules. All of these problems require around 10^{15} calculations to be performed. Such a problem will be solved in about 3 hours by a computer which can carry out 100 billion floating point calculations per second. Such a computer is classified as a supercomputer today (1998). By about the year 2000 computers which can carry out 10^{12} floating point operations per second on 64 bit floating point numbers would be available and would be the ones which will be called supercomputers. Such a computer is built by interconnecting several high speed computers and programming them to work cooperatively to solve problems. Recently applications of supercomputers have expanded beyond scientific computing. They are now used to analyse large commercial databases, produce animated movies and play games such as chess.

Besides arithmetic speed, a computer to be classified as a supercomputer, should have large main memory of around 8 GB and a secondary memory of 1000 GB. The speed of transfer of information from the secondary memory to the main memory should be at least a tenth of the memory to CPU data transfer speed. All supercomputers use parallelism to achieve their speed. In Sec. 12.9 we discuss the organization of parallel computers.

12.8 DISTRIBUTED COMPUTER SYSTEM.

A configuration in which several workstations/PCs are interconnected by a communication network is called a distributed computer system. A common use of distributed computers is the so-called *client-server computing*. In this mode several specialized services are provided by servers. For example, there may be workstations providing high speed CPU for numeric intensive programs, another with high speed printers, third with plotters and a fourth with a large disk to store big files. A user having a PC or a smaller workstation may do some local computing, debug etc., and may then requisition the services of the other workstations for storing files, providing language translators and carrying out intensive numeric computing. The workstation requisitioning services is called the *client* and the workstation providing the services is known as a *server*.

Sometimes there are problems requiring either large storage or high speed processing which cannot be solved using a single workstation in a network. In such a case it may be possible to get a set of workstations connected in the network to cooperate and solve the problem. In a distributed computer systems it often happens that many workstations are not fully utilized; either they are idle because no one is presently logged on or the user may be doing tasks such as editing or word processing which does not use the available computing power. In such a case a user requiring more CPU resources than what he has in his workstation can steal CPU cycles from idle processors to do his job. Software systems have been designed which permit this.

The communication network connecting the computers in a distributed system is normally slow and allows only one message to be communicated between two computers at a time. The network is usually a Local Area Network (to be discussed in the next chapter). For applications discussed above such a communication networks is adequate.

12.9 PARALLEL COMPUTERS

A set of computers connected together by a high speed communication network and programmed in such a way that they cooperate to solve a single large problem is called a *Parallel Computer*. There are two major types of parallel computers. One of them is called a *shared memory parallel computer*. In this case a number of processing elements are connected to a common main memory by a communication network (see Fig. 12.2). A program for this computer is written in such a way that multiple processors can work independently and cooperate to solve a problem. The processes are allocated to different processors and they read and modify data accessible to all of them in memory. Programming such a computer is relatively easy provided the problem can be broken up into parts which can be solved concurrently. The main problem with this architecture is that it is not scalable beyond about 16 processors as all the processors share a common memory. This memory is accessed via single communication network which gets saturated when many processors try to read or write from memory.

The other type of parallel computer is called a *distributed memory computer*. In this a number of processors, each with their own memory, are interconnected by a communication network. A program is divided up into many parts and each computer works independently. Whenever they need to exchange data to continue with computation they do so by sending

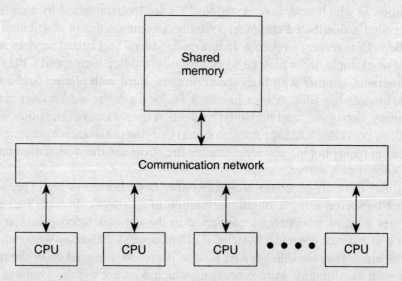

Fig. 12.2   A shared memory parallel computer.

messages to one another via the communication network. Such computers are also known as *message passing multicomputers*. Distributed memory parallel computers are scalable to over 1000 processors as each computer works reasonably independently and there are multiple communication paths to exchange messages. A popular interconnection network is called a *hypercube* (see Fig. 12.3).

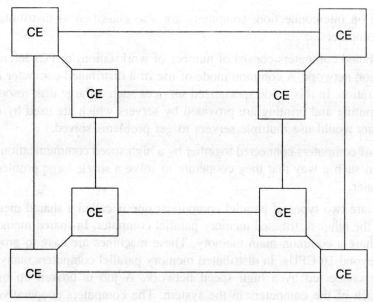

Fig. 12.3 A Distributed memory parallel computer (each CE is a computing element with its own CPU and memory).

SUMMARY

1. Computers are classified into a number of generations based on the electronic technology used in constructing the computer, the associated system software and applications.

2. Table 12.1 summarizes the characteristics of four generations of computers.

3. An empirical law known as Moore's law predicts that the number of components in integrated circuits (such as DRAM and microprocessors) will almost double every 18 months. The law has been found to be reasonably correct. It has been observed that the capacity of hard disks also increase at about the same rate. The cost of computers, however, has been going down. The implication of this is computers will be employed in a larger number of very complex applications and will be very widely used. Software will also become very complex as applications become complex.

4. Computers may be classified based on their mode of use and the way individual computers are interconnected.

5. Based on the nature of use computers are classified as Palmtop computers, Laptop computers, Personal computers, Workstations, Mainframes or Supercomputers. Palmtop and Laptop computers are portable. Personal computers are low cost computers used for word processing, small data base maintenance and executing small programs. Workstations are used by professionals for intensive computation, computer aided design, simulation and graphical visualization. Mainframes are used for massive transaction processing. Supercomputers are primarily used for intensive numerical computation.

6. Based on interconnection, computers are also classified as distributed computers and parallel computers.

7. Distributed computers consist of number of workstations or PCs interconnected by a communication network. A common mode of use of a distributed computer is in a client-server configuration. In this mode specialized services such as large disk resource, numeric intensive computing and printing are provided by servers which are used by clients in the network. Clients would use multiple servers to get problems solved.

8. A set of computers connected together by a high speed communication network and programmed in such a way that they cooperate to solve a single large problem is called a parallel computer.

9. There are two types of parallel computers: one is called a shared memory parallel computer and the other distributed memory parallel computer. In shared memory computer many CPUs share a common main memory. These machines are easy to program but are not scalable beyond 16 CPUs. In distributed memory parallel computers many independent computers are connected by a high speed network. A job is broken up into parts and allocated to each of the computers in the system. The computers cooperatively solve the problem by locally computing and by exchanging messages among them. Distributed memory parallel computers are also known as message passing parallel computers. They are scalable upto about 1000 computers.

REVIEW QUESTIONS

12.1 Who fabricated the first electronic computer and what was it called?

12.2 When was the first electronic computer fabricated?

12.3 Who invented the concept of stored program?

12.4 Which was the first stored program computer and where was it made?

12.5 Which was the first commercially produced computer?

12.6 What was the switching device used in the first generation computers?

12.7 What type of memory was used in first generation computers?

12.8 What languages were available in first generation computers?

12.9 What new switching device led to the emergence of second generation computers?

12.10 What is the main difference in characteristics between the first and second generation computers?

12.11 What was the main memory technology used in second generation computers?

12.12 What important developments in software took place during the second generation of computers?

12.13 What was the important peripheral memory device invented in the second generation of computers?

12.14 What type of operating system was used with second generation computers?

12.15 What main technological change ushered in the third generation of computers?

12.16 What are the advantages of integrated circuits compared to transistors?

12.17 What was the main memory technology in the third generation computers?

12.18 What improvements in peripheral memory took place during the third generation of computers?

12.19 What was the most significant development in software in the third generation computers?

12.20 What technological change ushered in the fourth generation of computers?

12.21 What development in computer architecture took place during the first decade of the fourth generation?

12.22 What significant developments in software took place during the first decade of the fourth generation?

12.23 Answer question 12.21 for the second phase of the fourth generation.

12.24 Answer question 12.22 for the second phase of the fourth generation.

12.25 What major new applications were undertaken during the first decade of the fourth generation?

12.26 What is Moore's law?

12.27 What are the implications of Moore's law in the development of computer technology?

12.28 What are the special features of Palmtop computers?

12.29 What are the main parameters used to classify computers?

12.30 What do you understand by a Laptop computer?

12.31 What do you understand by a Personal Computer?

12.32 What hardware facilities are normally available in a Personal Computer?

12.33 What do you understand by a Workstation?

12.34 In what way is a Workstation different from a Personal Computer?

12.35 What are the important applications of Workstations?

12.36 What is a mainframe computer?

12.37 When are mainframes useful?

12.38 What do you understand by the term supercomputers?

12.39 What are the applications of supercomputers?

12.40 What do you understand by a distributed computer?

12.41 What is client-server computing?

12.42 What is a parallel computer?

12.43 How is it different from a distributed computer?

12.44 Why do we need parallel computers?

12.45 What are the two types of parallel computers called?

12.46 What are the main differences between them?

12.47 Which type of parallel computer is scalable?

13
Computers and Communications

Early computers were being used as "stand-alone" systems in organizations fulfilling their own requirements. With widespread use of computers there was a realization that it would be advantageous in many situations to use computers from remote points. It was also felt that connecting computers together via telecommunication lines will lead to widespread availability of powerful computers. Advances in computer technology also made these interconnections possible. In this chapter we will discuss various aspects of communications technology and examine how this technology can be used along with computer technology to provide powerful networks of computers.

13.1 TYPES OF COMMUNICATIONS WITH AND AMONG COMPUTERS

We saw in Chapter 10 the need and advantages of time sharing a computer among many users by using interactive terminals. Users would prefer to have access to a computer from their place of work or even their homes without having to go to the computer centre. Such access can be provided by connecting the users' terminals by communication lines to the computer. As a user working at a terminal enters program and data manually, the speed of communication to the computer is slow. The method does not place heavy demands on the communication lines.

Another type of communication between computers would be necessary when a number of computers close together (within 10 km radius) are to be connected together. An organization may have a number of computers in different locations in a campus, each computer fulfilling a function. For instance, an office may have a computer which is used as a word processor and a filing system, the stores department may have a small computer for inventory control, the accounts department may have a computer to compute payroll, prepare budgets, etc. An interconnection of these machines would be useful to share files, to transfer the load from one of the machines to the other when a machine breaks down and to exchange messages between departments. Such a connection of computers is called a *Local Area Network, LAN* for short. In this case fast communication is required between machines. Besides this, the traffic between computers will be in short bursts of intense activity.

Suppose an organization has a powerful computer with large disks for file storage, fast printers etc. It may have many branch offices in many cities with their own smaller computers, small disk, printer etc. For many applications in the branch office it may find its local computer and database sufficient. There may be instances when branch offices need a more powerful computer. In such a case it would be necessary to use the computer in the main office from terminals in the branch offices and transfer the result files back to the branch office for printing locally. Very often information such as local sales reports, accounts etc., may have to be transferred to the main office by the branch offices to update the organizational database. Another example is the ticket reservation in the Railways. A city normally would have a database of seats/berths available from it to several other cities. Reservation offices would be located in various suburbs of the city in addition to that in the main station. A customer may go to any of these locations to book tickets. The computer(s) in the local ticket offices must be connected to the database in the main computer to check availability of tickets/berths and update the database when a ticket is issued. Such a connection of a number of computers in known as *Computer Network*. In this case it would be necessary to use communication media maintained by post and telegraph or telephone companies. Such communication networks are known as *public networks* or *common carrier networks*. These networks usually have land telephone lines, underground coaxial cables, microwave communication and satellite communications. These networks are normally designed for human telephone conversation or low speed telegraph transmission and need to be adapted for computer to computer communication.

In view of the increasing requirements for high speed data communications, the public networks in various countries of the world are being improved. Data communication lines which transmit data at 64K bits/second are now easily available. New systems are being introduced which will communicate data at 34M bits/second over long distances.

Another type of communication which is becoming very important is transmission of *data between computer networks*. This is called internetworking. Various networks within a country can be interconnected. Country networks can in turn be connected to networks in other countries. In this case one needs *interoperability*. By interoperability we mean the ability of diverse computers from different vendors and with different operating systems to cooperate in solving computational problems. It should be possible for users to use the network without knowing the details of the hardware, communication method etc. Such a worldwide network is now available and is called the *Internet*. Internet is now widely used all over the world including India.

13.2 NEED FOR COMPUTER COMMUNICATION NETWORKS

We will discuss in greater detail the need for each of the types of computer communication discussed in the last section. Remote time sharing terminals are most useful for program development. The rapid turnaround provided by such a use increases programmer productivity. A user who has a personal computer at home would use it for most of his work and connect the video terminal of the personal computer to a big computer for solving larger programs and to access special library programs and data resident in the big computer.

Another use is by smaller organizations which may not have the work load to justify an in-house computer. In such a case they buy a workstation or a PC, place it in their premises and connect it as a time-sharing terminal to a larger computer via a telephone line.

This allows them to conveniently access a larger machine without having to make frequent trips to the computer centre.

Another important remote terminal application is for information retrieval. Some information centres store large amounts of data on patents, technical reports, journal articles, etc., in an organized fashion. A user requiring specific information, say on patents in a specified area, can connect his terminal through a telephone line to a large computer and retrieve the information using appropriate descriptors. Some information centres are connected to the international fax networks and it would be possible to send enquiries via fax to such centres. Rapidly many such centres are being connected to internet. Enquiries and replies would then be by electronic mail.

As we saw in the last section, local area networks are used to interconnect many computers within an organization. The purpose of interconnection would be to share files, share programs, and decentralize specialized functions. Another reason for creating a local network is also to share the use of expensive peripherals such as fast printers, large disks, graphics workstations, etc. Similar local networks are useful in a laboratory environment where each sophisticated instrument has a built-in microprocessor. These can be interconnected and the network connected in turn to a general purpose computer with powerful I/O devices and storage devices. The general purpose computer and the peripheral devices enhance the power for analyzing the output of each of the instruments. Besides this, data gathered and processed by each instrument may be correlated.

Local area networks are also used in factories for controlling plants and processes. Individual small computers would be usually installed to monitor and control critical processes in the plant. These computers may be interconnected and connected in turn to another computer which would perform supervisory functions. Such a network provides an integrated control of the plant.

The communication lines interconnecting the computers in LAN are short. It is also localized to "private" area and one need not use a public telephone network. As distances are small and as faster communication between processors in the LAN is desirable, high speed communication lines which can transmit around ten million to hundred million bits per second are used to interconnect them.

Computer networks are mainly used to connect a number of widely dispersed computers. The main objective of such an interconnection is to allow users of the network to access specialized library programs, databases, languages and special facilities available in any of the computers in the network. For example, it would not be possible for many organizations to install a supercomputer which may cost 15 million dollars. If a supercomputer is connected to a network then it is possible for many organizations to access it from their location. This will enable the organizations to use their own local computer for most purposes and utilize the supercomputer only for those problems which require its speed and memory capacity. Another use would be when one of the computer centres in the network provides specialized services such as patent information database or bibliographic database. Such databases would be accessible to any of the computers in the network. Two big networks of this type which were operational for several years (since 1969) were the ARPAnet and TYMENET in USA. The ARPAnet interconnected about 50 computers in USA including supercomputers and has now been superseded by Internet.

NICNET in India connects PCs located in all district headquarters with a large computer at the National Informatics Centre in Delhi. This network is used to gather data for national planning. Another network in India is the ERNET (Educational & Research Network) which is used to connect computers at Indian Institutes of Technology, Indian Institute of Science, National Centre for Software Technology and many educational and research organizations in India. It is also connected to Internet so that academics and researchers in India can have access to their counterparts elsewhere in the world.

Another major network is the network maintained by Indian Railways for railway reservations. Using this network a passenger can book tickets on most major trains anywhere in India. Indian Airlines also maintains a network for airlines reservations.

World airlines also interconnect their computers which are used primarily for passenger reservations. Such a networking is essential because a passenger may change many airlines during international travel and the reservation status of each of the airlines would be required. Thus the database containing reservation status of individual airlines must be accessible via the network to all the cooperating airlines. Two international networks of this type are the SITA network and the British Airways network. International banks have their own network called SWIFT to reconcile their accounts and for electronic funds transfer.

13.3   INTERNET AND THE WORLD WIDE WEB

We saw in the last section that local computer networks can be connected together to constitute a wide area network. Wide area networks located in all parts of the world can in turn be connected to form a world wide network of computers known as the internet. Internet provides the following services which are possible due to the inter-operability between networks.

Electronic Mail

Electronic mail is an application in which any user on a network can send/receive letters on his computer terminal to/from any person in the world who has an electronic mail address. Internet provides a worldwide electronic mail facility. For example, any person in the world having access to the Internet from his work place or home can send me email to my email address rajaram@serc.iisc.ernet.in. The general format of internet email address is: <name of addressee>@<identity of his dept>.<institution>.<identity of Indian network>.<country code>. Mail can be sent not only to individuals but to groups, by using group identity. The network takes care to see that the mail is delivered safely if it leaves the user's terminal.

File Transfer

Mail is intended for short messages. A file transfer program is available on the Internet which allows transferring a large file containing programs or data from a computer in any part of the world to another. The files can be quite large (a few Mbytes). The system provides authorization of persons allowed to copy the file. The file transfer is reliable. The rules used in Internet for file transfer is called *file transfer protocol* or *ftp* for short.

Remote Login

By remote login (or telnet access) we mean a user sitting on his terminal logging on to a machine located anywhere in the world. Remote login allows a user's workstation or terminal to behave as though it is directly connected to the machine where the user is logged in. The user must have login account and password to access the remote computer. This is an extremely useful facility. For example, a company in India can develop and install software for a company in U.S.A. and continue to maintain it from India. Two researchers in two countries can collaborate using email, file transfer and remote login.

World Wide Web

Information is normally dispersed over many computers connected to the internet. If a user wants to obtain information from any of these computers they must be logically linked. The information stored in computers is not only text but also graphics (images), sound and video. This is called *multimedia information.*

Each document can be indexed using a number of keywords and the keywords can be used to link it through pointers to related multimedia items. For example, if there is a document describing Taj Mahal it can be linked to a picture of Shah Jehan stored in an image file. The designer of a document can choose the keywords and also provide links to similar keywords and items related to the keywords. Such a document annotated using keywords along with links (or pointers) linking it to other related documents is called a *hypertext*. A special notation is used to mark the keywords and links in hypertext. This notation is known as *hypertext mark up language,* abbreviated html. A computer connected to internet can store multimedia information indexed using html. This is called a web page. A computer located at an internet address can store many web pages. Such a computer is called a web site. The collection of all web sites linked together by hyper text links is known as the world wide web. Every web page has a unique address called Universal Resource Locator (URL). In order to transfer files on the web a special set of rules called hypertext transfer protocol (http) is used. All web pages are thus addressed starting with http. For example, the web address of the Supercomputer Education & Research Centre at the Indian Institute of Science containing web pages describing SERC is

http://www.serc.iisc.ernet.in

To obtain information from the web a software called a browser is used which normally has a good graphical user interface (GUI) pronounced Gooyee. Some popular GUI browsers are Netscape, Mosaic and Internet Explorer. Browsers provide a very powerful method of accessing information which may be located anywhere in the world. Thus most organizations and even individuals maintain a web page (called a home page) containing information about themselves. Literally millions of web pages are maintained today and it is increasing rapidly.

13.4 CHARACTERISTICS OF COMMUNICATION CHANNELS

By a communication channel we mean a medium through which electrical signals can be transmitted. Signals transmitted may be classified as either analog or digital. An *analog channel* transmits continuously varying signals such as sine waves. A *digital channel*, on the other hand, transmits binary digits represented by voltage pulses. For example, a +12 volts pulse may represent a 1 and a –12 volts pulse a 0.

Analog signals are continuously varying voltages of the type shown in Fig. 13.1. Such

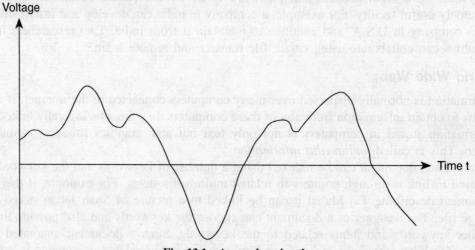

Fig. 13.1   An analog signal.

signals may be represented as a sum of sine waves. A sine wave is specified by the expression: $V \sin 2\pi f t$. Thus an arbitrary analog signal $h(t)$ may be represented by the equation:

$$h(t) = V_1 \sin 2\pi f_1 t + V_2 \sin 2\pi f_2 t + \ldots + V_n \sin 2\pi f_n t \qquad (13.1)$$

In order to describe the characteristics of an analog channel (which transmits analog signals) it is necessary to understand the characteristics of a sine wave signal. A sine wave signal $V \sin 2\pi f t$ is shown in Fig. 13.2. The *amplitude* of the sine wave is defined as V and

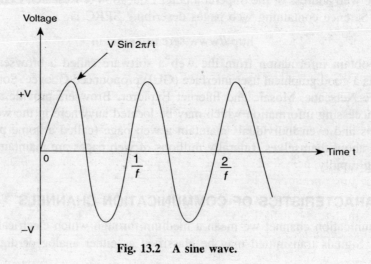

Fig. 13.2   A sine wave.

its *frequency* is defined as f. The amplitude of electrical signals is measured in volts and its frequency in *Hertz* (in honour of Heinrich Hertz who first generated electromagnetic waves) and is abbreviated as Hz. Sine wave signals may be generated in a laboratory with an instrument called an *oscillator*. The amplitude and the frequency of signals generated by an oscillator can be varied. For low frequencies the number of times a sine wave crosses the time axis (Fig. 13.2) will be small. In the limit when $f = 0$ the signal is said to be direct current (d.c.) signal. For high frequencies the number of times a sine wave crosses time axis will be very large.

The capacity of an analog channel is specified by its *bandwidth*. We may measure the bandwidth of an analog channel by connecting an oscillator at one end of the channel and send a sine wave of amplitude V_s through it. The amplitude of the sine wave received at the other end V_r is measured. The frequency of the sine wave is varied and at each frequency V_r and V_s are measured. The ratio V_r^2/V_s^2 is plotted as shown in Fig. 13.3. As may be seen from Fig. 13.3 the ratio (V_r^2/V_s^2) at low frequencies is small and it increases and remains

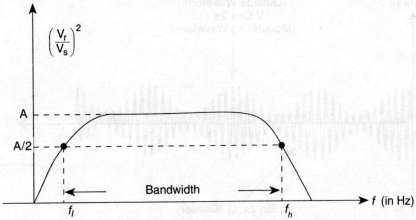

Fig. 13.3 Illustrating bandwidth of an analog channel.

constant over a range of frequencies and again decreases at very high frequencies. The lowest frequency where (V_r^2/V_s^2) reaches 50% of the value in the 'flat' portion of the curve (Fig. 13.3) is called the *low cut off frequency* f_l of the channel. The highest frequency where (V_r^2/V_s^2) again becomes 50% of the value in the flat portion of the curve is called the *high cut off frequency* f_h of the channel. The difference between these two frequencies $(f_h - f_l)$ is known as the *bandwidth* of the channel. The physical significance of bandwidth is that sine waves with a frequency in the range f_l to f_h would be transmitted without considerable loss of power. Most telephone lines used for communication within a city have a bandwidth of about 3000 Hz. The value of f_l would be about 300 Hz and f_h about 3300 Hz. This bandwidth is appropriate for local telephone lines as these lines are meant to transmit conversations whose frequency range is between 300 Hz and 3300 Hz. Thus human voice will be transmitted by such lines without loss. Such lines are known as *voice grade communication channels*.

The larger the bandwidth of a channel, the higher its capacity to carry information. For example, the bandwidth of coaxial cables used for inter-city trunk telephone calls (STD calls) is about 300 MHz. Such channels are used to transmit several conversations simultaneously using a *carrier modulation* scheme. We will now explain the term carrier modulation.

There are two basic ways in which analog signals may be transmitted over a channel. They may be sent in their original form as they arise physically. This is known as *baseband signal*. Another way is for them to be *modulated* or carried by a higher frequency called a *carrier* frequency and transmitted at the new frequency. For example, if $V \cos 2\pi ft$ is the original signal and $V_c \sin 2\pi f_c t$ is a carrier frequency signal then the *amplitude modulated* signal is (see Fig. 13.4).

$$(V_c + V \cos 2\pi ft) \sin 2\pi f_c t \tag{13.2}$$

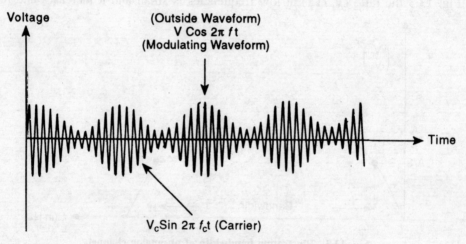

Fig. 13.4 An amplitude modulated waveform.

In other words, the baseband signal $V \cos 2\pi ft$ is added to the amplitude V_c of the carrier signal. We may express (13.2) as:

$$V_c \sin 2\pi f_c t + \frac{V}{2} (\sin 2\pi(f_c + f)t + \sin 2\pi(f_c - f)t) \tag{13.3}$$

The frequency of the carrier gets shifted to $(f_c + f)$ and $(f_c - f)$. The frequencies in the amplitude modulated signal are: $f_c - f$, f_c and $f_c + f$. If a voice signal in the frequency range f_l to f_h amplitude modulates a carrier f_{c1} the range of modulated signal frequencies and amplitude, would be as shown in Fig. 13.5. If another voice signal modulates another carrier f_{c2}, this modulated signal will be in the frequency $f_{c2} - f_h$ to $f_{c2} + f_h$ as shown in Fig. 13.6. If the channel bandwidth is large then by using several carrier frequencies and modulation, several conversations may be carried by the channel.

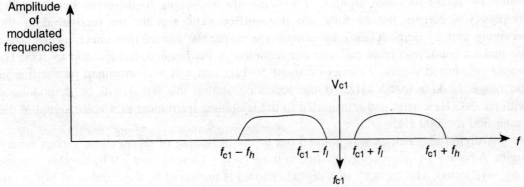

Fig. 13.5 Frequency spectrum of a modulated carrier.

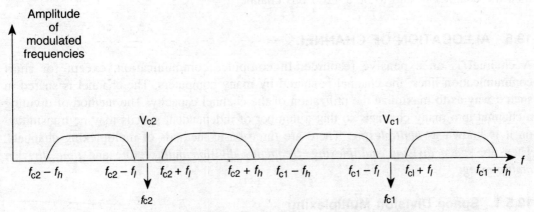

Fig. 13.6 Frequency spectrum of two modulated carriers.

To recover the conversation at the receiving end of the channel, the signal is *demodulated*. This is done by multiplying the received signal by the carrier and by rejecting higher frequencies using an electrical circuit called a *filter*. For example, if we multiply (13.3) by $2 \sin 2\pi f_c t$ we obtain (remembering that (13.2) and (13.3) are different forms of the same expression):

$$(V_c + V \cos 2\pi ft)\, 2 \sin^2 2\pi f_c t = (V_c + V \cos 2\pi ft)(1 - \cos 2\pi 2 f_c t) \qquad (13.4)$$

If we filter high frequencies around $2f_c$ and subtract the constant we will obtain from (13.4) the expression:

$$V \cos 2\pi ft \qquad (13.5)$$

which is the original signal which was modulated by the carrier.

To summarize, we saw that an analog channel carries continuously varying signals. The bandwidth of the channel specifies the range of frequencies that the channel can faithfully transmit. Higher the bandwidth of a channel, larger is its capacity to carry information. In order to use the larger bandwidth available in some channels several carriers may be used which modulate message signals, translating the messages to different bands in the frequency spectrum before they are transmitted. The signals are recovered at the receiving end by demodulating them with the respective carrier frequencies. Thus when we make a trunk telephone call, our conversation in the frequency range 300 to 3000 Hz would get shifted around a carrier of about 50 kHz and will be transmitted on the line in the range 47 kHz to 53 kHz. At the receiving station the signal will be demodulated with the 50 kHz carrier and transmitted to the telephone instrument as a voice signal in the range 300 to 3000 Hz.

A digital channel, as was pointed out at the beginning of this section, carries binary digits. A binary 1 is represented by one voltage (say, + 12 volts) and a 0 by another voltage (say, – 12 volts). The capacity of a digital channel is measured by the number of bits it can carry per second and is expressed as *bps*. Thus if 1200 bits can be transmitted per second then the channel is said to be a 1200 bps channel.

13.5 ALLOCATION OF CHANNEL

A channel is an expensive resource. In computer communication, except for short communication lines, the channel is shared by many computers. The channel is shared in such a way as to maximize the utilization of the channel capacity. The method of dividing a channel into many channels so that a number of independent signals may be transmitted on it is known as *multiplexing*. There are three basic methods of multiplexing channels. They are *space division multiplexing, frequency division multiplexing* and *time division multiplexing*.

13.5.1 Space Division Multiplexing

Space division multiplexing is creating a communication channel by grouping together a number of individual communication lines. For example, a number of subscribers' lines are packaged in a multiwire cable at a telephone exchange. Near the subscribers' premises they are separated into individual lines. This type of multiplexing is inefficient as a number of physical twisted wire pairs are used per telephone instrument and a bandwidth of only 3 kHz is used in each line. Each line is capable of being operated at a much wider bandwidth. The advantage of this method is that it allows individual connection to each user. When this method is used, transmission of information will be in the baseband for short distances. The system is simple to implement and use.

13.5.2 Frequency Division Multiplexing

Frequency division multiplexing (FDM) is the technique used to divide the bandwidth available in a physical medium into a number of smaller independent logical channels with each channel having a small bandwidth. The method of using a number of carrier frequencies each of which is modulated by an independent speech signal (which was discussed in the last section) is in fact frequency division multiplexing.

The best example of FDM is the way we receive various stations in a radio. The physical channel in this case is the 'ether', an unbounded medium. Many radio stations use the medium. Each radio station is assigned a frequency range within a band of radio frequencies. For example, Bangalore station is assigned the carrier frequency 720 kHz whereas Madras 'A' broadcasts at 612 kHz. The carrier, amplitude modulated by speech, music, etc., is transmitted by the radio station. A radio receiver's antenna receives signals transmitted by all stations. The tuning dial in the radio isolates the station tuned, demodulates the signal and converts it to the audio baseband signal. This is amplified by the radio and converted to sound by the loudspeaker.

In a bounded medium such as a telephone cable, the cable is connected between exchanges of main cities. In this case a cable has a bandwidth of about 200 kHz. Each telephone conversation would need a bandwidth of around 4000 Hz. We can transmit around 10 different conversations simultaneously on this channel by using a FDM scheme. We pick ten carrier signals of 50 kHz, 60 kHz, 70 kHz, ... 140 kHz and modulate the ten individual speech signals. This is transmitted over the cable and at the receiving telephone exchange they are demodulated using the respective carriers, filtered and routed to the appropriate telephone instruments (see Fig. 13.7).

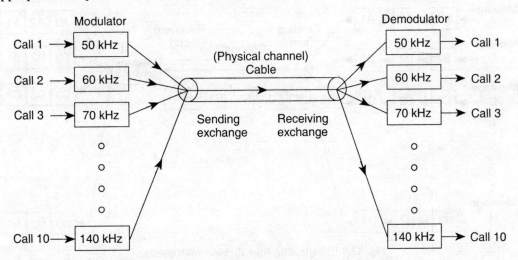

Fig. 13.7   Illustrating frequency division multiplexing.

We will now look at the characteristics of FDM. In order to use FDM the signals to be transmitted must be analog signals. Thus digital signals, if they are to use FDM, must be converted to analog form. We will see how this is done later in this chapter.

The second important characteristic of FDM is that all the signals in the physical channel travel *simultaneously*. Thirdly, the *physical* channel is split into a number of *logical channels*. Each logical channel is distinct and carries an independent signal. The available bandwidth of the physical channel is efficiently utilized. Finally, we need a modulator at the sending end and a demodulator at the receiving end for each logical channel. If we need two way communication, that is, if both ends of the physical channel are to be used to send messages as well as receive messages then we need a modulator and a demodulator at each end. A modulator-demodulator pair is known as a *modem*.

13.5.3 Time Division Multiplexing

Time division multiplexing (TDM) is another popular method of utilizing the capacity of a physical channel effectively. Each user of the channel is allotted a small time interval during which he may transmit a message. Thus the total time available in the channel is divided and each user is allocated a time slice.

In FDM a number of users send messages in parallel, simultaneously. The channel bandwidth is divided and allocated. In TDM, on the other hand, users send messages sequentially one after another. Each user can, however, use the full channel bandwidth during the period he has control over the channel. The channel capacity is fully utilized in TDM by interleaving a number of messages belonging to different users into one long message. This message sent through the physical channel must be separated at the receiving end. Individual chunks of message sent by each user should be reassembled into a full message (see Fig. 13.8).

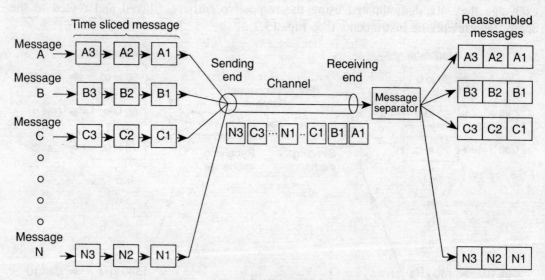

Fig. 13.8   Illustrating time division multiplexing.

TDM may be used to multiplex digital or analog signals. For digital data communications it is more convenient to transmit data directly in digital form and thus TDM is more appropriate. Besides this, communication between computers occurs in short fast bursts. Each burst would thus need the full channel bandwidth and in TDM this bandwidth is available.

Another aspect of allocation of channel which we should consider is, for how long the channel is allocated and how much data may be transmitted during this time. In TDM a time slice is allocated and the amount of data that can be transmitted during this time slice is a function of bandwidth of the channel. Suppose the bandwidth of the channel for digital data is 9.6 kilobits per second and the allocated time slice is 100 milliseconds, then a *"packet"* of 960 bits may be transmitted during the allocated time. Observe that the channel is "switched" between different users quickly and frequently. For example, if there are 10 users of the 9.6 kbps channel and each user gets 100 milliseconds slice, the user will get the channel to send the next packet after a second. A reallocation of time slice may be made as necessary to ensure an equitable use of the channel.

In contrast to this in voice transmission, in an FDM telephone channel, once a circuit is allocated to a sender and he is connected to the intended receiver of his message, he can have exclusive use of the logical channel as long as he wishes.

13.6 PHYSICAL COMMUNICATION MEDIA

Physical communication media are the physical channels through which information is transmitted between computers in a network. Media may be classified as *bounded,* for example, wires, cables and optical fibres; or *unbounded,* for example, ether or airwaves through which radio, microwave, infrared and other signals are transmitted.

13.6.1 Bounded Media

Twisted-pair of wires is the main media used in local telephone communication and short distance (less than 1 km) digital data transmission. Pairs of wires are twisted (see Fig. 13.9) together to reduce interference by adjacent wires. Wires are usually made of copper. This medium is inexpensive and easy to install and use.

Fig. 13.9   A twisted pair.

The twisted pair is used for audio telephone communication with speech signal bandwidth of 4 kHz. It, however, has a much higher bandwidth of about 50 kHz. The typical speed of digital signal transmission using local telephone lines is 1200 bits per second (bps) (Also commonly quoted as 1200 *bauds*). Twisted pairs used to connect terminals to a computer may be used up to 9.6 kbps if the length is less than 100 metres. Noise pick up by twisted wires limit their use. Error rates become high when the line length goes beyond 100 metres.

Coaxial cables offer much higher bandwidths and noise immunity. They are widely used in long distance telephone lines and as cables for closed circuit TV. Coaxial cables consist of a central copper wire surrounded by a Teflon or PVC insulation over which a sleeve of copper mesh or extruded aluminium is placed. The metal sleeve is covered by an outer shield of thick PVC material (see Fig. 13.10). The signal is carried by the inner copper wire. The signal is electrically shielded by the outer metal sleeve. Coaxial cables have a very high bandwidth. A 3/8 in. television cable has a bandwidth around 300 Mega Hz. The cable can carry digital signals at very high rates of 10 Mega bits per second.

Physically an *optical fibre* consists of a glass core, a plastic or glass cladding and a protective coating. The core diameter is between 8 and 200 micrometres. The refractive index of the cladding is less than that of the core. If the core has a single refractive index then there is an abrupt change in the index between the core and the cladding. Such a fibre is called a *step index fibre*. When the refractive index of the core changes gradually, the fibre is known as *graded index fibre*.

Light is propagated along an optical fibre as a set of guided light waves called the *modes* of the optical fibre. Depending on the geometry of the fibre and refractive index variations either a number of modes propagate or a single mode propagates. The first one is called *Multimode fibre* and the second a *single mode fibre*. Single mode propagation requires a small core dimension (1.5 to 5 micrometres), whereas multimode propagation

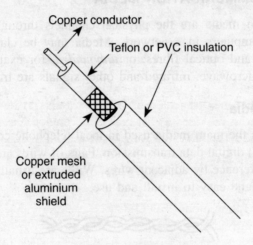

Copper conductor

Teflon or PVC insulation

Copper mesh
or extruded
aluminium
shield

Fig. 13.10   A coaxial cable.

requires a larger core dimension (50 to 200 micrometres) as only with a larger core diameter the refractive index can be graded. The most popular fibres are single mode and multimode graded index. Single mode fibre has lower losses and higher bandwidth (100 GHz per km) whereas multimode graded index fibre has higher losses and lower bandwidth (200 MHz to 2 GHz per km). The single mode fibre is more expensive compared to multimode fibre. For long distances single mode fibre is used and for shorter distances multimode fibre is used. It is difficult to have tappings on a single mode fibre whereas it is possible in multimode fibres. Multimode fibres are used to interconnect computers close together.

Optical fibres have several advantages. They are:

(i) Very high bandwidth.

(ii) Protection against electromagnetic interference.

(iii) More secure as they cannot be tapped easily.

(iv) Light weight and no corrosion.

The major disadvantages of fibres are:

(i) It is difficult to align and join two fibres in the field without special equipment.

(ii) They are fragile and cannot have sharp bends.

In fibre optic communications, electrical signals are transformed into light pulses by a modulator, transmitted over the fibre as light waves, detected and converted back to electrical signals by photoelectric diodes. Figure 13.11 illustrates this.

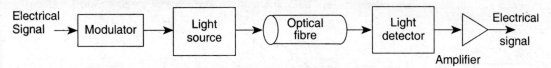

Fig. 13.11   Fibre optic transmission.

The light source used is either light emitting diode (LED) or a laser diode. For transmission of light over long distances with low dispersion it is necessary to have coherent monochromatic light. Lasers provide this whereas LEDs do not. Lasers are however expensive compared to LED. With LED, 15 Mbps transmission has been achieved whereas with lasers the speed is 2500 Mbps.

At the receiving end of the fibre optics system, light signals are detected and converted back to electrical signals by photoelectric diodes. One may either use PIN diodes (*P* Insulated *N* channel) or Avalanche photodiodes (APD). APDs are more sensitive and effective but are expensive compared to PIN diodes.

Optical fibres may be used to communicate either analog or digital signals. In analog transmission the light intensity is varied continuously whereas in digital transmission the light source is turned *on* or *off*.

13.6.2   Unbounded Media

Radio waves in the Very High Frequency band (VHF) (about 300 MHz) which are not used for commercial broadcasting may be used for communication between terminals and computers and between computers. Allocation of radio frequencies is controlled by the Government in most countries. One method of using radio waves is to use a *packet radio*. This is a combined transmitter and receiver with different transmission and receive frequencies. A packet radio is attached to each terminal and the computer (Fig. 13.12). Information entered on a terminal is transmitted using the packet radio and received by the computer. Processed results are transmitted back to the terminal by the computer. One of the main disadvantages of an unbounded medium is lack of security. The radio messages may be received by any one within the range of the transmitter. The main advantage is high data rates which may be achieved as the usable bandwidth on a carrier of 300 MHz would be about 100 kHz which can give digital transmission speeds of around 24 kilo bits per second. The other advantage is the possibility of reaching rural and hilly areas not covered by land telephone lines. VHF waves are corrupted by atmospheric noise and special error control schemes are necessary for reliable data communication.

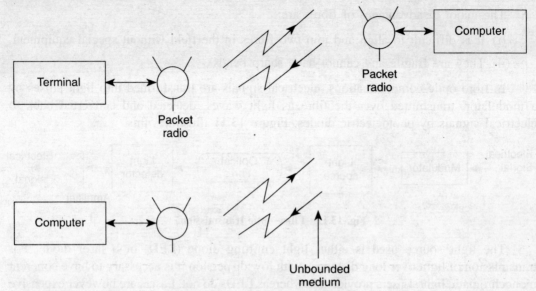

Fig. 13.12   Packet radio transmission.

Wireless communication is also becoming very important for communicating between portable computers (laptop or notebook computers) and servers. Laptop machines cannot have large disks and thus cannot store large files. With wireless connection a laptop computer can access files from stationary servers situated nearby. Further, portable computers can send and receive electronic mail from mail servers if wireless connection is available.

Microwave (2 to 40 GHz) communication using wave guides and repeaters is another useful unbounded medium. At microwave frequencies the electromagnetic waves cannot "bend" or pass obstacles like hills. The transmitter and receiver should be in "a line of sight". The microwaves are also attenuated in transmission and require power amplification. Thus receivers are placed at intervals of about 50 km. The receivers receive and retransmit the signal after amplification. These are called *microwave repeaters.* The great advantage of microwaves is the large bandwidth of 40 to 200 MHz available which will permit data transmission rates in the region of 250 Mbps. The capital investment needed to install microwave links is very high. They are mostly used to link big metropolitan cities with heavy telephone traffic between them. The link can support about 250,000 voice channels. Some of the voice channels may be used for data communication. Figure 13.13 illustrates microwave links.

Communication satellites are now becoming very popular for data communication between computers. Communication satellites are now launched either by rockets or by space shuttles and parked in a *geostationary* orbit at 36000 km above the equator. The speed of the satellite in this orbit equals the speed of rotation of the earth and thus the satellite is stationary relative to earth. The Indian national satellite INSAT-2B is parked so that it is accessible from any place in India including the islands of Andaman, Nicobar and Lakshadweep.

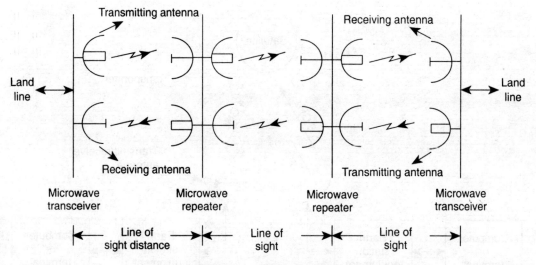

Fig. 13.13   Microwave relay.

A communication satellite is essentially a microwave relay station in the sky. Microwave signal at 6 GHz is beamed to it from a transmitter on the earth. It is received by the satellite as a feeble signal due to 36000 km travel. It is amplified and retransmitted to the earth at 4 GHz by a system called a *transponder* mounted on the satellite. The retransmission frequency is different as otherwise the powerful retransmission signal will interfere with the weak incoming signal. The main advantage of the satellite is that it is a single microwave relay station visible from anywhere in a country. Thus transmission and reception can be between any two randomly chosen places. The bandwidth of signals which can be handled by a transponder is about 36 MHz which would give 1200 voice channels, each supporting 4800 bps data rate or 400 digital channels of 64 kbps each.

A satellite has many transponders thus providing enormous communication capability at costs which favourably compete with microwave links on earth. Figure 13.14 illustrates a satellite communication link.

The interesting features of a satellite communication link are:

(i) There is a 270 msec propagation delay between the sending of data from one terminal or computer and its reception in another computer or terminal.

(ii) The transmission and reception costs are independent of the distance between computers.

(iii) Very high bandwidth is available if a user has an antenna in his own premises or a radio link to an earth station. The cost of receive-transmit ground stations has considerably reduced and now one may install a "private station" for about Rs. 10 lakhs.

(iv) A signal sent to a satellite is broadcast to all receivers within the satellite's range. Thus special security precautions would be necessary.

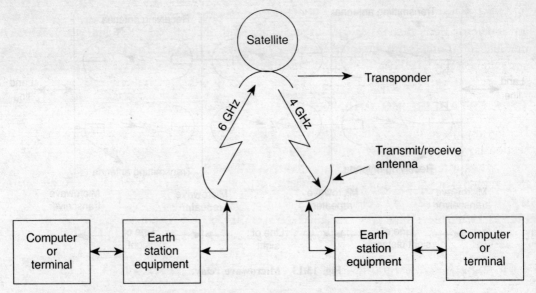

Fig. 13.14   Illustrating satellite communication.

(v) A transmitting station can receive back its own transmission and check whether the transponder has transmitted the information correctly. If an error is detected the data would be retransmitted.

(vi) Recently higher frequencies for uplink (i.e. earth station to satellite) and down link (satellite to earth station) are being used. The band 4 GHz to 6 GHz is called the C-Band and the higher frequencies 12 GHz and 14 GHz is called the K_u band. Use of K_u band transmission is, however, affected more by atmospheric disturbances particularly during the monsoons.

(vii) When a satellite system is to service a large number of users it is desirable to reduce the cost of the earth stations to be located in each user's site. This can be done provided the transponders in the satellite are improved and provide higher power output. Recently systems of this type are being built with Very Small Aperture Terminals (VSATs) at users' sites. The aperture refers to the diameter of the dish antenna which is about 1 to 2 metres. Smaller antennas and lower power transmitters and receivers at users' sites make VSATs affordable.

13.6.3   Infrared technology

For short distance line of sight communication Infra Red light (IR) can be used to transmit data. The most common IR device used is the hand held remote control of consumer goods such as TV, VCR, Audio Systems, Airconditioners etc. IR is in the frequency range 1000 to 3000 GHz and allows high speed data communication upto around 50 Mbps over a few metres in experimental systems. Commercial systems available now have 10 Mbps band. The most common use is thus in Local Networks. A portable computer with an IR communication interface can communicate with a stationary computer a few metres away provided there are no walls or similar obstructions in the line of sight path. The main advantage of IR is that it has a restricted range and thus the same frequency can be used in adjacent rooms without interference. Commercial IR-based products to interconnect computers today (1998) are marketed by IBM.

13.7   ESTABLISHING CHANNELS FOR COMMUNICATION

Having discussed the various methods available for communication we will discuss in this section how the media may be used to set up communication channels.

When a terminal is to be connected to a computer located at a distance of the order of 100 metres it can be done using a twisted pair. The information originating at a terminal will be in digital form. When it is transmitted over the line it is distorted as shown in Fig. 13.15. For low speeds of transmission of up to 300 bps the distortion is not severe up to about 5 km. If the speed of transmission is increased, the distortion would increase. For 9600 bps transmission the distance should be less than 100 metres. One may go up to about 500 metres for 1200 bps speed.

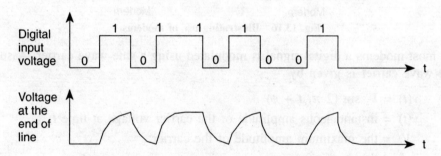

Fig. 13.15   Illustrating distortion of a digital signal.

When terminals are kept at a distance of the order of 1 km from a computer, transmission errors due to electrical disturbances may occur if no special precautions are taken. A *line driver* is often used for distances up to 5 km for transmission speeds up to 1200 bps. The line driver converts a digital 1 to a + 20 milliampere current and a 0 into a – 20 milliampere current and transmits the current. This is known as a current loop and has a better immunity against electrical disturbances.

When digital signals are to be transmitted over distances greater than 5 km via public telephone lines maintained by the Department of Telecommunications (DOT), the signals should be converted to analog form before transmission. This is due to the fact that DOT lines are designed to transmit telephone conversation. They are voice grade lines with a bandwidth between 300 Hz and 3000 Hz and will severely distort digital signals at 1200 bps. If digital signals are to be transmitted from a terminal to a computer, they are converted to analog signals before transmission. This is done by a *modulator*. The analog signals received by the computer are converted back to digital form by a *demodulator* to permit processing by the computer. The processed digital information is modulated to analog form and returned via the telephone line to the terminal where the analog signals are demodulated to digital form for display on the terminal. We thus need a *modulator-demodulator* pair at both ends of the telephone line. This equipment is called a *modem*. Figure 13.16 illustrates the use of modems. There are two main reasons for using modems. They allow higher speeds of transmission on a given analog line, and they reduce the effects of noise and distortion.

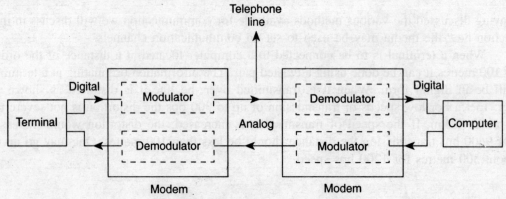

Fig. 13.16 Illustrating use of modems.

In most modems a digital signal is modulated using a sine wave carrier. Assume that the sine wave carrier is given by

$$v(t) = V_c \sin (2 \pi f_c t + \phi)$$

where $v(t)$ = instantaneous amplitude of the carrier voltage at time t;

         V_c = the maximum amplitude of the carrier;

         f_c = the carrier frequency;

         ϕ = the phase.

There are three ways of modulating the sine wave carrier by a digital signal. The first method is to modulate the amplitude of the carrier with the digital signal as shown in Fig. 13.17. Observe that when the digital bit is 1, the carrier is transmitted and when the bit is 0, it is not transmitted.

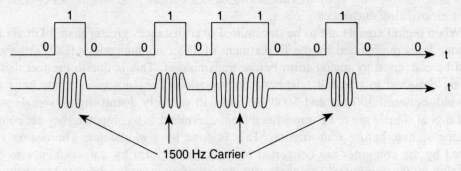

Fig. 13.17 Amplitude modulation of a digital signal.

The second method is to send a sine wave of frequency f_1 when the digital signal is 1 and a sine wave of different frequency f_0 when it is zero. This is called *frequency modulation* and is illustrated in Fig. 13.18. Frequency modulation of digital signals is also known as *frequency shift keying* and abbreviated as *FSK*. Frequencies in the range 1000 Hz to 2000 Hz are appropriate.

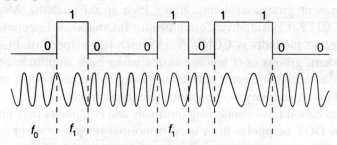

Fig. 13.18 Frequency modulation of a digital signal.

The third method is to send a sine wave with phase = 0 when the digital signal is 1 and a sine wave with phase = 180° when the digital signal is 0. This is called *phase modulation* and is illustrated in Fig. 13.19. Phase modulation is also known as Phase Shift Keying (PSK). Frequencies in the range 1000 Hz to 2000 Hz are appropriate for PSK. When only 2 phases are used for modulation PSK is termed 2 PSK.

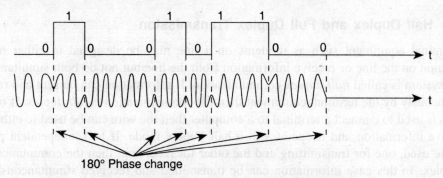

180° Phase change

Fig. 13.19 Phase modulation of a digital signal.

Amplitude modulated signals are sensitive to impulse noises picked up by the transmission line. Impulse noises arise due to electrical sparks near the transmission line. Frequency and phase modulated signals, on the other hand, are not sensitive to large impulse noise. In these modulation schemes an amplitude limiter is used, as the binary information is detected by the frequency or the phase values and not by the amplitude. Frequency modulation modems (FSK modems) are easier to design because, discrimination between two frequencies is simpler than detecting phase changes. Thus for medium speed modems (1200 to 2400 bps) the FSK scheme is preferred. For higher speed transmission of 9600 bps it is found that phase modulation is more reliable. We described PSK with 2 phases, a phase of 0 to represent binary 0 and a phase of π for representing 1. We can use 4 phases $\pi/4$, $3\pi/4$, $5\pi/4$ and $7\pi/4$ to represent 00, 01, 11, 10 respectively of the input bit string. The carrier frequency is not changed. With this encoding the speed of transmission in bits per second can be doubled as 2 bits are sent for each phase change. Note that a single frequency is used thereby conserving bandwidth. This modulation is known as 4 PSK as 4 phases are used. Instead of 4 phases we can use 8 phases to represent groups of 3 bits but detection of phase difference becomes more difficult. 8 PSK is combined with amplitude modulation (2 levels) to represent groups of 4 bits giving high speed modems. Modems have been standardized by CCITT (Consultative Committee for International Telephone and Telegraph) and one of the recent modems is CCITT V.33 which has a speed of 14.4 kbps on leased lines. In this modem, groups of 7 bits are coded using both amplitude and phase. Recent modems incorporate arithmetic error correction (using redundant codes) and are capable of working at 32 kbps on ordinary voice grade telephone lines.

The communication lines connecting terminals and computers may either be dedicated lines leased from DOT or public lines used in normal telephone communication. Leased lines normally bypass mechanical switching equipment in telephone exchanges and are more reliable. Communication lines have distributed inductance and capacitance which distort the amplitude of signals and also delay the signals at different frequencies by different amounts. For reliable communication, the attenuation and delay over the range of frequencies of transmission should be constant. This is achieved by *line conditioning*. Special circuits are added at both ends of the leased line by DOT to compensate for unequal attenuation and delay. This is essential to achieve reliable communication up to 9600 bps.

13.7.1   Half Duplex and Full Duplex Transmission

The terminal equipment such as modems on a line may be designed to either transmit information on the line or receive information from the line but not do both simultaneously. Such a system is called *half duplex* communication. If information can be sent and received simultaneously by the terminal equipment then the communication is *full duplex*. If one pair of wires is used to connect a terminal to a computer then the wire can be used to either send or receive information and it operates in a half duplex mode. If two independent pairs of wires are used, one for transmitting and the other for receiving, then the communication is full duplex. In this case information can be transmitted and received simultaneously.

One pair of wires may be used in full duplex mode by a modem provided 4 distinct frequencies (assuming FSK) are used. One pair of frequencies may be used to represent 1 and 0 in one direction and another pair for the reverse direction. This method, however, requires a large bandwidth if the transmission speeds in both directions are to be same. If data transmission in one direction is slow, then a lower bandwidth is sufficient. Typically 4 wire full duplex modems for 1200 bps are used on public telephone lines. 4 or 8 PSK using 2 frequencies can also be used for full duplex communication on a pair of wires. Some recent modems standardized by CCITT (e.g., V.32) use this method and work at 9600 bps.

13.7.2   Asynchronous and Synchronous Transmission

Information may be sent on a line in one of two modes. These are called *asynchronous* transmission mode and *synchronous* mode. In asynchronous transmission information is transmitted character by character. At the beginning of a character, a start signal is sent. The nature of the start signal is standardized and is "understood" by the receiving end equipment which prepares to receive the coded character. The start signal is followed by the bits of the coded character. If ASCII code is used, the seven coded bits and a parity bit are sent. Following the character code is stop signal. Figure 13.20 illustrates this.

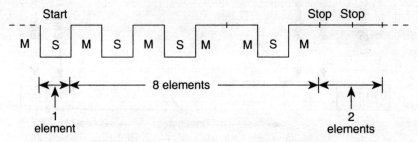

Fig. 13.20 **Asynchronous start-stop transmission-coding of a character.**

As each character is "framed" by a distinct start signal and a stop signal the time taken between transmitting any two characters may be arbitrary. When a terminal is connected to a computer and a programmer manually presses keys on the terminal, the time spent between successive keystrokes would vary. Thus asynchronous transmission is appropriate. This method does not require any local storage at the terminal end as each character is transmitted as soon as it is keyed in.

The main disadvantage of asynchronous transmission is that the transmission line is idle during the time intervals between transmitting characters. If the lines are short, this is not bad because line cost would be low and idle time not expensive. The advantage of asynchronous transmission is that it does not require any local storage at the terminal or the computer and is thus cheaper to implement.

In synchronous transmission blocks of about 100 characters are sent at high speed on the transmission line. This mode is particularly suitable for computer to computer communication. A distinctive synchronization pattern is sent at the beginning of the block. This is used by the receiving device to set its clock in synchronism with the sending end clock. The synchronization pattern is followed by codes to identify sender and receiver and the message characters. The number of characters in the message may be variable with a maximum of 100 characters. The message is terminated by an end of message character followed by a check character to aid detection of any transmission error. The format of a data block for synchronous transmission is shown in Fig. 13.21.

The main advantage of synchronous transmission is efficient utilization of the transmission line. The periods between blocks is kept small and the block itself is sent at nearly the maximum line speed. The main disadvantage is the need for local buffer storages at the two ends of the line to assemble blocks and also the need for accurately synchronized clocks at both ends.

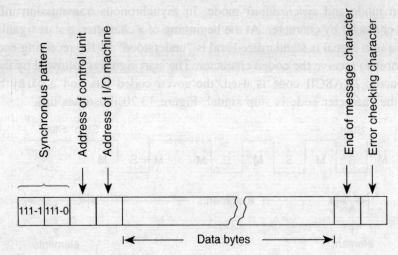

Fig. 13.21   Typical format of a data block for synchronous communication.

13.7.3   Establishing Communication Paths

When computers are connected to transmission lines they may communicate with one another in one of three ways. The simplest method is known as *circuit switching*. This is the method used to interconnect telephones in a telephone network. In a telephone network when a subscriber dials a number, the telephone exchange establishes a circuit between the calling and the called subscribers. This circuit is exclusively used by the two parties till the caller hangs up the phone. Computers and terminals connected to a telephone network may also use this method of establishing communication paths among them. This method is however very inefficient in utilizing the communication lines because communication among computers occur in bursts for a short period with long silent periods in between, during which the communication line is not used. In circuit switching a connection is established between a sender and a receiver for their exclusive use for the duration of communication. In the literature this is known as *connection oriented service*. As the connection is for the exclusive use of the two parties, the entire bandwidth is available for their use. This is particularly important for audio and video communication as they need high bandwidth and cannot tolerate delays in transmission. Data communication, on the other hand, can tolerate delays and exclusive reservation of a circuit is not necessary. Thus for data communication a method called *packet switching* is more appropriate. In this method a block of information to be communicated from a computer to another is formatted by the computer as a group of packets. A packet contains, besides the block of data to be sent (of the order of 1000 bytes), bits for synchronization, control information, message number, number of the current and last packet, destination and source addresses, acknowledgement and error checking bytes. The packet is sent on the transmission line and when it reaches another computer in the network the packet is examined and is routed to the next node based on an available free channel. The actual path taken by the packet to its destination is dynamic as the path is established as it travels along. When a packet reaches a node, the channel on which it came is released for use by another packet. As channels are used only when packets are transmitted, this method uses the channels very efficiently. This method is thus more suitable for "bursty" computer to computer communication. Figure 13.22 illustrates a packet switched system. In this figure the information to be sent from the source to the destination is broken up into three packets A, B, C. Observe that each packet takes a different route but all of them combine at the destination. As each packet has a serial number it is possible to reassemble the packet in the right order at the destination computer. Packet switching is not appropriate for audio or video data as delay on the network is unpredictable. Remember that telephone conversation takes place in real time and delays are not tolerated.

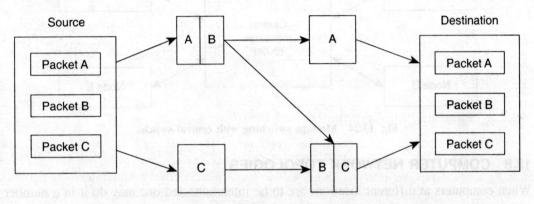

Fig. 13.22 Illustrating store and forward method of packet switching.

The packet switching method described above is known as a *store and forward* method as each node in the network temporarily stores a packet reaching it and forwards it using an available channel to the next node. It is also possible to *broadcast* each packet over a medium. In this case all the nodes check the destination address of each packet as they pass by and accept only those addressed to them (see Fig. 13.23). This approach eliminates routing delays inherent in store and forward systems. In this scheme, however, all nodes must be connected to the channel.

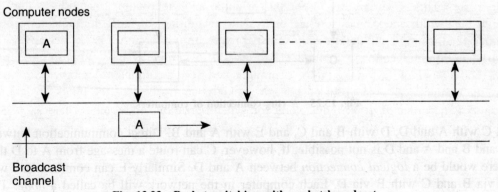

Fig. 13.23 Packet switching with packet broadcast.

Message switching is a variation of packet switching. In this case all message packets are received and stored by a central node connected to all the terminals. This central node then routes messages to their addresses. This method is used when message delays are not critical. Figure 13.24 illustrates message switching.

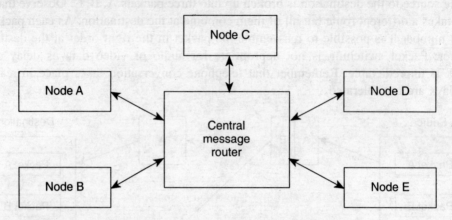

Fig. 13.24   Message switching with central switch.

13.8   COMPUTER NETWORK TOPOLOGIES

When computers at different locations are to be interconnected one may do it in a number of ways. For example, if five computers A, B, C, D, E are to be interconnected we may do it as shown in Fig. 13.25. In this case there are *physical links* between A-C, A-E, D-C, B-E and B-D. Assuming full duplex links, A can communicate with C and E, B with E and

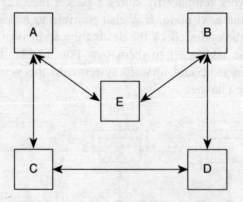

Fig. 13.25   A ring connection of computers.

D, C with A and D, D with B and C, and E with A and B. Direct communication between A and B and A and D is not possible. If, however, C can route a message from A to D then there would be a *logical connection* between A and D. Similarly E can communicate with D via B and C with B via D. Each computer in the network will be called a *node*. This interconnection pattern (Fig. 13.25) is known as *a ring network* and AEBDC form a ring.

Two other interconnection patterns are shown in Figs. 13.26 and 13.27. The pattern of Fig. 13.26 is called a *star network* and that of Fig. 13.27 a *fully interconnected network*. Different patterns of interconnections are known as *network topologies*.

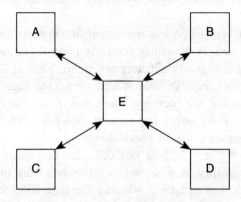

Fig. 13.26   A star connection of computers.

The main considerations in selecting a particular topology are:

(i) The availability and cost of physical communication lines between nodes and line bandwidth.

(ii) The capability of a node to route information to other nodes.

(iii) Delays due to routing of information.

(iv) Reliability of communication between nodes when there is a breakdown of a line or a node.

(v) Strategy of controlling communication between nodes in the network—centralized or distributed.

The fully connected topology of Fig. 13.27 has a separate physical connection for connecting each node to any other node. It is the most expensive system from the point of

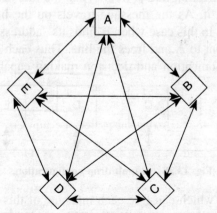

Fig. 13.27   A fully interconnected network.

view of line costs, as there are 10 separate point-to-point lines. It is, however, very reliable as any line breakdown will affect only communication between the connected machines. Each node need not have individual routing capability. Communication is very fast between any two nodes. The control is distributed, with each computer deciding its communication priorities.

The star topology of Fig. 13.26 has minimum line cost as only 4 lines are used. The routing function is performed by E which centrally controls communication between any two nodes by establishing a logical path between them. Thus if A wants to communicate with D, E would receive this request from A and set up the logical path A-E-D based on line availability. Delays would not increase when new nodes are added as any two nodes may be connected via two links only. The system, however, crucially depends on E. If E breaks down the whole network would break down.

The ring topology of Fig. 13.25 is not centrally controlled. Each node must have simple communication capability. A node will receive data from one of its two neighbours. The only decision the node has to take is whether the data is for its use or not. If the data is not addressed to it, it merely passes it on to its other neighbour. Thus if E receives data from B (see Fig. 13.25) it examines whether it is addressed to self. If it is, then it uses the data, else it passes the data to A.

The main disadvantage of a ring is larger communication delays if the number of nodes increase. It is, however, more reliable than a star network because communication is not dependent on a single computer. If one line between any two computers breaks down, or if one of the computers breaks down, alternate routing is possible.

One may use a hybrid approach to interconnection. In other words, the interconnections may not be a pure star, loop or full interconnection. The physical links may be set up based on the criteria specified at the beginning of the section to have an optimal communication capability for the specified network functions.

Another interconnection method is a *multipoint* or *multidrop* linkage of computers shown in Fig. 13.28. The main advantage of this method is the reduction in physical lines. One line is shared by all nodes. If computer A wants to communicate with E then it first checks whether the communication line is free. When the line becomes free it transmits the message addressed to E on it. As the message travels on the line, each computer checks whether it is addressed to it. In this case when E finds its "address" in the message it accepts it, sends an acknowledgement to A and frees the line. Thus each computer connected to the line must have good communication and decision making capability.

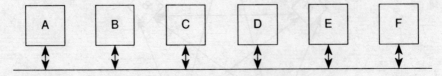

Fig. 13.28   A multidrop configuration.

An alternate approach which can free each machine of this task is to have one master computer overseeing communications on the line. The master would receive all messages and route them to appropriate machine. This approach would however create a bottleneck when computers connected to the link increase and consequently the master computer becomes too busy.

The method whereby each computer in a multidrop configuration places a message with the source and destinations addresses, to be picked up by the addressee, is known as a *broadcast scheme*. This method is appropriate for use in a local area network where a high speed communication channel is used and computers are confined to a small area. This method is also appropriate when satellite communication is used as one satellite channel may be shared by many computers at a number of geographical locations. In this method it is easy to add new computers to the network. The reliability of the network will be high with distributed control because the failure of a computer in the network will not affect the network functioning for other computers.

13.9 COMMUNICATION PROTOCOLS

When a number of computers and terminal equipment are to be connected together to form an integrated system, a well understood standard method of communication and physical interconnection should be established. This becomes particularly critical when equipment supplied by different vendors are to be connected since each vendor would have his own standards. If computers in different countries are to be connected together, yet another problem arises due to the need to use communication systems belonging to different nations which would have their own telecommunication regulations. Common agreed rules followed to interconnect and communicate between computers are known as *protocols*.

A universally used standard method of interconnecting user terminals to computers is the one proposed by Electronic Industries Association (USA) standard RS 232-C. This standard has been endorsed by CCITT (*Commite' Consultatif International Telegraphique et Telephonique*) recommendation V24. It completely specifies the interface between data communication devices (for example, modems), computers, and terminals. The RS 232-C interface consists of 25 connection points which specify the physical pin connections, voltage levels, signal transmission rates, timing information and control information such as ready and send.

The interconnection protocol for computer to computer communication is much more complex. It should define, besides the physical characteristics such as voltage levels, speeds, etc., the following:

1. How to begin and terminate a session between two computers?

2. How the messages in a session are to be framed?

3. How errors in transmission of messages are to be detected?

4. How messages are to be retransmitted when errors are detected?

5. How to find out which message block was sent by which terminal/computer and to whom?

6. How the dialogue on the communication line proceeds?

The most common method of sharing communication lines in a network is for a central communication controller to allocate unique addresses to computers and terminals in the network and allocate resources by *polling*. In polling, the communications controller asks a terminal or computer, using its address, whether a message block is to be sent. If the answer is 'yes' it accepts the message and routes it to the computer or terminal specified, if it is free to receive it.

An interconnection protocol for computer to computer communication as recommended by International Standards Organization (ISO) is gaining wide acceptance. It is an approach based on defining a number of distinct layers each addressing itself to one aspect of linking. This is known as the ISO model for *open systems interconnection*. The ISO model is made up of seven layers as shown in Fig. 13.29. Each layer has a specific independent function. The standardization achieved by each of the layers is explained in what follows.

Physical link layer: This layer defines the electrical and mechanical aspects of interfacing to a physical medium for transmitting data. It also defines how physical links are set up, maintained and disconnected.

Data link layer: This layer establishes an error-free communications path between computers over the physical channel. It gives the standard for framing messages, checking integrity of received messages, accessing and using channels and sequencing of transmitted data.

Network control layer: This determines the setting up of a logical path between computers in a network, message addressing to computers, and controlling message flow between computer nodes.

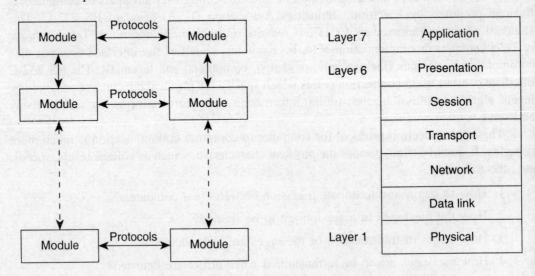

Fig. 13.29 ISO seven-layer model for open system interconnection.

Transport layer: Once a path is established between computers it provides control standards for a communication session for enabling processes to exchange data reliably and sequentially, independent of which systems are communicating or their location in the network.

Session control layer: This establishes and controls system dependent aspects of communications session between specific computers in the network and bridges the gap between the services provided by the transport layer and the logical functions running under the operating system of a particular computer in the network.

Presentation control layer: This layer provides facilities to convert encoded transmitted data into forms which can be displayed on a video terminal or printed.

Application/user layer: This provides services that directly support users such as file transfers, remote file access, data base management, etc.

The main advantage of the layered approach is that each one can be improved and modified independent of other layers. With changes in communication technology and standards, easy adaptation is important. One standard which defines the first three layers of ISO is the CCITT X.25 protocol. This standard has been integrated in the network architecture of many vendors.

Another commonly accepted standard which roughly corresponds to the bottom 4 layers of the ISO standard is known as TCP/IP (Transmission Control Protocol/Internet Protocol). It is now used as the standard in Internet which has now encompassed the whole world. We will describe the details of this standard later in this chapter.

In an ideal computer network, a user working at any one of the computers at any location in the network should be able to utilize the special facilities, languages, etc., available in any other computer in the network without having to know the detailed filing methods, the type of operating system commands, etc. of that machine. In other words, there should be a standard user interface at all locations. The network operating system should be able to decide and provide the optimal computing facility to a user to fulfil his requirements wherever he may be in the network without his having to even know from where and how his requirements are met.

13.10 LOCAL AREA NETWORKS

When computers located within a small geographical area such as an office or a University Campus (within a radius of 10 kms) are connected together we call it a Local Area Network (LAN). The topology of connection of computers in a LAN are:

(i) A star network (Fig. 13.26).

(ii) A multidrop (or a bus based) network (Fig. 13.28).

(iii) A ring (Fig. 13.25).

Among these the star network usually uses a local telephone exchange to connect computers. In other words the node E (in Fig. 13.26) is a telephone exchange. This is not a very popular arrangement as an exchange failure leads to LAN failure. Data transmission rates via an exchange is also restricted. Among the other two LAN topologies, the multidrop or bus topology is very popular as it is not expensive, standardized and supported by all computer vendors. It is called an *Ethernet* connection. (Ether was originally thought of the medium through which electromagnetic waves are propagated). Ethernet allows data transmission at the rate of 10 Mbps (10 million bits per second). Newer versions of Ethernet have come in the past 4 years and are fast Ethernets which provide a data transmission rate of 100 Mbps and Gigabit Ethernet which allows a data rate of 1 Gbps.

The ring topology is now being used for highly reliable high speed LANs using fibre optic transmission medium. A standard has emerged known as Fibre Distributed Data Interface (FDDI) for ring networks using Fibre Optic cables. It is now supported by all vendors of workstations. This standard allows transmission speed of 100 Mbps.

Another emerging standard which is applicable for both Local Area Networks and Wide Area Networks (WAN) is known as Asynchronous Transfer Mode (ATM). One of the main characteristics of ATM is its ability to handle multimedia traffic over both long haul and local networks.

In the rest of this section we will discuss in detail the characteristics of Ethernet LAN, FDDI LAN and ATM.

13.10.1 Ethernet Local Area Network

Ethernet is a standard developed by Digital Equipment Corporation, Xerox and Intel for interconnecting computers within a small geographic area. This was later refined and standardized as IEEE standards 802. The original standard specified interconnection of computers using a bus. The physical layer was specified as a shielded coaxial cable supporting a data rate of 10 million bits/second. Ethernet has advanced much beyond the earlier standard. Many versions have appeared and we will discuss them briefly later in this section.

The data link layer defines controlling access to the network and how data packets are transmitted between stations connected to the network. Referring to Fig. 13.30 we observe that all the stations are connected to the bus and each station communicates with the bus

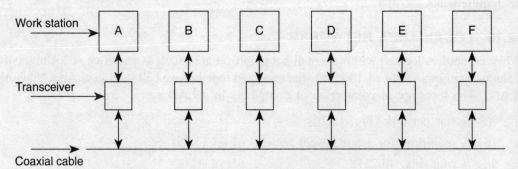

Fig. 13.30   An ethernet LAN.

via a transceiver, that is, a combined transmitter and receiver. Each station sends packages as a set of coded bits which are not modulated. Modulation is not necessary as the maximum length of the cable is small. Transmission of bits on the cable without modulation is known as *base band transmission.* Exchange of data between stations proceed as per the following protocol. When a station wants to send data its receiver listens to the bus to find out whether any signal is being transmitted on the bus. This is called *Carrier Serve* (CS). If no signal is detected it transmits a data packet. As the bus is accessible to all stations connected to it, more than one station could find no signal on the bus and try to transmit a packet on the bus. If more than one station transmits a packet on the bus then these packets will collide and both packets will be spoiled. Thus the receiver part of the transceiver of a station must listen to the bus for a minimum period T to see if any collision occurred. The period T is that time which the packet will take to reach the farthest station in the bus and return back to the sender. Collision is detected if the energy level of signal in the bus suddenly increases. Once a collision is detected the station which detected the collision sends a *jamming* signal which is sensed by all other stations on the bus so that they do not try to transmit any packet. The station also stops transmitting and waits for a random time and retransmits the packet. As it waited for a random time the probability of another collision is low. If there is again a collision it waits for double the previous random period and transmits. By experiments and analysis it is found that this method is quite effective and collisionless transmission will take place soon. This method of accessing the bus and transmitting packets is known as *Carrier Sense Multiple Access* with *Collision Detection* (CSMA/CD) system. It is called Multiple Access as any of the stations can try to send a packet on the bus or receive a packet from the bus.

The format of a packet consists of some bits for clock synchronization followed by the address of sender, address of the receiver, data packet and check bits (Fig. 13.31). A packet sent by a station is monitored while it is in transit by all other stations on the bus and the

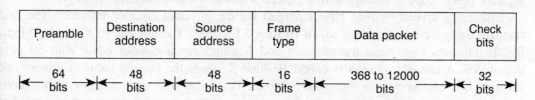

Fig. 13.31 The format of a frame or packet in ethernet LAN.

station to which it is addressed receives the packet and stores it. Other stations ignore it. It is possible to *broadcast* a packet to all stations. A packet can also be *multicast,* that is, sent to a subset of stations.

The length of the data packet is between 46 and 1500 bytes. The length is based on the length of the bus and number of stations connected to the bus. Currently ethernet is one of most popular Local Area Networks used as it is well proven, standardized and supported by all vendors of computers.

Ethernets may be extended using a hardware unit called a *repeater.* A repeater reshapes and amplifies the signal and relays it from one ethernet segment to another. A typical use of repeaters is shown in Fig. 13.32 in an office. A backbone cable runs vertically up the

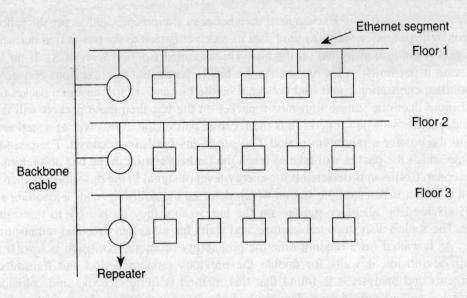

Fig. 13.32   Use of repeaters to extend ethernet connection.

building. A repeater is used to attach ethernet segments running in each floor to the backbone. Each ethernet segment is usually limited to 500 metres. No two workstations can have more than 2 repeaters between them if they have to communicate reliably. Use of repeaters is an inexpensive way of interconnecting ethernets. The main disadvantages of repeaters is they repeat any noise in the system and are prone to failure as they require separate power supply and are active elements unlike a cable which is passive.

Recently several options have emerged for the physical layer of Ethernet. The first standard using a coaxial cable is called 10 Base 5 Ethernet. The number 10 stands for Mbps, BASE indicates base band transmission and 5 stands for a coaxial cable with 50 ohm impedance. A cheaper version is called 10 Base 2 where the coaxial cable is thinner and cheaper. It is also known as *thin-wire Ethernet*. This Ethernet supports fewer workstations over a shorter distance compared to the Ethernet standard. A popular scheme which appeared in 1994 is called 10 Base T which is a 10 Mbps Ethernet using unshielded twisted wire (similar to the ones used in telephone lines).

In 10 Base T, unlike a cable which is a bus connection, each node is connected to a central *hub* using twisted pair of wires (see Fig. 13.33(a)). The hub has electronic circuits which receive signals from the twisted pair connected to it, amplifies and reshapes it and broadcasts it to all the other connections. The protocol is the same as ethernet, namely (CSMA/CD). The hub detects collisions and sends this information to all the nodes connected to it. Each hub can normally handle upto 16 nodes. (This number is increasing with improvements in technology). The distance between node and hub must be less than 100 metres. The main advantage of this type of connection compared to cable connection is higher reliability and ease of trouble shooting. Unlike a cable connection where if there is a fault in cable all nodes are affected and troubleshooting is time consuming, in a hub connection if a node fails it can be isolated and repaired while other nodes work. Other advantages are that most buildings are wired with twisted pair telephone lines and it is easy to connect it to a hub. Hub based wiring is much more flexible compared to cable wiring. Adding new computers to the LAN is easy. If the capacity of hub is exhausted more hubs may be used as shown in Fig. 13.33 (b). Recently 100 Base T, Local Area Networks (100 Mbps) using unshielded twisted pairs have emerged. By mid 1999 it is expected that gigabit Ethernet LANs will be standardized using CSMA/CD protocol. The physical medium for gigabit networks will normally be fibre optic cables.

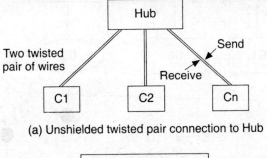

(a) Unshielded twisted pair connection to Hub

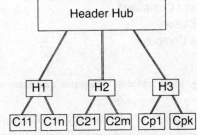

(b) Use of two level hierarchy of hubs

Fig. 13.33   Ethernet using unshielded twisted pair of wires and hubs

13.10.2   Wireless LAN

The use of wireless media to transmit digital information started in late 60s with the ALOHA Project at the University of Hawaii. The motivation was the requirement of communication between computers located in a number of scattered islands of Hawaii. ALOHA network was set up which used an early version of CSMA protocol. The situation changed dramatically in the 90s with the emergence of portable computers and better wireless technology. Executives moving around with their laptops wanted to be connected to the computers in their organization to look at their email and retrieve information from databases and also send email, purchase orders etc. Wireless technology also improved leading to widespread use of cellular telephones. Thus cellular radio technology used by telephones has been adopted to communicate between mobile laptop computers and stationary Local Networks.

In order to communicate using radio waves between a mobile computer and a fixed LAN, the mobile computer should have a transceiver (a combination of a wireless transmitter and receiver) and the LAN must have a base station with a transceiver to transmit and receive data from the mobile computer (see Fig. 13.34). The transmitter uses frequency in the so-called unlicensed band (915 MHz to 2.4 MHz) which is not used for commercial radio and other purposes. The power should be low to avoid interference with other transmitters. This technology currently provides a peak bandwidth in the range 1 to 4 Mbps.

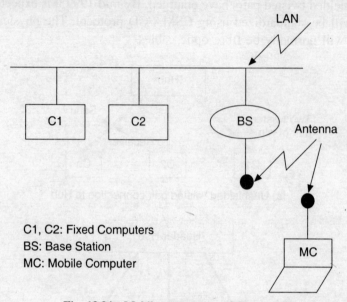

C1, C2: Fixed Computers
BS: Base Station
MC: Mobile Computer

Fig. 13.34   Mobile computer and Base station.

Early systems used *narrowband* technology in which a low power carrier signal was modulated by digital data using amplitude modulation. It was necessary for the transmitter power to be low to avoid interference with other systems using this frequency. It was thus affected by noise and special coding methods and error detection/correction algorithms were implemented. To reduce error while maintaining low power transmission a newer method called *spread spectrum* is now being used. In this method the input signal is transmitted (at a low power level) over a broad range of frequencies. This spreading of frequencies reduces the probability of jamming of the signal and makes it difficult for unauthorized persons to acquire and interpret data. Thus it is more reliable and secure. Wireless technologies today (1998) provide a bandwidth of 1 to 4 Mbps but the speed is bound to increase as usage builds up.

We considered above a laptop use near a wired LAN. It is also possible to communicate with a laptop moving anywhere using cellular technology similar to the ones used with cellular phones. In the cellular technology a wireless network is organized as a honeycomb of hexagonal cells. Each cell has a base station with an assigned address and is connected to a local network (see Fig. 13.35). A mobile laptop sends and receives data from a base station in a cell in which it is currently situated. As the mobile laptop moves between cells the mobile station has to be handed over by the current base station to the new base station. This is achieved by each mobile laptop having a unique identity which is acquired by the base station in whose cell the laptop is currently situated. A protocol called Mobile IP protocol is used to control the hand off of a mobile computer from one base station to another.

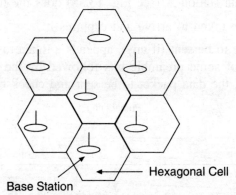

Fig. 13.35 **Cells in a cellular wireless network.**

13.10.3 FDDI Local Area Network

Fibre Distributed Data Interface (FDDI) is a standard defined by ISO/ANSI and IEEE for Local Area Networks using Fibre Optic cables to interconnect workstations/computers in the network. The standard defines the two lowermost layers of the ISO protocol. The physical layer medium dependent standard defines the specifications of optical transmitters and receivers, fibre optic cable, media interface connectors and optical bypass relays (optional). The transmitter is a light emitting diode (LED) and the receiver a photodetector. LEDs are inexpensive. The fibre optic cable defined in the original standard is 62.5 micrometre core diameter multimode, graded index, fibre optic cable with a cladding diameter of 125 micrometre (known as 62.5/125 cable). The connectors' mechanical details are given to connect to workstation ports. A relay is used to bypass the workstation/computer when the workstation fails. The media standards are being modified to include both copper cables (known as Copper Distributed Data Interface—CDDI) and single mode optical fibres. The other part of the physical layer standard specifies the methods of encoding data and synchronizing signals between workstations.

The next layer, namely, the data link layer, defines how the workstations are connected and how they access the network and communicate with one another. FDDI network consists of *dual counter rotating rings*. The stations are connected by a primary ring and a secondary or back up ring (Fig. 13.36). The primary ring carries the data between stations whereas the secondary ring aids in initializing the ring, reconfiguring and provides backup to the primary ring. Each ring in FDDI standard cannot exceed 100 km. The dual ring allows transmission if one of the stations fail or a cable breaks. This is done by wrapping around using the secondary ring (Fig. 13.37). Thus the FDDI standard provides excellent fault tolerance. If both faults occur then FDDI can be broken up into multiple independent rings. The FDDI ring is designed to transmit data at 100 Megabits per second (100 Mbps).

Frames are transmitted between stations in a FDDI ring using a protocol called the *Timed Token Protocol* (TTP). A *token* is a unique symbol sequence which circulates around the ring. To transmit a data station A (see Fig. 13.38) does the following:

(i) It waits for a free token to arrive and captures it.

(ii) It sets up a frame to be sent (if any), appends a token to it and puts it out on the ring. The frame consists of some preamble bits followed by the addresses of destination station and source station, the data packet to be sent and check bits.

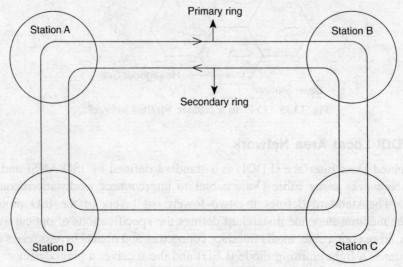

Fig. 13.36   An FDDI ring.

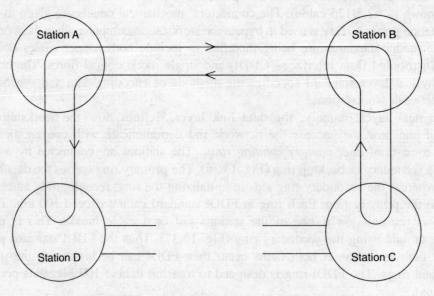

Fig. 13.37(a)   Reconfiguring ring when fibre breaks.

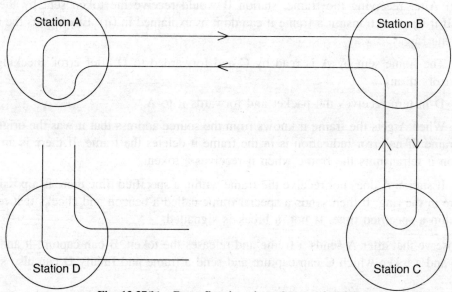

Fig. 13.37(b)   Reconfiguring ring when station fails.

(iii) When station B in the ring receives the frame it checks if it is intended for it by matching the destination address with its own address. If it is meant for it, it copies the packet and puts it back on the ring. It also checks for errors, if any, and notes it in the frame. If the frame is not addressed to it, it just forwards the frame to the next station C.

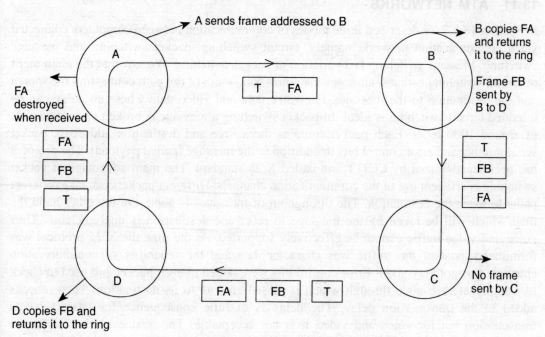

Fig. 13.38   Transmission of frames in FDDI ring.

(iv) After receiving the frame, station B would receive the token sent by the first station. If it wants to transmit a frame it can do it as explained in (ii). Else it puts the token back in the ring.

(v) The frame sent by A is read by C and forwarded to D after error checking and noting errors if any.

(vi) D in turn receives the packet and forwards it to A.

(vii) When A gets the frame it knows from the source address that it was the originator of the frame. If no error indication is in the frame it deletes the frame. If there is an error indication it retransmits the frame when it receives a token.

(viii) If station A does not receive the frame within a specified time there is a possibility of failure in the ring. It then sends a special frame called a beacon and checks if it returns to it within a specified time. If not, a break is signalled.

Observe that after A sends a frame and releases the token, B can capture it and send a frame and a token which C can capture and send a frame and finally D can also send a frame.

The FDDI standard allows all stations synchronous data transmission for a specified period followed by asynchronous transmission. The time allowed for each of this is dependent upon the time taken by a token to complete one rotation of the ring. The protocol allows a fair allocation of time to all the stations in the ring to transmit data.

13.11 ATM NETWORKS

In Section 13.7.3 we described three modes of communication between computers connected via a communication network, namely, circuit switching, packet switching and message switching. Message switching is a variation of packet switching. We saw that the main merit of circuit switching is that it allocates the entire bandwidth of the path connecting the source and the destination to the message. For voice data and video data where no delay can be tolerated circuit switching is ideal. In packet switching a message is broken up into packets of around 1000 bytes. Each packet contains the source and destination addresses, packet serial number and error control bits in addition to the message (called payload). The protocol has been standardized by CCITT and called X.25 standard. The main advantage of packet switching is efficient use of the communication channels. Different packets can take different paths to reach the destination. The throughput of messages is good. On the other hand the time which will be taken by the message to reach the destination is unpredictable. Thus voice and video traffic cannot be effectively supported. At the time the X.25 protocol was formulated most of the traffic was character data and the reliability of communication channels was not very good. Error control bits were added to each packet and used to check its validity at each node through which it passed enroute to its destination. These checks added to the transmission delay. The delay is of little consequence for character data transmission but for voice and video it is not acceptable. The next evolution of packet switching was called *Frame relay*. By the time this standard came, communication systems had become more reliable. Error checking at each intermediate node was considered not necessary. This reduced processing at intermediate nodes and consequently increased the speed of the system. Frame relay based systems are designed to deliver 2 Mbps to the end user whereas Packet switching systems deliver only upto 64 kbps. Packets in Frame relay system called frames are also long and of variable length. Thus frame relays also have unpredictable delays as packets take different paths to reach the destination. Error checking is done at the destination and not at intermediate nodes.

The next evolution in packet switching technology was *cell relay* also known as *Asynchronous Transfer Mode* (ATM). It may be thought of as an improvement over frame relay. Unlike a frame relay, the data packets in cell relay are short fixed length packets called *cells* which are 53 bytes long. Instead of using the terminology bytes for 8 bit groups, communications literature calls it an *octet*. A cell of 53 octets is divided into two parts; 5 octets for control and addressing and 48 octets for message. Observe that the cells are small and of fixed size as opposed to long variable length packets used in frame relays and packet switching. In ATM a message is divided into a number of cells. The structure of a cell is shown in Fig. 13.39. The message is preceded by a control cell (also 53 octets long) which specifies the type of cells which will follow, their priority and the bandwidth needed. The control cell is first sent from the source to the destination. This cell navigates through the

Octet #	Bit 8	Bit 7	Bit 6	Bit 5	Bit 4	Bit 3	Bit 2	Bit 1
0	Generic flow control				Virtual path identifier (VPI)			
1	VPI				Virtual channel identifier (VCI)			
2	VCI							
3	VCI				Payload type		Cell loss priority	
4	Header Error Control							
5 to 52	Payload							

(Message is called Payload)

Fig. 13.39 ATM cell structure.

nodes of the network and sets up a virtual path for the cells belonging to the message. The control packet returns to its source and places the virtual path identifier in all the cells belonging to the message. For the entire session (i.e, during the time the message from the source reaches the destination) the path is fixed. Thus it is like circuit switching because all cells will follow the same path. There is no need for packet serialization and the cells will travel in their natural sequence from source to destination. Thus the delay is predictable and could be made small if required. Thus video and audio data can be sent without degradation. ATM also assumes that the communication system is relatively error free and thus intermediate nodes do not check for errors. Only at the destination the message is checked for any errors (using a check sum). If there is an error, the entire message is retransmitted. ATM is like packet switching as a message is packetised and many packets (cells) can share a virtual path by Time Division Multiplex. A particular virtual path may be taken by cells belonging to different messages. Each message is allocated a virtual channel within a virtual path. In summary we see that the ATM protocol delivers all the cells belonging to a message in the right order via a fixed path. This is possible as the cells are short and finding a channel in a path is relatively easy. The control packet specifies the *quality of service* needed and while allocating a path the system guarantees (in a statistical sense) this quality.

One of the major advantages of ATM protocol is that it is a unified protocol and can be used (in theory) for both LANs and Wide Area Networks (WANs). In practice ATM switches are too expensive (as of now) for LAN use but is gaining acceptance for long distance communication in a wide area network. ATM based systems can work in the range of 100s of Mbps for frame relay based systems. The physical layer normally used with ATM is fibre optic cable, single node fibres for long distance networks and multimode fibres for short distance networks.

13.12 INTERCONNECTING NETWORKS

We examined Local Area Networks in Section 13.10. LANs connect machines in a small geographical area (around 10 km radius) and can operate between 4 Mbps to 2 Gbps (Giga bits per second).

Networks which connect machines in larger geographic areas are known as Metropolitan Area Networks (MANs) and Wide Area Networks (WANs). MANs operate over an area of around 100 km radius at a speed between 56 kbps and 100 Mbps. Wide Area Networks, also known as *long haul networks,* operate over the entire world with speeds in the range of 9.6 kbps to 45 Mbps.

To build a large network, smaller networks are interconnected. We already saw in Section 13.10 how small ethernet segments in a building can be connected together using *repeaters* to create a larger LAN. Repeater is the lowest level interconnect device which connects physical layers. It amplifies and reshapes electrical signals (bits) and retransmits them. The next level interconnect device is called a *bridge.* A bridge is designed to store and forward frames from one LAN to another. Bridges extend addresses of nodes connected to a LAN. If suppose 10 nodes are in LAN segment 1 with addresses 1 to 10 and ten more are in another LAN segment 2 with addresses 11 to 20. If node 5 in LAN segment 1 wants to send a frame to node 12 in LAN segment 2 it sends it as though it is in the same segment. As the destination address is not in that segment the frame is taken by the bridge which routes it to node 12 in LAN segment 2. The LAN segments need not know that a bridge exists. In other words the bridge is invisible to the end stations which communicate and are located in different LANs. *Routers* steer traffic through multiple LANs and ensure that the least congested route is taken. Traffic within a LAN are not disturbed by a router. Unlike bridges, routers are known to the end stations so that they can send messages to them to find out about frames sent by them. Routers have features for error and congestion control.

When larger networks are built interconnecting smaller networks one should have as the main goal *interoperability.* By interoperability we mean the ability of software and hardware of multiple machines from multiple vendors to communicate and operate together meaningfully. This is achieved to a great extent by a world wide computer network known as *Internet*. This network is a collection of interconnected *packet switched* networks using a protocol called Transmission Control Protocol/Internet Protocol abbreviated TCP/IP. This protocol does not follow the ISO/OSI protocol. It may be thought of as dealing with the higher layers, namely, the transport and application layers of ISO/OSI mode. TCP/IP defines· the unit of data transmission as a *datagram* and specifies how to transmit datagrams on a particular network.

13.12.1 TCP/IP

Internet allows any pair of computers attached to it to communicate. Each computer is assigned an address which is universally recognized throughout the network. Every datagram carries the address of its source and destination. Intermediate switching computers (routers) use destination address to route datagrams. TCP/IP provides acknowledgements between source and destination. The other transport level service provided by TCP/IP besides packet delivery is a reliable stream transport service. In other words, it "connects" an application program on one computer with that in another, and allows sending of large volumes of data between them as though they were connected directly by hardware. In order to achieve this, the protocol makes the sender divide the stream of data into small messages (datagrams) and send them, one at a time, waiting for the receiver to acknowledge receipt. In addition to providing basic transport-level services the TCP/IP includes standards for many common applications including electronic mail (E-mail), file transfer (ftp), and remote login. Thus when designing application programs using internet all the communication services needed are already provided by TCP/IP. For all practical purposes TCP/IP has become the standard for internetworking in Wide Area Networks (WANs).

13.12.2 Internet, Intranet and Extranet

We saw that any computer in the world can be connected to others by using a Public Switched Telephone Network. When the computers use TCP/IP protocol and have their own IP address they are said to belong to the internet, an international network of computers. There are many problems with the internet. One of them is lack of security. Vandals known as 'hackers' are known to have logged on to computers breaching password security (by exploiting weaknesses in the operating system of certain computers) and stolen or erased files. The other is slowing of the entire network due to very high traffic problem as the number of computers connected to the internet is increasing very rapidly. The strength of internet is its protocol which has proven to be robust. Many other services available on the internet such as email, ftp, remote log-in are found very useful. Many organizations thus felt that all the computers in their organization can be connected using the same protocol used by internet, namely TCP/IP. In many large organizations this will be a wide area network. Such a network is called an *intranet*. Observe that intranet is private to the organization. This 'isolationist attitude' can be counter productive as most organizations cannot work in isolation. They have to interact with their business partners. For example, a manufacturer has to interact with suppliers and distributors. A connection is required between the computers of these organizations. When computers of a group of organizations are interconnected using TCP/IP protocol such a network is called an *Extranet*. Extranet is a little more secure than internet and better security and traffic controls can be implemented.

SUMMARY

1. Access to a computer may be provided from a remote location by connecting a terminal to the computer via a telecommunication line.

2. A local area network (LAN) is an interconnection of many computers and terminals located near one another (within 10 km radius) via a fast communication link.

3. Computers in a LAN can be used to share data files, share computing resources and peripherals.

4. An interconnection of widely dispersed computers via a public telecommunication system is known as a wide area computer network.

5. Computer networks located in different organizations, cities or countries may be interconnected. This is called internetworking.

6. Internetworking is useful if we can ensure interoperability, that is, allow diverse hardware and software of different computers to work cooperatively.

7. Internet is a worldwide computer network which interconnects computer networks of many countries. Internet provides three important services, namely, electronic mail, file transfer between any two computers and remote login.

8. Information dispersed on many computers connected to the internet can be logically linked using *keywords* and such connected information is called hypertext and the links hypertext links.

9. Each computer in the internet which can be referenced by a hypertext link is called a web site. A collection of web sites is known as the world wide web.

10. A computer network allows its users to share library programs, databases, languages and special facilities such as an expensive supercomputer.

11. Communication channels required to interconnect computers may be classified as analog channels and digital channels. Analog channels are designed to transmit continuously varying signals whereas digital channels transmit two levels of voltages.

12. An analog channel is characterized by its bandwidth. The bandwidth specifies the range of frequencies of sinusoidal waves which the channel can transmit without attenuation. Larger the bandwidth, higher is its capacity to carry information.

13. The larger bandwidth available in some channels may be utilized by modulating message signals using several high frequency carriers. Modulation shifts each message signal to a different frequency band in the frequency spectrum and transmits it. The individual message signals may be reconstructed at the receiving end by demodulating with the respective carriers.

14. The capacity of a channel to carry digital signals is specified by the maximum number of bits per second (bps) which can be reliably transmitted via the channel.

15. A channel may be shared by several independent signals by multiplexing the channel. In frequency division multiplexing different signals are transmitted in a set of distinct bands in the available bandwidth. In time division multiplex, each signal is allocated a time slice during which it can use the full bandwidth of the channel exclusively. Available time is shared by various signals.

16. Physical communication media may be classified as bounded and unbounded media. Twisted pair of wires, coaxial cables, and fibre optic cables are examples of bounded media. Radio communication media, microwave communication and satellite communication are examples of unbounded media.

17. Twisted pairs of wires are inexpensive media used in voice grade telephone lines. They may be used for low speed transmission of signals of the order of 9.6 kbps.

18. Coaxial cables have wide bandwidth of the order of 300 MHz. They may be used in LAN and at transmission rates of about 10 Mbps. Recently unshielded twisted pairs of wires have been introduced as communication media in 10 Mbps LANs by improving error control techniques.

19. Fibre optic cables are plastic or glass fibres and provide high quality transmission of signals at very high rates, upto 1 Gbps. They are also used in LANs.

20. VHF radio at about 300 MHz is used for communication between computers in inaccessible locations or for short range communications. Speed of transmission of about 24 kbps is usually available when this medium is used.

21. Microwaves are used for wide bandwidth line-of-sight communication. Rates of transmission upto 250 Mbps is possible with this medium.

22. Communication satellites are microwave relay stations in the sky. Transponders on the satellite are used to receive, amplify and retransmit signals sent from an earth station. The main advantage of satellite is its wide coverage of a large area and thus it may be used from inaccessible locations. A transponder has a very large capacity and can handle about 400 channels, each channel having 64 kbps speed.

23. Computers separated by a few metres (in the same room with no intervening obstacles) can communicate using Infrared light (1000 to 3000 MHz) at a speed around 50 Mbps.

24. Direct digital communication between a terminal and a computer is possible using a twisted pair of wires at short distances (500 metres).

25. Communications between terminals and computers located at larger distances (5 km) is carried out using voice grade public telephone lines. Digital signals are modulated and converted into sine waves by a modulator and transmitted by the line. The received signals are converted to digital signals by a demodulator. As each end of the line has to both send and receive signals, modulator-demodulator pair known as modem is used at both ends.

26. The most common modem uses frequency shift keying. Digital 0 is converted to a sine wave around 1000 Hz and a 1 to a frequency around 1200 Hz.

27. Recently faster modems have been made using phase shift keying with 8 different phase shifts to represent groups of 3 bits.

28. A communication channel which allows a computer to either receive information or send information but not both simultaneously is called a half duplex channel. A channel which allows a computer to receive and send messages simultaneously is called a full duplex channel.

29. When messages are sent character by character and each character is framed by independent start and stop signals the transmission is called asynchronous.

30. In synchronous transmission blocks of about 100 characters are sent at high speed. A distinct synchronizing pattern is sent at the beginning of each block.

31. Computers connected to transmission lines may establish a path by either circuit switching, packet switching or message switching. Circuit switching connects the two machines via a line and this line is used exclusively by the two machines as long as they communicate. In packet switching, blocks of messages to be transmitted between machines are formed into a packet with source and destination addresses, error detection and control bits, and placed on the channel. Packets are routed using the address information. In message switching, all packets are sent to a central computer by all other machines. The central computer stores and forwards the messages to the appropriate destination addresses. It is more economical to use packet switching for most computer to computer communications as such communication is usually in bursts.

32. Computers in different locations may be interconnected in a star, ring, fully connected or intermediate configurations. A fully connected net connects every computer to the other with a physical link. It is reliable but expensive. A star net uses minimum number of lines but its reliability is critically dependent on the central computer in the star. In a ring connection each computer must have communication capability.

33. Another configuration is a multidrop linkage of computers. This linkage reduces the number of communication lines. Communication between computers is through a

broadcast scheme in which each computer places a message with source and destination address on the interconnecting bus.

34. Common agreed rules followed to interconnect and communicate between computers in a network are known as protocols.

35. A protocol defines how a session between two computers is begun and terminated; how messages are framed; how errors are detected and communicated; identifies source and destination computers and how the dialog between computers proceeds.

36. International Standards Organization has suggested a protocol. This is a layered approach where each layer addresses itself to one aspect of the communication problem. This approach allows each layer to be independently developed.

37. Ethernet is a very popular LAN. Ethernet uses a multidrop coaxial cable or unshielded twisted pair of wires to interconnect computers and can communicate at 10 Mbps. It uses a protocol called CSMA/CD (Carrier Sense Multiple Access with Collision Detection) to communicate between computers connected to the LAN.

38. Communication between a mobile computer such as a laptop computer and computers connected to a LAN is established by using wireless communication. Wireless transceivers are added to a mobile computer and to a base station connected to the LAN. The mobile computer communicates with base station which communicates with other computers connected to the LAN.

39. FDDI (Fibre Distributed Data Interface) is a standard for interconnecting computers as a LAN using fibre optic cable. FDDI network consists of dual counter rotating rings which provides highly reliable communication even when computers in the ring fail or cable is cut. It uses a protocol called the Timed Token Protocol which uses tokens with each data packet. FDDI allows data transfer at 100 Mbps.

40. Asynchronous Transfer Mode (ATM) is a recent unified standard to interconnect computers both in a wide area network and a local area network. ATM breaks up a message into short cells (each 53 bytes long) and sends *all* packets from a source to a destination along a fixed path. The path is negotiated before message transmission begins by a control packet with the intermediate nodes based on quality of service needed, bandwidth and tolerable delay . ATM thus has the advantages of both circuit switching and packet switching. It is particularly suited to transmit multimedia messages over fibre optic networks with a speed of several gigabits per second.

41. Table 13.1 gives a summary of nature of computer interconnections, distance and transmission speed.

Table 13.1   Summary of computers and communications

Distance in metres	What are interconnected	How connected	Nature of communication	Speed bps
1	Memory and processor	Buses	Bit parallel	100 M
10	Fast I/O and processor	Buses	Bit parallel	10 M
100	Video terminal and computer	Twisted pair	Serial asynchronous	19.2 K
1000	Video terminal and computer	Twisted pair Private line	Serial asynchronous current loop	9.6 K
10000	Video terminal and computer	Telephone line (within city)	Serial asynchronous modems	2.4 K to 9.6 K
100 to 1000 K	Video terminal and computer	Leased telephone line	Serial asynchronous modems	4.8 K
10 K	Computer and computer (LAN)	Fibre optic cable	Token ring	100 M
1 K	Computer and computer (Local area network)	Television cable multidrop	Bit serial broadcast	10 M
10 to 50 K	Computer and computer (Computer network)	VHF radio	Serial synchronous high speed modems	64 K
10 to 50 K	Computer and computer (Computer network)	Microwave link	Serial synchronous high speed modems	10 M
1000 K	Computer and computer (Computer network)	Satellite link	Serial synchronous high speed modems	256 K
100 to 1000 K	Computer and computer (Computer network)	Leased telephone line	Digital packet switching or store and forward packets	64 K to 2 M
100 to 1000 K	Computer and computer	Fibre optic Cable	Asynchronous Transfer Mode	1 to 10 G

REVIEW QUESTIONS

13.1 What is the purpose of using a remote interactive terminal connected to a computer?

13.2 What is a local area network?

13.3 What are the objectives of a local area network?

13.4 What is a computer network?

13.5 What are the objectives of a computer network?

13.6 What is internetworking? Why is it useful?

13.7 Give some examples of computer networks and their applications.

13.8 What is the world wide web?

13.9 What is a web page?

13.10 What is html?

13.11 What is URL?

13.12 What do you understand by the terms analog channel and digital channel?

13.13 How is the capacity of an analog channel specified?

13.14 Define the terms low cut off frequency, high cut off frequency and bandwidth of an analog channel.

13.15 What are the characteristics of a voice grade telephone line?

13.16 What do you understand by the term baseband transmission and carrier modulated transmission?

13.17 Describe how a signal is amplitude modulated and demodulated.

13.18 Why is modulation used in signal transmission?

13.19 How do you specify the capacity of a digital channel?

13.20 Why are channels multiplexed for signal transmission?

13.21 What is space division multiplexing?

13.22 What is frequency division multiplexing (FDM)?

13.23 Give an example of FDM.

13.24 How are voice signals frequency division multiplexed in a wideband channel?

13.25 Describe the characteristics of FDM transmission via a channel.

13.26 What is a modem?

13.27 What is Phase shift keying (PSK)?

13.28 What is 8 PSK and how is it useful in designing high speed modems?

13.29 What is time division multiplexing (TDM)?

13.30 Can TDM be used for digital channels?

13.31 Explain the operation of a TDM channel.

13.32 Explain the differences between FDM and TDM.

13.33 What is a bounded communication medium?

13.34 What is an unbounded communication medium?

13.35 What is a twisted pair? What is its capacity for analog and digital transmission?

13.36 What is a coaxial cable? What is the typical bandwidth of a coaxial cable?

13.37 What is the capacity of typical coaxial cables for digital transmission?

13.38 What is a fibre optic cable? What is the bandwidth of a typical fibre optic cable?

13.39 What is the typical digital speed of a fibre optic cable?

13.40 How is information transmitted via a fibre optic cable?

13.41 Give some examples of unbounded media.

13.42 Give the method by which VHF radio is used for terminal to computer communication.

13.43 What is the capacity of typical VHF links to transmit digital information?

13.44 Explain how microwaves can be used for computer to computer communication.

13.45 What are the advantages and disadvantages of using microwave communication?

13.46 Explain how communication satellites may be used for communication.

13.47 What are the advantages of using a communication satellite?

13.48 What is a transponder?

13.49 What is the typical bandwidth available per satellite transponder?

13.50 How many and at what speeds can digital signals be normally transmitted via a satellite?

13.51 What method of connecting a terminal to a computer is appropriate when they are separated by about 1 km and a transmission speed of 1200 bps is desired?

13.52 When are public telephone lines used to connect a terminal to a computer?

13.53 What is the normal speed of transmission of digital signals on a telephone line?

13.54 Why are modems necessary when telephone lines are used for digital data communication?

13.55 What are the modulation methods used to modulate digital data?

13.56 Explain the term frequency shift keying.

13.57 What is line conditioning? Why is it necessary?

13.58 What do you understand by the terms half duplex and full duplex transmission?

13.59 Is full duplex transmission essential for terminal to computer communication?

13.60 What is asynchronous transmission?

13.61 What are the advantages of asynchronous transmission?

13.62 What is synchronous transmission?

13.63 What are the advantages of synchronous transmission?

13.64 What is circuit switching?

13.65 What is the disadvantage of circuit switching?

13.66 What is packet switching?

13.67 Why is packet switching useful in digital data communication between computers?

13.68 Explain how packet switching method is implemented.

13.69 What is message switching?

13.70 What is the difference between packet switching and message switching?

13.71 What do you understand by the term computer network topology?

13.72 What is a fully connected computer network? What are its advantages and disadvantages?

13.73 Distinguish between physical and logical paths in a computer communication network.

13.74 What criteria are used in selecting a computer network topology?

13.75 What are the advantages and disadvantages of a star network?

13.76 What are the advantages and disadvantages of a ring network?

13.77 What is a multidrop interconnection of computers?

13.78 How do computers communicate in a multidrop configuration?

13.79 What do you understand by the term broadcast scheme for multidrop interconnected computers?

13.80 What is a communication protocol?

13.81 When is RS 232-C standard interconnection used? Explain the characteristics of the RS 232-C interface.

13.82 What characteristics need to be defined in a communication protocol?

13.83 What do you understand by the term polling?

13.84 What is system data link control?

13.85 What is the ISO model for open systems interconnection?

13.86 Why is a layered approach to protocol design adopted by ISO?

13.87 What are the various layers and their functions in the ISO proposal?

13.88 What topologies are appropriate for LAN?

13.89 What is an Ethernet LAN? What is the speed of communication on Ethernet?

13.90 What protocol is used to establish communication between computers in Ethernet?

13.91 Why is jamming signal needed in CSMA/CD protocol?

13.92 How long should a computer sending a packet on an Ethernet wait to find out whether there is any collision or not?

13.93 What do you understand by broadcast and multicast on an Ethernet LAN?

13.94 What is a thin-wire Ethernet?

13.95 How can one connect Ethernet segments in a building?

13.96 What do you understand by the terminology 100 BASE T Ethernet?

13.97 What is a hub? How is it used in an Ethernet using unshielding twisted pair wires?

13.98 What is wireless LAN? Explain why it is needed and how it is used?

13.99 What is spread spectrum and where is it used?

13.100 What is cellular wireless technology?

13.101 What are the advantages of using counter rotating rings in an FDDI network?

13.102 How are data packets transmitted and received in an FDDI ring?

13.103 Can there be more than one token at time in a FDDI ring?

13.104 What is the maximum bit rate at which frames can be propagated in a FDDI ring?

13.105 What is a frame relay?

13.106 What is ATM? What are the advantages of ATM?

13.107 What is the size of ATM Cell? What are the advantages and disadvantages of having a small cell size?

13.108 What is a MAN? At what speed does a MAN normally operate?

13.109 What is a repeater? When is a repeater used?

13.110 What is a bridge? When are bridges used?

13.111 What is a router? When is a router used?

13.112 What do you understand by interoperability? Why is interoperability essential in Internet?

13.113 What do you understand by TCP/IP?

13.114 How is communication between computers established in Internet?

13.115 What is an Intranet? How is it different from Internet?

13.116 What is an Extranet? How is it different from an Intranet?

14
Computer Graphics

Till recently the output obtained from a computer has been alphanumeric. It is well known that information presented in graphical and pictorial form tremendously aids human comprehension. For example, bar charts, pie charts, sales graphs, etc., are commonly used by managers. Building plans, perspective views, cardboard models, etc., are used by architects. Engineers use mechanical drawings, circuit diagrams, scale models, contour maps, etc., in their work. Thus it would be desirable to have outputs from a computer in a pictorial form. It would also be desirable to feed graphical inputs and process them. Advances in computer hardware and software have led to the development of inexpensive graphic input and output devices and associated software. Computer graphics is concerned with the generation, representation, manipulation and display of pictures with the aid of a computer. With the emergence of Graphical User Interface (GUI pronounced Gooyee) computer graphics has become an integral part of all computers today. These interfaces use graphical icons to represent operations. By pointing to an icon using a mouse and clicking buttons, various operations are initiated. Most application programs such as word processors now have GUI which make them easy to use. As this area has become extremely important in both the design and use of computers, we will devote this chapter to the discussion of computer graphics.

14.1 COMPUTER GRAPHICS APPLICATIONS

Computer graphics may be subdivided into three broad areas. These are:

1. *Generative graphics* which deals with creation of 2D and 3D pictures from mathematical representation of the objects. For example, numerical results obtained from computations may be transformed to graphs and pictures. Pictures may be transformed, rotated, contracted and expanded for display. Animations, namely rapid changes of pictures to depict changes (as in movie projection), are useful in some applications. For example, in pilot-training the graphic display may be used to mimic the approach of an aircraft to an airstrip as the pilot manipulates the landing controls.

Another very important application of generative graphics is in Computer Aided Design and Computer Aided Manufacturing (abbreviated CAD/CAM). In CAD, graphics is used to design electrical, electronic, mechanical and structural components and systems. For example, extensive use of graphics is made in designing printed circuit board layouts, design of LSI/

VLSI chips, aircraft structures, ships' hulls, building structures, chemical plant piping layouts, etc. Very often the emphasis is only on producing precise mechanical drawings, architectural drawings, etc. Based on the drawings, manufacturing information such as parts list, subassembly list, etc., are automatically generated and used in CAM. The great advantage of computer graphics is the possibility of very quickly modifying drawings based on design changes, creating immediately accurate assembly drawings and associated part lists.

A more important, and rapidly growing graphics application is the actual design of engineering systems based on models simulated on the computer. Design ideas may be quickly checked interactively, and graphics provides the immensely useful pictorial model required in conceptualization. After the engineering system has been designed, the clerical jobs of creating assembly-drawings, parts list, tapes for controlling numerically controlled machines, etc., are done by a post-processing program.

2. *Cognitive graphics* deals with algorithms to recognize and classify pictures. For example, algorithms to classify pictures of thumbprints by their "features" may be developed. Such a thumbprint file stored in a computer would be very useful in criminal investigations. Other similar applications are: classifying peoples' faces, microscope pictures of bacterial colonies, ECG patterns, Bubble chamber photographs obtained by physicists, etc. In such applications, the pictures are converted to digital form by devices called *optical scanners*. The digital information is transformed and classified by specially written *pattern recognition programs*.

3. *Image processing* deals with cleaning up noisy or blurred images and creating clear pictures. For example, X-ray pictures of certain human organs may be obscured by intervening tissues. The X-ray is digitized with a scanner. The digital information is transformed with appropriately chosen algorithms which sharpens the image. This digital information is converted back to a picture and displayed. The new image would be much clearer to comprehend. Another application is to compress the bandwidth needed to transmit images such as television pictures by appropriate algorithms. Image processing methods are also extensively used in enhancing the visual quality of pictures obtained from satellites, and in mapping ocean boundaries, lakes, rivers, etc.

In Table 14.1 we summarize the above points. As the techniques used in cognitive graphics and image processing are primarily special computer algorithms, we will not discuss these in this book. We will discuss in greater detail the hardware and software aspects related to generative graphics in the rest of this chapter.

14.2 DISPLAY DEVICES

The most commonly used display device in computer graphics is a cathode ray tube (CRT). A simplified diagram of a CRT showing its essential parts is given as Fig. 14.1. It consists of an evacuated glass tube enclosing a source of electrons, an electrode to accelerate the electrons emitted by the source, a focussing system to constrain the accelerated electrons in a narrow beam, a horizontal and vertical deflection system to deflect the beam, and a phosphor coated screen which glows when an electron beam strikes it. There are two

Table 14.1 Computer graphics classification

		Inputs and Outputs	System objective	Devices used
C O M P U T E R G R A P H I C S	G E N E R A T I V E	*Inputs*: Numbers, mathematical formulae, digitized pictures. *Outputs*: Monochrome and colour computer generated 2D and 3D pictures, and animations.	Computer aided generation of pictures from mathematical representation. Transformation of picture information. Classification, storage and retrieval of pictures.	Interactive video displays, light pens, graphic tablets and plotters.
	C O G N I T I V E	*Inputs*: Photographic images or computer generated pictures. *Outputs*: Images and pictures transformed and classified by computer programs.	Recognition of pictures as belonging to a certain class. Classification of images. For example, recognizing thumb prints, their classification and storage.	Optical scanners, picture grammars, special recognition algorithm.
	I M A G E P R O C E S S I N G	*Inputs*: Photographic images. *Outputs*: Computer enhanced photographic images.	Sharpening blurred "noisy" images by noise filtering and image enhancement. Picture transmission bandwidth reduction. Feature extraction and recognition. For example, improvement of medical X-ray images, removing noise from satellite pictures, recognition of features such as lakes, rivers, etc. in pictures taken from satellites.	Optical scanners. Gray level digitizers. Gray scale displays.

methods used to focus and deflect the electron beam. One of them is an electrostatic method using voltages applied to sets of conducting plates. The other is an electromagnetic method which uses electrical currents passed through focussing and deflection coils. We will describe both the methods and compare them in what follows.

Referring to Fig. 14.1 an oxide-coated metal called a *cathode* is heated by a heating filament. The cathode emits a large number of electrons when heated. These electrons are accelerated by applying a positive voltage to a *control grid.* The control grid voltage determines the number of electrons which ultimately strike the phosphor coated fluorescent screen. If the grid voltage is negative then no electrons are allowed to pass the grid and the beam is said to be *blanked.* A large positive voltage applied to the grid attracts many electrons which will ultimately strike the screen. This increases the intensity of the emitted light when the electron beam strikes the screen. Thus the voltage applied to the grid controls the beam's intensity.

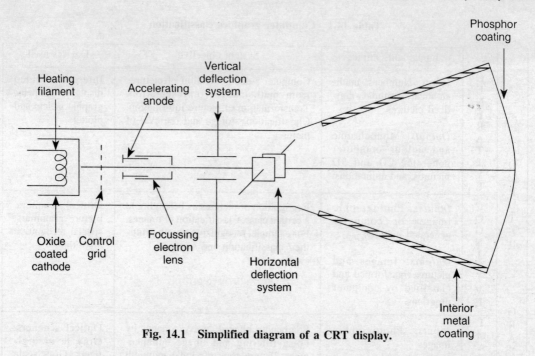

Fig. 14.1 Simplified diagram of a CRT display.

The electrons accelerated by the grid are further accelerated by an accelerating anode to which a positive voltage is applied. These are focussed by a focussing electron lens assembly which consists of a cylindrical metal enclosure with a hole (Fig. 14.1) through which the electron beam proceeds towards the screen. The assembly of electron source, accelerator and focussing system is known as an *electron gun.*

The beam from the electron gun passes between a set of vertical deflection plates. By applying a positive voltage to the top plate the beam can be moved up. It can be moved down by applying a positive voltage to the bottom plate. The beam can thus be made to trace a line along the vertical or *Y*-direction by controlling the voltage applied to the vertical deflection plates.

Following the vertical deflection plates is a pair of horizontal deflection plates. If a positive voltage is applied to the left plate, the beam will move left along the horizontal direction. It moves right if a positive voltage is applied to the right plate. Thus the beam can be made to trace a line along the horizontal or *X*-direction by controlling the voltage applied to the horizontal deflection plates. These deflection plate assemblies are sealed inside the neck of the CRT.

The electron beam, when it emerges from the deflection system, is further accelerated by applying a high positive voltage to a metallic coating inside the sides of the conical part of the CRT.

When the focussed and accelerated electron beam hits the phosphor coated screen at a high velocity at one point, this point lights up. The colour of the light emitted depends on the type of phosphor used. Phosphor types known as P1, P4 emit white light and are used in black and white television tubes.

Another important property of the phosphor is its *persistence.* The time taken for the spot to disappear when the beam is blanked is known as the persistence time. In a high persistence phosphor this time would be a few seconds. The phosphors used in graphic displays have a persistence time between 10 and 60 microseconds. If a line is traced from left to right, this line would thus be visible only for a few microseconds, unless the line is traced repeatedly. In order to see a flicker-free stationary line, the line should be drawn again and again. The number of times it is to be drawn depends upon the persistence of human vision and persistence time of the phosphor. Normally the line has to be redrawn 30 to 60 times a second to create a flicker-free image when P1, P4 or P7 phosphor is used. The number of times a picture is drawn in a second is known as the *refresh rate.*

A high-persistence screen would require a smaller refresh rate. A higher persistence would, however, keep an image on the screen longer and it would be difficult to rapidly change the images. Thus only relatively static applications in which an image need not be changed often would use high persistence screens.

The deflection system we have discussed so far is known as an electrostatic deflection system as the electron beam is deflected by a static electric field. Instead of using an electric field a magnetic field may also be used to focus the beam as well as to deflect it. Focussing may be achieved by surrounding the neck of the CRT tube with a coil carrying a current. This produces a magnetic field and focusses the beam. Two other coils are wound around the neck of the tube. As an electron beam travels along the axis of the tube, the field due to a current in one of the coils deflects the electron beam horizontally, while the field from the other deflects it vertically. The main merits of magnetic deflection system are the ease of construction of the CRT as the coils are outside the tube and better focussing leading to sharper spots and brighter images. As opposed to this the electrostatic deflection is superior in three respects. As voltages are used for deflection, higher deflection speeds can be achieved. The position of beam can be controlled more accurately and image distortion can be made lower. Most commercial display systems use magnetic deflection primarily because of their relatively simple construction and lower cost.

14.2.1   Colour Display Tube

Home colour TV sets use a method of displaying colour known as *shadow mask technique.* The inside of the CRT's viewing surface is coated with three different phosphors. The three phosphors are coated as patterns of three dots or triads covering the whole screen. Each of the three phosphors emits a different colour. One of them is red, the other green and the third blue. The dots in the triad are so close that when the CRT is viewed from a distance, the three dots do not appear distinct. The three colours merge into one and different colours may be obtained by controlling the intensity of each of the individual colours in the triad.

The individual phosphors in the triad are independently struck by three independently generated beams of electrons. The three beams are also arranged as a triad. The three beams are deflected synchronously and are focussed on the same triad on the tube surface. A shadow mask is placed in front of the tube surface. This mask has one small hole accurately aligned at each triad position on the screen. The acceleration voltage applied to each electron beam controls the intensity of each of the corresponding colours. Thus by controlling the individual acceleration voltages, a range of colours may be obtained. Figure 14.2 illustrates a shadow mask colour TV.

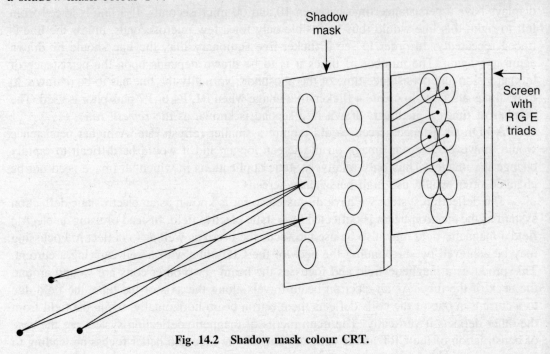

Fig. 14.2   Shadow mask colour CRT.

The resolution of colour display tube is limited by the need to precisely align the shadow mask. In high resolution displays, the distance between the centres of triads is 0.35 mm whereas in home TV tubes, this distance is 0.6 mm. The cost of colour tubes has come down rapidly. Users have a marked preference for colour displays. Thus the majority of VDUs today are colour displays.

14.3 OVERVIEW OF DISPLAY METHOD

To display images in an interactive computer graphics system the following methods are followed:

Step 1: The picture to be drawn is visualized by a user, perhaps by drawing a rough sketch on a graph sheet.

Step 2: A graphics program is written to draw the picture using the primitives of a graphics language or by using functions in a general purpose language such as C. The primitives normally available are to draw a point, a line, a polygon, arc of a circle, ellipse, dotted line, fill areas with colour etc. For example, to draw the picture shown in Fig. 14.3 one may write in a graphics language instructions as follows:

Draw_ polygon(x_0, y_0; x_1, y_1; x_3, y_3; x_4, y_4)

Draw_line $(x_1, y_1; x_2, y_2)$
Draw_line $(x_2, y_2; x_3, y_3)$
Draw_circle $(x_5, y_5; R)$

The values x_0, y_0 etc. are to be given in a coordinate system which will be later transformed to actual points on a display device.

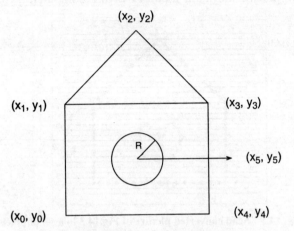

Fig. 14.3   A picture to be displayed.

Step 3: Almost all current displays are known as *raster scan displays*. In these displays the electron beam of the CRT sweeps and draws a line from the left edge of the screen to the right edge of the screen (see Fig.14.4), returns to the next line and again sweeps across the face of the tube. During the return sweep the beam is blanked as shown by the dotted lines of Fig. 14.4. After the bottom line of the display has been traced the beam returns to

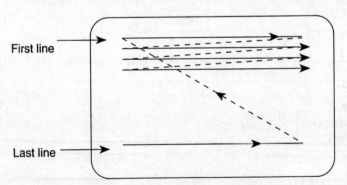

Fig. 14.4   Principles of raster scan display.

the top left corner of the screen. During this return also the beam is blanked. A medium resolution display will have 480 scan lines and a high resolution display around 1000 lines. The scanning rate in modern display is around 60 times/second.

The line drawing generated by the graphics program is sliced along the parallel horizontal scan lines generated by the raster scan CRT. All the points where the drawing cuts the horizontal scan line is called a *pixel* which is an abbreviation for a picture element (see Fig. 14.5). This procedure is called *scan conversion*. The coordinates of each pixel is stored. If it is a colour display the pixel will have bits to represent colour and intensity. The pixels are stored in a memory called a *frame buffer*. The frame buffer may be an independent memory or it may be part of the main memory of the computer.

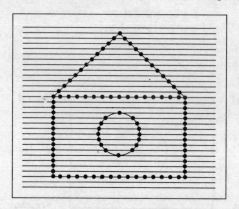

Fig. 14.5   Scan converted picture of Fig.14.3 to a set of pixels.

Step 4: The information stored in the buffer is retrieved by a video controller which drives the CRT display. The pixels are retrieved from the frame buffer and used to illuminate corresponding points on the VDU with appropriate colour.

A general block diagram of the components of a graphic display system is given in Fig. 14.6.

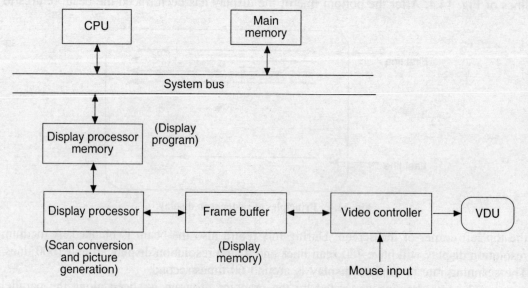

Fig. 14.6   Block diagram of an interactive computer graphics system.

14.4 RASTER-SCAN DISPLAY PROCESSING UNIT

As we saw in the last section in a raster-scan display device the electron beam is swept from left to right starting from the top of the screen. It then returns to the next line. During its return the beam is blanked. The scan is continued till the bottom of the screen is reached. The beam is then returned to the top left corner of the screen again for the next scan (see Fig. 14.4). A picture to be displayed is sliced along parallel horizontal lines corresponding to the raster. The beam is intensified at all the points where the picture cuts the raster (see Fig. 14.5).

The screen of the VDU may be assumed to be superscribed by a grid of 1024×1024 points. Each intersection point of the grid is used to display a pixel.

A display memory (also called a frame buffer) is associated with the raster-scan display in which one bit per pixel is stored. One bit defines either beam on or beam off. One bit per pixel is used in monochrome CRT. In colour terminals more bits per pixel are used which will explain later in this section. The video controller cycles through the display memory row by row, starting from the top row, at the rate of 60 times per second. Memory reference addresses are generated in synchronism with the raster-scan. The bit retrieved from the memory is used to control the intensity of the beam striking the CRT screen. Figure 14.7 depicts the contents of a small frame buffer and the corresponding picture displayed by the raster-scan display.

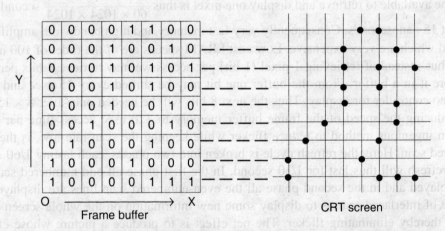

Fig. 14.7 A refresh buffer and the picture generated by it in a raster-scan display.

The organization of a video controller is shown in Fig. 14.8. The raster-scan generator produces the appropriate deflection signals to generate the raster. It also controls the X and Y address registers, which are used to fetch from the frame buffer the pixel value to control the beam intensity.

Assuming that a 1024×1024 pixel display is used, the X and Y addresses of the frame controller buffer will each range between 0 and 1023. At the start of the refresh cycle, the video will set X address register to zero and the Y address register to 1023 (the top scan line). The raster-scan generator, besides generating the first scan line, increments X address

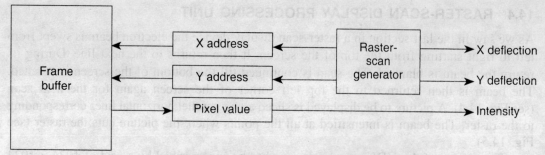

Fig. 14.8 A raster-scan video controller.

register in synchronism. These X addresses and the Y address are used to fetch the appropriate pixel to control the beam intensity. At the end of the first scan line, X address is reset to zero and the Y address is decremented by one. The next scan line is then generated and corresponding pixels are displayed. The process continues until the bottom scan line (Y address = 0) is generated.

The top to bottom scanning is repeated 60 times a second, for a flicker-free display.

With 60 repetitions of the picture per second one scan line is retrieved in $\dfrac{1}{60 \times 1024}$ second.

The time available to retrieve and display one pixel is thus $\dfrac{1}{60 \times 1024 \times 1024}$ second, which is about 15 nanoseconds. Consequently very fast memory and high bandwidth amplifiers are required which are very expensive. Low cost SRAM speeds are of the order of 100 nsec per byte. Thus instead of retrieving 1 pixel (1 bit) per access we may retrieve 8 bits per access and store it in a buffer. From the buffer one bit may be shifted every 15 nsec and sent to the video controller for display. Thus the next 8 bits will be needed only after $8 \times 15 = 120$ nsec reducing the speed of the frame buffer memory to 120 nsec access time per byte.

An ingenious method to reduce flicker while keeping the scan rate low, is the use of interlaced scan. Here, the refresh cycle is broken into two phases, each lasting 1/60 second. A full refresh will thus last for 1/30 second. In the first phase all odd-numbered scan lines are displayed and in the second phase all the even-numbered scan lines are displayed. The purpose of interlaced scan is to display some new information on the whole screen in 1/60 second thereby eliminating flicker. The net effect is to produce a picture whose effective refresh rate is closer to 60 per second. This interlacing method is based on the idea that the pixels in adjacent scan lines are almost the same. With interlaced scanning, 512 lines are

scanned in each 1/60 second. Thus the time needed to display one pixel is $\dfrac{1}{60 \times 512 \times 1024}$ which is about 30 nanoseconds. In this case also frame buffer speed may be reduced by retrieving 8 pixels per access. In this case we need a RAM of access time 240 nsec which is quite inexpensive by current day standards. Even though interlaced scanning leads to lower cost it is not commonly used in computer graphics as one may perceive some jitter in the images due to interlacing.

After a picture is displayed, if a new picture is to be displayed, the bit pattern for the new picture should be placed in the frame buffer replacing the old contents. This may be conveniently done during the time the raster takes to return from the bottom right corner of the screen to the top left corner. This raster *flyback* time is about 1.3 milliseconds. If replacing the frame buffer takes longer, picture refresh may by suspended and new information placed in the buffer.

The main reasons for the low cost of raster-scan display are the low cost of a TV monitor, semiconductor RAM and simple logic. The use of expensive analog components is avoided. For medium quality (256 × 256) display, inexpensive commercial TV monitors used in home TV sets may be used.

Another advantage of raster-scan display is the ease with which several shades may be displayed. This may be achieved by storing a group of bits rather than one bit per pixel. If a byte is used per pixel, 256 intensity levels may be displayed at each point. This allows shading, display of solid objects and also animation. Besides this, video information from such a display can be easily recorded on video tapes and replayed.

It is also possible to easily display colour pictures when this method is used. If we use 3 bits per pixel, each bit can activate one colour (red, green or blue). If proper mixing and shading of colours is needed 24 bits per pixel may be stored with 8 bits per colour. This gives excellent colour images. In the case of colour graphics we need to retrieve 24 bits/ pixel every 30 nsec if we use interlaced scan. If we retrieve 96 bits per access then we will need a frame buffer memory with 120 nsec access speed per 96 bits. This is feasible but quite expensive compared to a monochrome display. A 1024 × 1024 display will require 3 MB frame buffer with access time of 120 nsec for 12 bytes. Special techniques are used to organize high speed memories for graphic displays. An interested reader may read the book by Foley and Van Dam given in the References at the end of this book.

All display applications require, besides pictures, annotations to be written as a string of characters. Thus *character generators* are essential units in a display generator. The simplest hardware solution is to use a dot matrix display. In this method, each character to be displayed is defined as a pattern of dots on a small grid as in Fig. 14.7. In order to display all letters, special characters and digits, at least 7 × 9 grid of points is needed for each character. A ROM is used to store a string of 63 bits for each character. Given a character code, the appropriate string of bits is retrieved from the ROM which modulates the intensity of the CRT display to display the character.

In our discussions so far we have assumed that a separate display processor, display memory and frame buffer are added to a computer to give it graphics capability. This is not essential. A part of the main memory may be used as both display memory and frame buffer. Similarly, CPU may execute graphics programs and perform scan conversion. This, even though feasible, would put too much demand on the CPU and memory of a general purpose computer and consequently slow down computation as well as graphics speed. Thus nowadays even Personal Computers use special purpose graphics systems (such as VGA, SVGA cards in PCs and processor enhancement such as MMX processor of Pentium processor) to facilitate graphics applications on computers.

In this section we have discussed how a raster scan display device can be used to display graphics. There is another type of display called a *random scan display* in which points are plotted by applying appropriate voltages (or currents) to X and Y deflection systems of a CRT display. This display is more expensive compared to raster scan and is not used extensively nowadays.

14.5 INPUT DEVICES FOR INTERACTIVE GRAPHICS

There are a variety of devices used as input devices in graphics applications. These devices may be logically divided into four classes: locators, pickers, keyboards and function (or choice) keys.

A *locator* is used to move a *cursor* around the CRT screen to locate a desired point in a picture. A cursor is a small cross or underline or a small bright rectangle which may be superposed on the picture and can be separately controlled. The main purpose of a locator is to change a portion of a picture once it is located. A locator may also be used to locate a part of a picture and expand it for perceiving greater detail. Another application of a locator is to convert the information in a picture to digital form and store it in memory. This is known as *digitizing* a picture. For example, the *x* and *y* coordinates of points in a drawing may be stored in a database in digital form. This enables retrieval of the information, recreation of the drawing as well as introduction of changes as required.

There are two popular devices used as locators. They are: a *graphical tablet* with an associated *stylus* or a *cursor* or a *"mouse"* and a *joystick*.

A graphic tablet is a flat surface which may be kept on a table. Most tables use an electrical sensing mechanism to measure the position of a stylus or a cursor placed on the tablet. In one method, a grid of fine wires is embedded below the tablet surface to carry a current. When a stylus, which is like a pencil (Fig. 14.9), is pressed down at a point on the tablet, a switch is closed and its tip is electromagnetically coupled to the current-carrying grid wires. The strength of the picked up voltage indicates the (x, y) coordinates of the point. When the stylus is moved, the cursor on the CRT screen moves simultaneously to a corresponding position on the screen, to provide visual feedback.

For digitizing pictures, a lens-like cursor with a cross hair is used (Fig. 14.9). This is positioned over the point to be digitized. The voltage picked up by a coil embedded in the cursor is used to estimate *x* and *y* coordinates. Digitizers are marketed with tablet sizes up to 48" × 72" and a resolution of up to 0.001".

A mouse is a small plastic box mounted on two metal wheels whose axes are at right angles (Fig. 14.10). Each wheel of the mouse is connected to a shaft encoder which emits an electrical pulse for every incremental rotation of the wheel. The mouse is rolled around a flat surface. The flat surface need not have any embedded wires as in a tablet. As the mouse is rolled, its movement is sensed by the two wheels in two perpendicular directions. The distance moved is found by counting the pulses received from the shaft encoders. These are stored in registers. The values stored in the registers are sampled by the video controller 30 to 60 times a second. Visual feedback is provided by the cursor on the CRT screen which moves in synchronism with the mouse. Push buttons are mounted on top of

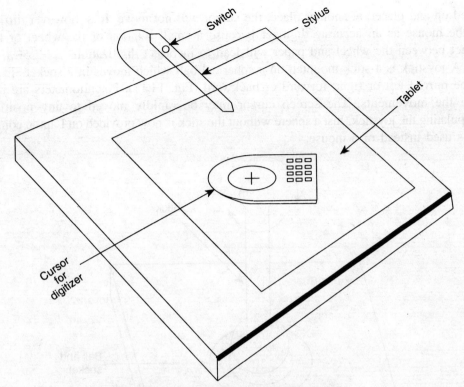

Fig. 14.9   A graphic tablet with stylus/cursor.

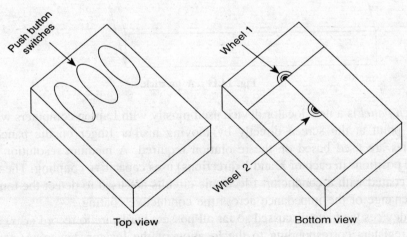

Fig. 14.10   A mouse.

the mouse and the user can press them as he moves the mouse. The (x, y) coordinates of the mouse, when the button is pressed, are stored by the computer.

The mouse is simple to make, and is inexpensive. In contrast to a stylus, the user need not pick up the mouse in order to use it. It is thus more convenient to use. If a mouse is picked up and placed at another place, the cursor will not move. It is, however difficult to use the mouse as an accurate digitizer because a small rotation of the wheel or loss of contact between the wheel and paper will lead to incorrect digitization.

A joystick is a stick mounted on a spherical ball which moves in a socket. The stick can be moved left or right, forward or backward (Fig. 14.11). Potentiometers are used to sense the movements. The screen cursor may be rapidly moved to any position by manipulating the joystick. Just a sphere without the stick is now provided on Laptop computers and is used instead of a mouse.

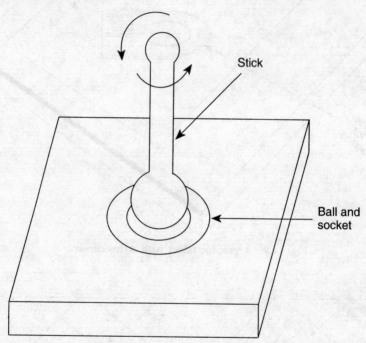

Fig. 14.11   A joystick.

Touch panel is a new locator device used mostly with Laptop computers which allows a user to point at the screen directly by moving his/her finger on the panel. Different technologies are used based on the resolution required. A medium resolution panel (100 resolvable positions in each of X and Y directions) uses capacitive coupling. The touch panel is a glass coated with a conductor. Electronic circuits are used to detect the touch position from the change of the impedance across the conductive coating.

The devices we have discussed so far all possess hardware to record (x, y) coordinates in buffer registers corresponding to the location of the locator device. At fairly regular intervals, the x and y coordinates are read from the buffer by the computer. These values can be used to modify the display file in any desired fashion.

In contrast, a *picking device* when pointed at an item on the CRT screen generates information from which the item can be identified by the program. The most important picking device is a *light pen*. The two main elements of a light pen are a photocell and an optical system which focusses onto it any light in its field of view. The lens and photocell assembly is mounted in a pen shaped case which can be held in hand and pointed at any point on the CRT screen (Fig. 14.12). The pen case has a finger operated switch which either opens or closes the electrical path from the photocell to the amplifier. The

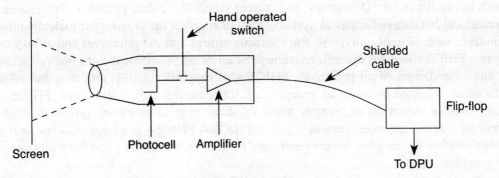

Fig. 14.12 A light pen.

photocell output is amplified, shaped and fed to a flip-flop which is set whenever the pen is pointed at a sufficiently bright source of light. The state of this flip-flop can be read and cleared by the computer. When the flip-flop is set, it interrupts the computer and the contents of the X and Y registers are read to determine which item in the picture is currently being viewed by the light pen.

Alphanumeric keyboards are used to input text and numbers to a graphic display unit. These are typewriter like keyboards described in Chapter 3 on I/O devices.

Function keys are specially programmed keys which may be used to pick some options from a menu. Preprogrammed pictures may also be displayed by depressing appropriate keys to generate them. For example, in an application to display electronic circuit diagrams, symbols for registers, capacitors, diodes, etc. may be stored in a special ROM or in memory and invoked by pressing appropriate function keys. Specially designed graphic workstations normally provide a large number of function keys appropriate for the application area.

14.6 PROGRAMMERS' MODEL OF INTERACTIVE GRAPHICS SYSTEMS

We have seen in the previous sections that graphic display and input systems have made rapid advances. The hardware of such systems has become versatile and inexpensive. They are rapidly becoming as popular as alphanumeric terminals and are now a standard device for interactive computer use. The question which arises is whether software for the use of graphic devices has kept pace with hardware advances. The answer is "not quite". In the early days software was highly *device-dependent* and special low level language routines unique to the specific device were supplied by each manufacturer. The present trend is towards *higher-level, device-independent* subroutines developed by independent software companies. These routines can drive a variety of display devices. The primary objective of such routines is to ensure the portability of application programs written in a high-level graphics oriented language to different machines.

The first attempt at standardization of device independent graphics was the one specified by a group formed by the Association for Computing Machinery (ACM), U.S.A., in mid 70s. This was called 3D Core graphics standard. It was refined and standardized by the International Standards Organization (ISO) as a Graphical Kernel System – 3D (GKS-3D) which has facilities for 3D graphics. The current standard is called PHIGS + (Programmer's Hierarchical Interactive Graphical System). PHIGS supports the grouping of logically related primitives such as lines, polygons, and character strings and 3D primitives and allows their nesting. PHIGS simulates dynamic movement by allowing geometric transformation (scaling, rotation, translation) of all primitives. PHIGS also supports creating, retaining and editing a database of nested hierarchical grouping of 3D primitives called *structures*. PHIGS has been extended with a set of features which facilitate realistic rendering on raster graphics terminals and this extended version is called PHIGS+. PHIGS+ is a large package as it has a large number of complex features and runs best on systems with good hardware support for graphics.

The general conceptual framework on which core standards are being formulated is shown in the block diagram of Fig. 14.13. There are three major blocks in the system:

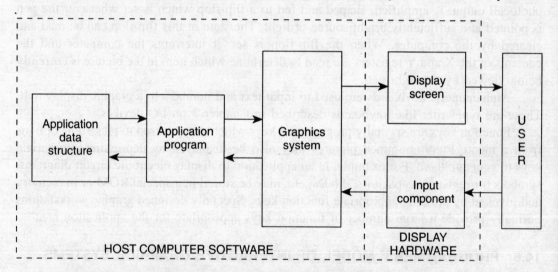

Fig. 14.13 Block diagram of programmers' model of interactive graphics system.

1. The display hardware which includes the display device, its screen and all the logical input devices, namely, the locator, the picker, keyboard and function keys.

2. The software on the host computer consists of an *application program* which interacts with the *application data structure or data base* and sends graphics commands to a set of routines called the *graphics system*.

3. The *user* who interacts with the graphics hardware terminal equipment and uses the software implemented on the host computer to get his job done.

We have already discussed in detail the display hardware. We will now discuss briefly the software. The data structure component of the software holds descriptions of objects whose pictures are to be displayed on the screen. This description typically consists of the following:

(i) *Geometric* coordinate data that define the shape of the object.

(ii) *Attributes* of the object such as surface texture, colour and line style.

(iii) *Connectivity* relationships and *positioning* data which defines how various parts of the object fit together. For example, in a circuit layout one has to specify how the various components are to be interconnected.

(iv) Non-geometric *text* or *property* data which give information on the geometric components to assist in further numerical processing. For example, for a circuit layout the *values* of various components such as capacitance, resistance, etc. would be needed to analyze the electrical properties of the circuit.

The application program describes to the *graphic system* the two or three dimensional (2D or 3D) geometry of the object whose picture is to be displayed. The 2D and 3D geometry of graphical objects have to be described in a manner which is quite different from those used in normal numerical and non-numerical programming as the types of data to be represented are quite different. Making "true to life" 3D pictures with shading, animation are particularly challenging tasks. Thus a whole new body of relevant mathematics and associated algorithms is rapidly evolving. For simpler problems, on the other hand, high-level device-independent graphics packages have matured and have made the interactive plotting of graphs, charts and drawings extremely simple and straightforward.

The application programs' description of 2D and 3D objects is fed to the *graphics system*. The graphics system contains a collection of *output* display routines compatible with a high-level language such as FORTRAN or Pascal. These routines create appropriate display files from the users' description of pictures to drive the display device (vector, or storage or raster-scan).

The graphics system has a function similar to that of an operating system in non-graphic application programming. Just as an operating system shields a high-level language programmer from the details of input-output programming, the graphics system shields the high-level language application programmer from the intricacies of the display hardware, the screen size and other physical parameters. The programmer is allowed to have a logical view of the display when he writes his program. The transformation from the logical to the actual physical device parameters is performed by the graphics system software. One part of the graphics system provides routines for output display. Another part contains input routines which pass user-supplied input data to the application program during an interactive session. Thus an application program can request the system to read the inputs from a locator input device. Alternately, the application program may receive inputs through interrupts generated from a keyboard or a light pen or a similar device.

Good graphics programming requires:

1. Creation of interactive "languages" for man-computer dialogues. Besides providing simple "menus" for interaction, graceful and informative error handling procedures are essential.

2. Removal of hidden surfaces, colour, lighting and shading methods to make pictures realistic.

3. Proper use of mathematics of geometric transformations and of shape and surface description for 3D display.

4. Good software engineering methodology for developing well documented, extensible, reliable and maintainable graphics programs.

SUMMARY

1. Computer graphics is concerned with the generation, representation, manipulation, and display of pictures with the aid of a computer.

2. As graphical presentation of results tremendously aids human comprehension and since graphic display hardware has become versatile and inexpensive, this area is gaining importance in computing.

3. Three broad classes of computer graphics are: generative graphics, cognitive graphics and image processing. Generative graphics deals with the creation of 2D and 3D pictures from the mathematical representation of objects. Cognitive graphics deals with algorithms to recognize and classify pictures. Image processing deals with cleaning up blurred images and creating clear pictures. We are mainly concerned with generative graphics.

4. An interactive graphics hardware system consists of a display device for outputting pictures, a display file memory in which the program to display pictures is stored, a display processing unit (DPU) which uses the information in the display file to generate signals to drive the display device, and a graphical input unit to feed information to the processor to store and interactively manipulate displayed pictures.

5. Cathode ray tubes similar to the ones in home television sets are used to display (or output) computer generated pictures. In the CRTs employed currently in computer graphics a picture should be repetitively displayed 30 to 60 times per second to produce a stationary image.

6. To display an image in an interactive graphics systems, a graphics program is first written to represent it using the primitives of a graphics language.

7. This program is translated into a set of instructions and stored in the display memory of a display processor. In cheaper computers such as PC, a part of the main memory is used as display memory.

8. Almost all current computer displays are raster scan displays in which the electron

beam of CRT sweeps and draws a set of lines from top to bottom. The number of lines varies between 480 to 1000 depending on the cost of the VDU.

9. The image drawn by the display program (stored in display memory) cuts the scan lines generated by the raster at a number of points. Each point is called a pixel (picture element). The number of bits used to represent a pixel depends on the number of intensity levels used to represent it. In monochrome CRT, it is around 8 bits and in colour CRTs it is around 24. The number of pixels stored depends on the resolution of the display required. In high resolution display it is (1024 × 1024) pixels.

10. The conversion of a display program to a set of pixels is called scan conversion.

11. The memory where the pixel are stored is called a frame buffer (or a refresh memory). The pixels in the frame buffer are retrieved in synchronism with the raster of the CRT display (60 times a second) and used to control the intensity of the beam(s), thereby displaying the picture.

12. Raster-scan displays are superior in displaying realistic 3D shaded images, excellent colour images and animated pictures. As they widely use TV display tubes, and as RAMs are becoming cheaper, they are becoming highly popular because they provide versatility at low cost.

13. Input devices used in computer graphics may be logically divided into four categories: locators, pickers, keyboards and function keys. Locators are used to move a cursor around on the display screen and point to a portion of a picture. They may also be used to digitally represent (digitize) pictures. Physical devices used as locators are: a graphic tablet with an associated stylus, a "mouse" and a joystick. Details of these devices are given in Sec. 14.5.

14. A picking device, when pointed at an item on the CRT screen, generates information from which the item can be identified by the program. A light pen is the most common picking device.

15. Alphanumeric keyboards with additional preprogrammed function keys are used to input character information, commands and to display preprogrammed pictures or text.

16. Software to use graphic display systems is being standardized with the evolution of higher-level device-independent subroutines using a standard proposed by the International standards organisation (ISO) called PHIGS (Programmers' Hierarchical Interactive Graphics System). Such subroutines have matured and interactive drawing of graphs, charts and drawings have become extremely simple. For complicated problems involving display of appropriately shaded 3D systems, colour display of 3D systems, animation, etc., a new body of appropriate mathematics and associated algorithms is rapidly evolving.

REVIEW QUESTIONS

14.1 What is computer graphics?

14.2 Why is graphics gaining importance in computers?

14.3 What is generative graphics?

14.4 Give some examples of generative graphics applications.

14.5 What do you understand by the term CAD/CAM?

14.6 How is graphics useful in CAD and in CAM?

14.7 What is cognitive graphics?

14.8 Give some applications of cognitive graphics.

14.9 What is image processing?

14.10 Give some applications of image processing.

14.11 Sketch a cathode ray tube and explain the purpose of each of the important components of the tube.

14.12 How is the intensity of the light emitted by a CRT beam controlled?

14.13 How is an electron beam deflected in a CRT?

14.14 What is the difference between electrostatic and electromagnetic deflection systems? Which is superior for computer graphics applications and why?

14.15 What is the advantage, if any, of using a high persistence screen?

14.16 Explain how a colour CRT functions.

14.17 "The rate of image refreshing could be reduced if a high persistence screen is used in a CRT". Is this statement true? If true what are the disadvantages of using a high persistence screen?

14.18 Give the block diagram of a raster-scan Display Processing System. Explain how images are stored in a refresh buffer.

14.19 Write a program to draw the picture of Fig.14.14 using graphics primitives for drawing circle, points, line etc.

14.20 Give the contents of a 16×16 refresh buffer to display the image of Fig. 14.14.

Fig. 14.14   Image for review question, 14.19, 14.20.

14.21 Define a pixel.

14.22 For a high quality 4096×4096 colour raster-scan display with a refresh rate of 60 per second, what should be the frame buffer access time? How can you reduce it?

14.23 How much time is normally available in a raster scan display to replace a picture to be displayed by another stored in the frame buffer.

14.24 In a high performance 4096×4096 raster-scan display it is required to display 16 intensity levels. What should be the capacity and organization of the frame buffer?

14.25 Repeat 14.24 if 8 colours of fixed intensity are to be displayed.

14.26 Repeat 14.24 if 8 colours with 16 intensity levels each are to be displayed.

14.27 Explain how alphanumeric characters are displayed in a raster scan VDU.

14.28 What are the four basic logical input devices in computer graphics?

14.29 What are the main differences between a mouse and a stylus based locator device?

14.30 What are the differences between a joystick and a mouse? Which is more versatile?

14.31 Explain how a picture may be digitized using a locator device. Use Fig. 14.14 for your explanation.

14.32 What is a picking device? How does it differ from a locator?

14.33 Explain how a light pen device works.

14.34 What are the applications of function keys in a graphics oriented computer?

14.35 What do you understand by the term device-independent high level graphics software?

14.36 What is the *de-facto* standard in graphics software?

14.37 What are the software components in a graphics system?

14.38 How is picture information described in a graphics data structure?

14.39 What are the qualities of a good graphics programming system?

References

(Books which will be useful for further reading relevant to topics in each chapter are listed below).

CHAPTER 1

1. D.E. Knuth, *The Art of Computer Programming—Vol. I: Fundamental Algorithms*, Addison-Wesley, Inc., Reading, Mass., 1969.

2. V. Rajaraman, *Computer Programming in Pascal,* Prentice-Hall of India Private Limited, New Delhi, 1983.

3. N. Wirth, *Systematic Programming—An Introduction*, Prentice-Hall, Inc., Englewood Cliffs, N.J., 1976.

CHAPTER 2

1. W.I. Fletcher, *An Engineering Approach to Digital Design,* Prentice-Hall of India Private Limited, New Delhi, 1990.

2. V. Rajaraman and T. Radhakrishnan, *An Introduction to Digital Computer Design,* 4th Ed., Prentice-Hall of India Private Limited, New Delhi, 1997.

CHAPTER 3

1. D.H. Saunders, *Computers Today,* McGraw-Hill, New York, 1985.

2. R. Jourdain and P. Norton, *The Hard Disk Companion,* 2nd Ed., Prentice-Hall of India Private Limited, New Delhi, 1992.

3. P. Pal Chaudhuri, *Computer Organization and Design,* Prentice-Hall of India Private Limited, New Delhi, 1994.

CHAPTER 4

1. J. Eimbinder, *Semiconductor Memories,* John Wiley and Sons, New York, 1971.

2. W.B. Riley, *Electronic Computer Memory Technology,* McGraw-Hill, Inc., New York, 1971.

3. M.E. Sloan, *Computer Hardware and Organization,* Science Research Associates, Inc., Chicago, 1976.

CHAPTER 5

1. W. Stallings, *Computer Organization and Architecture,* McMillan, New York, 1987.

2. C.W. Gear, *Computer Organization and Programming,* McGraw-Hill, Inc., New York, 1980.

3. M. Mano, *Digital Logic and Computer Design,* Prentice-Hall of India Private Limited, New Delhi, 1993.

CHAPTER 6

1. Y. Chu, *Digital Computer Design Fundamentals,* McGraw-Hill, New York, 1952.

2. J. Flores, *The Logic of Computer Arithmetic,* Prentice-Hall, Inc., Englewood Cliffs, N.J., 1963.

CHAPTER 7

1. M. Marcus, *Switching Circuits for Engineers,* 3rd Ed., Prentice-Hall, Inc., Englewood Cliffs, N.J., 1975.

2. J.E. Whitesitt, *Boolean Algebra and its Applications,* Addison-Wesley, Reading, Mass., 1961.

3. T.R. Viswanathan, G.K. Mehta and V. Rajaraman, *Electronics for Scientists and Engineers,* Prentice-Hall of India Private Limited, New Delhi, 1978.

CHAPTER 8

1. J.P. Hayes, *Computer Architecture and Organization,* McGraw-Hill, Inc., New York, 1978.

2. M. Mano, *Computer System Architecture,* 3rd Ed., Prentice-Hall of India Private Limited, New Delhi, 1994.

3. D.A. Patterson and J.C. Hennessy, *Computer Architecture—A Quantitative Approach,* Morgan Kauffman, CA, U.S.A., 1990.

CHAPTER 9

1. E. Balaguruswamy, *Programming in BASIC,* Tata McGraw-Hill Publishing Co. Ltd., New Delhi, 1983.

2. T.W. Pratt, *Programming Languages,* 2nd Ed., Prentice-Hall, Inc., Englewood Cliffs, N.J., 1984.

3. V. Rajaraman, *Computer Programming in Fortran 77,* 4th Ed., Prentice-Hall of India Private Limited, New Delhi, 1997.

4. V. Rajaraman and H.V. Sahasrabuddhe, *Computer Programming in COBOL,* Prentice-Hall of India Private Limited, New Delhi, 1984.

5. V. Rajaraman, *Computer Programming in C,* Prentice-Hall of India Private Limited, New Delhi, 1994.

CHAPTER 10

1. D. Comer, *Operating System Design,* Prentice-Hall, Inc., Englewood Cliffs, N.J., 1984.

2. B.W. Kernighan and R. Pike, *The UNIX Programming Environment,* Prentice-Hall, Inc., Englewood Cliffs, N.J., 1984.

3. S.E. Madnick and J.J. Donovan, *Operating Systems,* McGraw-Hill, New York, 1974.

4. H.M. Dietel, *An Introduction to Operating Systems,* Addison Wesley, Reading, Mass., 1984.

CHAPTER 11

1. H. Garland, *Introduction of Microprocessor System Design,* McGraw-Hill, Inc., New York, 1979.

2. L.A. Leventhal, *Introduction to Microprocessors: Software, Hardware, Programming,* Prentice-Hall of India Private Limited, New Delhi, 1982.

3. A.P. Mathur, *Introduction of Microprocessors,* Tata McGraw-Hill Publishing Co. Ltd., New Delhi, 1983.

CHAPTER 12

1. C.G. Bell and A. Newell, *Computer Structures: Readings and Examples,* 2nd Ed., McGraw-Hill, Inc., New York, 1980.

2. B. Randell (Ed.), *The Origins of Digital Computers: Selected Papers,* Springer Verlag, New York, 1973.

3. A.S. Tanenbaum, *Structured Computer Organization,* 2nd Ed., Prentice-Hall of India Private Limited, New Delhi, 1984.

CHAPTER 13

1. J. Martin, *Computer Networks and Distributed Processing,* Prentice-Hall of India Private Limited, New Delhi, 1981.

2. T. Viswanathan, *Telecommunication Switching Systems and Networks,* Prentice-Hall of India Private Limited, New Delhi, 1992.

3. A.S. Tanenbaum, *Computer Networks,* 2nd Ed., Prentice-Hall of India Private Limited, New Delhi, 1981.

4. W. Stallings, *Local Network,* 3rd Ed., McMillan, New York, 1990.

CHAPTER 14

1. J.D. Foley, A. Van Dam, S.K. Feiner and J.F. Hughes, *Interactive Computer Graphics,* 2nd Ed., Addison-Wesley, Reading, Mass., 1996.

2. W.K. Giloi, *Interactive Computer Graphics,* Prentice-Hall of India Private Limited, New Delhi, 1978.

3. W.M. Newman and R.F. Sproull, *Principles of Interactive Computer Graphics,* 2nd Ed., McGraw-Hill, Inc., New York, 1981.

GENERAL

1. J. Frates and W. Moldrup, *Computers and Life,* Prentice-Hall, Inc., Englewood Cliffs, N.J., 1983.

2. A. Freedman, *The Computer Glossary,* Prentice-Hall, Inc., Englewood Cliffs, N.J., 1983.

3. D.L. Slotnick and J.K. Slotnick, *Computers: Their Structure, Use and Influence,* Prentice-Hall, Inc., Englewood Cliffs, N.J., 1979.

4. P.V.S. Rao, *Perspectives in Computer Architecture,* Prentice-Hall of India Private Limited, New Delhi, 1992.

Glossary

Access time: Time required to retrieve a specified data from a computer's memory.

Accumulator: A register in the computer's processor where arithmetic operations are performed and results are stored.

Ada: A computer language standardized by U.S. defence department for complex command and control applications.

Address: A unique identification of a location in memory.

Address bus: A set of wires which is used to transmit the address. One wire is used for each bit in the address.

Algol: A computer language standardized by an international committee (*Algo*rithmic *l*anguage). It was mainly used to program numerical applications. It is extinct.

Algorithm: A finite sequence of precise and unambiguous instructions to solve a problem.

ALU: *A*rithmetic *L*ogic *U*nit of a computer which is used to perform arithmetic and logic operations.

Analog channel: A communication path used for transmitting and receiving continuously varying electrical signals.

Applet: A small object oriented program which can be used as a part of a larger application program.

ASCII: *A*merican *S*tandard *C*ode for *I*nformation *I*nterchange. This code is a string of seven bits used to code characters.

Assembler: A program which translates an assembly language program to its machine language equivalent.

Assembly language: A low-level language for programming a computer in which mnemonics are used to code operations and alphanumeric symbols are used for addresses.

Asynchronous communication: Communication between units operating independently with their own independent clocks.

ATM (Asynchronous Transfer Mode): A method of transmitting messages between computers in a LAN or a WAN. It breaks up the message into fixed size packets each

327

53 bytes long (called cells) and finds a fixed path from source to destination through which all cells of the message travel. It is particularly suited for transmitting multimedia data.

B

BASIC: Beginner's All-purpose Symbolic Instruction Code. A simple high level language for computers.

Base: The number of distinct symbols used to represent numbers in a system for enumeration.

Base address: An address to which the address in an instruction is added to find the absolute address in memory for storage or retrieval.

Base register: A register which stores the base address.

Batch operating system: A system program which facilitates the execution of a series of user programs without any manual intervention.

Binary: One of two possibilities.

Binary coded decimal: A representation of decimal digits which uses a unique string of 4 bits to represent each digit.

Bit: A binary digit which is either 0 or 1.

Block: A set of items handled as one unit in storage and retrieval.

BNF: Backus Naur Form is a notation used to precisely define syntax rules of a programming language.

Boolean algebra: An algebra to check the logical consistency of propositions which are either *true* or *false* and to simplify such propositions.

Boolean variable: A variable which can assume a value *true* or *false*.

Bridge: It is a circuit which stores and forwards frames received from one ethernet segment to another ethernet segment of a LAN.

Byte: A group of eight bits used to represent characters.

C

C: A high level programming language whose features allow one to write efficient programs.

C++: An object oriented version of C.

Cache memory: A small high speed memory which is used to temporarily store a portion of a program or data from the main memory. The processor retrieves instructions or data from the cache memory. Instruction and data caching speeds up computation.

CAV (Constant Angular Velocity): Recording method used in magnetic disks (Winchester hard disks). In this method the angular velocity is same for all tracks. Thus tracks with smaller radius have a high linear velocity. The density of recording is higher in the innermost tracks.

Chain printer: A printer (to output results from a computer) in which the characters to be printed are embossed on a chain or a band. The chain is fashioned as a loop and print heads are activated to print specified characters.

Channel: A small special purpose computer used to control the transfer of information between I/O units and the memory of a computer.

Circuit switching: Method used to interconnect two computers in which the communication channel connecting them is exclusively allocated to them for the duration of information inter-change.

CLV (Constant Linear Velocity): Recording method used in CDROM in which the angular velocity of the disk is reduced as the recording head moves to the inner tracks. This maintains constant recording density on all the tracks of the disk.

COBOL: *Co*mmon *B*usiness *O*riented *L*anguage. A high level language used for business data processing.

Cognitive graphics: This deals with algorithms to recognize and classify pictures.

CDROM (Compact Disk Read Only Memory): A shiny metal disk in which strings of bits are written along spiral tracks using a laser beam. The beam creates a tiny circular pit on the surface when a 1 is written and no pit is created for a 0. A 5.25 inch CDROM stores around 650 Mbytes (1995). Once data is written on this disk it cannot be erased. Newer versions of CDROM with read/write capabilities are now emerging. They are called CDROM-R

Communication channel: A medium through which (electrical) signals are transmitted and received.

Communication protocol: Common agreed rules followed to interconnect and communicate between computers.

Compiler: A system program to translate a high level language program to machine language.

CISC (Complex Instruction Set Computer): A processor which has variable length instructions, variety of addressing mode and many instructions.

Client server computing: A methodology of architecturing computer applications in which required functions are grouped as service requestors and service providers. Clients request services and servers provide them. This method is particularly suited for applications implemented on distributed computers.

Computer: This is a machine which executes an algorithm stored in its memory to process data fed to it and produces the required results.

Computer graphics: The area is concerned with the generation, manipulation and display of pictures with the aid of a computer.

Computer network: A group of geographically distributed computers which are interconnected using communication lines in such a way that any computer in the group may be used from any other computer location.

Control bus: A set of wires used to transmit signals to control the operation of various units of a computer.

Control program: A set of system programs to perform I/O operations, dumping memory on a printer to aid in error detection and to supervise exchange of parameters between programs.

CPU: Central Processing Unit of a computer. It consists of circuits to perform arithmetic and logic and also has circuits to control and coordinate the functioning of the memory and I/O units of a computer (also known as Processor).

Cross translator: A program to translate a high level language to the machine language of some machine X and run on another machine Y.

Cycle stealing: The method used to transfer data from I/O units to memory by suspending the memory — CPU data transfer for one memory cycle.

Cycle time: The time interval between the instant at which a read/write command is given to a memory and the instant when the next such instruction can be issued to the memory (also known as memory cycle time).

D

Data entry unit: A system with a keyboard to enter data and a magnetic medium such as a floppy disk to store the entered data.

Demand paging: A procedure used to bring from the disk memory to the main memory of a computer the portion of a program (a page) to be executed.

De Morgan's theorem: A theorem in Boolean algebra which states how to complement a Boolean expression.

Destructive read out: A memory cell in which the stored information is destroyed when read.

DAT (Digital Audio Tape): Uses 4 mm wide magnetic tape in a cartridge to back up contents of disk.

Digital channel: A communication medium through which information in binary (digital) form is transmitted.

Digital Signal Processor: A microprocessor which is optimized to process real-time audio and video signals.

Direct address: The address of an operand in main memory specified in an instruction.

Disk memory: A backup or peripheral memory in which information is stored as magnetized spots on the surface of disks coated with magnetic material. In hard disks the disks are not flexible. In floppy disks the disk is a circular platter made of flexible magnetic coated plastic sheet.

Display file: A file containing a sequence of instructions (program) to draw a picture on a graphic output unit.

Distributed computers: A configuration in which several workstations or PCs are interconnected by a fast communication network.

DMA: Direct memory access. This is a method in which data from I/O devices to memory and vice-versa is transmitted without the involvement of the central processing unit of a computer.

DPU: Display processing unit consists of a set of electronic logic circuits to generate signals to drive a display device using the program in the display file. It also accepts inputs from graphic input device(s) to store and interactively manipulate displayed pictures.

Drum printer: A printer in which the characters to be printed are embossed on a drum. Used to output results from a computer.

DVDROM: Digital Versatile Disk Read Only Memory uses a technology for storing data on a disk similar to CDROM except that 2 to 4 layers are used to record information. Data is also packed on the tracks much closer compared to CDROM. The maximum capacity of 4 layer DVDROM is 17 GB. Rewritable versions are also emerging.

E

EEPROM: Electrically Erasable Programmable Read Only Memory in which information may be erased and written using electrical signals.

Effective address: The address in main memory, calculated by the CPU, which is used to retrieve operands.

Electronic mail: Electronic mail is an application in which any user on a network can send/receive letters on his computer terminal to/from any person in the world who has an electronic mail address.

EPROM: *E*rasable *P*rogrammable *R*ead *O*nly *M*emory. A semiconductor memory where programs are semi-permanently stored. The program may be erased and new information written in it.

Ethernet: A standard for local area network connection (IEEE 802) which uses a Carrier Sense Multiple Access with Collision Detection (CSMA/CD) protocol.

Executive program: A system program used to monitor I/O from devices and to allocate computer resources to user programs.

Extranet: An internet connection between a predetermined number of member organizations.

F

FDDI (Fibre Distributed Data Interface): It is a standard defined by ISO/ANSI and IEEE for local area networks using Fibre Optic cables to interconnect workstations/computers.

Fibre optics cable: A cable made of glass fibres used to transmit light signals.

File: A collection of records relating to an object such as stores, personnel, user programs, etc.

File transfer protocol (ftp): Rules used in a computer network to copy large files (Mbytes) from a remote computer to a requestor's computer.

First generation computers: Computers built between 1949 and 1955 which used vacuum tubes. Programming was in assembly language.

Flat Panel Displays: Computer displays whose thickness is much smaller than VDU. Normally used in Laptop computers. They use liquid crystal display technology. Emerging flat panel displays are Plasma displays and Field Emission displays.

Flip-flop: An electronic circuit which can be placed in one out of two stable states. Each state may be used to represent a binary digit.

Floating point number: A number representation in which real numbers are expressed as a mantissa and an exponent. The mantissa is less than one. The exponent is an integer. The mantissa is multiplied by the base of the number raised to a power equal to the exponent. For example 44.86 in floating point is $0.4486E2 = 0.4486 \times 10^2$.

Floppy disk: A circular magnetic disk made of flexible plastic sheet coated with magnetic material.

Flow chart: A pictorial representation of a computational procedure.

FORTRAN: *For*mula *Tran*slation; a high level language used for scientific and engineering calculations.

Fourth generation computers: Computers built between 1975 and now. They use large scale integrated circuits, semiconductor memories and powerful high level languages and operating systems.

Fourth Generation Languages: Also known as 4GL, these provide query languages (e.g. structured Query Language) to access data from databases and manipulate them.

Frame Relay: A method of transmitting messages between computers in a WAN in which a message is broken up into variable size packets and sent via the least congested route. The packets need not be received in any specified order. Error detection is performed only by the receiving computer and not by the intermediate computers.

Frequency division multiplexing: A method in which a communication channel is shared by a number of independent messages. Each message is allocated a distinct range of frequencies.

FSK: *F*requency *S*hift *K*eying. A method of transforming digital signals 1 and 0 to two sine waves of different frequencies. This is done to transmit digital signals via an analog channel.

Full adder: An adder which adds three binary digits and outputs a result bit and carry bit.

Full duplex communication: A method of using a communication channel in which signals can be transmitted between a source and a destination in both directions simultaneously.

Functional Language: (Also known as Applicative language). Problems are solved using this language by applying a sequence of functions to an input state to transform it to the required output state.

G

Generative graphics: This deals with the creation of 2D and 3D pictures from the mathematical representation of the objects.

Giga: A word used to represent 10^9. Abbreviated form G.

H

Half adder: An adder which adds two bits and gives the result bit and the overflow bit (if any).

Half duplex channel: A communication channel in which signals may be transmitted at a time in only one direction from source to destination or vice-versa.

Hexadecimal system: A number system using 16 as base. The 16 symbols in this system are 0 to 9 and A, B, C, D, E, F.

High level language: Computer language in which each statement is translated into many machine language statements.

html (Hypertext markup Language): A notation which locates keywords in web pages and thereby indexes the page for easy location and retrieval.

Hub: A box to which unshielded twisted pair wires from the ethernet interfaces of computers are connected. It receives signals, reshapes and broadcasts them to all computers connected to it. CSMA/CD protocol is used.

Hypertext: A document in which keywords are marked and pointers used to link it to other documents which have the same keywords.

I

IBG: *I*nter *B*lock *G*ap. The gap left in a magnetic tape store between blocks of data.

IC: *I*ntegrated *C*ircuit. An electronic circuit fabricated on a single chip of silicon.

Image processing: This deals with cleaning up blurred images and creating clear pictures.

Immediate addressing: An instruction in which the address part of an instruction is the operand and not the address of the operand.

Index register: A register in CPU whose contents are added to the operand address specified in an instruction to find an effective address in memory from where the operand will be fetched.

Indirect address: An instruction in which the address part of an instruction gives the address where the address of the operand would be found.

Input unit: A part of a computer used to feed programs and data.

Instruction: A command or order given to a computer. It normally consists of a code to indicate the operation to be performed and address(es) in memory where the operand(s) would be found.

Instruction register: A register in CPU which is used to store an instruction.

Interface logic: Electronic circuit used to interconnect I/O devices to a computer's CPU or memory.

Internet: A world wide network of computers. Several thousands of individual computer networks are interconnected to form the internet. Internet provides electronic mail, telnet (remote login to computer), file transfer services and enormous amount of information through various discussion groups and information retrieval facilities.

Interoperability: Ability of diverse computers from different vendors with different operating systems to cooperate in solving computational problems.

Interpreter: A translator which translates a statement of a high level language to machine language and immediately executes it.

Interrupt service routine: A computer program stored in the computer which is invoked when an interrupt is sensed by CPU. This program is usually used to transfer data from or to I/O devices to or from memory.

Interrupt signal: A signal sent to the CPU by an external event such as when information from an input device is ready to be read.

Intranet: A network of computers within an organization which follows the same protocol as the internet and provides the same services as the internet.

I/O spooling: A technique in which the information to be read from slow input devices or those to be written on slow output devices are stored in a faster peripheral device such as a magnetic disk. Information is transferred to or from memory via this peripheral device.

I/O units: Input/output units of a computer.

ISO protocol: A communication protocol to interconnect geographically dispersed computers. This protocol has been standardized by the International Standards Organization.

ISCII (Indian Standard Code for Information Interchange): An 8-bit common code standardized by the Bureau of Indian Standards to represent characters of all Indian languages.

J

JAVA: An object oriented language which is easily portable. It is normally used to program on the internet.

Job control language: A special purpose language used to describe to a computer's operating system the resource requirements of programs fed to the computer.

Joy stick: A stick mounted on a spherical ball which moves in a socket. Used to move the cursor on the screen of a display device.

K

Kilo: Used to represent $1024 = 2^{10}$ in computers. Abbreviated form K.

L

LAN: *L*ocal *A*rea *N*etwork is an interconnection of many computers and terminals located within 10 km radius via a fast communication link.

Laptop (or Notebook) computers: A portable computer which weighs around 2 kg and runs all PC applications. It uses a liquid crystal display and is usable by a person while travelling.

Latency time: The time taken for a record stored in a disk track (which is to be read) to come under the read/write head positioned over that track. Maximum latency time equals the time taken by disk to rotate once.

LEX : A tool used to perform lexical analysis of a programming language.

Lexical rules: Rules to specify syntactic elements or words of a programming language.

Light pen: A pen shaped device which has a lens assembly. It is pointed towards an image displayed on a cathode ray screen. It picks up the light and determines the position of the picture element picked up.

Line conditioning: A method in which special circuits are added at both ends of a leased analog telephone line to compensate for unequal attenuation and delay of different frequencies. This ensures digital signals to be sent reliably on an analog telephone line.

Line driver: An electronic amplifier used to increase the power of a digital signal to be transmitted over a communication line.

Linker: It is a system program which processes and combines a set of independently created object modules to produce a ready-to-execute object program .

Linux: A version of Unix Operating System whose source code is maintained by voluntary efforts and available free of cost.

LISP: A *Lis*t *P*rocessing language. This high level language is used in applications such as theorem proving, game playing, etc.

Loader: It is a system program which accepts a linked object program produced by a linker and loads it in the memory ready for execution.

LSI: A *L*arge *S*cale *I*ntegrated circuit. An electronic circuit with about 10,000 transistors fabricated on a silicon chip.

M

Machine independent language: A high level programming language which is designed to be used with a variety of computers.

Machine language: A language which uses numeric codes to represent operations and numeric addresses of operands. Each model of a computer has a unique machine language.

Machine readable form: Information which can be read by input devices connected to a computer.

Magneto resistive head: Heads used to read data from magnetic disks. They depend on the change of resistance of head when a magnet is taken near it. They are more sensitive compared to traditional inductive coil heads.

Mainframe computers: Large computers used by organizations such as banks. They process hundreds of millions of transactions per second, have hundreds of gigabytes of disks and very fast data transfer rate between disk and main memory. They can be accessed simultaneously by hundreds of terminals.

MATHEMATICA: A problem oriented language used to simplify complex algebraic expression symbolically. Also used for indefinite integration.

MATLAB: A problem oriented language used by scientists and engineers to solve algebraic and differential equations.

Mega: Used to represent $1024 \times 1024 = 2^{20} \cong 10^6$. Abbreviated form M.

Memory: An organized collection of cells used to store data and programs in a computer.

Memory cell: A circuit which can store information. A binary memory cell would store a 0 or a 1.

Message switching: A method whereby messages to be transmitted between computers are all sent to a central computer, which gathers them and routes them to the appropriate destination(s).

Micro: Used to represent 10^{-6}.

Microcomputer: A computer which is fabricated using a microprocessor, and other integrated circuits, namely, a ROM, RAM, and I/O interface chips.

Microcontroller: An inexpensive special purpose microprocessor which is optimized for control applications. It has an in-built ROM to store control programs and also has built-in I/O controller.

Microkernel: A very small machine dependent core of an O.S. which coordinates the activities of device drivers, file server, scheduler and memory manager.

Microprocessor: A LSI chip which contains the entire CPU of a computer.

Milli: Used to represent 10^{-3}.

Modem: *Mo*dulator-*dem*odulator units used to convert digital signals (to be communicated over an analog channel such as telephone line) to sine waves at the sending end and back to digital signals at the receiving end.

Moore's Law: A prediction that the number of transistors in a microprocessor will double every 18 months.

MOSFET: *M*etal *O*xide *S*ilicon *F*ield *E*ffect *T*ransistor. This is used as an electronic switch.

Mouse: It is a small plastic box mounted on two metal wheels whose axes are at right angles. The mouse is moved around on a flat surface called a tablet. As the mouse is moved, a cursor on the screen is moved and (x, y) coordinates of the cursor may be determined.

MS-DOS: Microsoft Disk Operating Systems designed by Microsoft Corporation for IBM compatible Personal Computers.

MS-WINDOWS: An operating system with a good graphical interface and multitasking facility developed by Microsoft Corporation for PCs.

MSI: *M*edium *S*cale *I*ntegrated circuit. A circuit with about 100 transistors fabricated on a single silicon chip.

Multiplexing: A method in which a communication channel is shared by a number of messages or signals.

Multiprogramming operating system: An operating system in which a number of programs are kept in memory and CPU and I/O resources are dynamically allocated to programs with the objective of keeping all the units of a computer simultaneously active.

Multitasking: Executing multiple programs residing in memory concurrently in a CPU. Each task is allocated a time slice to use CPU.

N

Nano: Used to represent 10^{-9}.

Network topology: The structure of interconnection of nodes of a computer network.

Normalized floating point number: A floating point number in which the most significant digit of the mantissa is made non-zero.

Notebook computer: See Laptop Computer.

O

Object: A programming model to represent a real world object. All the necessary data structures and procedures needed to model it are encapsulated. An object is invoked by sending a message to it requesting its services.

Object Oriented Language: A programming language having facilities to model objects and methods to invoke objects.

Object program: The machine language program resulting from the translation of a user program.

Octal system: A number system whose base is 8.

On-line system: A computer system which has terminals connected to it and allows direct access to user files from terminals. The files are updated as soon as a transaction is completed.

Operating system: A set of system programs used to control input/output devices of a computer, select appropriate software requested by users, allocate computer resources such as memory, CPU time and schedule user programs.

Operation code: A group of bits used to represent operations to be performed by a CPU.

Output unit: A unit of a computer used to print or display computed results.

Overflow: An overflow is said to occur if the result of an arithmetic operation is larger than the largest number which can be stored in the computer.

OS/2: A multitasking operating system with good graphical user interface developed by IBM for PCs.

P

Packet switching: A procedure for communicating between computers in a network in which blocks of messages to be transmitted between machines are formed into packets with source and destination addresses, synchronizing, error correction and control bits and placed on the channel. The packets are routed using the source and destination addresses.

Palmtop Computer: A computer with capabilities of a PC which can be accommodated on a person's palm (Size: 16 cm × 12 cm × 5 cm).

Parallel adder: An adder in which all the bits of the two operands are added simultaneously.

Parallel computers: A set of computers connected together by a high speed communication network and programmed in such a way that they cooperate to solve a single large problem.

Parity bit: A bit appended to a string of bits to enable detection of errors.

Pascal: A high level programming language named after Blaise Pascal. Used for a variety of applications, particularly suitable for non-numeric programming.

PC (Personal Computer): A small inexpensive self-contained desk top computer intended for an individual user. Most often used for word processing and small database applications.

PCB: *Printed Circuit Board*. A phenolic or glass epoxy board on which electronic components are mounted and interconnected by conducting copper strips bonded to the board.

Phase modulation: A method of modifying a sine wave 'carrier' in which its phase is changed in accordance with the message to be transmitted.

Physical address space: Addresses in main memory which are directly addressable and available for storing program and data.

Pixel: A picture element. It is used to represent one point in a raster-scan display device.

PPU: *Peripheral Processing Unit.* A special purpose computer which controls the transfer of information between peripheral devices (disk, tape, printer, etc.) and the main memory of the computer independent of the CPU (same as channel).

Printer: An output unit to print the results of computation. Line printers print one full line at a time using a character, chain or drum. Character printers print one character at a time serially.

Problem oriented languages: High level languages designed to solve a narrow class of special problems. The language does not describe the detailed algorithm to solve the problem but precisely states the problem and its data.

Procedure oriented languages: High level languages with the structure to describe in detail a general class of algorithms.

Processor: A unit of a computer which interprets instructions, executes them using arithmetic and logic circuits and controls the operation of all the other units of the computer (also known as CPU).

Program: An algorithm expressed using a precise notation which can be executed by a computer.

Program counter: Also called PC. A register in CPU which stores the address of the next instruction to be carried out by it.

Programming language: A precise notation (with precisely specified syntax and semantic rules) to express algorithms.

PSK (Phase Shift Keying): Another terminology used for phase modulation. In PSK the phase of a sine wave carrier is 0 or π depending on whether a 0 or a 1 is to be transmitted. In n PSK, n values of phase of the carrier are used to represent n strings of bits (0..0 to 1...1).

Q

Quarter inch cartridge tapes: Magnetic tape of width 0.25 inch sealed inside a cartridge in which bits are recorded along 9 to 30 serpentine tracks.

R

Radix: The number of distinct symbols used to represent numbers in a system for enumeration (same as base).

RAID (Redundant Array of Inexpensive Disks): An array of inexpensive disks from which data can be retrieved in parallel from each disk in the array thereby increasing speed of data retrieval. Reliability of data retrieved is improved by storing error detecting bits in addition to the information carrying bits.

RAM: *R*andom *A*ccess *M*emory. A memory used as the main memory of a computer in which the time to retrieve stored information is independent of the address where it is stored.

Random scan display: Also known as vector display or calligraphic display. This displays images by breaking them up into points, lines, and segments of standard curves. The image is refreshed.

Raster scan display: In this display the image to be displayed is stored as a matrix of pixels. A pixel is usually several bits, the number of bits depend on whether the display is a colour or monochrome display. The pixel storage is called a frame buffer or a refresh buffer. As an electron beam scans a CRT from left to right the pixels are retrieved from the frame buffer and used to modulate the beam and display the image.

Real-time system: A system in which a computer is used to control a physical system operating independently. The time taken to compute should match the needs of the physical system.

Record: A collection of related items of data treated as one unit.

Refresh display: A cathode ray tube in which images are to be repetitively displayed 30 to 60 times per second to perceive a stationary image.

Register: A serially interconnected group of memory cells.

Remote login: The facility to login and use a remote computer in a network from a user's terminal.

Response time: The time elapsed between entering a command and getting the result of computation (normally) on a terminal in a time shared computer system.

RISC (Reduced Instruction Set Computer): A processor architecture which uses uniform instruction length, simple addressing mode, references to memory only to load and store operands, small number of instructions to simplify control unit design, pipelined instruction execution to enable at least one instruction to be executed in each clock cycle.

RJE system: A *R*emote *J*ob *E*ntry system. A small computer and I/O units located at a geographically remote point connected to another larger computer via a communication channel.

RLE: Run Length Encoding is a method used to compress data to be stored usually on disks.

ROM: *R*ead *O*nly *M*emory. A memory in which information is permanently written. The information can be read quickly but not changed.

Router: It is a circuit which steers messages through multiple LANs and ensures that the least congested route is taken by messages.

RS 232-C standard: A standard defined by Electronics Industries Association (USA) which specifies the interface between computers, modems and terminals.

S

Sampling Theorem: A theorem which states that if an analog signal $s(t)$ has f_h as its highest frequency component, then $2f_h$ samples of $s(t)$ must be taken every second to preserve all the information contained in $s(t)$.

Scripting Language: Language which has facilities to glue existing applications to create new ones.

Second generation computers: Computers built during the period 1956–65 which used transistors in CPU, magnetic core main memories and high level languages FORTRAN and COBOL for programming.

Seek time: The time required for a read/write head of a disk to move to the track where the record to be read or written is stored. Maximum seek time is the time taken for the head to move from the outermost track to the innermost track.

Semantic rule: Rules to assign meanings to valid statements of a language. These rules define what computations are to be carried out for each valid statement.

Serial access memory: A memory from which information is retrieved sequentially one bit after another.

Serial adder: An adder in which the bits of the operands are added one after another.

Single address computer: A computer in which a machine instruction specifies only one operand address.

Software: Programs for a computer.

Source program: A program written in a symbolic or high level language.

Speech input unit: A unit which will recognize spoken words and convert it to ASCII code. These units are classified as single word recognition or continuous speech recognition. A further classification is speaker dependent or speaker independent.

Speech output unit: A unit which will accept strings of ASCII bytes and convert them into spoken words or sentences.

SSI: *S*mall *S*cale *I*ntegrated circuit. An electronic circuit with about 20 transistors fabricated on a silicon chip.

Stack: A memory in which information which is stored last is on top and is retrieved first. Also known as LIFO (Last-in-first-out) store.

Store and forward system: A system of computers and/or digital equipment in which messages or signals are sent to a central computer which receives and stores them and forwards them to the specified destinations.

Stored program computer: A computer where the program to solve a problem and the necessary data are stored in its memory.

Supercomputers: They are the fastest computers available at any given time and are normally used to solve problems requiring intensive numerical computation.

Superscalar processor architecture: A processor architecture in which multiple instructions are executed in one clock cycle.

Symbol table: A table used by a programming language compiler to allocate memory to store variables.

Synchronous: The time between successive bits, bytes or events is constant. All equipment connected together in such a system are strictly controlled by a clock.

Syntax rules: Rules which specify how valid syntactic elements of a programming language can be combined into legal statements of the language.

System software: General programs written for a computer. These programs provide the environment to facilitate the writing of application programs.

T

TCP/IP (Transmission Control Protocol/Internet Protocol): A protocol used to interconnect computer networks. This protocol is used by internet and includes standards for common applications such as electronic mail, remote login (telnet) and file transfer (ftp).

Telnet: See Remote login.

Third-generation computer: Computer built between 1966 and 1975 which used integrated circuits in CPU, high speed magnetic core main memories, powerful high level languages and saw the advent of time sharing operating system.

Throughput: The number of jobs completed by a computer in a specified period.

Time division multiplexing: A method of sharing a communication channel in which the channel is allocated to each signal successively for a specified period.

Time sharing system: A computer system designed to allow many users to simultaneously use it.

Touch panel: A locator device used in laptop computers as a replacement for a mouse. It is operated by moving a finger over a capacitively coupled glass panel to point to a location on the screen.

Transistor: A controlled electronic switch fabricated using a semiconductor.

Transponder: Device mounted on a communication satellite which receives, amplifies and retransmits signals from earth stations.

Trap: An interrupt signal sent to CPU by an event within a computer such as hardware error, arithmetic overflow, etc.

Truth table: A table which gives the input/output relationship of a logic circuit.

Turnaround time: The time elapsed between the submission of a program by a user to a computer and getting the results.

U

Underflow: Condition occurs when the result of an arithmetic operation is smaller than the smallest number which can be stored in the computer.

Unibus: A single bus which interconnects I/O units, CPU and memory of a computer.

UNIX: An operating system designed by AT & T Bell Telephone Laboratories (USA). It is a time sharing O.S. written in C.

Unix Kernel: The inner most core of Unix OS which performs various primitive operations requested by user processes.

Unix Pipe: A facility available in Unix to feed a stream of bytes which are output of a program as input to another program.

Unix Shell: A command interpreter supported by the Unix operating system.

URL (Universal Resource Locator): The unique address used to locate a web page.

UVEPROM: *U*ltra *V*iolet light *E*rasable *P*rogrammable *R*ead *O*nly *M*emory.

V

VDU: A *V*ideo *D*isplay *U*nit. An I/O device which consists of a television tube for presenting outputs and a keyboard for entering inputs.

Virtual machine: A computer as it is available to a user, which is not merely the hardware but the hardware made usable by an operating system software, high level languages and application programs.

Virtual memory: A hierarchy of a fast main memory and a slower peripheral memory managed by a software system in such a way that the user has an effective addressable memory which equals the sum of capacities of the two memories with an access time approaching that of the faster main memory.

VLSI: *V*ery *L*arge *S*cale *I*ntegrated circuit. An electronic circuit with about 100,000 transistors fabricated in a silicon chip.

Volatile memory: A memory in which the information stored is lost unless energy is continuously fed to it.

VSAT (Very Small Aperture Terminal): An earth station which uses a very small diameter dish (1 to 2 metre) antenna to transmit and receive digital data from satellites.

W

Winchester disk drive. A disk memory in which non-interchangeable disks are used and the read/write heads are built-in with the disk.

Windows NT Operating System: A multi-user, multitasking portable OS designed by Microsoft for high end PCs used as servers.

Wireless LAN: A LAN in which a mobile computer such as a Laptop computer can send or receive messages to or from a base station connected to the LAN.

Word processor: A computer program which facilitates the creation of well formatted neat looking reports.

Workstations: Desktop computers which can perform fairly intensive numerical computation. Typical workstations use a powerful processor 10 to 100 times faster than PCs, 256 MB of main memory, 10 GB disk, and a 19 inch colour monitor. They use UNIX as their Operating System.

World Wide Web: Each computer in the Internet which can be referenced by a hypertext link is called a web page. A collection of web pages is known as the World Wide Web.

Y

YACC: Yet Another Compiler Compiler is a programming tool which generates the parser for a high level language when the rules of syntax of the language are given.

Index

345